Fatefully, Faithfully Feminist

CRITICAL
MEXICAN STUDIES

Critical Mexican Studies
Series editor: Ignacio M. Sánchez Prado

Critical Mexican Studies is the first English-language, humanities-based, theoretically focused academic series devoted to the study of Mexico. The series is a space for innovative works in the humanities that focus on theoretical analysis, transdisciplinary interventions, and original conceptual framing.

Other titles in the series:

Fatefully, Faithfully Feminist

A Critical History
of Women, Patriarchy,
and Mexican
National Discourse

Carlos Monsiváis

Translated and edited
by Norma Klahn and Ilana Luna

Vanderbilt University Press
Nashville, Tennessee

Originally published as Carlos Monsiváis and Marta Lamas, *Misógino feminista* (Oceano, Mexico: Debate Feminista, 2013).

Library of Congress Cataloging-in-Publication Data

Names: Monsiváis, Carlos, 1938–2010, author. | Klahn, Norma, translator. |
   Luna, Ilana Dann, 1978– translator.
Title: Fatefully, faithfully feminist : a critical history of women,
   patriarchy and Mexican national discourse / Carlos Monsiváis ;
   translated and edited by Norma Klahn and Ilana Luna.
Other titles: Misógino feminista. English
Description: Nashville, Tennessee : Vaderbilt University Press, 2024. |
   Series: Critical Mexican studies
Identifiers: LCCN 2023036848 (print) | LCCN 2023036849 (ebook) | ISBN
   9780826506337 (paperback) | ISBN 9780826506344 (hardcover) | ISBN
   9780826506351 (epub) | ISBN 9780826506368 (pdf)
Subjects: LCSH: Feminism—Mexico. | Feminism—Mexico—History—20th
   century. | Feminism. | Feminism—History—20th century. |
   Misogyny—Mexico. | Misogyny.
Classification: LCC HQ1191.M6 M6613 2024 (print) | LCC HQ1191.M6 (ebook)
   | DDC 305.420972—dc23/eng/20231109
LC record available at https://lccn.loc.gov/2023036848
LC ebook record available at https://lccn.loc.gov/2023036849

We dedicate this book to our daughters Jennifer, Elizabeth, and Amy Corsun Klahn and Isabella Luna Dann

Contents

Notes on Translation

"To translate Monsiváis is to keep him alive," we wrote in an article that formed part of a homage to Carlos Monsiváis that appeared in *Inundación castálida: La Revista del Claustro de Sor Juana* in June 2020, and we not only believe this to be true, but we believe his words are needed today more than ever. Of course, the crucial and seemingly heroic undertaking of translating Monsivais could not have taken place without the work of groundbreaking Mexican feminist scholar and activist Marta Lamas, editor of the original anthology *Misógino feminista* (2013) that today you read in translation with a new introduction and extensive notes. It was both a labor of love and memory and an exercise in bringing Monsiváis's feminist writings together in one place in order to disseminate the most important work on women's rights, representation, and political participation that he penned.

We, Norma and Ilana, first met as members of UC-Mexicanistas, a research group based in California that has been active for more than two decades researching and promoting Mexican literature and cultural studies under the directorship of Professor Sara Poot-Herrera. Belonging to different generations has benefited this project. At the time of Norma's earlier readings, Monsiváis's articles spoke to her epoch, a post-1968, postmodern, and decolonizing one—deconstructing hierarchical binaries, crisscrossing the entire social structure of Mexican society—and to her experiences as a girl on the Texas-Mexico border, steeped in Mexican popular culture. Norma first met Monsi in 1980 as a newly minted assistant professor at a conference in Jalapa, and even though Onetti, García Márquez, Fuentes, and other Boom writers were there, the author she most wanted to meet was Monsiváis. It was the beginning of a beautiful friendship, and of an ongoing dialogue that was mutually nurturing and productive. Her approach to the essays included in this book was to read them in their immediacy as they appeared, many of them in *Debate Feminista*, paying attention to their content and their contextualization. They were an exploration and critique of the origins of patriarchal power and its legacies, and an update to the ongoing struggles of women, gay men, and other excluded minorities for equal rights. Ilana, born in the Pennsylvania of the late 1970s to a mixed Jewish family, whose Spanish was not native but was a family language nonetheless, came to the writings of Monsiváis from a very different position. Ilana's initial contact with Monsiváis was through his writing, read in classrooms at the Universidad Iberoamericana in Mexico City in the late 1990s, when, for example, the recent papal visit, condemning the use of condoms despite the AIDS epidemic, loomed large. Monsiváis's writing provided Ilana essential insight into the character of Mexican culture, both political and popular, as she navigated living among the "rituals of chaos." She would later also read his work in graduate seminars at the University of California, Santa Barbara. The one and only time she was fortunate enough to speak with Monsiváis in person was at UC-Irvine, when he gave the keynote to the annual UC-Mexicanistas conference in 2007.

Given the current interest in literature and cultural productions from Latin America in translation and the impetus toward a global culture (in the academy and outside), and as professors and researchers at public universities in the borderland states of Arizona and California, we share an urgent personal and ethical commitment to making Carlos Monsiváis's lucid and timely essays available to a US public. Given the ongoing dialogue that Monsiváis himself maintained with an international English-speaking audience, it seemed inconceivable to us that these chronicles and essays on women's struggles, rights, and representation were not known beyond the Spanish-speaking world.

It's our belief that these texts we have translated will continue to influence not only the cultural and political debates in Mexico today, but writing itself. To capture the tone of his writing has been one of the greater translating challenges we encountered, forcing us to consider how to most effectively convey his unique style and methodology, and the precise form (genre) in which to articulate his content (exclusionary practices and the movements of an inclusionary democracy). Monsiváis actively engages a myriad of genres, all with their particular conventions, linguistic registers, and purposes to achieve varied literary effects: the open-endedness of the chronicle as he follows the feminist and other civil rights movements; the parodic use of sentimentality to dismantle traditional poetic expressions, whether in the male idealization of women or by women themselves; humor and irony in making transparent the effects of the melodramatic imagination in film; the celebratory language of popular culture in reviewing Sontag's "Notes on Camp," followed by an academic analysis in his bio-bibliographical attention to her life; confessional in his self-reflexivity; laudatory in his epistolary eulogy to Nancy Cárdenas where his admiration knows no bounds (an unusual characteristic of his persona); irreverent and ironic when critiquing the Church, but turning to revised biblical verses in his praise of exceptional women; acerbic sarcasm in the critique of the State and the discourses of power; satirical in exposing the hypocrisy of the bourgeoisie; humor and parody to critique the role and power of media and culture; an unhampered denunciatory tone in describing the unrelenting devastation brought about by "savage capitalism"; and an accusatory voice condemning the impunity exercised by the State as continued femicides remain unpunished.

Our poetics of translation also focuses on his particular use of language itself. Monsiváis has a particular style that is inimitable and often referential, metareferential, and ranging between the erudite and the popular. We chose to respect the diversity of his vocabulary, often searching for parallel poetic and semantic structures, while implementing a systematic preference for clarification of his abundant ellipses, both material and alluded. The challenges we experienced in translating Monsiváis were due to his complex syntactical phrasing, which we addressed by using parenthetical asides and em-dash clarifications. He uses words and turns of phrase beyond the habitual or predictable, beyond received ideas and stagnant paradigms; he coins neologisms, which we take the liberty of doing in English (i.e., beatañol becomes sanctimonyish). His complex thinking and ideas lead to long sentences, at times serial ones that contain lists of three or more words, phrases, or clauses, and that oftentimes in mid-sentence address the reader directly through asides and parentheses. His writing often gives a sense of urgency due to the staccato punctuation of sentence fragments that are intercalated with extended, frequently paragraph-length, multi-clausal phrases and the occasional bullet-point lists.

To assure that our readers could capture his recurrent use of irony, humor, and sarcasm, we oftentimes used italics or scare quotes. We left words in foreign languages where a sense of globality is implicit, and decided to leave many words in Spanish, such as *cursi*, *huarache*, *charros*, *rumbera*, and *granaderos*, words that both defy simple translation and also let the reader know that these essays, although relevant to a global audience, are coming from a specific historical and cultural milieu. Monsiváis's writing is geographically situated in Mexico, and such Mexicanness, we did not want to abandon.

Finally, because Monsiváis was a public intellectual, essayist, and chronicler, not necessarily bound by the rules of the academy, we spent quite a bit of time hunting down complete citations, sometimes originally in English, and others culled from a vast archive of sources that we parsed and documented in our notes. Perhaps what is foregrounded in the process of translating Monsiváis, in the rearticulation of a vibrant present when it is now past, is that his writing represents a chronicle of events that was very relevant at the time but that was not easy to re-create far from the zeitgeist of the moment.

Such "problems" lead us to a particular politics of translation: we chose to make this anthology a scholarly, critical edition in order to explain the historical, political, and cultural references for an English-language audience. Why did we choose to intervene so heavily, with substantial footnotes, rather than leave the text as it stood? In this context we were not attempting to seamlessly hide our role as translators, but rather to enter into a critical and intellectual debate across space, time, and generations. We contextualized the shifting notions of gender, political representation, and the canon in Mexico for an international audience, and we believe that the repercussions of our work will be greater for having fleshed out the "unspoken" Mexican cultural knowledge that is often alluded to with a wink and a nod. We also recognize the dialogue Monsiváis himself had with the international—US in particular—feminist writings of his time, and have attempted to respect the linguistic genealogy of these feminist epistemologies as they would have emerged in time, alongside Monsiváis's observations of particularly Mexican phenomena. We also chose to foreground translation itself in the creation of knowledge, and the cross-cultural/transborder dissemination of ideas. Therefore in many of our extensive commentaries, we offer the reader references to works in English translation to which Monsiváis has referred and always name the translators when possible.

Early on, it was clear to us that while the title in Spanish, *Misógino feminista*, spoke to a Mexican audience familiar with Monsiváis and his acerbic wit and would thus be understood as playful and ironic, when translated into English, the title *Feminist Misogynist* fell flat. The oxymoronic logic, far from the clever irreverence conveyed in Spanish, would appear to reinforce misplaced stereotypes when brought into the English-language context. We were concerned that the target audience, unfamiliar with his uncanny ability to hold multiple and seemingly opposing positions, and his profound commitment to revealing and critiquing the often hidden-in-plain-sight systems of power at play in the Mexican setting, would simply shrug him off as just another "Mexican Macho." Therefore, our first major choice—to change the title to *Fatefully, Faithfully Feminist*—becomes, then, a way to playfully engage Monsiváis's writing: referring to both the inevitability of, and his abiding commitment to the rights of minorities and women, then and now.

We would like to thank and acknowledge the following people who have supported our work, and with their expertise and enthusiasm for the project, have seen us through to the end. Our deepest thanks first go to Ignacio Sánchez Prado, Marta Lamas, and Rubén Sánchez Monsiváis and the Monsiváis family, for believing in the importance of this scholarly edition and translation. Thanks to Gabriel Guerra for permission to reprint poems by Rosario Castellanos, and to the Bilingual Press/Editorial Bilingüe for the reproduction of the epigraph in Chapter 10, taken from Julian Palley, *Meditation on the Threshold: Anthology of Poetry* (Tempe, AZ: Arizona State University, 1988). Irena Polic and Karen Brooks at the Humanities Institute, UC Santa Cruz, and Melissa Weimer in Research Advancement at New College, Arizona State University, were instrumental in its early stages. Special thanks to Joell Smith-Borne for her excellent copyediting, and the whole Vanderbilt University Press team. We are grateful to Sara Poot Herrera, who first invited us to speak about our translation at the annual UC-Mexicanistas conference, and subsequently published our first meditation on the translation process. Guillermo Delgado-P. and Gaspar Orozco offered important technical, linguistic, and scholarly contributions. We would also like to acknowledge the support of our families for their patience as we single-mindedly pursued this work to their neglect, and our friends and colleagues including Raquel Serur, Max Parra, Cheyla Samuelson, Sara Potter, Amanda Petersen, Rebecca Janzen, Rebecca Ingram, Suzanne Jill Levine, Jacobo Sefamí, Cristina Rivera Garza, Irmgard Emmelhainz, María Elena Díaz, Annika Mann, Anita Huizar, Ron Broglio at the Institute for Humanities Research (ASU), Margaret Brose, Olga Nájera-Ramírez, Pedro Castillo, Carla Freccero, Hunter Bivens, Cristina Venegas, Carlos Vargas, José Manuel Valenzuela, Louis Mendoza, and Lois Brown whose insight, whether into Monsiváis, feminism, or translation, inspired us to continue our task.

Foreword

Marta Lamas

The second wave of Mexican feminism that emerged at the beginning of the seventies found in Carlos Monsiváis an impressive ally. Few intellectuals have responded as he did to feminist issues about the subordinate place of women in society, and none have rivaled his analysis of the evolution and impact of the feminist movement.

Monsiváis stands out not only for the aforementioned, but for the symbolic effectiveness of his interpretations and observations about the social and political marginality of women, which produced both a clarifying and legitimizing effect. Nevertheless, in spite of his writings on these issues, Monsiváis's thinking on feminism has not figured centrally in the extensive critical work by those who study him, and is almost unknown to his readers. Feminism was one of his causes and for it, he deployed his customary keen insights, as well as physically accompanying us during marches and conferences.

The essays collected here run the gamut of his penetrating critique on feminism, gender, and women; they do not, however, exhaust his texts on these topics. Missing in this selection is much of what he published in *Siempre!* and in the magazine *El Machete*, as well as other historical writings, such as the interesting foreword "When Gender Can't Be Seen amid the Symbols: Women and the Mexican Revolution," published in *Sex in Revolution: Gender, Politics, and Power in Modern Mexico* by Jocelyn Olcott, Mary Kay Vaughn, and Gabriela Cano. Since his appointment in 1972, as director of the literary supplement of *Siempre!*, *La cultura en México* (Culture in Mexico)—with Rolando Cordera, David Huerta, and Carlos Pereyra as editors, and Vicente Rojo in design—and specifically in the sections "Para documentar mi optimismo" (Documenting my optimism), "El consultorio de la Dra. Ilustración" (Dear Dr. Wisdom), and "Por mi madre, bohemios"

(Here's to my mother, bohemians), Monsiváis made scathing commentaries using selected clips from photo-novels and advertisements that today constitute a unique register of the shifting relationship between the sexes and the transformation of machista discourse. Monsiváis also used that platform to publish the first Spanish translations of second-wave feminists, as well as essays by Mexican feminists, in addition to their first manifesto, "Por la legalización del aborto" (In support of the legalization of abortion), signed by more than two hundred personalities from the intellectual, artistic, and feminist world, which, in fact, resulted in a strong admonition from the director of *Siempre!*, José Pagés Llergo.

The majority of the essays, chronicles, and varied notes and reviews that appear in this volume were proposed by Carlos Monsiváis himself, although I know that some of these texts were produced under pressure exerted by one of his close feminist friends. Carlos compiles a wide repertory on Mexican women's shifting mindsets; he dissects the ways feminine sensitivities are constructed; he makes fun of macho men; he critiques the sentimentality of Mexican cinema beginning with the "poor, long-suffering mother;" he analyzes the strategies of the Right and the Vatican in their campaign against the decriminalization of abortion; he writes about the work of five famous women; he reviews two seminal texts: *Mujeres y poder* (Women and power) and *Huesos en el desierto* (Bones in the desert); he reiterates, time and again, his convictions on the importance of the feminist movement. Thus, in all his writings, adorned with brilliant aphorisms and surprising metaphors, one discovers sound diagnoses and accurate prognoses that he invariably prescribed to us feminists.

Carlos accompanied us from the very first public conferences. In 1972, he participated in a series of talks, "Imagen y realidad de la mujer" (Woman's image and reality), that took place at La Casa del Lago, where he spoke on sexism in Mexican literature. In that presentation, published later in Supplement 579 of *La Cultura en Mexico* (March 14, 1973) using the provocative title "Dreamy, Flirty, and Fiery: Notes on Sexism in Mexican Literature," he laid out the best definition that I have ever read on discrimination based on sex: "Neither a conspiracy nor a trap, but rather a more methodical and established structure. It's the deliberate, watchful, exalted, melancholic, merciless, tender, and paternalistic structuring of inferiority. Sexism is none other than an ideological sum total that is a praxis, and a technique that is a world view."[1]

Monsiváis was very good friends with Margarita García Flores. When she founded the magazine *fem* with Alaíde Foppa in 1976, they created a space for reflection where two years later Carlos would publish "A New Salute for the Optimist." In that essay Monsiváis considers that "feminism's greatest victory is happening through social contagion or contamination." Later in that essay he would say, "In fewer than ten years, the feminist and sexual liberation movements, in spite of the enormous internal and external hurdles, have become an irreplaceable element in the construction of civil society, in the critique of capitalist exploitation, and in the vision of a democratic socialism."[2] His interest in the movement has made him our most important ally, and by placing value on our feminist objectives—which appear as guiding principles across several of these texts—he restores our faith in the work that we've been doing: "Feminism quickly advances (not the movement specifically, but the irrefutable condition of many of its points of view, and its influence on social conduct) and upsets the rules of the game, the general consensus on the role of women."[3]

Despite the limited mobilization we had on the streets, the legitimacy that he bestowed on our movement was very comforting. "Regardless of the ostensible weakness of the feminist movement today, if we measure its achievements by the level of social and cultural influence attained, the results are impressive."[4] Years later, he would scold us for the "timidity" that kept us from claiming the victory of having changed "the social perspective." In 2005, during the fifteen-year celebration of *Debate Feminista* that took place at the Programa Universitario de Estudios de Género (PUEG, University Program on Gender Studies) of the UNAM (Universidad Nacional Autónoma de México-National Autonomous University of Mexico), Monsiváis pronounced the following with his customary conviction:

> Feminism is an element that upsets patriarchal control, revisits family traditions, rejects the idea of women's bodies as terrains of masculine conquest, reclaims bodily autonomy, frees itself from moralistic tyranny, and gives rise to a discourse that forces a newfound eloquence—no matter what one thinks of the scant presence of feminism in Mexico in terms of organized groups, what is true is that it has changed society's outlook. One can no longer exclude the feminist perspective from the social and political gaze, and this is a considerable breakthrough that is not recognized as such, among other things, because of the timidity of the feminists in proclaiming their victories. What I don't understand at this stage is how a movement that has radically changed the social perspective in thirty short years can still remain timid.

But Monsiváis did much more than praise us. His critique of machismo was categorical. Not only did he dedicate an essay—published in this volume—to analyzing "the macho" ("But Were There Ever Really Eleven Thousand

Machos?"), but he also explored these ideas in other essays, such as "On Constructing 'Feminine Sensitivity,'" where he declares: "Mexican culture, since its inception, has been structured by machismo."[5] Just as harsh was his critique of the Vatican's interference in Mexico. In the writings selected here, two texts may not appear as specifically "feminist:" the one about the pope's visit, "The Fourth Papal Visit: The Spectacle of Faith Fascinated by Its Own Spectacle," and "Mexico at the Dawn of the Twenty-First Century: Globalization, Determinism and the Spread of Secularism." The reason for their inclusion in this anthology goes beyond the fact that Carlos had selected *Debate Feminista* to publish them. The first, an analysis of the effect that the pope's visit had on Mexican culture, responds to a political fact: the Vatican has become the principal adversary of feminism. And the chronicle that Carlos writes about the staging of the Vatican's anti-abortion stance, especially regarding the popular response, was a valuable tool for understanding which strategies to pursue. In the second text, Carlos summarizes many lines of thought regarding the major gender struggles that must be undertaken, among them, feminism. In this text, Carlos repeats a long paragraph that had previously appeared in his critical reading of *Huesos en el desierto*. Given his longstanding habit of continuously reworking his ideas, Monsiváis deliberately used some sections of previously published texts. In this collection, you will find very few repetitions. Some have been left the same, however, as is the case in "Mexico at the Dawn of the Twenty-First Century," since what is repeated is central to the argument at hand. This is also the case for other essays that offer a glimpse into Monsiváis's writing process. For example, Pablo Martinez Lozada demonstrated that a stanza by Salvador Díaz Mirón quoted twice by Carlos, although the same words, is imbued with different meanings due to the commentary and placement in Monsiváis's text. On the other hand, we decided to eliminate an appendix included in his essay on Simone de Beauvoir while keeping it in its entirety in "On Women's Representation." Its absence in the de Beauvoir text does not affect his thinking on *The Second Sex*, while the appendix is essential to the essay on women's representation.

Besides backing us with his writings, Monsiváis also supported us by participating as a speaker in the events we organized. For example in 1991, before midterm elections, the importance of having more representatives in congress was debated, because it wasn't enough to merely include "women's issues" on the electoral agenda, it was necessary to incorporate more women in decision-making positions. Therefore, *Debate Feminista* organized a forum titled "¿De quién es la política? Crisis de representación: Los intereses de las mujeres en la contienda electoral" (Who owns politics? The crisis of representation: Women's interests in electoral campaigns). The high point was the discussion between Monsiváis and Beatriz Paredes, then governor of Tlaxcala. In his talk that is included in this anthology as "On Women's Representation," Monsiváis mixed historical facts and hysterical anecdotes, positing a very critical conclusion:

> Women's cause (their rights, their leadership training, and their response to the serious problems of inequality and subordination) is reaching its limits, and is constrained by the same forces that oppose democratization. In politics, as far as I know, feminists' specific objectives (from decriminalizing abortion to wage parity) will become more effective only when organically included in a larger project. Otherwise, the cause loses strength due to its unpredictability, the activists end up as petitioners, the struggles become myths, and their achievements always seem profoundly dissatisfying when compared to the totality of the machista monopoly.
>
> Does this mean renouncing their principles? Rather, it means broadening their radius of action. For women in politics, the feminist perspective, even if it is the touchstone, should only be a part of their agenda. Otherwise, they will perpetuate exclusionary practices in the name of theory.[6]

This was one of the many prophetic pronouncements made by Monsiváis, both harsh and optimistic at the same time. Then, during the debate and the panelist's interventions, Monsiváis fired off this question, "Where do politics take place in Mexico?" He answered his own question immediately: "Up until now in spaces where only a few women are allowed to enter, for short periods, with a restricted invitation and without much power."[7]

Carlos laid out possible political scenarios, he envisioned plans of action and would reveal to us—the activists— the reasons for our own militancy. We looked to him for explanations, and he would say, "I'm not a prophet." Nevertheless, I don't remember a single time that he wasn't on the mark in his appraisals and predictions. He used his notoriety as a political strategist to the benefit of activist groups. His fame opened doors for us that, without him, we would never have been allowed to enter.

He always insisted that a commitment to political transformation finds its truest ally in the field of culture, to such an extent that if a cultural war is not being waged, the political struggle might well be lost. He was the political compass for broad sectors of our country, as well as a tireless fighter on all fronts where he was needed. He was both our ethical and political mentor, and we would hound him to draft a manifesto, to attend a meeting, to correct a flier, to get us an appointment with such-and-such a politician or

bureaucrat. His commitment to the cause was evident in his open participation in and founding of Diversa, in the Campaign for Chosen Maternity,
in the launching of the feminist party México Posible, and in his contributions to *Debate Feminista*.

Maybe his bid for a cultural transformation explains his sustained interest in a publication like *Debate Feminista*, where he collaborated in different
ways, suggesting themes, proposing texts by others, and writing his own.
He knew very well that he could send an essay, no matter what length, and
we would jump for joy. Thus, besides his participation in the round table
on politics and his dialogue on censorship with the Chilean writer Diamela
Eltit, we published twenty-six of his texts, among which twelve are explicitly
feminist. The others, mainly about sexual diversity, have already been collected in *Que se abra esa puerta: crónicas y ensayos sobre la diversidad sexual*
(Open that closet: Chronicles and essays on sexual diversity).

In his unrelenting, persistent, and stubborn struggle for justice, Monsiváis decidedly supported many other endeavors. He was also characterized
by the way he defended diverse "lost causes" in the majority of his writings
and conferences. On his seventieth birthday, in 2008, the Universidad de la
Ciudad de México (University of Mexico City) organized a colloquium in
his honor. In the lecture he gave that day, he said, "Lost causes share many
features with defeated movements, but not all; they run deeper, making
ethical choices with aesthetic resonances, adhering to demands and vindi-
cations doomed to immediate failure but valid in themselves, and imbuing
the moment with, above all, dignity." Later on he stated, "What defines this
kind of 'lost cause' is the belief in the inherent value of the demands for
justice and the struggles necessary to reach it." And, with his incomparable
style, he offered this definition: "A lost cause is one that we never expect to
benefit from."

In the journal *Debate Feminista*, we ask our collaborators to write their
own biographic profiles. At the time, Carlos Monsiváis described himself
(in the third person) saying, "He alternates his misogyny with an incendiary defense of feminism." In effect, Monsiváis is a true oxymoron: a feminist misogynist. It isn't a surprise that there were only five women—Rosario
Castellanos, Nancy Cárdenas, Simone de Beauvoir, Susan Sontag, and Frida
Kahlo—to whom he dedicated an essay. I knew that he wanted to write about
Elena Poniatowska, his great friend and the only one who could scold him,
and also about Jean Franco, whom he cared for and admired. His departure
was premature, given that he still had so much more to give to this Mexico
so in need of his intelligent and courageous interventions.

Carlos was, as he titled his biography of Salvador Novo, a "marginal figure in the center." Unlike many intellectuals, he persevered in his ethical and radical stance. During the mournful homage in his honor that was held at Bellas Artes (Palace of Fine Arts) the day after his death, and reflecting the feelings of thousands, Elena Poniatowska asked, "What are we going to do without you, Monsi?" Today, I answer: we must continue to read him, because reading him is to recover his clarity and his combative spirit. Reading these texts is also a way of understanding why so many of us feminists are so profoundly grateful to him.

I want to thank Beatriz Sánchez Monsiváis for all her support in the completion of this book. She was the first to see these texts, and has been, more than any other friend, the woman that most shared in Carlos's life and work. Thanks also to Guillermo Osorno, who put me in contact with Oceano, which has been a welcoming and efficient publishing house. There, I have had the privilege of working with Pablo Martinez Lozada and Guadalupe Ordaz, and under Rogelio Villarreal Cueva's caring attention. Finally, my thanks to the *Debate Feminista* team, most especially Alina Barojas.

NOTES

1. Ch. 1, "Dreamy, Flirty, and Fiery," page 17 in this volume
2. Ch. 2, "A New Salute for the Optimist," page 44 in this volume.
3. Lamas quotes Monsiváis from a source cited as (1981:20) that neither she nor we have been able to trace or verify.
4. Ch. 4, "We Don't Want Mother's Day, We Want Revolution!," page 59 in this volume.
5. Ch. 6, "On Constructing 'Feminine Sensitivity,'" page 81 in this volume.
6. Ch. 9, "On Women's Representation," page 114 of this volume.
7. Ch. 9, "On Women's Representation," page 113 of this volume.

Introduction

Fatefully, Faithfully Feminist: A Critical History of Women, Patriarchy, and Mexican National Discourse is a critical edition and translation of *Misógino feminista*, a collection of Carlos Monsiváis's feminist writings collected by Marta Lamas and published in 2013 in Mexico. It compiles a foundational set of texts published in two well-known and prestigious feminist journals, *Debate Feminista* and *fem*, as well as the important cultural supplement *Siempre!*, that span over four decades (1973–2008). These essays effectively address both the ongoing struggles of the feminist movement for equality and bodily autonomy and their connections to other marginalized communities within the Mexican National Project, including Indigenous Peoples, the LGBTQ+ community, and religious minorities. This collection, thus, situates the urgencies of these social movements as they developed in real time. Monsiváis explores the ways Mexican national literary, historiographic, religious, political, and filmic discourses have represented women (and minorities) within patriarchal paradigms.

Known to many as the "Chronicler of Mexico City," Carlos Monsiváis (1938–2010) was a leading intellectual and fundamental cultural critic whose legacy lives on and is considered foundational to the production of knowledge in the latter half of the twentieth century in Mexico. A prolific and extensively published chronicler and essayist, his work was a constant in newspapers, journals, and cultural supplements such as *Debate Feminista*, *El Día*, *El Universal*, *Este País*, *Eros*, *Excélsior*, *fem*, *La Jornada*, *Letras Libres*, *Nexos*, *Novedades*, *Personas*, *Proceso*, *Siempre!*, *Uno Más Uno*, among others. He is widely cited and referenced in Latin America for his chronicles (influenced by US New Journalism), cultural criticism (literary, film, radio, visual art, mass media, etc.) as well as for his incisive and lucid analyses of Mexico's watershed events (1968 student movement, 1985 earthquake, 1994 Chiapas insurgency), and the exclusionary politics that led to these.

1

Carlos Monsiváis authored more than sixty books: chronicles; literary, visual, musical, cultural essays; biographies and autobiographies; and major poetry and short story anthologies. In addition, he co-authored numerous books with other distinguished Mexican writers, critics, and intellectuals; and more than four hundred essays and articles, prologues and introductions. This expressive talent earned Monsiváis the most prestigious literary prize in Mexico, the National Science and Arts Prize in Linguistics and Literature (2005). In addition, he received myriad other recognitions including the Jorge Cuesta Prize (1986), the Xavier Villaurrutia Prize (1996), the International Latin American and Caribbean Prize for Literature Juan Rulfo (2005), the Sor Juana Inés de la Cruz Award (2008), and ten *Doctor Honoris Causa* from universities in various Mexican states, Europe, and the US. Carlos Monsiváis founded the Museo del Estanquillo in Mexico City's Historic Center in 2006 as a place to house his personal collections from paintings to photography, albums to film and music posters, handicraft toys, calendars, advertising, and other ephemera. His childhood goal of acquiring a library rather than "capital" became a reality, and his "Monsiteca," an archive of about twenty-seven thousand volumes and nineteen thousand articles from newspapers, magazines, and journals, originally sheltered in his house, is now located in the west wing of the José Vasconcelos Library at La Ciudadela in Mexico City, available for public consultation since circa 2016. The writer and essayist Adolfo Castañón, who has compiled Monsiváis's vast bibliography, considers him to be, perhaps, the last public intellectual in Mexico.[1]

As a member of the generation that began writing in the 1960s, Monsiváis was influenced by the civil rights movements in the US and Europe, and he was marked by the events surrounding the Tlatelolco Massacre of 1968 and the corollary state violence (both preceding and following the massacre and the Summer Olympics). Since then, his critique has been crucial in the redefinition of the Nation-State and its relationship with civil society in the process of democratization. For his project, it has been fundamental to place the marginal at the center. Although his activism and writing about feminism in Mexico was a constant, the posthumously published collection *Misógino feminista* was the first collection of his writings to be published in one place.

We are indebted to the work of pioneering academic and activist feminist Marta Lamas, who compiled and wrote the original Foreword to *Misógino feminista*, which has been a fundamental contribution to the study of his work on gender equity, and the women's reproductive and legal rights and LGBTQ+ movements, among others.[2] In fact, her selection is crucial for

disseminating dispersed and not easily available essays on women's continued struggle for equality in Mexico, an area of Monsiváis's critical interest
that has been much less known and studied than his other areas of specialty
such as urban and popular culture including film, music, literature, and art,
and politics in general. This critical translation intends to generate compar-
isons in the US and beyond, and foment a cross-cultural feminist dialogue
in the Americas, where women and other marginalized groups continue
to face many of the same challenges that Monsiváis elucidates. In this way,
Monsivais's writing, which draws from the lived, embodied experiences of
innumerable women and minorities living under patriarchy, is in fact highly
translatable and legible in new contexts. Monsiváis theorizes in such a way
as to offer a model for dismantling cultural inequities. In fact, as scholars of
Mexican culture, we have both previously engaged with Monsiváis's work
on feminist issues and questions of translation.[3]

As we know, translations from English to other foreign languages have
been much more prevalent than from foreign languages into English. Lately,
however, there has been a "translation turn" or better, as Susan Bassnett
and André Lefevere signal, a "cultural turn in translation studies."[4] This
shift considers broader issues of context, history, and conventions, displaying more interest in hemispheric studies of the Americas, interdisciplinary
perspectives, and other-than-European thinkers and theorists. This has led
to more interest (still not enough in our opinion) in translating the critical
work of contemporary intellectuals, cultural critics, and theorists from Latin
America. While the translated work of novelists and poets has had much
better circulation in English, this has yet to be the case for cultural criticism.
Nevertheless, there is a growing number of such translations, most notably
among them, Angel Rama's 1984 *The Lettered City*, translated in 1996; several by Néstor García Canclini: *Transforming Modernity* (1993), *Consumers
and Citizens* (2001), *Hybrid Cultures* (2005), and *Imagined Globalization*
(2014); Beatriz Sarlo's *Scenes from Postmodern Life* (2001); Elizabeth Jelin's
State Repression and the Labors of Memory (2003); and more recently the
posthumously published essays by Bolivian intellectual René Zavaleta Mercado, *Towards a History of the National-Popular in Bolivia, 1879–1980* (2018).

In the case of Monsiváis, there are only two book-length translations of
his work into English: John Kraniauskas's *Mexican Postcards* (1997), a selection of twelve of his chronicles and essays; and Jeffrey Browitt and Nidia
Esperanza Castrillón's *A New Catechism for Recalcitrant Indians* (2007), a
fictionalized narrative by Monsiváis that acts as a contestation of neoco-
lonialism in Mexico and a revalorization of Indigenous cultures. In the
appendix to this edition, we list fifty-two works by Monsiváis that have

been translated and published in English, none of which explicitly address feminist issues, although Monsiváis often celebrates the accomplishments of women in the artistic sphere.

In light of his immense body of work, translations are relatively few and far between. We attribute this dearth of translation to two key factors: first, to the Mexican contextual specificity of Monsiváis's literary, cultural, historical, and social references, and second, to the elaborate polyphonic style and satirical nature of much of his writing. Gabriela Valenzuela Navarrete, one of the few critics who makes note of this, laments the lack of translation of his work while underscoring the inherent risks and roadblocks to translating Monsiváis's complexities.[5]

While a considerable body of critical writing has been produced in the US academy on Monsiváis, there is only one monographic study of Monsiváis's life and work, by Linda Egan.[6] Considering the current backlash against progressive movements in the world, and more particularly in the US where rights so arduously fought for and won in the late 1970s through the 1990s are currently under attack, our critical commentary on and translation of these essays is not only relevant but timely. What were considered "settled debates" on women's reproductive and LGBTQ+ rights are suddenly being legally challenged.

In his 1994 essay in this volume, "An Open Letter to Nancy Cárdenas, Exemplary Activist," Monsiváis recalls how the Stonewall uprising was a catalyst for the emergence the LGBTQ+ movement in the US—and an inspiration for the movements in Mexico and around the world. Fifty years later, in 2019, this major event was celebrated at the New York Public Library with their exhibit "Love and Resistance," and yet today hate crimes against the LGBTQ+ community persist. It will be fifty years since *Roe v. Wade*, the landmark decision by the US Supreme Court, which ruled that the Constitution of the US conferred women the ability to make decisions about their own bodies with regards to reproduction based on a right to privacy. This ruling was overturned in 2022 by the Supreme Court's *Dobbs* decision, which exposes women to the repeal of their rights by their respective state governments. In Mexico, on the other hand, abortion was decriminalized only in 2007, in Mexico City, though many states failed to follow suit. It wasn't until 2021 that Mexico's Supreme Court dictated the decriminalization of the practice at a national level, trailing their 2015 ruling in favor of same-sex marriage in the country.[7] On September 6, 2023, Mexico's Supreme Court decriminalized abortion nationwide, building on previous rulings to declare that any state law that prohibits abortion is unconstitutional and a violation of women's civils rights.[8]

In Mexico, feminism is "having its moment," and women are, more and more, taking to the streets to protest the impunity of police and a state that systematically ignores the fact that femicide—the explicit killing of women because of their gender—is at an all-time high, with ten women a day murdered nationwide. Social media and #hashtag activism has accelerated the sharing of information across borders and among women who are fighting for their rights and their lives all over the world, as the writer and critic Cristina Rivera Garza notes.[9] In 2019, in tandem with similar campaigns across the globe, the #MeToo movement made it to Mexico's cultural milieu, causing scandal and outrage because it made evident that women continue to face discrimination and harassment at every level of society. Since 2019, there have been yearly March 8 marches—on International Women's Day—that have flooded the streets and public plazas, as well as national women's strikes, "a day without women" events held on March 9, to massively underscore their invisible labor in the upkeep of society and to note the tragedy of women's forced disappearance and murder. This translated critical edition allows us to trace the historical roots of patriarchal domination and honor the forerunners and pioneers of today's Mexican feminist practices who have struggled to dismantle the systemic structures and strictures of state, church, and family.

To this end, Monsiváis dedicates several chapters to individual women whom he considered crucial to feminism writ large: Simone de Beauvoir, Rosario Castellanos, Susan Sontag, Nancy Cárdenas, and Frida Kahlo. Throughout, he denounces the imposed silencing of women's voices, he highlights and praises illustrious women who challenged stereotypes, such as Tonantzin, Sor Juana, Josefa Ortiz de Domínguez, Laureana Wright, Las Adelitas, Nellie Campobello, Lucha Reyes, Chavela Vargas, Sara García, Rosa Luz Alegría, Elena Poniatowska, Elena Garro, Lourdes Portillo, Comandante Elisa, and the Zapatista revolutionaries, among many, many others. Monsiváis reminds us of the longstanding presence of feminism and feminist movements in Mexico, and of institutional interactions with feminist theories and gender perspectives including the First Feminist Congress of Mérida in 1916, the granting of women's suffrage in 1953, and Mexico City's hosting of the United Nations International Year of the Woman in 1975. Nonetheless, he does not avoid interrogating and decrying the terrible realities that persist despite struggle and feminist gains, including women's economic inequality, political impunity in cases of violence against women, intra-familial violence, femicide (with a particular attention to Ciudad Juárez), and the constant pushback by the Catholic Church against women's hard-won bodily autonomy. Throughout, Monsiváis analyzes how men have represented women's place in Mexican society versus how women have and can represent themselves based on radically different lived experiences than those shown in films and literature. Likewise, he examines women's political representation and the pitfalls of accessing power via patriarchy. In fact, Monsiváis attends to the ways that the "Macho Mexicano" was culturally constructed, breaking down how such mythologies play out socially and politically, and inviting men to become allies with the feminist movement for their own benefit, as well as for the sake of justice.

The essays in this volume speak to their particular historical moments, important as chronological documents of Monsiváis's perspective at the time. Their analytical and theoretical frameworks also offer a critique and exploration of the origins and legacies of patriarchal power, colonialism, racism, classism, authoritarianism, church dogma, and the resistance—both collective and individual—to all of these. His writing here serves as a model for disentangling complex issues around social and cultural constructions of gender as he breaks down binaries and offers concrete alternatives for other ways of thinking about gender, class, and social standing, while offering the reader the tools and language to posit and defend their political beliefs.

It is important to note that Carlos Monsiváis was one of the first Mexican writers to introduce the work of US and European women and feminist thinkers into Mexican society in general. We believe that this translation will solidify Monsiváis's legacy in the English-speaking world with respect to the trajectory of the ideas and concepts that he elucidates. His overarching project was deeply invested in an inclusive, democratizing process, and his ethical and political commitment to the rights of minorities, and Human Rights in general (lest we forget that the International Declaration of Human Rights just turned seventy), continues to be relevant in the construction of a more just world.

In *Fatefully, Faithfully Feminist*, Monsiváis, besides documenting the feminist movement from its early stages as both an observer-chronicler and an active participant, systematically condemns "sexism," "as a universal problem and condition confronting machismo," which he calls "the cult of hyper-virility" and "phallocentric masculinity."[10] The essays in this collection chart a map from the Conquest of Mexico to the turn of the twenty-first century in order to identify patriarchal authoritarianisms, and to defy the essentialisms that excluded alternative narratives and realities. In his efforts to change sexist, classist, and racist mindsets, he critiques the Paterfamilias, the State, and the Church (which he says powerfully regulated social life from the pulpit), in order to abolish the persistent prejudices present in society, culture, literature, film, and so on, whose discourse—based on sexism— stereotypes women as the idealized selfless mother, the subservient wife, or the berated libertine. Always proactive and purposeful, Monsiváis takes note of women's tangible and emerging achievements, recording the changes that are being attained such as the right to their own bodies, the decriminalization of abortion, and the ground gained by their political participation. Throughout, Monsiváis focuses on the intellectual, creative, and political accomplishments of women, to place them on equal footing with men.

With few exceptions, Monsiváis sees 1968 as a watershed moment when sexism as masculinist chauvinism becomes increasingly contested and he offers alternatives based on deconstructing what were essentialist adjudications on women's perceived nature. His theorization and analysis demonstrate his faith that literature, art, and writing itself are spaces that can *either* uncritically re-cement women's subordinate position *or* open up alternative possibilities to undo long-time patriarchal structures. For over four decades, across the span of these essays, his message is clear: a response to sexism (as well as to racism, classism, and homophobia) has to be political not moral.

Each essay in this collection is autonomous; however, collectively they critique patriarchal power, recognizing feminist epistemologies as crucial to advancing women's rights and democratization in the Mexican context and beyond. It is important to note that Monsiváis masters multiple literary genres, effectively exploring different modes of writing to produce a specific impact on the reader. Whether in the form of chronicle, eulogy, biography, review, or epistolary (among others), or by following the rhetorical devices of the bible, journalistic investigation, or scholarly analysis, Monsiváis is always keenly aware of the effect his writing will have on the public—all this with the presence of an autobiographical "I" who is attentively engaging his reader. We have briefly summarized each essay to demonstrate the breadth and depth of Monsiváis's cultural critique.

In Chapter 1, "Dreamy, Flirty, and Fiery: Notes on Sexism in Mexican Literature" (1973), Monsiváis presents a historical account from pre-Columbian times to the present focusing on literary works that have uncritically cemented women's subordinate position in society, whether through continued mythification (Virgin/Tonantzin), idealization (the virtuous virgin or the self-sacrificing mother), or exploitation (the sinful temptress). Saving Sor Juana as the exception in a range of literary works that spans several centuries, he is careful not to blame the authors as they are, he notes, reproducing the prevalent social mores of the period.

Chapter 2, "A New Salute for the Optimist" (1978), is an assessment of the early accomplishments of the feminist movement in Mexico. Monsiváis points out that there's no going back: the movement has reached large sectors of the population. The feminist and sexual liberation movements are contributing a critical perspective to the "feminine" and "masculine" condition as historical constructs. The biggest headway has been the campaign to decriminalize abortion, an advance in vindicating the right to one's own body, even as the Catholic Church (the majority religion) continues to condemn it. Monsiváis follows the continued resistance by feminists who reject familial, governmental, and ecclesiastical authoritarianism, and refuse to be subjected to any "moral lynching."

Chapter 3, "But Were There Ever Really Eleven Thousand Machos?" (1982), examines the meanings of "macho" and "machismo" in the Mexican context. It briefly explores cultural production in the context of filmmakers of Mexico's Golden Age of film in order explore the roots of ingrained gender roles. And in Chapter 4, "We Don't Want Mother's Day, We Want Revolution!: On the New Feminism" (1983), he examines the tokenism of celebrating women as mothers while failing to recognize their other myriad contributions to Mexican society; he outlines the actions taken in 1983 by feminist groups on Mother's Day as a way to discuss the history and genealogy of women's movements in Mexico from 1975 (the International Year of the Woman in Mexico City) to the present day (1983).

Chapter 5, "Mexico's Young Women in the International Youth Year" (1985), examines the intersections of gender and youth culture, discussing the ways Mexico has historically been constructed on the notions of female innocence and purity and obedience to a patriarchal order. It traces tendencies from the nineteenth century to the 1980s of Mexican literary and film narratives in popular culture to show how they circumscribe the lives of young women through the imposition of limited imaginaries. Subsequently, Monsiváis examines how popular culture addresses grave problems for Mexico's modern young women, such as questions of rape and abortion, and how they are processed by the legal system, which is steeped in patriarchal tradition.

Chapter 6, "On Constructing 'Feminine Sensitivity'" (1987), examines how machismo has structured "women's sensitivity" (one based on her being passive, spiritual, virtuous, or sinful, etc.) and the exclusionary politics that this marginalization brings about, not only for women, but also for Indigenous peoples. Neither were included as citizens in the constitutions of 1857 or 1917. Monsiváis proceeds to study women's poetry and novels from the nineteenth century to the present with a focus on those women who refused the male gaze in order to become the early pioneers of twentieth century literary contestation: Rosario Castellanos, Elena Garro, and Elena Poniatowska.

Chapter 7, "Love on (the Eternal Eve of an Impending) Democracy" (1990), meditates on whether love and democracy are compatible concepts, going on to explore the state-sanctioned versions of romantic and familial love. Monsiváis explores the notion of "the personal is political," considering the sexual revolution of the 1970s, and the way its impact on Mexican women was quickly curbed with the AIDS crisis of the 1980s. And Chapter 8, "How One Day Pro-Lifers Woke Up to the News That They Were Living in a Secular Society" (1990), focuses on the debates that the feminist movement brought to the fore: the decriminalization of abortion, which opened a heated discussion among the political Right, the Catholic Church, conservatives (pro-life groups), and Leftist political parties that believed in women's right to their own bodies. He points out that the position of the conservative Right, beyond opposing decriminalizing abortion (even in cases of rape), was also against the use of birth control and sexual relations outside of marriage.

Chapter 9, "On Women's Representation" (1991), begins with a look at the double standard in Mexican politics at the cusp of the neoliberal era, in which women, along with children, Indigenous peoples, and homosexuals, were considered an afterthought. Their condition as "protected groups" was minimally discussed by those in power, who claimed that a "right to work" was part of the protected groups' basic "liberation," with no specific legal provisions to attain such a noble task. Monsiváis puts into clear relief the problem of Mexican women's suffrage (attained in 1953), and their lack of representation in politics. He questions the manipulative power of tokenism and the practices that continue to keep women out of the upper echelons of power.

In Chapter 10, "A Crying Lesson" (1992), Monsiváis analyzes the poetry of Rosario Castellanos, an early and fundamental feminist writer whose 1950 MA thesis, *Sobre cultura femenina* (On feminine culture), spoke directly about women's marginalized condition, educated to obey rather than develop their full potential. Her poetry astutely contested male poetic imaginaries that idealized women by placing them on pedestals. With textual citations, Monsiváis demonstrates the critical distance that Castellanos assumes as a poetic persona by taking on the "real" and varied roles of women of that era, be they unhappily married, abandoned, on valium, unmarried, or single mothers—all from an ironic stance that showed the harsh reality lived by most women under patriarchy then and now. And Chapter 11, "Let Us Now Praise" (1994), is a lyrical essay in honor of the unsung heroines at the close of Mexico's nineteenth century. It attempts to revive the names and acts of women from a time that refused to record their participation in history. He lists the achievements of precursors to the present feminist struggle, women who dared to push the envelope; to study and work in fields where they were not welcome, like medicine, literature, politics, and publishing; women unafraid of tongue-lashings, social isolation, and prison in their struggles to win the rights of present-day women at the turn of the twenty-first century. Chapter 12, "An Open Letter to Nancy Cárdenas, Exemplary Activist" (1994), is an epistolary essay addressed to Nancy Cárdenas, a well-known Mexican writer, playwright, poet, theater actress, stage manager, director, journalist, essayist, radio host, and activist. A pioneer in the 1970s for gay rights, she was one of the first to publicly declare her lesbianism. This essay acts as a eulogy in praise of a close friend, bringing her back to life as he stages her unique biography.

Chapter 13, "The Fourth Papal Visit: The Spectacle of Faith Fascinated by Its Own Spectacle" (1999), chronicles Pope John Paul II's visit to Mexico in 1999, exploring the ways tradition and capitalism intersected and highlighting certain hypocrisies and social exclusions fomented by the alliance between the Catholic Church and neoliberal politicians. With acerbic humor, he outlines the copious preparations made in honor of the papal visit, underscoring the ways the supposedly "lay nation" is still influenced by its deeply conservative Catholic roots. Monsiváis highlights the aspects of spectacle and showmanship that hide or bury the underlying problems of a deepening social class divide in Mexico, making evident how this blind national faith continues to work against women's best interests with respect to their ability to choose their own fate in the face of faith.

In Chapter 14, "*The Second Sex*: One Is Not Born a Feminist" (1999), Monsiváis offers a rereading of *The Second Sex* followed by an analysis of its relevance today. When *The Second Sex* appeared in 1949, it went unnoticed in Mexico, which he claims is undoubtedly because Mexico was still a feudal empire: women didn't yet have the right to vote, divorce was still illegal, adultery continued to shake the (hypocritically) "good families," women wearing pants still provoked a heated discussion, and the presence of women at the university was almost nil. The book, he says, still retains its vitality because even if there are advances, women continue to be in grave disadvantage.

Chapter 15, "Women in Power" (2000), is an extended review of Sabina Berman and Denise Maerker's book *Mujeres y poder* (2000; Women and power), which attempts to understand the underpinnings of power in Mexico through interviews with women who have attained a certain level of political power in the nation: Elba Esther Gordillo, Commander Elisa (of the EZLN), Rosa Luz Alegría, Silvia Hernández, and Rosario Robles.

Monsiváis presents the major findings of the book and its accompanying documentary, which address how women can take political power and use it for the betterment of society in general, and for women's lived experience in particular. He sees that it will take time before the words "women and power" become so commonplace as to not require a book of their own. And Chapter 16, "Bones in the Desert: Listening through the Eyes of Dead Women" (2003), is a review of *Huesos en el desierto* (Bones in the desert) by Sergio González Rodríguez; published in 2002, it was the first significant investigative journalistic book that denounced the femicides in Ciudad Juarez in the 1990s and 2000s, enacted mainly on the bodies of maquila workers. Monsiváis analyzes this violence as a result of the systemic misogyny of a still-feudal patriarchal regime in Mexico. He saw the physical mutilation of young women as a perfect dystopia that was dehumanizing, and that deterred the civilizing project, hindering women's newly won freedoms. Monsiváis classifies these brutal murders as hate crimes, not only due to unpunished sexism, but also to classism and racism, considering that most of the young women were poor and Indigenous. For Sergio González Rodríguez, it was an active remembrance; for Monsiváis it became a call to action.

In Chapter 17, "The Saintly, Long-Suffering Mother: The One Who Loved Mexican Cinema before She Ever Saw It" (2004), Monsiváis examines the ways mass media of the twentieth century transformed the nation, and how women's bodies, and the iconicity of certain actresses, acted as a moral guide for women, shaping the way they would imagine themselves by virtue of how they were portrayed in popular culture. He analyzes how the Mexican film industry, especially in melodramas of the "Golden Age" (1932–1950), responded to Hollywood with their own brand of misogyny and sexism. Monsiváis explores stereotypes, citing examples from many famous films, to finally analyze the role of the paradigmatic actress Sara García and her iconic "white head" of hair, as the eternally long-suffering grandma of Mexican cinema. This essay puts into question the idea of maternity as the ultimate ideal for women, and questions the way that this ideal is upheld by the film culture of the twentieth century.

Chapter 18, "Susan Sontag (1933–2004): Imagination and Historical Conscience" (2005), is a biographical and bibliographical essay on Susan Sontag's life and work, written after her death as a critical eulogy that highlights the milestones she achieved as a major writer and political activist. Monsiváis follows her life and work from her first major radical essay, "On Camp" (1964), until her death in 2004, focusing on her most important works and political interventions. Monsiváis was an early follower of her work and was crucial in making her writings and activism on feminist and gay movements known in Mexico. In this essay he differentiates between the feminist and gay movements in Mexico, which emerged influenced by Anglo and European events. In both contexts legacies of feudalism and colonialism are still present, as well as heteronormativity that circumscribes individual lives differently.

Chapter 19, "Mexico at the Dawn of the Twenty-First Century: Globalization, Determinism, and the Spread of Secularism" (2006), is a historical essay that acts as an overview of the entire collection, taking as a starting point the major political changes that occurred when Vicente Fox, from the far-right Partido de Acción Nacional (PAN) political party, became the first president to break the seventy-one-year rule of the Partido Revolucionario Institucional (PRI). Monsiváis then reflects on the use of big ideas for political ends, noting the use of key words such as "civil society, tolerance, transition to democracy, inclusive programs, diversity, plurality and empowerment," all terms culled from the women's movement and its subsequent "gender perspective." This essay outlines major events that brought to the fore the plight of Indigenous peoples on the occasion of the fifth centenary of "discovery" [encounter]—commemorated in 1992 and extended by the UN as the First International Decade of the World's Indigenous People (1995–2004), as well as the social interventions of religious minorities in the national imaginary. He examines social groups, especially the gay community, who fought for their visibility and their lives, and the rise of femicides in Ciudad Juárez as corollaries to the spread of "secularism."

And finally, Chapter 20, "Frida Kahlo: The Stages of her Renown (2008)," is a portrait of Mexico's most reproduced artist, showing how her fate changed in the hearts and eyes of the art world from the time of her active painting to the years following her death. It is particularly compelling because it demonstrates how an artist and her work can be adopted posthumously for political and social purposes, and how Fridamania came to be. In particular, Frida Kahlo became a household name after the publication of Hayden Herrera's biography and Kahlo's own *Diary*, the release of various biopics, and the subsequent mass reproduction of her paintings on all manner of objects, which lead to a practical sanctification of her image internationally.

This critical edition and translation into English offers the opportunity to reread Monsiváis and his overarching project: casting women as agents in their own liberation rather than focusing on victimization. It provides a deep reflection on how even in the face of insurmountable odds, women were and are capable of representing themselves. Monsiváis effectively traces the struggles and successes of the women's movements, bringing his readers to a place of ethical and political commitment. He writes, "One is not born a woman. Neither a feminist."[11]

NOTES

1. Adolfo Castañón, *Nada mexicano me es ajeno: Papeles sobre Carlos Monsiváis* (Mexico City: Bonilla Artigas, 2017), 19, 249–55.

2. Marta Lamas is considered one of the foremost academics in Mexico with regard to feminism and women's rights movements. She has published extensively on these topics in both English and Spanish. See Marta Lamas, *Feminisms: Transmissions and Retransmissions*, trans. [J. D.] Pluecker (New York: Palgrave Macmillan, 2011).

3. Norma Klahn and Ilana Luna, "Traducir a Monsiváis es mantenerlo vivo," in *Inundación Castálida: La Revista del Claustro de Sor Juana*, no. 15 (June 2020): 34–38. See also Ilana Luna, *Adapting Gender: Mexican Feminisms from Literature to Film* (Albany, NY: SUNY Press, 2018); Norma Klahn, "Carlos Monsiváis," in *Encyclopedia of Mexico: History, Society and Culture*, 2nd ed., ed. Michael S. Berner, 937–39 (Chicago, IL: Fitzroy Dearborn Publishers, 1977); Norma Klahn and Guillermo Delgado-P. "Lágrimas Negras" en una nota para Monsiváis," *Debate Feminista*, no. 43 (April 2011): 201–8; Norma Klahn, "Locating Women's Writing and Translation in the Americas in the Age of Latinoamericanismo and Globalization," in *Translocalities/Translocalidades: Feminist Politics of Translation in the Latin/a Américas*, ed. Sonia Alvarez et al., 39–56 (Durham, NC: Duke University Press, 2014).

4. Susan Bassnett and André Lefevere, *Constructing Cultures: Essays on Literary Translation* (Bristol, UK: Multilingual Matters, 1998), 123. This concept originally from Susan Bassnett and André Lefevere, eds. *Translation, History and Culture* (London: Pinter, 1990).

5. Gabriela Valenzuela Navarrete, "¿Traduciendo o traicionando a Monsiváis . . .?" In *La Conciencia Imprescindible: Ensayos sobre Carlos Monsiváis*, Ed. Jezreel Salazar, 278–92. (Mexico City: Tierra Adentro Fondo Editorial, 2009).

6. Linda Egan, *Carlos Monsiváis: Culture and Chronicle in Contemporary Mexico* (Tucson: University of Arizona Press, 2001).

7. Stephania Taladrid, "Mexico's Historic Step toward Legalizing Abortion." *New Yorker*, October 28, 2021, https://www.newyorker.com/news/news-desk/mexicos-historic-step-toward-legalizing-abortion.

8. Simon Romero and Emiliano Rodríguez Mega, "Mexico's Supreme Court Decriminalizes Abortion Nationwide," *New York Times*, September 6, 2023, https://www.nytimes.com/2023/09/06/world/americas/mexico-abortion-decriminalize-supreme-court.html.

9. Cristina Rivera Garza, "On Our Toes: Women against the Femicide Machine in Mexico," *World Literature Today* 94, no. 1 (Winter 2020), https://www.worldliteraturetoday.org/2020/winter/our-toes-women-against-femicide-machine-mexico-cristina-rivera-garza.

10. Chapter 1: Dreamy, Flirty, and Fiery: Notes on Sexism in Mexican Literature, 17.
11. Chapter 14, "*The Second Sex*: One Is Not Born a Feminist," 166.

REFERENCES

Bassnett, Susan, and André Lefevere. *Constructing Cultures: Essays on Literary Translation*. Bristol, UK: Multilingual Matters, 1998.

Castellanos, Rosario. *Sobre cultura femenina*. Mexico City: Ediciones de América, 1950.

Castañón, Adolfo. *Nada mexicano me es ajeno: Papeles sobre Carlos Monsiváis*. Mexico City: Bonilla Artigas, 2017.

Egan, Linda. *Carlos Monsiváis: Culture and Chronicle in Contemporary Mexico*. Tucson: University of Arizona Press, 2001.

García Canclini, Nestor. *Tranforming Modernity: Popular Culture in Latin America*. Translated by Lidia Lozano. Austin: University of Texas Press, 1993.

García Canclini, Nestor. *Consumers and Citizens: Globalization and Multicultural Conflicts* [In Spanish, 1995]. Translated and with an introduction by George Yúdice. Minneapolis: University of Minnesota Press, 2001.

García Canclini, Nestor. *Hybrid Cultures: Srategies for Entering and Leaving Modernity* [In Spanish, 1989]. Translated by Christopher L. Chiappari and Silvia L. López. Minneapolis: University of Minnesota Press, 2005.

García Canclini, Nestor. *Imagined Globalization* [In Spanish, 1999]. Translated and with an introduction by George Yúdice. Durham, NC: Duke University Press, 2014.

Jelin, Elizabeth. *State Repression and the Labors of Memory* [In Spanish, 2002]. Translated by Judy Rein and Marcial Godoy-Anativia. Minneapolis: University of Minnesota Press, 2003.

Klahn, Norma. "Locating Women's Writing and Translation in the Americas in the Age of Latinoamericanismo and Globalization." In *Translocalities/ Translocalidades: Feminist Politics of Translation in the Latin/a Américas*, edited by Sonia Alvarez, Claudia de Lima Costa, Verónica Feliu, Rebecca Hester, Norma Klahn, and Millie Thayer, 39–56. Durham, NC: Duke University Press, 2014.

Klahn, Norma. "Monsiváis entre la nación y la migra(na)ción." In *El arte de la ironía*, edited by Mabel Moraña and Ignacio Sánchez Prado, 176–90. Mexico City: Era/ UNAM, 2007.

Klahn, Norma, and Guillermo Delgado-P. "'Lágrimas Negras' en una nota para Monsiváis." *Debate Feminista*, no. 43 (April 2011): 201–8.

Klahn, Norma, and Ilana Luna. "Traducir a Monsiváis es mantenerlo vivo." *Inundación Castálida: La Revista del Claustro de Sor Juana*, no. 15 (June 2020): 34–38.

Lamas, Marta. *Feminism: Transmissions and Retransmissions*. Translated by [J. D.] Pluecker. New York: Palgrave Macmillan, 2011.

Luna, Ilana. *Adapting Gender: Mexican Feminisms from Literature to Film*. Albany, NY: SUNY Press, 2018.

Monsiváis, Carlos. *A New Catechism for Recalcitrant Indians* [In Spanish, 1982]. Translated by Jeffrey Browitt and Nidia Esperanza Castrillón. Mexico City: Fondo de Cultura Económica, 2007.

Monsiváis, Carlos. *Mexican Postcards*. Translated by John Kraniauskas. New York: Verso, 1997.

Monsiváis, Carlos. *Misógino feminista*. Edited by Marta Lamas. Mexico City: Océano/Debate Feminista, 2013.

Rama, Angel. *The Lettered City* [In Spanish, 1984]. Translated and edited by John Charles Chasteen. Durham, NC: Duke University Press, 1996.

Rivera Garza, Cristina. "On Our Toes: Women against the Femicide Machine in Mexico." *World Literature Today* 94, no. 1 (Winter 2020). https://www.worldliteraturetoday.org/2020/winter/our-toes-women-against-femicide-machine-mexico-cristina-rivera-garza.

Sarlo, Beatriz. *Scenes from Postmodern Life* [In Spanish, 1994]. Translated by John Beasley-Murray. Minneapolis: University of Minnesota Press, 2001.

Valenzuela Navarrete, Gabriela. "¿Traduciendo o traicionando a Monsiváis . . .?" In *La Conciencia Imprescindible: Ensayos sobre Carlos Monsiváis*, edited by Jezreel Salazar, 278–92. Mexico City, Tierra Adentro, 2009.

Zavaleta Mercado, René. *Towards a History of the National-Popular in Bolivia, 1879–1980*. Translated by Anne Freeland. New York: Seagull Books, 2018.

CHAPTER 1

Dreamy, Flirty, and Fiery

Notes on Sexism in Mexican Literature

1973

Neither a conspiracy nor a trap, but rather a more methodical and established structure. It's the deliberate, watchful, exalted, melancholic, merciless, tender, and paternalistic structuring of inferiority. Sexism is none other than an ideological sum total that is a praxis, and a technique that is a world view. A society (in this case, any society, because sexism is a universal problem and condition, it doesn't automatically depend on a social and political system, it transcends ideologies and militancies) overwhelmingly presupposes its founding convictions: whoever doesn't subscribe to this behavioral pattern (because they can't or won't) will inevitably be deemed an inferior being. When does sexism emerge? Historically, maybe it is when, in lieu of pleasure or personal development, reproduction becomes the sole objective of sexual relations. Patriarchy decided this, backed by biology for all eternity: God says to Eve (according to Genesis): "I will greatly multiply your sorrow and your Conception; In pain you shall bring forth children; Your desire shall be for your husband, and he shall rule over you."[1] Adam, in command of the situation, looked at the woman and saw an object, a valuable tool because of her ability to spark a demographic explosion, and her ability to please, and be companion to, the masters of the world. A syndrome of the fundamental evils and the record of events of any system, sexism—this kind of imperialism that is doubly exercised against *at least* half of humanity—has been making its history through submission, slavery, and the continuous exercise of rules and repression. Sexism is a mirage: even if a woman is privy to an education, wealth, and independence, as if she were (truly) an autonomous being equal to man, all the meaningful influences in her life show her that education is only justified if used in service to her husband. Sexism is a distorted mirror that legitimizes the caudillo's posturing, making it appear like civilized behavior; its distortions assure the woman that her only possible reality lies in the care of her children and the creation of a supportive environment for the "true" human beings, the men who aggressively traipse around the world to better lead it.[2]

SEXISM AS FIXED ROLES

Sexism, a widespread phenomenon, is only comprehensible in very general terms. Any inquiry at this stage runs the risk of becoming overly simplistic and of promoting new kinds of clichés. The term covers a wide range: the dominance of one sex (and of those who within that sex are more aptly aligned to the dominant mindset, and possess the necessary characteristics to exercise power); the preference of society for that sex; the transformation of a declared inferiority into a real inferiority; the attribution of privileged qualities and behaviors to the dominant sex; and an emphasis on control in any personal relationship of a sexual nature. Sexism, through subjugation, divides the world into "masculine" and "feminine" roles, attributing to each role characteristics that must be fatalistically fulfilled. The "feminine" must embody, for example, tenderness, modesty, patience, sweetness, intuition, abnegation, resistance to pain, abject passivity, inertia, lack of initiative, frivolity, an inability to connect to History (with a capital *H*), and a willingness to view reality through the lens of gossip. Thousands of years of these ideas, forcefully imposed, along with invigorated and reinvigorated models of behavior, has rendered this definition of the "feminine" a "natural" and "instinctual" response. Sexism infantilizes, robs, and strips autonomy, self-confidence, and agency from a whole sector of humanity. For thousands of years, an exchange has been negotiated that demands servitude, and "charitably" offers protection.

So, what constitutes sexism? It's an ideology based on the necessities and values of the dominant group, and it is normalized according to what the members of this group admire in themselves, and what they find useful in their subordinates: aggression, intelligence, strength, and effectiveness in men; passivity, ignorance, docility, "virtue," and ineffectiveness in women. It's a psychological framework that presupposes a card-carrying membership to patriarchal ideology, and diminishes—through social beliefs, ideology, and tradition—any possibility for equality for the feminine ego. It's a phenomenon of social class, a sociological truth, an economic and educational fact, a theory of strength, a biological assumption, and an anthropological structure that suppresses myths and religions. Sexism recognizes its most successful political form in patriarchy, and its most evident institution in the family.

WOMAN AS AN INSTRUMENT

By its very nature and definition, Mexican culture is a sexist culture. Fundamentally, it relies on the belief that because women are inferior beings, they must be exploited. Octavio Paz, in *El laberinto de la soledad* (1949; *The Labyrinth Of Solitude*), provides an excellent first mapping of the process:

> No doubt an element of masculine vanity, the vanity of the "señor," of the lord or chieftain (it is an inheritance from both our Indian and Spanish ancestors), enters into our conception of feminine modesty. Like almost all other people, the Mexican considers woman to be an instrument, sometimes of masculine desires, sometimes of the ends assigned to her by morality, society and the law. It must be admitted that she has never been asked to consent to these ends and that she participates in their realization only passively, as a "repository" for certain values. Whether as prostitute, goddess, *grande dame* or mistress, woman transmits or preserves—but does not believe in—the values and energies entrusted to her by nature or society. In a world made in man's image, woman is only a reflection of masculine will and desire. When passive, she becomes a goddess, a beloved one, a being who embodies the ancient, stable elements of the universe: the earth, motherhood, virginity. When active, she is always function and means, a receptacle and a channel. Womanhood, unlike manhood, is never an end in itself.[3]

These lines by Octavio Paz, with his innate talent for synthesis, are precise. Among us, the pre-Hispanic tradition that assigned women a disdainful, servile role meshed easily with the culture brought by the conquistadores.[4] The first pact among those responsible for the origins of our national identity was about women's place in society. And, drawing here from the testimonies of indigenous poetry, there is a certain—neither emphatic nor eluded—identification between being conquered (weakness), and wailing and fleeing (femininity). From a typical poem:

> Is suffering my destiny?
> Oh my friend, my heart cries out in anguish:
> We live among afflictions on earth.
> How can we live with others?

> If we live in vain we offend others!
> One must live in peace, one must surrender
> and walk with a bent-down head among others.[5]

And in *Visión de los vencidos*, in one of the best-known post-Conquest poems, "The Mexicatl people have vanished," the poet states:

> Our cries of grief rise up
> and our tears run down,
> for Tlatelolco is lost.
> The Aztecs are fleeing across the lake;
> they are running away like women.[6]

From the Viceroyalty on, a worldview is firmly established that uses, in its demand for supremacy and privilege for a certain class and a certain gender within that class, moral and political repression, education, and government. The Viceroyalty conceives of an order of things in which obedience is the primary requisite for any situation, and where notions of honor and virtue become social and political responses. During the three centuries of Spanish rule, patriarchal structures and conducts are reinforced, and remain *essentially* intact today through family education, which continues to be the unifying principle of power relations in societies like ours.

RETROACTIVE EFFECTS

Therefore, to talk about sexism is to retrospectively evaluate our entire historical process: the Colonial, Independent, Liberal, Revolutionary, Post-, and Counter-Revolutionary periods. Can our managing and deployment of the notion of sexism allow for retroactive ramifications? Isn't it a historic contradiction or a parodic gesture to label Juan Ruiz de Alarcón or Pedro Castera, author of the romantic novel *Carmen*, sexist?[7] To a certain degree, yes. However, upon thoroughly reviewing what's within our grasp, that is, the history of our culture with new and revised approaches and perspectives, it's not a contradiction at all. This re-examination becomes a useful and urgent task, not because of a bloodthirsty desire to disinter defenseless writers and enact an avenging trial, but rather for the purpose of interrogating our cultural upbringing, and its manipulation of our reactions and sense of morality today. All of us—to a greater or lesser degree—rely on sexism to parse reality, and an awareness of this problem will only be possible once we accept its existence. As with many things, we are only beginning to scratch the surface, and these notes, while attempting to acknowledge the roots of sexism, are inevitably steeped in it as well.

In Mexican literature (and it couldn't have happened any differently) sexism finds a necessary and effective collaborator. In this case, the reflection of reality is almost always a direct representation, without nuance. If other phenomena of national life can allow for artistic reimagining and modification, this is not the case for sexism. It is a point of view that is too deeply engrained, so fundamentally rooted that—judge it as you may—it constitutes an idiosyncrasy, a "natural" response to external and internal demands. Hence, at this stage, any purely moral reaction to the institution of sexism is useless. The moral offensive tends to stop just short of demonization, at the gates of condemnation. And sexism, like all secular conditioning, like all our deep cultural responses, is rife with judgment and outrage; it undoes or ridicules all attempts at criticism. In confronting sexism, the response must be political, not moral. The fight against the pre-determined servitude of one sex, against such unrelenting rules of conduct, must organically become a part of the present struggles for liberation. The sexual revolution is yet another (classical) phase of revolution in our time.

But these thoughts are taking a dogmatic, judgmental, and precipitous turn. This title does not proclaim a plan of action, but rather proposes a survey. Let's revisit my supposed line of argumentation, with this assertion: the task of identifying the impact of sexism on our literature is of utmost importance. Today, while a revision of our historical process is taking place—a demythifying and demystifying moment—it is important to consider the scope and foundational roots of systems of exploitation, among which sexism is essential and definitive.

FEMALE CHARACTERS

Women, in our literature, are assigned a fundamental role: that of landscape. Men are always the central figures, the be-all and end-all of existence. On the margins, exalted or tainted, women move—accordingly—with dignity or seductively. She can be the mother (who suffers everything), the wife (who forgives everything), or the prostitute (who degrades everything). She is, by necessity, only a pretext or an excuse to write. Antonio Machado once expressed in a concise tone (this time not put to music): "Woman is the obverse of being."[8] What is the obverse of being? A nonbeing, a nonentity? Or is it akin to ontology, where affirmations or negations are reproduced as inverted, imaginary, or nonexistent by virtue of their opposition to true reality? According to this conception, the essence of woman is that she is a derivative, appropriated being. In our literature (and in our painting, popular music, and later, radio, film, and television), women exist insofar as men are represented as not being (officially) alone. The first manifestation of this is Tonantzin, "Our Mexica Mother," who later emerges as Guadalupe in a process unique to our nation.[9] When the miracle of Tepeyac is decreed and politically established, the terms of feminine idealization are fixed: the "Virgin," with or without a capital *V*, is the worshipped and venerated woman ("I swear no one is more sacred to me than you"). If this interpretation weren't suspiciously tinged with psychologism, one might notice in a whole area of literature (or reality) a pan-virginal project. To be immaculate is the sign of respectable womanhood: my mother, my wife, my daughter, have been and will continue to be perfect virgins, because virginity, more than a physical condition, is an essential attribute of that which belongs to me. As my possession, she is inaccessible, sheltered from and beyond any desecration. Ultimately, virginity becomes sacred because of the complex and evident way in which it is a manifestation of property rights.

Invented, portrayed, and obscured by literature, woman takes on and embodies different roles: she is the reticent beloved to whom men should dedicate their musings and reminiscences (the idolatrous object of some modernista poets, like Lopez Velarde's Fuensanta); the chaste betrothed (Emilio Rabasa's Remedios, Ignacio Manuel Altamirano's Clemencia); the selfless and understanding mother who is radiant in her pain and loss (the ubiquitous and omnipresent being that appears everywhere from serialized fiction to popular poetry, from the style of Guillermo Aguirre y Fierro's "El brindis del bohemio" ["A Bohemian Toast"] to Efrén Hernández's sweet and steadfast characters); the repentant sinner, a Mary Magdalene aware that only by death is she redeemed for her loss of virginity (like the heroine of the serialized novel *Santa* by Federico Gamboa); and the man-eater, who takes on men's predatory spirit, deploying masculine techniques of subjugation to avenge her spoiled virginity (this widely disseminated cliché manifests itself as a secondary character in novels, and especially in film: María Félix will make it her hallmark, as will the *rumberas* in their earthy abundance: Ninón Sevilla, Meche Barba, etc. Recently, in *La Martina*, Irma Serrano has revived the man-eater, conflating nymphomania with consumer mentality).[10]

Other archetypes are the faithful soldadera, who admirably sacrifices her life for her man's (La Codorniz in Mariano Azuela's *Los de abajo*); the vulnerable flirt who gambles with her honor and loses (Micaela in Agustín Yáñez's *Al filo del agua*); the sickly and withdrawn woman (Susana San Juan in Juan Rulfo's *Pedro Páramo*); the crazed lover, victim of passionate love who in her surrender redeems her shamelessness (Adriana in José Vasconcelos's *La tormenta*); the venerated goddess, so magnificent that she's comparable to the mother (Rosario in Manuel Acuña's "Nocturno"); the long-gone earthy woman (the brave, dark-haired Indian in Manuel José Othón's "Idilio salvaje"); and the purest nymphet, whose love of an adult can only be consummated in tragedy (in Pedro Castera's novel *Carmen*).[11]

What might be a rudimentary and general conclusion? To this day, our literature is lacking in female characters whose reality is portrayed realistically. They're not constituted as whole beings: instead they're represented as mythic figures, as models from a previous era. Even in what is possibly our best novel, *Pedro Páramo*, next to the raw, obsessive, and blunt presence of the *cacique*, a double spectrality appears: the mad, disembodied presence of Susana San Juan, who never transcends her isolated and reclusive condition, always evoking an intense and imprecise eroticism, a ghostly silence, an intangible love. Pedro Páramo will possess all women, violate them, tame them, and ultimately discard them. As long as women are treated as inferior, they become possible prey: Dolorita Preciado or Damiana Cisneros. When Pedro Páramo sees Susana as his equal and loves her without the use of physical force, at that moment, Susana San Juan is divested of any defined characteristics: she becomes a delirious, mystical project, an erotic abandon that longs for eternity; she becomes, definitively, a nonentity.

It's inevitable. For even if there's a minimal relationship between what can be (in conventional terms) designated as literary reality and real reality, that tenuous connection links literature with a space where women hold no specific weight and always occupy a secondary and dependent position. For women to finally be represented in literature with their own center of gravity, they must transcend their invented construction, that pact between the author and the reader's suspension of disbelief. It's not a question of misogyny: everything that happens comes both before and after the hatred of women. Culture and Literature perceive women as child-like, only conceivable or granted a place through writing, given that if they were portrayed realistically, they would lack interest and spiritual substance. If women in Mexican literature are to be represented in complex ways, they will be, almost fatalistically, an abstraction.

THE HISTORICAL PROCESS

On the cusp of the eighteenth century, Sor Juana Inés de la Cruz in her splendid "Respuesta a Sor Filotea de la Cruz," (The response to Sor Filotea) engages in a battle: that of an exceptional woman who chooses to exercise her intelligence in a society that only allows women to be gracious, enchanting, flustered, or submissive.[12] The letter to Sor Filotea is an exemplary document: an ultimate act of resistance by someone condemned to ignorance and silence, to the renunciation of her intellect and to the "quiet of the cloister." Sor Juana, in a society where "many parents would rather leave their daughters uneducated and uncultured, rather than risk exposing them to such notorious peril as this familiarity with men," painfully and zealously defends her right to read, her right to know, her right to write.[13] "And if the evil lies in their being used by a woman, we have just seen how many women have used them most laudably, then what evil lies in my being one?"[14] In Sor Juana's question, the response is implicit: the intrinsic evil of being a woman is simply to be one, "her baseness and turpitude" as she herself establishes, are synonymous with her feminine condition.[15]

Between the knowledge of her inevitable failure and her will to resist—to the bitter end—subjugation (extinction), we find Sor Juana's greatness, a greatness that is at once a defense (both personal and gendered) of knowledge. Her uniqueness brought her face to face with repression, with a lack of understanding that has persisted in essays and analysis. Sor Juana's maladies continue today: on the one hand, the members of those "cultural associations" that still see women as "man's biggest supporter" have made her their symbol, ignoring the radical meaning (both intellectual and political) of her work; on the other hand, the superficial or disdainful readings (both sexist attitudes) have turned her "redondillas" into mere amusing expressions of a complaint, rather than the cogent criticism of her gender's institutional disadvantages that her polemic declaration made. Therefore, "O foolish men / who accuse women with so little cause . . ." has been read as a derisive reference to a minor protest, "not seeing you are the reason / for the very thing you blame."[16]

NINETEENTH-CENTURY RULES AND REGULATIONS

José Joaquín Fernández de Lizardi (1776–1827), acclaimed as the first Mexican novelist, outlines an intransigent code of conduct for women in his classic novel *La Quijotita y su prima* (1818; The Quijotita and her cousin).[17] To prove his point, he contrasts the education of two young girls, Pomposa and Pudenciana.[18] The colonel, character and alter ego of the author, explains the rebel Lizardi's point of view as follows:

> Whether by natural law, divine law, or civil law, woman, as a rule, is always inferior to man. Let me explain this to you. Nature [. . .] created women as

weaker than men, maybe because that physical weakness of which I am speaking either spares them energy or excuses them so they may carry out their role as mothers and secure the world's continuity. [. . .] I don't think you're understanding me: [of course, the colonel is monologuing with a woman] I'll say it more clearly. Nature, or speaking as Christians, our most wise author, didn't accord women the same strength as men, so that removed from the particular work of men, women would become, as intended, the delight of the world, and therefore would be the first and foremost protagonists in the propagation of our human lineage.[19]

Woman's mission has been stipulated: she is a luxury item, with reproductive capacity. Her first virtue: docility. Her second: gratitude. In this rich anthology of nineteenth-century sexism, *La Quijotita y su prima*, the colonel (a highly qualified summary of the liberal mindset of the first half of the nineteenth century) asserts his criteria:

Truly they [women] are worthy of the appreciation and esteem of the cultured man, and this regard makes men pay their respect, and cede, on many occasions, their own preferences to the woman's; but these respects and attentions must be accepted by the sensible woman; either as a reward for her virtue, or as a result of the generosity of men, and she should never demand such rights owed to her as a woman.

Lizardi's generosity doesn't end there. He also has a scathing thesis regarding the division of labor:

Taking into consideration this same weakness [that is, women's, which makes them inferior to men by natural law], civil laws have denied them priesthood, governance, participation in politics and the art of war, which have been entrusted to men, an exclusion that turns out to be a just reward owed the fair sex, and so just that men excluding them from these burdens have done nothing but reward their particular activities, recompense their wearisome tasks, and procure what best suits them.

The man who vilifies women on the grounds of their different sex should be declared foolish and ungrateful; but in the end, we must confess that quite justifiably women are inferior to men by civil law. How could a woman hold a child to her breast in one arm and in the other a rifle? I would say the same for a pen, a chisel, a plow, or other tools particular to men: it would be necessary to let go of either the tool or the child.

It doesn't make much sense to blame an author for the prevailing social mores of his era. Lizardi, a typical product of the liberal codes of conduct of viceregal society, does nothing but summarize a general line of thought. It so happens that this patriarchal vision that joyously relegates women to the *metate*, the *comal*, and the *tortilla* doesn't end with Lizardi.[20] In order to sustain itself, it has an admirable sounding board: the family, a monolithic unit contrived for the convenience of the ruling classes, and the Church, which continues, almost unchanged, until today. Society is founded on the family and, in exchange, society imbues marriage with its moral, religious, social, and economic bases— the foundations that make continuity possible. The novelists of the nineteenth century (and many of the twentieth century) identify happiness with marriage, and demand of the bride and groom rigid requirements: wealth and monetary credit; nobility (birth, lineage); certain prestige; influence and power; education; respectability; reputation, temperament, and personal qualities (physical, moral, intellectual, spiritual); and even race and color. This literature fortifies the systematic defense of marriage, its advantages and demands. There is nothing more just, points out the theorist of the novel of that era, Ignacio Manuel Altamirano, since the novel must be "easily comprehended by all, and particularly by the fair sex, it's primary readers, and to whom it should be addressed, as it is their genre."[21] The novel, being the domain of women because they constitute its principle market, provides them with fruitful feedback that portrays them as economically valuable, and confirms their virtue in achieving a suitable (that is, financially respectable) marriage. The novelistic genre has its own rules: the moral values of the novel strengthen the bourgeois economic reality in which women are completely dependent on marriage to survive materially. (The income of a Mexican woman in the nineteenth century was, in the best of cases, approximately one sixth of a man's income, and a woman's property, upon marrying, was automatically transferred to her husband.) In this economic system, still present, honor is awarded to the highest bidder, and a virginity lost before marriage means (inevitably) declining odds for the woman in question to be marketable, thereby decreasing her chances of survival. Neither the María of Jorge Isaacs, nor the Amalia of José Mármol, nor the Clemencia of Altamirano had their own income, and that helped them to suffer better and more nobly, according to the way they were conceived by their creators.[22]

SPIRITUAL SURRENDER

Distant, solemn, ethereal, admirable, sweet, serene, marvelous, or slow-moving, woman cycles through our literature like a vast utopic project. Her initial capital is her passivity; marriage, her goal and accomplishment; adultery, her expulsion from paradise; and promiscuity, her death. As a ritual, she represents two extremes of a consumerist theology: she is either the Fall from Grace or Grace itself. If representing the Fall, she will tend to be conflated with the cityscape, becoming suspiciously comparable to a victim of a work accident. If seen as Grace embodied, solely with her presence she will restore purity to those who behold her. In this order of things, there is no manipulation more demagogic (nor more evident) than the one that identifies "woman" with spirituality and satisfying her with verbal praise, making her both origin and redemption. If "woman" is Spirituality incarnate, she is once more a magnificent unreality, a mere point of departure for literary fantasies. And the eternal Eve, prestigious and perfect, full of fruitful virtues, who broadens horizons, at the end of the lyrical rambling returns to her domestic space confined to the three "ghettos" at her disposal: the kitchen, the bedroom, and the confessional. Sexism also has ennobling rhetoric for its enslaving actions, and one of its preferred exercises is the metamorphosis of "woman" into Spirituality itself, that honorable and vacuous romantic being, an entity that permits humiliations and contrition, repentance and prostrations. Kneeling before Woman-as-Spirit—and there is abundant proof of this in romantic poetry and in the "modernista" poetic recitations, then and now—it isn't (must I point this out?) an act of self-criticism, but rather a self-exaltation that requires witnesses.

On the other hand, that kind of hidden literary Priísmo, where the Spirit replaces the Mexican Revolution in its totalizing representation, continues to manifest its classism.[23] In this narrative and poetry, the village women can be ingenious, chatty, feisty, loyal, or funny. But never spiritual. The spirit is the domain of the elite, and the gift of the upper classes.

AT THE MARGINS OF SEX

The rhetoric that sees Woman-as-Spirit is part of a relentless reality: asexuality, the anti-sexuality of our literature, a literature that—still at the beginning of the 1960s—preserved its feudal structure almost intact, its negation of the body and of orgasm, and its extreme aversion to using sexual intercourse as a logical explanation of reality. This sanctimonious prudishness functioned for over a century and a half as both aggression and defense: there was no reference to the sexual act because relationships existed only on an ideal plane; the vision or glorification of the human body did not yet exist because it had not yet been conceptualized as literary reality. It isn't surprising, then, that writers less contaminated by sexism would be more erotically charged. Sexism, in its most evident and apocalyptic instance, tends to deny any exploitation, rendering invisible what it considers profane. For sexism, in its hypocritical and consequential form, virginity is the most laudable condition for a woman as she represents the exalted fiction of purity, and a kind of public redemption of the object that is possessed, humiliated, worn-out, and degraded to the point of uninterrupted child-bearing.

Therefore, the writers who have most profoundly assumed their eroticism don't and can't be understood within the usual parameters of sexism. In a society such as ours, eroticism is explosive and subversive, and even passionate love, with its weight of naiveté and primitive performativity, has played a revitalizing role. A puritanical, feudal, and Porfirian society doesn't indulge in obsessions.[24] Obsession (with its persistent monomaniacal burden, inflexibility) is at once a reproach and a challenge. In 1904, Efrén Rebolledo insists repeatedly:

> You know not what it is to be a slave
> of a fiery and impetuous love,
> to endure desire like a nail
> like a nail in my forehead lodged.
> You know not of greed
> of biting the longed-for mouth
> hands sliding in restless caress
> over contours of snowy flesh.
> [. . .]
> And you know not of despair
> of conjuring your figure divine
> in bed, tossing and turning, there
> that insomnia has strewn with spines[25]

In this poetry—without the knowledge of literary history—a revolt of considerable proportions is taking place. At the height of the Porfiriato, a sex-obsessed poet, one who publicly recognizes his love of lust, a writer that covets an actual body. The sacralizing tradition of Mexican poetry had gone from the mythological abstention of Ignacio Ramírez—"Ara es este álbum: esparcid, cantores, / a los pies de la diosa incienso y flores" (This album is a harvest: spread, oh bards, / incense and flowers at the goddess's feet)—to the accounting of Manuel Gutiérrez Nájera, the first to believe in literature's purchasing power, and a faithful worshipper of the woman as object:

> Yesterday's lovers are empty glasses,
> in which we poured a bit of love

We drank their nectar . . . the days flew by . . .
Bring me new glasses, with fresh liqueur!

Champagne, the blondes with porcelain skin;
Burgundy the lips of vivid carmine;
Dark eyes are Italy's wines,
those green and light, wines from the Rhine[26]

Or to the authoritarian exaltation of Salvador Díaz Mirón, who in his poem "A Gloria" declares his creed:

Don't try to convince me of confusion
with the delusions of your insane mind!
My reason is both light and strength
Strength and light, like a crystal rock

Which ends:

Be content, woman! We are here
in this crushing valley of tears,
You, like a dove, for the nest,
And I, like a lion, for combat![27]

Against that tradition, Rebolledo chooses another path, a hidden path that is diminished by the need to contain and repress. According to official culture in Mexico, base instincts are nonexistent, there are only sound and steadfast principles; there is no eroticism, only sexual frenzy. Such decency erases Rebolledo's message, as it will later intervene to soften or suppress the erotic aspects of the poetry by López Velarde, who today (after exhausting official tributes, and a film biography that promises to become a television series) has become the perfect provincial beau, the feverish and chaste suitor that nostalgically clings to a pure love. On the contrary, in López Velarde, I find subterranean tensions, an accursed poet (blasphemous and profane, protected by his frankness and baroque style), defeated "over a riot of nymphs and a moaning chorus of ghosts," and immersed in his idolatry "of erotic and mystical bosoms."[28] However, his arch-heretical possibilities (his "lustful barometer"[29]) could not be integrated into a culture that continues to see in pornography (albeit, occasionally delightful) an enemy, and continues to formally praise a feudal monogamy. López Velarde was purified, whitewashed, returned to a state of innocence, identified with the provincial spirit. And this purifying process is not unrelated to that applied to Flores Magón, who was refashioned as a mere lyrical precursor to the Revolution.[30] Following that conception, the fate of the unorthodox, in the best of cases, is just a romantic aura.

REVENGE AS SUBMISSION

"For power," asserts D. H. Lawrence, "is the first and greatest of all mysteries. It is the mystery that is behind all our being, even behind all our existence. Even the phallic erection is a first blind movement of power."[31] And maybe this systematic suppression of sexual reality could also be seen as the first act of weakness or, at least, as a mutilated quest for power. For Mexican literature, as well as for much of Latin American literature, the absence of sex and eroticism (hidden or evident) has made it imprecise, watered-down, and deceitful. The lack of tensions and distensions that drive sexual relations— the undercurrent of physical attraction—is coupled with a fixed portrayal of womanhood: a subject of domestic servitude (including sexual intercourse), she is also something of a permanent witness to her own existence and to that of others—someone who is always present, in a subdued manner, reiteratively performed by her own actions. Even now, with the novelty of explicit sexual depictions, women continue to be represented either as a pretense or as scenery—a passive territory, a trap to be outsmarted, a moan of surrender before the irrefutable force of the phallic will. Without a life of her own, "woman" becomes a construct of masculine design.

Are women capable of revenge? In any event, they are complicit with unleashing disaster. For the love of a woman, terrifying calamities may befall her lover. Her use of "spells" or "enchantments" are magical notions that already signal the impossibility of female dominance achieved via "normal methods," but the agent of destruction is never the woman, rather it is the character's will to self-destruct, it is his "feminine weakness." Only if someone is *like* a woman can he be defeated *by* a woman. Thus, abruptly hidden, repositioned, and minimized, women appear and reappear in this narrative in order to a) frustrate or temper heroism and political participation; b) confirm emotional blackmail as the only form of communication between masculine courage and feminine cowardice; c) become a catalyst for opportunism.

In her diminishment, woman grows as a negative element. She is either the forever imperfect beloved or the sensitive, infantilized creature with abundant domestic abilities who annuls or castrates the protagonist. Since she cannot have a life of her own, woman (in an act of revenge, which is a confession of impotence) will attempt to undo the lives of others.

A RESOURCE OR A VALIDATION

It is inevitable that almost all of the authors coincide in their contempt for, or their philanthropic paternalism toward, women. The culture of a colonial or colonized society (such as Mexico's) has required it to be so, and even now between disguises and euphemisms, demands it. As the subject of any moral experiment or any daily exercise of power, "woman" has existed literarily (and this generalization, I insist, does not begin to break down until the 1960s, albeit rhetorically) as a resource for men to use or as a validation of their status. And literary trends and ideological currents have coincided in this use and abuse. The idea of womanhood that the Marxist José Mancisidor fears isn't much different from that of the "Cristero," Antonio Rius Facius.[32] Naturalism and realism also concur. Santa, the idealized prostitute in the novel *Santa* (1903) by Federico Gamboa, is an accumulation of hesitations and sins that can only be resolved through death. The novel is not about canonizing Santa, but is rather a retelling of a just punishment. Gamboa, typically, is not interested in understanding or describing his protagonist, but rather in representing how society indicts marginalized people. Without virginity, social interactions are rendered impossible, as Santa's mother, Agustina, states when she finds out about her daughter's first misstep:

> She [the mother] did not curse her. No matter how impure, Santa was still her beloved daughter for whom she implored God's infinite mercy. But her mother did repudiate her, as must be done when a virgin leaves the path of righteousness and allows her cloak of innocence to be torn asunder; as must be done when an unworthy daughter stains the honor of an aging mother soon to meet her maker; as must be done when an ungrateful sister threatens to corrupt all that surrounds her, and she must be repudiated, cast out and regarded from then on as if no longer alive, may God have mercy on her soul.[33]

FROM THE MEXICAN REVOLUTION ON

If the Mexican Revolution considerably modified women's status, allowing them to participate actively as combatants and laborers, the Novel of the Revolution did not noticeably acknowledge this shift. Agustín Yañez, in *Al filo del agua* (1947), traced an excellent portrayal of women's mourning and confinement in a Porfirian province:

> The pious activities of old and young, of men and women, find expression in many societies. But the two most important are the Association of the Good

Death and the Daughters of Mary. The Daughters of Mary, to a large extent, in fact almost exclusively, shape the character of the village, exercising a rigid discipline over the dress, movements, speech, thoughts, and feelings of the young girls, bringing them up in a conventual existence that turns the village itself into a kind of convent. Any girl reading at the age of fifteen without belonging to the Association of the black dress and blue ribbon with high neck and long sleeves, its skirt reaching to the ankles, is regarded with grave disapproval. In this Association, all vie with one another in jealous vigilance, and expulsion from it constitutes a scandalous blot on the reputation that follows one through life.

There is strict segregation of the sexes. In church, the Gospel side is reserved for men, and the devout female sex occupies the Epistle side. It is not considered proper for men and women, even when related, to stand chatting in the street or doorway, not even for a moment. When a meeting occurs, brief greetings are exchanged, all the briefer if the man or woman is alone; but this rarely happens, especially if the woman is unmarried, since then she is always accompanied by another woman.[34]

However, the novelists of the Revolution did not produce a corresponding portrayal of that reality. Which is easily explained. By mobilizing the country, dealing a death blow to a sedentary lifestyle, and destroying feudal structures, the Revolution was the catalyst that initiated the dismantling of a culture, of a way of life. However, the process, as far as social mores are concerned, was cut short. Although freedoms were gained, and some of the most visible aspects of slavery were brought to an end, the structures and oppressive apparatus were left intact—the familial fiefdom. In a certain way, the Revolution famously legalized one aspect (at least) of this persistent inequality: the admirable figure of the *soldadera* who, just a few feet from her "Juan," drags food and children around, confirming her immutable submission.[35] Inevitably, the writers of the Revolution upheld this inherited order of things. "Woman" in Azuela is long-suffering and submissive; she believes in her man, follows him, defends him, kills and is willing to die for him, lives through him; hers is either a jubilant or melancholic surrender. For José Vasconcelos, "woman" is an indispensable and expendable passion, a place to consummate his lust, because—Vasconcelos notes with the carelessness of a prophet—"a pair of breasts are more powerful than a pair of oxen," Adriana, his lover, is a trophy *soldadera*, who follows her "Ulíses Criollo" with a frivolous and frenzied abnegation.[36] In the work of Martín Luis Guzmán, women are providers of children, pleasure, and food. They are combative prostitutes or housewives in the shadows. They're a repository and a public service. Nothing more.[37]

DURING, BEFORE, AND AFTER THE STORM

The country, however, continues to develop, and the most rudimentary and shameful forms of sexism tend to be, at the very least, hidden. With the government of Miguel Alemán, we see the rise of the bourgeoisie, and with them, the will to eliminate any excesses that remind them of their humble beginnings, now considered a source of shame.[38] What follows is the first critical examination of machismo, the first damming analysis, and also the creation and the grand mythification. The middle class and the bourgeoisie can allow themselves that luxury. Machismo, defined as mere posturing and arrogance, becomes superfluous. Or in any case, it's seen as a folkloric attitude that is pejoratively regarded. This in no way indicates an initial critique of sexism. As things stand, in journalism, and in the quest for a Mexican essence (the failed attempt of a philosophical and psychological nationalism), machismo is reviled only so far as its excesses—excesses that go against the national project of development by belligerently insisting on wastefulness and destruction.[39] Machismo, during the Mexican Revolution, was a desperate attempt for validation, an affirmation of self. During the era of political bureaucracy, machismo is both an unnecessary expense and a reassuring myth. The critique of machismo both honors and invents its object of inquiry. The macho (it's understood) is an abuse, a scourge, a returning home at three in the morning to beat the woman who meekly awaits him, a barroom brawl, an institutionalization of "If they're going to kill me tomorrow, let them kill me now." Machismo is the cult of hyper-virility, and the Mexican practice of violence. Or, that is, and this aspect will intensify gradually, a myth that functions as a compensatory technique. Movies, popular songs, and social critique are, then, responsible for the "invention" of machismo. Not that the characteristics that define the term didn't exist before. What didn't exist was the style that unified such characteristics. In identifying and condemning machismo, various objectives are at play: idealizing an increasingly impractical behavior (from a personal point of view) in an increasingly repressive society; giving the middle class—delighted with their discovery of pseudo-Freudian techniques—the opportunity to understand and name an extreme behavior that had reached its limits; the opportunity to feel superior to macho bravado, and also superior to (in the paternalistic belittling of) that other archetype, his companion,

the "long-suffering and abnegated Mexican woman"; and finally, position-
ing machismo thus allows for the public disparaging of a "Callista" political
style that was already reprehensible in an era of stability that required less
arrogant and dangerous methods.[40] This, however, does not contradict the
resurgence of those methods in 1968, when the governing regime saw them
as indispensable.[41]

It is there, perhaps, that one can find one of the reasons for the weakening
and death of the narrative genre of the Mexican Revolution. This epic project, this dramatic or melodramatic retelling of the lives that transformed the
country, highlighted, by contrast, the progressively grey, bureaucratic, depo-
liticized, and mundane atmosphere routinely being lived by its middle-class
readers. Accepted and admired for its epic quality, the culminating legend of
a country (that could well be this one), the novel of the Mexican Revolution,
at some point, no longer found an active and direct connection with its public.
Such epic incitement, in the aftermath of the corruption of the Alemán government, was excessive. The nation of heroes had become a nation of legislators.

CONTEMPORARY SEXISM

Although it's not as easy to identify or anthologize, sexism, the ideology of
male chauvinism—the repressive apparatus that sees women only as dominated and domitable objects—continues to manifest itself vigorously in our
literature today, not to mention in our way of life. A new stage begins that
could be called "sexual openness," and this means that Freudian discoveries
have not been in vain. But this tenacious intolerance, the militant oppression that characterizes sexism, continues unchecked. Where are the narratives that present alternatives to a rigid and hypocritical monogamy, to
patriarchal despotism, to that occasionally embarrassed machismo, worried,
more often than not, by its lack of opportunities to show off? Aside from a
few exceptional writers, neither in literature nor in real life can one say that
there is sexual freedom in Mexico. It's not even (of course) that society might
consider this freedom a desirable or valid goal. Neither international pressure, nor the progress of the miniscule sector of the country that profits from
the surrounding underdevelopment, nor post-Freudian revelations, nor the
impact of liberation movements, have managed to broaden our perspectives
about sexual freedom. We continue to operate under a rigid moral code that
represses and maintains the status quo in order to repress—with a morality of
raids, of social scandals, of secret pornographic recreation, and of the inability to accept unconventional or diverse life choices. There's no sexual freedom because relationships are not conceived of (not even imagined) as equal;
because virginity continues to be a fetish—a marketable commodity—that

defines life (and of course, honor); because theories and practices are not radically reexamined (there is still a belief in notions so dubious, so unverifiable, so futile as "lasciviousness," "impropriety," the "unnatural," and the "perverted"); because the sexual act continues to be immersed in notions of guilt and sinfulness that now (in order to be publicly acceptable) turn into references about social convention ("I won't ask an unwed mother to be my child's godmother"), about the impact on one's career ("It'll damage my reputation if I'm seen with you"), or in order to make a distinction between liberty and "licentiousness."

Without a doubt, this outlook isn't completely foreboding. Beyond the prohibitions and decrees of rigidity, there continue to be acts of spontaneity, defiance, heresy, rupture, and dissident positions, which in order to be organically transformative at the forefront of this shift, require a radical critique and an artistically valid portrayal of the sexism that insists on seeing in the eagle and the serpent one of the metaphoric variants of the matrimonial condition.[42] A radical and uninhibited criticism whose urgency Bertolt Brecht signaled with precision: "Art is necessary to make humanly practicable what is politically just."

COLOPHON – HOMAGE TO WOMEN

> 1. "A woman should be
> dreamy, flirty, and fiery
> She should give herself to love
> with an ardent frenzy
> in order to be a woman."

"A woman," lyric and music by Mario Clavel[43]

2. "Women, like purebred dogs, die of cold without caress. Their nature casts them into caresses, like their warmth to the coolness of water."

"A woman is capable of forgiving a day without money, but never a day without a caress."

"A good wife is like a fat cow in times of scarcity."

From *Meditaciones* (Meditations) by José López Bermúdez[44]

NOTES

1. Genesis 3:16 (King James Version).
2. In Spanish-speaking countries, a *caudillo* is a strongman, most often a military or political dictator.
3. This translated quote is taken from Octavio Paz, *The Labyrinth of Solitude: Life and Thought in Mexico*, Lysander Kemp (New York: Grove Press, 1961), 35.

4. Hernán Cortés and his troops of conquistadores arrived on the shores of Veracruz in 1519.

5. For the complete poem in English entitled "Sorrow and Life," see Eduardo Matos Moctezuma, *Life and Death in the Templo Mayor*, trans. Bernard R. Ortiz de Montellano and Thelma Ortiz de Montellano (Niwot, CO: University Press of Colorado, 1995), 115. According to this book, this poem pre-dates the Conquest; nevertheless, in Monsiváis's original text, he frames it as a post-Conquest poem. We have chosen to remove his reference to the post-Conquest to avoid confusion with the understanding that it indeed represents a Nahua cosmovision on life and death.

6. *Visión de los Vencidos: Relaciones indígenas de la conquista*, ed. Miguel López-Portillo, trans. Angel María Garibay K. (Mexico: UNAM, 1959). It was a groundbreaking collection that chronicled the events of the Conquest of Mexico from the perspective of Indigenous people. This translation comes from a modified version of this book: Miguel León-Portilla, ed., *The Broken Spears*, trans. Lysander Kemp (Boston, MA: Beacon Press, 1992), 146.

7. Juan Ruiz de Alarcón, born in New Spain in 1639, was a prolific dramatist, best known for his comedy *La verdad sospechosa* (*The Suspicious Truth*), which was debuted in 1624 and was published in his collected plays in 1634. It was considered a masterpiece of Spanish American Baroque theatre, and was first translated into English in 1927 in *Poet Lore*. See Juan Ruiz de Alarcón, *The Suspicious Truth*, trans. Alfred MacAdam, *Review: Literature and Arts of the Americas* 24, no. 43 (1990): 22–36. Pedro Castera (1846–1906) was a Mexican journalist, miner, and literary figure at the end of the nineteenth century known for his poetry, short stories, and novels. His novel *Carmen: Memorias de un corazón* was published in 1882.

8. Antonio Machado (1875–1939) is a major lyric poet and philosopher of the Spanish literary movement known as the Generation of '98. Much of his poetry was set to music by Spanish singer-songwriter Joan Manuel Serrat in an album entitled *Dedicado a Antonio Machado, Poeta* (1969). This is a verse taken from the *Cancionero apócrifo* (Apocryphal songbook) attributed to Abel Martín, heteronymous and alter ego of Antonio Machado that first appeared in his *Poesías Completas* (Spain: Espasa Calpe, 1928). Martín/Machado here sees women as the best face of mankind. This idealization of women is also found in another of Martín's verses, "Sin mujer / no hay engendrar ni saber" (Without woman / there is no procreation nor knowledge), and in a verse by Machado, "Dicen que un hombre no es un hombre / hasta que no oye su nombre / de labios de mujer," (They say a man is not a man / until he hears his name / from a woman's lips), quoted in Miguel Siguán, *El tema del otro en Antonio Machado* (Spain: Universidad de Barcelona, 1966), 281.

9. *Tonantzin*, meaning "our mother" as translated from the Nahuatl, is the venerated female goddess of the Mexicas. There is a debate as to whether the

Spaniards used the cult of Tonantzin in order to found the cult to the Virgin of Guadalupe, or whether the Mexicas continued their cult to Tonantzin symbolically concealed within Guadalupe. The cult to Tonantzin-Guadalupe continues today among many Indigenous groups.

10. Ramón López Velarde (1888–1921) is a prominent poet of the "post-modernista" movement, whose muse Josefa de los Ríos was the inspiration for the poetic persona Fuensanta. Emilio Rabasa (1856–1930), was a diplomat and politician best known as a novelist; Remedios occupies a major role in his tetralogy; Ignacio Manuel Altamirano (1834–1893), a prominent liberal writer and a principal promoter of Mexican literary nationalism, was famed for his romantic novels *Clemencia* (1869) and *El Zarco* (published posthumously in 1901). Guillermo Aguirre y Fierro (1887–1949) is best known for this poem, a tribute to and an idealization of the mother; Efrén Hernández (1904–1958), an important literary figure for the first part of the twentieth century, was a writer, poet, dramatist, screenwriter, and critic. Federico Gamboa (1864–1939), writer and diplomat, is famous for his novel *Santa* (1903), a nineteenth-century naturalist fiction (akin to Zola's *Nana*) that inspired several films and a song by Agustín Lara. María Félix was one of the most successful (also considered one of the most beautiful) stars of Mexican cinema in the twentieth century, known as La Doña for portraying strong, at times domineering women; Ninón Sevilla (Cuba, 1923–2015) and Meche Barba (US, 1922–2000) are both celebrated for their performances as *rumberas* (dancers of Afro-Caribbean rhythms known as rumba), which figured in that film genre during the Golden Age of Mexican Film; Irma Serrano (1933–) is a popular singer and performer of the *ranchera* and *corrido* (ballad) genres, and later a politician. She starred in *La Martina* (1972), a film based on a classic *corrido*.

11. The *soldaderas*, some also called *Adelitas*, were women who participated in the Mexican Revolution whether as officers, combatants, or camp followers. *Los de Abajo* (1916) by Mariano Azuela (1873–1952), considered the first novel of the Mexican Revolution, was first published as a serial in a Spanish newspaper in El Paso, Texas, from October to December 1915, and translated into English as *The Underdogs* by Enrique Munguía Jr. in 1929. *Al filo de agua* (1947) by Agustín Yáñez (1904–1980) was translated as *The Edge of the Storm* (1963) by Ethel Brinton. *Pedro Páramo* (1955) by Juan Rulfo (1917–1986) has been thrice translated, in 1959 by Lysander Kemp, in 1994 by Margaret Sayers Peden, and in 2023 by Douglas Weatherford. *La tormenta* (1936) by José Vasconcelos (1882–1959), author of *La raza cósmica* (1925), was translated by Didier T. Jaén as *The Cosmic Race* in a bilingual edition in 1997. Manuel Acuña (1849–1873) is best known for his poem "Nocturno a Rosario" (Nocturne to Rosario), which is dedicated to his muse, Rosario de la Peña, whose unrequited love, it is believed, led him to commit suicide. Manuel José Othón's (1858–1906) "Idilio Salvaje" (1906; Wild idyll), published posthumously, is considered one of the most famous poems of love

and landscape. Pedro Castera (1846–1906) was a journalist, miner, and literary figure at the end of the nineteenth century known for his poems, short stories, and a novel, *Carmen* (1882).

12. Initially published as a letter in 1691, "Respuesta a Sor Filotea de la Cruz" (The response to Sor Filotea) has been collected and anthologized in many selected works and also published as a book and critical edition.

13. This citation from Sor Juana's letter follows her observation that girls are not properly educated given the lack of learned older women, which obliges parents to employ men. See Juana Inés de la Cruz, *The Answer / La Respuesta, Sor Juana Inés de la Cruz*, 2nd ed., trans. Electa Arenal and Amanda Powell (New York: Feminist Press, 2009), 85. As Sor Juana's recognition grows internationally, so do translations of her work. For a more recent translation, see "Respuesta a Sor Filotea," in Juana Inés de la Cruz, *Sor Juana Inés de la Cruz: Selected Works*, ed. and trans. Edith Grossman (New York: Norton, 2014).

14. de la Cruz, *The Answer / La Respuesta*, 95, 97.

15. de la Cruz, *The Answer / La Respuesta*, 96.

16. Grossman, 33.

17. The full title is *La Quijotita y su prima: Historia muy cierta con apariencia de novela* (The Quijotita and her cousin: A true story that reads like a novel). There is no translation of this novel to date. Lizardi also wrote *El periquillo sarniento* (1816), considered the first novel written in Latin America. Its first partial English edition was published in 1942 by Doubleday, translated as *The Itching Parrot* by Katherine Anne Porter. Later an unabridged translation by David Frye was published as *The Mangy Parrot*, with an introduction by Nancy Vogley (Indianapolis, IN: Hackett Publishing, 2004).

18. *Pomposa* plays with the idea of pomposity and *Pudenciana* with the idea of "pudor," or modesty.

19. This is our translation of Lizardi. Throughout, brackets in quoted text refer to omissions and to interventions made by Monsiváis.

20. A Mexican saying suggesting that a woman's place is in the kitchen. The *metate* is a flat stone used for grinding maize by hand; the *comal* is a griddle to cook or reheat tortillas. These activities are labor intensive and often begin before dawn.

21. Our translation. *Revistas literarias de México* (Mexico City: T. F. Neve Impresor, 1868), 69. Only two texts by Altamirano have been translated into English: *Navidad en las montañas* (1871) as *Christmas in the Mountains*, trans. Harvey L. Johnson (Gainsville: University of Florida Press, 1961), and *El Zarco* (published posthumously in 1901) as *El Zarco: The Blue-Eyed Bandit*, trans. Ronald Christ (Santa Fe, NM: Helen Lane Editions / Lumen Books, 2006).

22. María is the eponymous protagonist of Jorge Isaac's novel, as is Amalia of José Mármol's, and Clemencia of Ignacio Manuel Altamirano's.

23. *Priísmo* refers to the monopoly of the ideological top-down doctrine of the PRI, or the Partido Revolucionario Institucional (Institutional Revolutionary Party), which held seventy-one years of uninterrupted single-party rule from 1929 to 2000.

24. *Porfirian*, or the *Porfiriato*, refers to the period of Mexican history when Porfirio Díaz was president and dictator of the country. There were two Porfirian periods: 1877 to 1880 and 1884 to 1911.

25. Our translation of these verses by "modernista" poet Efrén Rebolledo (1877–1929), from his book *Hilo de corales* (1904; Coral threads). This poem is quoted in its entirety in Carlos Monsiváis, *La poesía mexicana del siglo XX: Antología* (Mexico: Empresas Editoriales S. A., 1966), 237. Rebolledo is recognized for his short novel *Salamandra* (1919), about a femme fatale, and his poetry collection *Caro victrix* (1916) is considered his crowning achievement by the poets Xavier Villaurrutia, Carlos Montemayor, and José Emilio Pacheco.

26. Ignacio Ramírez (1818–1879), also known as the Mexican Voltaire, was a writer, poet, journalist, politician, lawyer, liberal, and atheist, who used the pen name "El Nigromante" in many of his writings. This couplet appears on the first page of an album gifted to Rosario de la Peña, known for her literary *tertulias* (salons) where the leading poets of the era met, and where some of their poems were collected. She was a muse to many who courted her in vain, as was the case with Manuel Acuña who committed suicide over unrequited love. Manuel Gutiérrez Nájera (1859–1895), an early promoter of *modernismo*, was a poet influenced by French poets like Verlaine, a writer, journalist, and chronicler, also known by his pseudonym "El Duque Job," made famous by his poem "La Duquesa Job." The verses (our translation) from "Para un menú" (A menu) appear in their entirety in José Emilio Pacheco, *La poesía mexicana del siglo XIX* (Mexico: Empresas Editoriales, 1965), 446.

27. This is our translation of verses from the poem "A Gloria" by Salvador Díaz Mirón (1853–1928), from *Poesías completas* (Mexico City: Fondo de Cultura Económica, 1997), which is said to have been influenced by Lord Byron and Victor Hugo, and was a very influential poem during this era.

28. Ramón López Velarde, *Songs of the Heart: Selected Poems by Ramón López Velarde*, trans. Margaret Sayers Peden, illus. Juan Soriano (Austin: University of Texas Press, 1995), 55. Our translation from his poem "Idolatría" (Idolatry).

29. Our translation from his poem "Ánima adoratriz" (Adoring soul).

30. Ricardo Flores Magón (1874–1922) was a member of the Partido Liberal Mexicano (Mexican Liberal Party), editor of the anarchist newspaper *La regeneración*, and active in the social movements leading up to the Mexican Revolution. Those who followed him and his two brothers, Enrique and Jesús, became known as *Magonistas*. Persecuted, he fled to the US where he remained active and was often imprisoned as a dissident. In 1945, his remains were repatriated to Mexico and are now in the Rotonda de los Hombres Ilustres (Rotunda of Illustrious Men).

31. D. H. Lawrence, "Blessed are the Powerful," in *Reflections on the Death of a Porcupine and Other Essays* (Philadelphia: Centaur Press, 1925), 156. His thoughts on this subject end with the following sentence: "Love is said to call the power into motion: but it is probably the reverse: that the slumbering *power* calls love into being."

32. José Mancisidor (1894–1956) was a prolific writer, dramatist, screenwriter, histo- rian, and politician. Recognized as a novelist and historian of the Mexican Revo- lution, he belonged to the Liga de Escritores y Artistas Revolucionarios (League of Revolutionary Writers and Artists) with David Alfaro Siqueiros, Diego Rivera, and Frida Kahlo, among others, and was an active promoter of the proletariat novel. Antonio Rius Facius (1918–2012) was a Catholic writer and historian who wrote about the Guerra Cristera (Cristero War). This rebellion from 1926 to 1929 took place in Central and Western Mexico in response to secularist articles of the 1917 Constitution that were perceived as anti-Catholic by the Church and members of its congregations, who took up arms in the name of Christ. This conflict between Church and State, dating back to the nineteenth century with the War of Reform between liberals and conservatives, ended in 1929.

33. Federico Gamboa, *Santa: A Novel of Mexico City* (Chapel Hill: University of North Carolina Press, 2010), 46. This is the first translation of *Santa* (1903) from Spanish into English, over one hundred years after its publication.

34. Agustín Yañez (1904–1980) is recognized as one of the initiators of the modern novel in Mexico, winning the National Prize in Literature in 1973. *Al filo del agua* (*The Edge of the Storm*) takes place just before the Mexican Revolution began in 1910, and is acknowledged as his masterpiece. Besides being a prolific writer, he served as governor of Jalisco and secretary of public education during the presidency of Gustavo Díaz Ordaz (1964–1970). Agustín Yañez, *The Edge of the Storm: A Novel*, trans. Ethel Brinton (Austin: University of Texas Press, 1963), 13.

35. Here *soldadera* references the camp followers of the Mexican Revolution who faithfully stood by their men, called *Juan*, a generic designation for the unnamed soldiers of the Revolution.

36. José Vasconcelos, in his epic autobiographical novel *Ulises criollo* (Mexico City: Ediciones Botas, 1935), references Ulysses, the epic hero from Homer's *The Odys- sey*. *Criollo* here is used to describe a person of Spanish peninsular descent.

37. Martín Luis Guzmán (1887–1976), a writer and politician who was considered a pioneer of the Novel of the Mexican Revolution, was awarded the National Prize in Literature in 1958.

38. Miguel Alemán was the first civilian president to lead Mexico from 1946 to 1952, a period of rapid industrialization.

39. Two influential books on this topic in that period are Samuel Ramos, *El perfil del hombre y la cultura en México* (1934), translated by Peter G. Earle as *Profile of Man and Culture in Mexico* (Austin: University of Texas Press, 1962); and Octa- vio Paz, *El laberinto de la soledad* (1950), translated by Lysander Kemp as *The Labyrinth of Solitude: Life and Thought in Mexico* (New York: Grove Press, 1961).

40. *Callismo* refers to the tactics of Plutarco Elías Calles, a general in the Mexi- can Revolution who served as president of Mexico from 1924 to 1928. Founder of the PRI in 1929, known as El Jefe Máximo (the commander in chief), he played a key role in politics between 1928 and 1934, a period referred to as el

Maximato, which ended when President Lázaro Cárdenas (1934–40) ousted him from the country.

41. This refers to President Gustavo Díaz Ordaz's regime (1964–1970), which in the months leading up to the 1968 Olympics in Mexico exerted increasing pressure on student protestors, culminating in the massacre at Tlatelolco on October 2.

42. This refers to the founding of the Mexica (Aztec) civilization. It was prophesied that the nomadic Mexicas would settle where they saw an eagle devouring a serpent perching on a *nopal* (cactus). This emblematic image is the symbol on the Mexican flag and currency, and persists in the Mexican cultural imaginary. In Monsiváis's metaphor, the eagle represents the masculine and the serpent the feminine.

43. Mario Clavel or Clavell (1922–2011, Argentina) was a writer, composer, popular singer, and actor of Argentine cinema, internationally recognized.

44. José López Bermúdez (1908–1971) was a poet, orator, essayist, and politician born in Guanajuato, Mexico.

CHAPTER 2

A New Salute
for the Optimist

1978

What has been achieved, in this decade of emerging militancy, by feminism and the sexual liberation movements in Mexico? The answers vary, depending on the "criteria of usefulness" that is applied to the question. If the measure is its organizational development, the landscape is certainly sparse, and above all factional; there are a small number of middle-class groups, frequently divided or ideologized to the point of paralysis. If the measure is its degree of social influence, the results are quite substantial especially with relation to feminism, which in a few short years has become a now indispensable point of view that far transcends its *deliberate* sphere of action, and in a wide-spread yet effective manner reaches vast sectors of the population. Though I am not unaware of its degree of influence, I am not referring here to the imitative and colonized zeal that finds in liberation (with or without air quotes) a way of staying relevant, taking advantage of feminism as a means to modernization. What I'm interested in underscoring is more important: in a country lacking independent organizations, without a democratic tradition, with a still-precarious civil society, feminism, and the sexual liberation movement in general, are offering society a critical perspective for understanding that the "feminine condition" and the "masculine condition" are historical artifacts that feed and invigorate labor exploitation, social repression, and political manipulation.

Until now, the greatest success of feminism has been the campaign for the decriminalization or the legalization of abortion, which has gone from being a taboo topic to a pressing cause, despite the unmoving opposition of the Church (nationally and worldwide) and the weak complicity of the (national) government. An exemplary anecdote (for me): five years ago, the director of a publication where I work threw a letter from pro-abortion feminists in the trash, saying, "This is dirty and immoral!" Now, in the very same publication, they frequently publish arguments in favor of abortion, with no opposition. This is not only attributable to the "spirit of the era" or the protracted terror of facing a demographic explosion, but rather the influence of feminist reasoning. Therefore, it makes no sense to try and determine the efficacy of the fight for free and legal abortions based solely on legal outcomes while avoiding the other fundamental criterion: *the reduction of social oppression.* This is demonstrable: the feelings of shame, embarrassment, humiliation, and grief generally associated with abortion have considerably diminished. Certainly feminism isn't responsible for the disappearance of Honor as the primary family value. But what *is* attributable, in large part due to advocacy and feminist struggle, is the change in attitude for tens of thousands of women who, when having abortions, no longer consider themselves "victims of sin" or "trash," but rather human beings who, in a consequential manner, choose the scope of their responsibilities.[1] Who could the bishop of Tlalnepantla possibly convince anymore by giving women a tongue-lashing for believing themselves to be "owners of their own bodies?" Only small fanaticized groups, as we shall see with the meager anti-abortion protest by Pro-Vida.[2] Neither explicit nor stated, those who have abortions (still an exclusively feminine ordeal despite the PRI claiming that men's and women's problems are identical), are imbuing the act of abortion with a political dimension: as resistance to family, government, or ecclesiastical authoritarianism; as insubordination to a future imposed from the outside.[3] It is a significant political gain to vindicate women's right to their bodily autonomy.

Therefore, feminism's greatest victory is happening through *social contagion* or *contamination.* Today, to make fun of "women who think they're men" is counter-balanced with an anxiety over being denounced for—or accused of— machismo. (Oh, irony of the 1970s: this term, not long ago a "Source of Pride for All Real Men," has become an incrimination!)

It could be said, and rightly so, that the lower classes are less visibly affected by this contagious persuasion: in that cultural milieu, neither do machos stop being macho because of cultural shame, nor do women feel authorized to use their bodies freely (and not only regarding abortion). Nevertheless, due to the fast pace of social change, the loss of machismo's *inherent prestige*, and the public discussions on the decriminalization of abortion, on women's de facto legal equality, on homemakers' salaries, on criminal punishment for rapists, on gay rights, and so forth, these advances cannot be downplayed. This is especially true when considering the criteria of capitalist exploitation, that is, if one thinks of the centuries of social invisibility suffered by women and marginalized minorities, or if one considers the strategy of traditional morality that, supported by the Church, continues to deny women the right to protest and also refuses to recognize— beyond tabloids or a basic compassion for the abject—the civil existence of homosexuals.

Traditional machismo, put on the defensive, attempts to update itself, to become sophisticated, and to reinstate its prestige. If machismo was previously used to discredit the popular classes (the treatise by Samuel Ramos in the 1930s[4]), today it is proof of a cultural anachronism. If "being macho" was a source of pride (bravado, an arrogant identity with no self-awareness), now, at the end of the seventies, anti-machismo is a cultural category rooted in the educated elite who, by disseminating terms like "sexism," limit the more reactionary forms of patriarchal ideology.

The Left has also suffered some important transformations. For many years, the "orthodox" Left, of Stalinist affiliations, disdained and fought feminism for being "petty bourgeois" and for "undermining the fight against the principal enemy." This Left opposed feminism with its famous *apocalypse of goodness*—everything will be resolved with the triumph of socialism; meanwhile, it's better to postpone partial or factional struggles, like feminism, for all to be delivered by the coming of a holistic liberation.[5] Now, only Stalinoid grouplets on the path to extinction, like the Partido Popular Socialista (Popular Socialist Party) shamelessly maintain these "theories," though they're a far cry from specifying situations like women's double political militancy or the "inter-classism" of feminist organizations. But many of the Left's "ancestral" prejudices are beginning to crumble, and proof of this is the recent founding of the Frente Nacional de Lucha por la Liberación y los Derechos de la Mujer (the National Front for the Fight for the Liberation and Rights of Women), with the participation of the Communist and Worker's Revolutionary Parties, university unions, and feminist groups, and so on.

If in Leftist spaces the principal debate focuses on the autonomy of the feminist movement, in the wider discussion, the most controversial point continues to be birth control. Even "respectable" militants advocate for unfettered fertility, and disengage from the fight for the legalization of abortion by arguing that the multiplication of the masses will signal the end of imperialism, or by simply opposing any demographic measures at all, calling them Malthusian and utilizing equally convincing hypotheses: homosexuality is a disease spread by the imperialists and the CIA to splinter or weaken the virile struggle of the peoples of the Third World (the thesis, for example, by Professor José Santos Valdés in an unintentionally humorous article).[6]

The strength of these movements must also be measured by their most extreme expressions. During two protests in which feminist and homosexual groups participated (July 26 and October 2, 1978), the response has been varied but generally surprisingly respectful. In the Left's tentative social and political acceptance, various factors are at play (social invisibility enforced by a continual sense of surprise, a distanced attitude toward "freaks," etc.). Also noticeable are genuine social developments. I don't ignore the grave inconveniences of "tolerance," a technique of political immobilization and a tactic of bourgeois modernization (see the lucid essay by José Joaquín Blanco, *Ojos que da pánico soñar* [Eyes I dare not meet in dreams][7]), but this risk is attenuated by the country's accelerated transformations and its militant decisions.

As for the rest, gains and battles are taking place primarily in the political arena. Feminism aims to inform women that their programmed inferiority is an essential part of their capitalist surplus value, and the sexual liberation movements clearly establish that the primary civil right is the use of one's own body. Hence, there is an obligatory linking of liberation movements to the country's general democratization processes and the collective fate of civil rights. If the Left comprehends—as it appears to be happening in its more progressive sectors—the very concrete and inalienable rights of the majorities and minorities that are marginalized and crushed by a sexism that is also an economic exploitation, then it will have taken a fundamental step forward. Additionally, there must be a reckoning with regards to the limitations of and disputes within the liberation movements themselves. This much is true: their circulation has diminished, and their publications are released irregularly; the groups are, actually, factions that tend to be divided by sectarian controversies or fights over leadership, etc. But all this means very little when compared to what has been collectively acheived, and for that very reason, it is worth revisiting the notions of *reformism* and *long-term strategies*. Regarding individual differences, every achievement can be radical. To reduce or limit personal humiliation and the familial desolation experienced by those who abort is enough in and of itself, as is unionization or any concrete use of constitutional and civil rights in the cases of women who are raped, beaten, or sexually exploited in their jobs, and of homosexuals who are harassed and blackmailed during raids, etc.[8]

I have tried to outline some of the undeniable advances made by the sexual liberation and feminist struggles in Mexico. We still need to examine other results (democratization and the seriousness gradually afforded to sex-ology, increasing respect for the discussion around mass media, the exhaus-tion of cheap humor and its sarcastic remarks about "liberated women" and "red gays," etc.), but fundamentally, you can summarize the gains made in this chapter of sexual liberation with the following points: a) a general and sectorial reduction of social and family pressure; b) a minimal reduction in both the invisibility and the oppression of marginalized minorities; c) a polarization in the "moral lynching" of minorities, which are now mostly found in tabloids (*Alarma, Alerta, Homicida*[9]), and are losing their cathar-tic attractiveness for many communities within Mexico; d) a recentering of the central theme (or problem) of sexual liberation that for the most part neutralizes manipulative fervors—Mrs. Griselda Álvarez, a gubernatorial candidate for Colima, is forced to distance herself: "I'm not a feminist, I'm a humanist") a significant decrease in victim passivity: there's an exponential growth in denouncements of rape, and there are incipient legal proceed-ings against the arbitrariness and unconstitutionality of homosexual raids; f) an adoption of the language used by the European and US movements that is "nationalizing" the shape of the struggles: for example, the expres-sion "the right to use one's own body," which began as an erotic expression and is today, for tens of thousands of women, the starting point for their understanding of reality.

In fewer than ten years, the feminist and sexual liberation movements, in spite of the enormous internal and external hurdles, have become an irreplaceable element in the construction of civil society, in the critique of capitalist exploitation, and in the vision of a democratic socialism.

NOTES

1. *Víctimas del pecado* was an iconic 1951 film by Emilio "El indio" Fernández, star-ring Ninón Sevilla. Much like many other films of the Golden Age, it cast "fallen" women as victims in order to make them redeemable. Women weren't sinners, they were "victims of sin."

2. Pro-Vida was a "pro-life" organization with ties to the Church formed in 1979 in response to Pope John Paul II's first pastoral visit to Mexico, and bolstered by groups such as the Legionnaires of Christ and the Opus Dei's desire to com-bat the state-issued national family planning program. See Andrzej Kulczycki, "The Abortion Debate in Mexico: Realities and Stalled Policy Reform," *Bulletin of Latin American Research* 26, no. 1 (Jan., 2007): 50–68.

3. The PRI was founded by President Plutarco Elías Calles to create a political place for the leaders and combatants of the Mexican Revolution, and it was plagued by corruption for the seventy-one years it was in power, first as the National

Revolutionary Party (Partido Nacional Revolucionario, PNR), then as the Party of the Mexican Revolution (Partido de la Revolución Mexicana, PRM), and finally as the PRI starting in 1946.

4. Monsiváis refers to Samuel Ramos (1897–1959) in *El perfil del hombre y la cultura en México* (1934), translated by Peter G. Earle as *Profile of Man and Culture in Mexico* (Austin: University of Texas Press, 1962), which was an influential book that meditated on the "Mexican condition."

5. Though we have been unable to find explicit reference to this so-called "apocalypse of goodness," we understand it in the sense that Marxist communism promised a messianically secular end to all suffering, and aligned its followers with the side of "goodness." For an interesting discussion on the shortcomings of this "extreme goodness" see Mauricio Rojas, "El marxismo y las desventuras de la bondad extrema" *Cuadernos de Pensamiento Político*, no. 24 (Oct.–Dec. 2009): 27–34.

6. Thomas Malthus (1766–1834) was an English economist and demographer known for his theory that population growth always tends to outrun the food supply and that any advancement for humanity would be impossible without strict control of population growth. This is a theory that has been debunked by Swedish economist Esther Boserup, among others. Santos Valdés wrote for publications such as *El Heraldo de Aguascalientes*, where he published articles like "Mal de nuestros días" (April 6, 1965) condemning homosexuality. Here Monsiváis refers to one of his many articles.

7. First published in *Sábado*, March 17, 1979, and later in *Cuadernos Magnus Hirschfield*, and finally as the fourth and final section of the collected work: José Joaquín Blanco, *Función de medianoche: Ensayos de literatura cotidiana* (México: Era, 1981), 183–90. This is a first-person essay on the marginality and political potency of homosexuality in Mexico. The title is taken from the translation of a verse "Eyes I dare not meet in dreams" by T. S. Eliot from the 1925 poem "The Hollow Men."

8. In Mexico, an element of social control was the raids carried out by the police on places where homosexuals gathered to socialize. For a recent fictional take on this practice, see the film *El baile de los 41* (*The Dance of the Forty-One*; 2020, David Pablos, dir.), which portrays a famous raid on a private home on November 17, 1901, in which twenty-one men were dressed as women and twenty-one as men. The forty-second attendee was excluded from arrest because, it is claimed, he was President Porfirio Díaz's son-in-law Ignacio de la Torre y Mier.

9. These are all titles of tabloid periodicals, translated as Alarm, Alert, and Homicide. In Mexico there is a long tradition of the *nota roja* (red news), or what in English is called "yellow journalism." This is a wildly popular genre of publication that is sold on street-corner newsstands, focusing on news of the sordid, the sexual, and the tragic, often times furthering misogynistic and homophobic views.

CHAPTER 3

But Were There Ever Really Eleven Thousand Machos?

1982

MACHISMO: IF THEY'RE GOING TO KILL ME TOMORROW, LET THEM KILL ME NOW

What is the historical meaning of the key word *machismo*?[1] Although I'm hesitant to respond, I'll outline the process. In Mexico, the term proliferates *after* the revolutionary battles to identify "men among men," those who boldly embody the spirit of the era, who are incensed by the deferral of death, who school others on how to stay calm when facing the firing squad or enemy artillery. The macho was the crowning achievement of a pact that represented the "courage of the species." If the concept *man* contained and exhibited grandiosity and fearless surrender, its antagonistic and complementary term affirmed this attitude, and turned it into a social legacy: no one may question the supreme value of *being macho* because virility is the greatest expression of any behavior, and virility manifests itself as an indifference to danger, a disdain for feminine qualities, and the imposition of authority at every level. Life has value as long as it isn't too highly prized. Anything that betrays the theatricality of being a macho is repulsive. He must show a disregard for physical exhaustion, only a fleeting tenderness in the presence of a beloved woman, and a contempt for anyone who fails to uphold the pact of courageous impenetrability.[2] What is ultimately nothing more than a basic requirement of Revolutionary-era violence, machismo manifests itself as a social conquest that, while reaffirming the inferiority of women, becomes a call to war.

MACHISMO: FOR THE LOVE OF YOUR MOTHER, DON'T LEAVE ME ALIVE!

Once the Mexican Revolution is written in capital letters, the cultural codes of the era reappear as popular mythology. Let's admire the macho for his style, let's watch him speak, let's look at the gallantry with which he holds our gaze in an antique photograph.... There's no good way to address themes of cruelty and barbarity; no convincing explanation nor acceptable excuse for them. It's better to downplay or ignore this violence, to forget about the ferociousness directed toward the losers, and to imagine it all like some festival of virtuosity and recklessness: "and without a word to anyone, he threw himself into the den of machine guns, exposing his chest to bullet fire."[3] Cruelty becomes picturesque, and heroic acts, when removed from their context, turn out to be the selling points for cultural industries and the circulation of historical deeds. Let's read, watch, and observe that time period in which the *manliest men* died, chin up, gallantly, sparing no details. Let's take a closer look at the macho who prefers to end his life once and for all, impatient for an ending.

PARADIGMATIC CONDUCT: "YOU'LL BE A MAN, MY SON"

The poem "If" by Rudyard Kipling ends heroically:

> Yours is the Earth and everything that's in it,
> And—which is more—you'll be a Man, my son![4]

Such is, to this day, the prevailing philosophy, above and beyond the slogans of machismo: *to be a man* is the pinnacle of conduct, to be able to both successively and simultaneously conquer adversity, selfishness, injustice, and a general bewilderment that taints your integrity. "Manhood is conferred"[5] is a widely used phrase for over a century that describes a canon that, in principle, excludes and condemns that which, in its very essence, is the opposite: the condition of *womanhood*. (And—which is less—you'll be a Woman, my daughter!) Patriarchal behavior takes what could be seen as a natural fact and makes it a coveted and prestigious goal: *a man* is he who shuns weakness, ineptitude, and limitations, left only with the air of superiority afforded to the victors. By defining manliness as "success in life," it unequivocally excludes women ... and failures. "Your father isn't much of a man, just look how we're living." / "He wasn't man enough to provide for your education."[6] He who doesn't triumph—defeated and frustrated—must settle for acting, merely performing masculinity—that privilege of so few.

THE MACHO: HE WHO SEES ME, HE WHO DOESN'T
SEE ME, AND HE WHO PRETENDS NOT TO

Posthumously, Pancho Villa is glorified as a symbol of machismo. His person-ality allows for such "social use" given his talents as a strategist, his "pictur-esqueness" rooted in classism, and his implacable resentment of exclusionary social practices. Over and over, journalism, literature, and film present the character's essence: his familiarity with death, his uncontrolled instinct, and his feudal voraciousness for women. What disappears from the frame, are the vindicating social demands that made it all possible. What is ignored is the fact that his attitude perfectly corresponded with his era, and instead, he is singled out as a symbol of barbarity, the "Revolutionary Macho."

Later, another more general criticism emerges. In 1934, just before mass media transforms Villa from "revolutionary" to "unbridled macho," in a book that would enjoy great influence, *Profile of Man and Culture in Mexico*, Samuel Ramos warns us that:

> the *pelado's* phallic obsession is not comparable to phallic cults and their underlying notions of fecundity and eternal life.[7] The phallus suggests to the *pelado* the idea of power. From this he has derived a very impoverished concept of man. Since he is, in effect, a being without substance, he tries to fill his void with the only suggestive force accessible to him: that of the male animal [macho]. He turns this popular concept of man into a dismal view of all Mexicans. When a Mexican compares his own nullity to the character of a civilized foreigner, he consoles himself in the following way: "A European has science, art, technical knowledge, and so forth; we have none of that here, but . . . we are very manly." Manly in the zoological sense of the term, that is, in the sense of the male enjoying complete animal potency.[8]

Cultural criticism casts a judgment: machismo represents a "popular" concept, an ill typically associated with the lower classes, another offense added to the crimes of poverty.[9] In theory, a macho is a poor man that has no resources other than flaunting his indifference to death or to the pain of others. The bourgeoisie feels "evolved" enough to smile ruefully at the construction workers that beat their wives, or who have too many children, in too many places. Furthermore, this country's processes of modernization are intersected by women, by their symbolic presence in politics and their effective presence in the workforce. Machismo, thus, remains a deformed mirror from which the subaltern classes peer out, smiling and subjugated.

THE MACHO: WE JUST DON'T LIKE THAT

In June 1963, film director Emilio "El Indio" Fernández stated:

> We [Mexicans] are sentimental by nature. When we have a full moon, we
> go out to see it. We like to see sunsets. We like to see nature. We like to see
> a beautiful flower. Sentimental? For the northern people [from the US], we
> are perhaps corny. It gives us a tremendous, wonderful feeling in our souls.
> It is natural for our people to burst into song. The more simple the people,
> the more beautiful they are. In them they have a contrast: they get angry, and
> they may kill, probably they will regret it afterwards, but they do not know
> how to hate [. . . On the other hand] I find this everwhere in the world. I see
> boys dressing up like women, women dressing up like men; and we just don't
> like that.[10]

THE MACHO: I PLEDGE ALLEGIANCE TO THE LAND WHERE I WAS BORN

The discrediting of a concept goes through a forced ideological process. Cinema, radio, and popular songs take the term "macho" and make it a show:

> I'm Mexican to the very core
> And pledge allegiance to the land where I was born
> To be macho among machos is my thing
> With great pride, it's to my country that I sing[11]

What is it to be a "macho among machos?" To show physical courage, to
prove one's amatory abilities, to not submit to anyone (outside of work hours),
to look as much like movie stars as possible: Jorge Negrete, Pedro Infante,
El Indio Fernández, David Silva, Arturo de Córdova, Pedro Armendáriz.[12]
Supreme virility is easily dramatized, it is a staged behavior in a society
excessively focused on individual gestures, and the reverberation of those
gestures, and the ways men carry themselves. In El Indio Fernández's films,
Pedro Armendariz is perfect: his face and his angry voice make his presence
felt; his imposing strength contrasts with the programmed weakness of his
partner Dolores del Río. In those mythical pictures of the 1930s and '40s,
about a world without history or reality, Jorge Negrete is spot on. He sings:

> Your men are real macho and oh, so reliable,
> They're valiant, fierce, their support, undeniable
> And when it comes to love, no rival can be viable[13]

The spectators know that he isn't advocating for a way of dressing or even a behavior, but rather something they can appropriate more easily: the arrogance necessary to affirm oneself, the essential path to a personality in a land where timidity is the byproduct of centuries of colonial domination.

NOTES

1. "Si me han de matar mañana, que me maten de una vez" is the closing lyric from the popular revolutionary song "La Valentina," based on the life of well-known revolutionary Lieutenant Valentina Ramírez, also known as "La Leona de Norotal," who was crucial in the siege of Culiacán. It was first sung by Jorge Negrete in the film *La Valentina* (Martín de Lucenay, dir., 1938). The film was then remade by Rogelio A. González in 1966, starring the iconic María Félix.

2. Here Monsiváis uses the phrase "no rajarse," which can be translated to mean "be courageous and invincible," as well as to mean "not allowing oneself to be open, vulnerable, or penetrable," which immediately refers us to Octavio Paz's concept of "no rajarse" as elucidated in his seminal book on Mexican identity *El laberinto de la soledad* (1950), *The Labyrinth of Solitude: Life and Thought in Mexico*, trans. Lysander Kemp (New York: Grove Press, 1961).

3. In his capacity as chronicler, Monsiváis captures the language, at times verbatim and at others as an amalgam of popular sentiment, found in the *corridos*, films, and novels of the Revolution as revolutionaries face execution.

4. Here we use Rudyard Kipling's English-language original of the poem "If," first published in *Rewards and Fairies* (Doubleday, Page, 1910). Monsiváis refers to a verse from Efrén Rebolledo's Spanish translation: "tuya es la tierra y todos sus codiciados frutos / y lo mas importante, ¡serás hombre, hijo mío!" (Antigua Imprenta de Murguía, 1919).

5. "Uno se recibe de hombre" is the well-known expression in Spanish that suggests the idea of manhood is a title that is earned through hard work and diligence, like a degree.

6. Here Monsiváis in his capacity of chronicler "captures" popular sayings.

7. The *pelado* figure is an urban man of the popular classes, who is seen as being vulgar, shifty, uncouth, and crude. This term does not have a one-to-one transfer to English, therefore, we respect Earle's decision to leave the term in Spanish.

8. Samuel Ramos, *El perfil del hombre y la cultura en México* (México: Espasa-Calpe, 1934). This quote is taken from Peter G. Earle's translation, *Profile of Man and Culture in Mexico* (Austin: University of Texas Press, 1962), 60–61.

9. *Popular* as referring to the "populace" and the masses who were generally seen as not cultivated or refined.

10. This quote is taken from Emilio Fernández, "After the Revolution," *Films and Filming*, June 1963, 20. Emilio "El Indio" Fernández was important in establishing gender roles and furthering the "Mexican" identity through his myriad films of the Golden Age.

11. "Yo soy puro mexicano / y me he echado el compromiso con la tierra en que nací / de ser macho entre los machos / y por eso muy ufano yo le canto a mi país." Our translation. These lyrics are from the song "Soy puro mexicano," composed by Pedro Galindo, featured in the film by the same name directed by Emilio "El indio" Fernández in 1942.

12. These are among the most famous male movie stars from the Golden Age of Mexican film.

13. "Tus hombres son machos y son cumplidores / Valientes y ariscos y sostenedores / No admiten rivales en cosas de amores." Translation ours. These are lyrics from the song "Jalisco no te rajes," composed by Manuel Esperón with lyrics by Ernesto Cortázar Sr., featured in the film ¡Ay Jalisco, no te rajes! (1941, Joselito Rodríguez, dir.).

CHAPTER 4

We Don't Want Mother's Day, We Want Revolution!

On the New Feminism

1983

The celebration of International Women's Day on March 8 turned out to be particularly dispirited in Mexico City. There was a "sparsely attended" (a euphemism of solidarity) march, articles, news coverage with post-mortem murmurings, and a few roundtables organized at a time of crisis, almost out of a sense of obligation to revive the cause.[1] Such "declining morale" coincides with observations made about feminist groups in the nation's capital: a loss of the early "enthusiasm of discovery," the weakness of autonomous projects (their integration into the agendas of political parties or government initiatives), the tacit certainty of some sectors regarding the ephemeral nature of "fashionable" Mexican feminism, the exhaustion of verbal repertoires, ideological close-mindedness, and clarity without a corresponding context for direct action.

What's left of the vehemence and brilliance deployed by feminism and, in general, the sexual liberation movements of the 1970s? What has become of their power to provoke and agitate, their political audacity, and the boldness with which they challenged taboos and explicit prohibitions in taking to the streets, the newspapers, the mass media, the student assemblies, and even religious demonstrations? What results have been yielded by the aggressiveness of slogans and public appearances, by the imagination that produced, seemingly out of nowhere, jubilant and combative marches, by the rage distilled on banners and in speeches, by the excellent documentaries, songs, and propagandistic theater, by the convictions that sustained endless debates and conferences, and by the first corrosive humor of a marginalized sensibility that burst onto the national scene with desperate vitality?

The phenomenon is so recent and so vast that it doesn't allow for categorical responses, nor simplistic optimisms or pessimisms. What is evident is that in great part due to the crisis's crushing individualism, the most common tactics have stopped eliciting enough of a response, and the attitudes of the groups—mainly middle class, college-educated, concentrated in the capital (DF²), and ideologized to the point of paralysis—split these groups into factions so much so that they no longer resonate among workers and peasants or don't manage to significantly reach working-class neighborhoods, where women's participation is so critical.

The aforementioned panorama, of backwardness and confinement, is contextualized by various facts:

- The outbreak of the [1982] crisis, into whose well-known tunnel we are only just entering, has frozen or demolished almost all the previous strategies of the entire Left. The demonstrations against poverty, for example, have mobilized the same small sectors as always, but in no way have they touched housewives.
- The feminist spirit that we knew between 1976 and 1980 in the Federal District is now being expressed in the countryside, in cities as unexpected as Puebla, Morelia, Durango, and Colima. All in all, the existence of feminist collectives in these places, and the tenor of discussions elsewhere, make evident that feminism is far from being a "fashionable foreign import," even if its initial success was inspired by the admiration that many women of the middle class felt for the vigor of the European and North American [US] movements.
- For the first time, the Mexican State—as much due to its obligatory modernization as to its chameleon-like tradition—recognized some feminist considerations during this past presidential campaign. In a ceremony held at the Instituto de Estudios Políticos, Económicos y Sociales (Institute of Political, Economic, and Social Studies) (of the PRI), the candidate de la Madrid admitted, "explicitly, if it's true that the Mexican Revolution has not been able to establish a principle and normativity of equality (between men and women), the reality is far from the political principle and the judicial norm," and he also declared, "freedom in Mexico is not the same for women as it is for men; there is no equal freedom for women if they cannot make decisions with any degree of choice."[3] This kind of discourse is already a far cry from the "chivalry and respect for the sublime mother" shown by previous PRI candidates, and proves the govern-

mental urgency to adopt the verbal formulas of feminism before proposing any type of political modification. This is something more than a "semantic plundering," it is the beginning of an imposed integration of points of view and programs. The complexity of Mexican society no longer tolerates "symbolic representations of woman" as a government tactic, and that is made evident by the rampant uselessness of the women representatives, senators, and functionaries who have taken on these positions only in their role as biological-ideological representatives.

Regarding the above, the rapid and often violent development of social processes and the very intensity of the crisis have made clear the end of a national project founded on total exclusions and minimal concessions. Since the beginning of an independent Mexico, the prevailing ethic reserved only one space for women, "the home," and in turn, the bourgeois philosophy, in founding the State over and against the individual, excluded women from the new Nation-State. Lacking citizenship and radically excluded from civic structure, women were not fully incorporated into the nation in 1953 (when Ruiz Cortines trusted the alliance with the Church so fully that he conceded the vote to "the females"), but rather later, once the feminist presence in the apparatus of production was already irrefutable.[4] This insertion into Mexican public life does not yet have sufficient institutional outlets and is marked by the governing party's mistrust and manipulation. Nevertheless, it is an economic, political, and social development that acts ubiquitously: female representatives from the PRI that demand the decriminalization of abortion; self-criticism regarding the now useless "women's associations;" criticisms from functionaries and leaders of workers and peasants that call out the Catholic Church as the "primary obstacle" to family planning due to its sermons against birth control and abortion, and the like. Whatever the case, the new national project that will emerge from this crisis will have to include, organically, women and their unrestricted rights.

FEMINISM AND THE WOMEN'S MOVEMENT

If anything, the sheer speed and range of developments underscores the differences between the women's movement and feminism. Marta Lamas explains this in her essay "The New Feminism in Mexico":

> In Mexico the women's movement is not synonymous with the feminist movement; it is only one of its manifestations. Parallel to their participation in

joint political and social movements, women in Mexico have also mobilized specifically as women, for diverse reasons and with extraordinary strength. From the labor and union struggles of workers and maids, and the fights of peasant women for their land, their water rights, and their means of production, to the recent attempts at organizing around specifically feminist demands (such as housewives fighting to have their husbands' workplaces recognize them as equal workers because they are being overloaded with tasks previously assumed by the companies; or maids refusing to use mini-skirted uniforms that they feel objectify them as sex objects), including the struggles that women, in active solidarity with their partners, have traditionally undertaken—forming auxiliary commissions or promoting committees for the family members of the disappeared, all of these mobilizations have taken place without an explicit feminist structuring or perspective.[5]

We might also add to what Lamas has described: that the housewives who in their own homes refuse to perpetuate the exploitation of their labor by their husbands, or the maids that won't assume that their physical attractiveness is part of their professional performance, are truly acting in accordance with the slogan "the personal is political."

WHAT EVER HAPPENED TO THE CHASTITY BELT?

Confronted by feminism, the traditional Right wing (inasmuch as it allows itself to be represented by the Partido de Acción Nacional (PAN), the Partido Demócrata Mexicano (PDM), and the organizations of ecclesiastical leadership, and not as it is expressed by the inertia of society in general) has not found a suitable response, except for an opposition to one basic demand: the decriminalization of abortion.[6] Their confidence is ever more tenuous (especially in rural areas) in that the paralyzing weight of the Church and the Family will do the work for them. Unfortunately for the Right, the policy of silence-as-denial-of-existence has not ushered in a flood of ankle-length skirts. Their idea of "acceptable femininity" only includes squalid and moribund examples (the bourgeois purity of yesteryear in the social-climbing of today's middle-classers), and the economic transformation of the country (with its impressive amount yet insufficient kinds of work for women) modifies the orthodoxy of the "Nuclear Family."

Perhaps the Right has been forced to confront feminism in an era in which—despite all the papal waffling—the defense of "Traditional Values" depends more on playing global politics than on any respect for the sacred teachings of our ancestors. Before the 1970s, feminism in Mexico had been the heroic and admirable position of a few women who were surrounded by incomprehension and general mockery. However, the mechanisms for its rapid and dazzling expansion were already in place, and that wasn't because of the middle classes' will to modernize, but rather because of the exigencies of national growth whose demographic explosion shocked a Right that had been forever confident in its negotiations and confrontations with the State, counting on an immutable familial institution (an ahistorical view of women).

"WE DON'T WANT MOTHER'S DAY, WE WANT REVOLUTION!"

I'll now return to where I began. Regardless of the ostensible weakness of the feminist movement today, if we measure its achievements by the level of social and cultural influence attained, the results are impressive. If we recall that the earlier feminism was severed from national life by the PRI's cooptation, and that the link between militant women socialists of the 1920s and 1930s and the new generations was only slowly rebuilt after 1968, what has been achieved in little over a decade of militant action is admirable. A new feminism—no longer charged with anarchism, rationalism, positivism, evolutionism, idealism, experiences of extreme social mutilation, and vague notions of Marxism—emerges (with its mix of heretical Marxism, youth-oriented ideology, unorthodox behaviors, rejection of the PRI's political system, hatred for machismo, and a critique of patriarchal society) and, in a few short years, fully transcends its deliberate radius of action to indirectly, but effectively, reach vast sectors of the population. In a country in which independent organizations are still weak, and in which civil society continues to be, to a great extent, an environment of opinion without any decision-making power, feminism rapidly became the indispensable perspective (and really the only one according to any rational criteria) to understand the "feminine condition" and the "masculine condition," those historical products that, once declared eternal, encourage labor exploitation, social repression, and political manipulation.

Many elements contributed to the speed with which the slogans and sermons of the new feminism were taken up: women's place in the production and growth of higher education (with considerable feminine participation); the demographic explosion with its ever-sprawling cities and its weakening of antiquated morals and parochial power; the spread of Marxism; the mimetic power of mass media; the dismantling of the outdated and the provincial (with its subsequent crumbling of traditions); the insertion of Mexico into a global landscape; the inability of the Church to contain the ideological and mental mobility exemplified in the rate of divorces and abortions; the sudden anachronism of once audacious terms like "free love"; the decision undertaken in 1968 to democratize national life that came at such a steep price; and the propagandistic intensity of the women's liberation and gay liberation movements in the United States and England.

In a remarkably brief period of time, feminism in Mexico made use of a theoretical scaffolding (not that extensive, but sufficient), a social space within institutions of higher learning and in the university-educated middle class, taking advantage of its unexpected irruption on the scene. First and foremost, the movement existed due to the strength of its demands: the questioning of patriarchal society; the locating and defining of sexism (a word that expressed both more and less than the previously used machismo, but that covered a much vaster terrain); the repeated insistence that "the personal is political"; the criticism and ridiculing of the sexual double standard (which up to that point had been set in stone, reified by the petulant quote by Don Luis Mejía to Don Juan Tenorio regarding a seduction: "You've spoiled her for you and for me"); the fight for the decriminalization of abortion; the questioning of the subordination of housewives; the first analysis of domestic labor; and the repudiation of rape.[7]

An entire subject—unknown, hidden, negated, buried by centuries of prejudice and conventions and fears—emerged to never again return to the shadows: class struggles; the battle of the sexes; invisible and unremunerated work; the obstacles and conditions of slavery that affect all women as a whole, and each one individually. A whole order of things was suddenly put on trial: the order that prohibited Sor Juana Inés de la Cruz from continuing her writing; that ignored Juana Gutiérrez Mendoza and the women-anarchists' liberatory efforts; that cancelled out the partisan life of Benita Galeana and women like her; that obligated many writers to assume the title of "women writers"; that turns housework into the unending inferno that Elena Poniatowska narrates in her admirable prologue to Ana Gutiérrez's *Se necesita muchacha* (Now hiring a maid)—a prologue that is, explicitly and implicitly, a magnificent feminist manifesto—the servant's inferno of unrelenting and colossal minutiae:[8]

> scrub again, pour out Holandesa or Bon Ami polishing cleanser, bleach, scrub for the third time, sweep, scrub, dust, mop, wash, rinse, scrub, shake out, put away, organize, all the verbs with bent knees are tied to domestic work. Pick up, mop, clean up, carry, cook, haul, answer the phone, uncap, open, serve, serve, serve, do everything that no one else wants to do, pick up everything that's left behind, gather the socks from the floor, scrub the golden-edged underwear against the washing stone, the grey rainbow of grime from the

shirt cuffs, the dust that collects in circles, the dust that swirls spherically over screens, the circular dust over the crystal ball of fortune, the dust on the apples, the round dust of things, the dust that becomes unbreathable and rolls around as a single ball called earth, what needs to be swept from the corners, what piles up on good intentions and needs to be taken out with the morning trash. . . .[9]

Much was already known and all of it was bitterly endured, but thanks to feminism, there is a broader coordination and an increasing ideological clarity regarding this situation. The slogan "the personal is political," despite the inevitable risks of any generalization, has slowly shifted perceptions about numerous activities, from the domestic sphere to the political, which, as was affirmed at the Foro Nacional de Mujeres del PSUM (February 1982; National Forum of Women of the Mexican Unified Socialist Party), "for the worker's movement it means recognizing the importance of the private sphere in the functioning of the public sphere, at the same time, it means the demand for a reconfiguration of the private and the public, of a politicization based on socialization."[10] Though the workers movement still doesn't seem to recognize such lessons, these women have indeed intervened powerfully in the daily life and in the political behavior of many thousands of women.

THE WORDS AND THE THINGS THAT NO LONGER WANT TO BE

It's not just a question of expanded nomenclature—sexism-phallocracy-male chauvinism; on a much deeper level, the different Mexican social strata have changed to varying degrees thanks to feminist reasoning and critique.[11] It's not yet possible to know how change will occur, but this process of radical change begins with naming the methods that have enforced and conditioned women's inferiority (the majority with a conditioned-minority mentality). Today it is known that all societies, to a greater or lesser degree, are aware of their founding belief in sexism that doesn't depend on the mechanics of power systems, that transcends ideologies and economic structures, and makes "the feminine" a natural and instinctive response. According to Susan Sontag:

The rules of the game in this society are cruel to women. Brought up to be never fully adults, women are deemed obsolete earlier than men. In fact, most women don't become relatively free and expressive sexually until their thirties. (Women mature sexually this late, certainly much later than men, not for innate biological reasons but because this culture retards women. Denied most outlets for sexual energy permitted to men, it takes many women *that* long to wear out some of their inhibitions).[12]

This has been made evident by feminist discourse. Sexism is also a psychology that, through beliefs and traditions, minimizes any egalitarian possibility in the feminine ego. It is a phenomenon of class, a sociological fact, an economic and educational system, a theory of strength, a biological presumption, and an anthropological structure subject to myths and religions. Sexism reaches its peak political form through patriarchy and becomes evident in the institution of the family.

BUT WERE THERE EVER REALLY ELEVEN THOUSAND MACHOS?

Among the greatest achievements of feminism, we find the extreme problematization of three themes: domestic work, abortion, and rape. In her essay "¿Salario para el trabajo doméstico?" (Salary for domestic work?), Alaíde Foppa cites the Italian feminist Giuliana Pompei:

> One of the principal discoveries we made as we were beginning to look at our surroundings as women was precisely the labor. We needed, therefore, to give a preferential place in our analysis to the "private" sphere, to those domestic walls before which a Marxist analysis of class stops short, as well as the praxis of Leftist political organizations, whether Parliamentarian or not. At home we came to see our invisible labor, that enormous amount of work that women are obligated to perform every day, to produce and reproduce the labor force, an invisible foundation—since it isn't paid—upon which the entire pyramid of capitalist accumulation rests. This labor is never presented as such, rather as a mission whose accomplishment enriches the personality of the one who does it. A woman is a mother, a wife, a loving daughter, only if she is willing to work for others, hours upon hours, on holidays, on vacations, at night, and without complaint. This labor relationship is seen, always and only, in personal terms: it is a personal matter between a woman and the man who has the right to appropriate her labor. Women are continuously told that their world is the family, not society: it is in the family that she must navigate the contradictions that the division of labor between men and women impose on her.[13]

THE RIGHT TO ONE'S OWN BODY

Once a taboo topic, and despite the ongoing opposition of the Church (national and global), and the complicity of the government (national), the campaign for the decriminalization or the legalization of abortion has become an urgent cause. An exemplary personal anecdote: ten years ago, the director of a well-known publication threw a letter from pro-abortion feminists into the trash, saying, "This is dirty and immoral!" Three years later, in the same publication, with frequency and without any opposition, they would print declarations in favor of abortion. This isn't just attributable to the "spirit of the era," or to the terror of confronting a demographic explosion, but rather to the influence of feminist reasoning, to their convincing and dramatic use of statistics: more than one and a half million abortions and twenty-five thousand deaths a year.

Rape is a related topic, and as feminists have shown, the extremely frequent occurrence of rape should not necessarily be seen as pathological (if that were the case, the Mexican Revolution with its hundreds of thousands of rapes would be a phenomenon more appropriately studied in psychiatry than in history). Rather, rape is an extreme demonstration of a patriarchal mentality that goes from brutal abuse to continued violation by other means: the terror of filing a complaint, the embarrassment of the family, the costs and humiliations that the judicial apparatus exacts from the plaintiff. Rape is a sexual crime in chain reaction. It doesn't begin with the rapist, nor does it end with committing the act itself. It emanates from a culture that makes any sexual relationship (from marriage to casual encounters) an unending chain of violations that "forcibly gives pleasure to the victim." (There is nothing more deplorable than a rape joke.) Educated in a shameful cult of "manliness," sincerely convinced that it's what a woman really desires, unable to receive any criticism or to truly confront their exploiters, overwhelmed by their hardships, many men resort to rape as a supreme act of affirmation of their Ego or as revenge. But that explanation, or many other similar ones, does not manage to become a justification. Women have the right to mobilize the State and society in defense of their bodily integrity, demanding strict adherence to the laws against rapists.

THE CODE OF HONOR AND THOSE WHO IMPOSED IT

It is, for the time being, useless to judge the effectiveness of the fight for accessible and cost-free abortion, or the application of the law against rapists, exclusively based on legal determinations. There is another basic criterion: the reduction of social oppression. The young woman who recently accused the chauffer from the Indian embassy of rape and succeeded in having him arrested rose above prejudices and inhibitions and demonstrated that the real shame should fall upon the rapist, not on the victim.[14] With respect to rape, victory doesn't depend as much on relativizing the social value of honor as it does on the courage and bravery of the accusers. This is verifiable: the feelings of shame, humiliation, and pain generally associated with abortion have diminished considerably, almost everywhere, and something similar will happen with rape, to the extent that there will be an increase in public denunciations and ideological and political understanding of the topic.

Certainly feminism hasn't been the major factor responsible for the disappearance of honor as the principal family value. Nevertheless, it is in good measure due to feminist propaganda and struggles that there is a change in the attitude of hundreds of thousands of women who after having abortions don't consider themselves "victims of sin" or "human trash," but rather beings that consciously choose the scope of their responsibilities.[15] Without a doubt, there are also hundreds of thousands of women that in respectfully exercising their beliefs think aborting would deprive a human being of life, but they also shudder to hear the bishops lash out at women for believing they "own their own bodies." For that reason, though the pro-life demonstrations only mobilize very small and fanaticized circles, the case against abortion still retains a large social consensus that publicly involves many who would otherwise privately support abortion rights. Though not in an explicit or verbalized way, those who abort (a situation still exclusive to women, even as some still declare men's and women's problems to be identical[16]) confer a political dimension to their action, one of resistance to family, government, or ecclesiastical authoritarianism, and of insubordination to a destiny shaped from the outside. The reclaiming of one's right to one's own body represents a major political advancement.

SOCIAL CONTAMINATION

This major victory of feminism is achieved through a two-fold process: by social transmission or contamination, and by cultural validation. Today, taunting "women who act like men" is mitigated by men's concern over being accused of machismo (oh, the irony of personal history: what was not long ago a great "Source of Pride" for a "Man's Man," is now an incriminating epithet). This primarily affects the "enlightened sector"; the popular classes are still not visibly impacted by this persuasive contagion: in those circles, machos don't stop being macho due to cultural shame, nor do women feel empowered to use their bodies freely (even if on a large scale they practice abortion). Remember Simone de Beauvoir's conclusion after meeting with workers: "When we talked about their oppression by their husbands, they gave us to understand very clearly that they felt a great deal closer to a worker husband than to a bourgeois woman."[17]

Nevertheless, the accelerated rate of change, the abrupt decline of machismo's prestige, and the public airing of topics such as decriminalizing abortion, effective legal and labor equality for women, salaries for stay-at-home mothers, legal punishment for rapists, rights for the homosexual minority, etc., are advancements that can't be downplayed if one considers the criteria of capitalist and post-feudal exploitation, if we think of the centuries of social invisibility for women and marginalized minorities, or if one pays attention to the strategy of traditional morality sustained by the Church and in the provincial praxis of family.

Put on the defensive, this patriarchal attitude attempts to update itself, sophisticate itself, renew its prestige in the face of the threat of becoming an anachronism. If being a macho was a source of pride (a defiant, arrogant identity never predisposed to self-criticism), now anti-machismo is a cultural category that has taken root in ever-growing social sectors, and insofar as these men need to adjust to the frenetic changes occurring in mass society, it has isolated and set aside the most reactionary forms of an ideology.

THE LEFTIST "MACHISTA" WILL NEVER BE "ALARMISTA"

On the left, these important transformations have yet to translate into an organic project that integrates women, or into a clarity regarding the double or triple political militancy of women and the "intersection of classes" in feminist organizations. For decades, the orthodox (Stalinist) Left fought feminism for being "petty bourgeois" and for "undermining the fight against the principal enemy." This Left opposed feminism with its well-known apocalypse of goodness: everything will be resolved with the triumph of socialism, the inequalities and sexist vices; meanwhile, it's better to postpone partial or factional struggles such as feminism so that all can be delivered by the coming of a holistic liberation. Now, only Stalinoid grouplets on their path to extinction, such as the Partido Popular Socialista (Popular Socialist Party), or proudly retrograde individuals support these "theories." Ancestral prejudices are beginning to crumble, and at least the PSUM, the PRT, and diverse labor unions now consider and respect a specifically feminist militancy.[18]

If within the space of the political Left, the primary debate has been about the autonomy of the feminist movement (why fight a separate battle when it's best to wait for a unified struggle?), in a wider context, the controversial points represent a fear of confrontation between the sexes, and the question of birth control. Not only the clergy, but also older and self-sacrificing militant men affirm that each and every child will be self-sustaining; they advocate for unending fertility, and they separate themselves from campaigns to legalize abortion (that are unrelated to birth control) by claiming that only the multiplication of the masses will extinguish imperialism, or by labeling any policy of demographic control as Malthusian.[19]

For better or worse, the Left is beginning to understand feminism as a permanent category. In this recognition, diverse factors come into play (the ideological development of large sectors of the population, the grudging acceptance of the fairness of some of their demands, the demands of urban life that become an "ideology of tolerance," etc.), and are organized thanks to a genuine progress that neutralizes the serious inconveniences of tolerance—a technique of political immobilization and a tactic of bourgeois modernization. (Compare to the lucid essay by José Joaquín Blanco "Ojos que da pánico soñar."[20])

A DECLARATION OF ASSETS

Feminism informs women that their programmed inferiority is a key component of capitalist surplus value which significantly overlaps with patriarchal surplus value, and the sexual liberation movements clearly establish that a fundamental civil right is the use of one's own body. Therefore, these battles depend on the general process of democratization and the collective fate of civil rights. It will be a major step in the right direction if the Left understands—as its frontrunners already do to a great extent—the concrete and inalienable rights of those majorities and minorities that are marginalized and crushed by a sexism that is also an economic exploitation. It will also be necessary to thoroughly update notions of reform and long-range strategy. With respect to individual lives, every gain is, or can be, radical. There are initiatives effective in and of themselves: reducing or eradicating the personal humiliation of those who abort or are raped; learning not to derive the meaning of life from other people; activating union consciousness or constitutional and civil rights in cases of sexually harassed and exploited women in the workplace, or in the case of prostitutes who are condemned to the most abject of living conditions.

I have attempted to summarize the unquestionable achievements of the feminist and the women's sexual liberation struggles in Mexico. Other advances remain to be addressed:

- the growing attention to, and democratization of, sexual education;
- the need for institutions to representatively include women;
- the increasingly respectful treatment of the topic in major mass media outlets;

- the recognition of the importance of historically situating women's struggles;
- the waning in crass humor and sarcastic comments about "liberated women";
- the enduring idea of "the movement" despite the diversity of the groups, their paltry and irregular publications, their sectarian controversies, etc.;
- the reduction of social and family pressures in general, and in specific social sectors;
- the gradual elimination (though the process is only just beginning) of the invisibility and oppression of marginalized minorities caused by sexism;
- the use of women's public voice to now speak about their bodies, their sexual desires, and their specific oppressions, and to write literature that is both important and unique;
- the polarization around the "moral lynching" of minorities that, when considering yellow journalist rags (like *Alarma* and *Alerta*[21]), has lost a good part of its cathartic attraction for distinct social strata in Mexico;
- the general politicization (and the progressive insertion into the nation) of feminists;
- the repositioning of the central theme (the question) of sexual liberation, in order to neutralize or shut down any possible manipulation;
- the clear evidence of the ways the streets are exclusively masculine (accentuated by the increase in urban violence);
- the reduction in victim passivity (rape is increasingly reported);
- the stark division between beliefs and the blind obedience to those who interpret said beliefs, based on rights and personal survival (the pill, abortion);
- and the incorporation of language derived from European and North American movements into the historical experience and current reality of Mexico.

The feminist past is recovered and the struggles are "nationalized." In this way, the expression "the right to the use of one's own body" began as a cryptic phrase, but today, for dozens of thousands of women, it is the guiding principle of their mindset.

NOTES

1. The crisis to which Monsiváis refers is the 1982 economic crisis under finance minister Jesús Silva Herzog, when Mexico defaulted on its external debt obligations,

marking the beginning of an economic crash that would result in the sharp devaluation of the Mexican peso.

2. Since 2016, the capital is no longer called Distrito Federal (Federal District) or DF, but rather is now designated politically as Ciudad de México (Mexico City) or CDMX.

3. Miguel de la Madrid (1934–2012) was president of Mexico from 1982–1986. It was during his presidency that Mexico suffered the economic crisis of 1982 and the devastating earthquake of 1985. His successor was Carlos Salinas de Gortari, who ushered in the era of neoliberalism in Mexican economic policy and was later accused of corruption.

4. Adolfo Ruiz Cortines (1890–1973) was a PRI president from 1952–58.

5. Carlos Monsiváis cites an unpublished Spanish version of this essay by Marta Lamas, which was published in French as "Le nouveau fémenisme au Mexique," in *Mouvements de femmes en Amerique Latine: nouveaux espaces de lutte*, ed. Angela Cunha Neves, Lena Lavinas, Helénè Le Doaré, *Cahier de Ameriques Latines*, no. 26 (1982): 71–89. Courtesy of Marta Lamas.

6. The Partido de Acción Nacional (PAN; National Action Party) is a conservative political party in Mexico founded in 1939. The Partido Demócrata Mexicano (PDM; Democratic Mexican Party) was an ultra-Catholic, socially conservative political party that existed between 1979 and 1997. These two parties represent the furthest right on the political spectrum in Mexico.

7. *Don Juan Tenorio* (1844) is a famous Spanish play by José Zorilla, which itself refers to the Golden Age play *El burlador de Sevilla y convidado de piedra* (The seducer of Seville and the stone guest (1630), attributed to Tirso de Molina. Both works relate the legend of Don Juan, a famous seducer of women. Here, the reference is to a conversation between Don Juan and his rival, Don Luis, in which a woman who has been with more than one man is considered "spoiled," as in "unmarriageable."

8. Sor Juana Inés de la Cruz (1651–1695) was a celebrated poet, playwright, philosophical writer, and a nun, first Carmelite, then Hieronymite, in colonial Mexico. She was ultimately silenced after an epistolary exchange with the bishop of Puebla, Manuel Fernández de Santa Cruz, in which she was unofficially censured for her interpretation and critique of a sermon by Portuguese Jesuit priest Father Antonio Vieira, and for her defense of herself and women's right to interpret sacred texts and participate in intellectual culture within and outside the Church. Juana Belén Gutiérrez de Mendoza (1875–1942) was an anarchist, feminist writer, and translator who founded the radical anti-Porfirian magazine *Vésper* and participated in the intellectual life of the Mexican Revolution. Benita Galeana (1903–1995) was a unionist, feminist, and suffragist member of the communist party in Mexico. Elena Poniatowska is an outspoken Mexican intellectual and cultural chronicler whose work often explores the points of view of Mexico's disenfranchised.

9. Elena Poniatowska, prologue to Ana Gutiérrez, *Se necesita muchacha: Historia de la formación del Sindicato Peruano de Trabajadores del Hogar* (Mexico City: FCE, 1983), 61. Gutiérrez's *Se necesita muchacha* (Now hiring a maid: The history of the founding of the Peruvian Domestic Worker's Union; our translation) is a study that takes testimony from twenty-four domestic servants in Cuzco, Peru, in order to explore the invisible and ill-paid labor that they provide to society.

10. An event that we assume Monsiváis attended in February of 1982 and chronicles here.

11. Monsiváis is engaging with the French philosopher Michel Foucault's (1926–1984) *Les mots et les choses* (1966), literally "The words and the things," though published in English as *The Order of Things*, translated by Alan Sheridan (New York: Vintage Books, 1994).

12. Susan Sontag, "The Double Standard of Aging," *Saturday Review*, September 23, 1972, 288–89.

13. Alaíde Foppa was born in 1914 in Barcelona and was a Guatemalan citizen. She lived her later life in exile in Mexico after the democratically elected Guatemalan president Jacobo Arbenz was deposed in a US CIA-sponsored coup (1954) and she and her husband were forced to flee. She was an outspoken writer, professor, translator, feminist, and along with Margarita García Flores, co-founder of the magazine *fem* in 1975. Foppa was disappeared in Guatemala in 1980, and to this day there have been no official responses by the government as to her final whereabouts. Pompei is cited in Alaíde Foppa, "¿Salario para el trabajo doméstico?" *fem* 1, no. 3 (1977): 14. Foppa notes that she quotes from a presentation of Pompei's that was later published as "Salario per il lavoro domestico," in *Femminismo e lotta di classe in Italia (1970–1973)*, ed. Biancamaria Frabotta, in the series Quaderni di Lotta Femminista (Rome: Savelli), 1973. Our translation.

14. This may refer to the case of Josefina Magaña accusing Joginder Singh. For details of this particular situation see Pink Scorpio's *Bite and Hate . . . Street Defense for Women* (self-published, Lulu.com, 2016).

15. *Víctimas del pecado* (Victims of sin) was a 1951 film by Emilio "El indio" Fernández in which Cuban-born star Ninón Sevilla plays the part of a cabaret dancer who rescues a brothel-born baby from the garbage and ends up killing her abuser in self-defense.

16. At the time of this writing, Monsiváis was not considering trans men in his category of analysis. We believe that if he were still alive and writing, he would explicitly support trans struggles today.

17. Simone de Beauvoir, "Queries to Jean-Paul Sartre," *New Left Review*, no. 97 (1976): 77.

18. The PSUM (Partido Socialista Unificado de México) is the Unified Socialist Party of Mexico, which later became the Partido Mexicano Socialista (PMS; Mexican Socialist Party) in 1988. It was a far-left labor party made up of a coalition of several previously existing parties: the Partido Comunista Mexicano

(PCM; Mexican Communist Party), the Movimiento de Acción y Unidad Socialista (MAUS; Movement of Socialist Action and Unity), the Partido del Pueblo Mexicano (PPM; Party of the Mexican People), and the Movimiento de Acción Popular (MAP; Movement of Popular Action). The PRT (Partido Revolucionario de los Trabajadores) is the Workers' Revolutionary Party, a far-left party that followed Trotskyite tendencies.

19. Thomas Malthus (1766–1834) was an English economist and demographer known for his theory that population growth always tends to outrun the food supply and that any advancement for humanity would be impossible without strict control of population growth. This is a theory that has been successfully refuted by Swedish economist Esther Boserup.

20. José Joaquín Blanco, *Función de medianoche.*

21. These periodicals translate as Alarm! and Alert! In Mexico there is a long tradition of the "*nota roja*" (red news) or what in English is called yellow journalism. This is a wildly popular genre of publication that is sold on street corner newsstands, focusing on news of the sordid, the sexual, and the tragic, often times furthering misogynistic and homophobic views.

CHAPTER 5

Mexico's Young Women in the International Youth Year

1985

1 How does one situate the perennial social and political marginalization of Mexico's young women and adolescent girls historically? In searching for an answer, let's consider two fundamental issues: a) the way the State and society obey a patriarchal ideology and temperament, organized around traditional morality and embodied in the priest and the politician who become the "collective father," and b) the prevailing factional and limiting vision that results in the succession of national projects in Mexico, whose greatest triumph is a State that drafted the Constitution of 1917, and legitimized the governments of Obregón and Calles, and in 1929, the Partido Nacional Revolucionario (PNR, National Revolutionary Party).[1] In the Nation marching toward progress, there is no place for women.

In the beginning, obedience. Throughout the nineteenth century—one of nation-building—very few people discuss pre-Hispanic and colonial traditions in relation to women, who weren't seriously considered subjects of the History that was being made. In the Nation that is imagined and mapped by its vanguard—neither the liberals, nor Indigenous Peoples, nor marginalized groups, nor women intervene, and this in spite of exceptional efforts. On drastically reducing the concept of Nation, and decreeing the constitutional nonexistence of women, a thesis that will be presumed unquestionable for over a century and a half is solidified: Mexico is, strictly speaking, a country made up of adult men who belong to the ruling classes. Whosoever doesn't meet these criteria will be, if they're lucky, second-class Mexicans, which affects a highly protected group: bourgeois women.

The Constitution of 1917 cannot escape this segregationist spirit. The political role and rights of women, separate from those of the family, are still unthinkable, which is tantamount to saying that half of the population simply has no juridic or moral autonomy. The situation shifts slowly over the course of "institutional" regimes, conditioned by ironic disbelief and mistrust. Women's civic status was studied from perspectives that were both republican and sexist, and the conclusion, sadly, was that if they were given the vote, they would just hand it over to the Church.[2] Whether or not that premise was true, those who affirm it are not concerned with women's political education and they don't even try, because that would be intruding (supposedly) on the strict dominion of men: their home. If in 1953, due to the pressures of modernity, granting women the vote is inevitable, nobody thinks—for either lack of interest or previous skepticism—to add any civic education to that vote. Not even the politicians trusted democracy, nor was it worth wasting their time "politicizing" women. If they're no longer voting in line with the priest, they'll still vote to maintain a sense of stability. At best, an entire gender is offered some representative positions (very few).

2 In the nineteenth century, banned from the Visible Nation, Mexican women (that is, the privileged ones) see their home as an inevitable confinement (with implacable extensions: in the confessional, which is proof of their daily vulnerability; and in their interactions with other women, which is the recurring reflection of their lack of free will). A piece of advice to the fortunate ones: consider yourselves lucky, how many women wouldn't want to inhabit a Nation that fits into a kitchen, a bedroom, a market, a conversation with the neighboring women, and interactions with housekeepers? In this *profane space*, young women's education goes through several stages. In the nineteenth century, the "debutantes" are educated to please and give thanks, they're experts in embroidery, culinary arts, sighing, dancing gavottes, reciting perfectly memorized long poems, and keeping their eyes down while leaving mass.[3] In the [1851] anthology *Presente amistoso dedicado a las señoritas mexicanas* (A friendly gift dedicated to young mexican ladies), edited by Ignacio Cumplido and written, overwhelmingly, by none other than Francisco Zarco, the liberal theorist, there is an insistence on the seraphic and ennobled idea of womanhood (an abstract angel who is, in practice, a concrete slave).[4] Advice is doled out to the maidens: they must possess an immense well of piety, compassion for the poor, an education of moral character through religion and virtue, and the embellishment of their "understanding of certain ideas, which although perhaps shallow, is not without its usefulness. [They] should steer clear of both equally

unpleasant extremes, that of vulgar ignorance and that of the vain ostentation of knowledge."[5]

Neither illiterate nor learned. To all these recommendations, two rules for conversation were added to make young women more agreeable: niceness and politeness. For dessert, the precious embellishments of music and singing. And the final gift, the supreme task: domestic order and caretaking: "Oh, women, know your mission in the world and make good use of it!"[6]

3 The young women who because of their social class don't qualify for the status of "Señoritas" receive no formal education. They're the raw material of sin, of slums, of exhausting workdays, of the interminable raising of children. Easily bedded, fertile, beasts of burden, these beings are in fact never "young ladies," they just stop being girls, that's all. And even their childhood is generally, to no one's great discomfort, a preparation for future work or an induction into exploitation. This situation also extends into the second half of the nineteenth century, and throughout the Porfiriato. You're either a "young lady" or you live those years with none of the associated prerogatives, faced with the merciless dilemma of either prostitution or mind-numbing submission, or a mix of the two.

This is the genuine legacy for the vast majority of young women in Mexico: the elimination of rights and the forced multiplication of obligations. The armed struggle, accelerating the great social upheaval of the 1910s, destroys feudal structures and establishes social mobility (with its own myth for the masses: the illusion of social advancement), but it still doesn't authorize women's education.[7] The process of opening up spaces (first and foremost, workplaces) is long and presents two possible paths: one for the middle class or the bourgeoisie, the pejorative or punitive label applied to "liberated women;" and the other, for the unspeakable world of the working-class women. In the first case, the necessities of modernization itself stimulate reforms, verbal recognitions of equality, endless criticisms of machismo. In the second case, the need to leave the working classes behind favors the fundamental presupposition of popular machismo: women are the primary resource of our basic patrimony.

4 Electronic mass media, charged with disseminating almost all the elements of urban popular culture, enthusiastically collaborates—albeit without much success—in maintaining the status quo. Their goal is unbridled sexism, the unrelenting internalization of woman-as-spectacle for the masses. But the new modalities of melodrama necessarily turn it into something quite different, and the tear-jerking didacticism ("Suffer for others so

they don't have to suffer for you") turns into a mix of pretext and sincerity, a trick of—and ultimately adherence to—tradition ("Let melodrama teach you new ways to behave"). Over three decades and throughout the entire nation, young women and adolescents go to the movies in order to learn about a variety of behaviors that their very existence denies them, and the radio and record industry become the vehicles for their sentimental expression.

The film industry is very interested in young women as a public, but not at all as a topic to explore (it's much more profitable to focus on the "souls of children," always threatened, always redeemable). Women's function is merely decorative. They can be saintly brides, still innocent on the brink of their Fall from Grace, flirts who are unaware that their coquettishness will devour them, or nothing but shadowy figures in the domestic sphere. The pre-established roles, requiring no dramatic development, are inscribed in an equally schematic setting in which strong men (tyrannical fathers, demanding boyfriends, insatiable villains) are the precise representation of their Destiny. Without further inquiry, the model offered to young women by Mexico's new industrial society is introduced: entertainment that isn't liberating; amorous surrender that doesn't imply free will; social disgrace that doesn't seek redemption.

In the mid-1950s, in direct relation to changes in the United States, there's a new way of treating young people in sight. The middle class has grown sufficiently and can allow itself to cooperate with the bourgeoisie in the invention of adolescents and teenagers that in their scheduled free time embody the virtues of a class utopia. A young man should be ambitious, athletic, family-oriented, fun, passionate, and capable of combining academic achievement with adventurous experiences. A young woman will need to be moderately ambitious, athletic, family-oriented and domestic, sentimental (the opposite of passionate), and capable of combining her life goals with her domestic duties.

In the 1960s, this tendency to illustrate class ideals with silly and tear-jerking movies produces convincing characters: Angélica María, Julissa, Patricia Conde, young women who go through a rough patch only to better hear Mendelssohn's victorious incitement—from misunderstandings and reprimands to the *Wedding March*.[8] Gone are the days when the young woman (Marga López) saw her entire existence shattered because her parents (Fernando Soler and Sara García, iconically) didn't accept her marriage to an atheist (Lalo Noriega) in *Azahares para tu boda* (Orange blossoms for your wedding, 1950); at the end of the movie, Marga, the spinster aunt, defends her niece, Silvia Pinal, and she urges her not to let them destroy her life like they did Marga's).[9] Gone too is the time of *Nosotros los pobres* (*We the Poor*, 1947), in which a young woman mired in "the muck" (Carmen Montejo) has no right to see her daughter, not even to inform her that she's her mother.[10] By the mid-sixties the problem of Honor no longer occupies a central place in the narrative.

5 While in film and literature the images and dialogues that will represent the "modern youth" are being debated, adolescents and young people are increasingly entering the work force, secondary schools, and institutions of higher education. (Clearly, the state's public fixation on social mores always lags behind reality). By definition, urban culture daily disintegrates traditional values, and the pharmaceutical industry provides a moral that does away with all the professionally virtuous fables: the pill.[11] With the mass production of contraceptive pills, the feeling of freedom spreads, diffuse and not generally ideologized while still effective in its reach. The fact that the media and mass culture only accept the dimensions of this change by force doesn't make it less totalizing.

A modest calculation: a million and a half abortions per year. In addition to the legal and social consequences, add the moral repercussions as evidence of the depth of the change. There are not—no matter what the "moral majority" says— a million and a half murderers, or a million and a half women living in mortal sin. There is a mass rejection of those morals that stand in the way of life, and millions of adolescents and young women are now making autonomous decisions about their bodies.

Why hasn't this translated into new legislation that includes abortion among women's fundamental rights? This is not only because of the (undeniable) political pressure exerted by the Church and traditionalists, but also because these decisions of bodily autonomy don't correspond with an organic development of women's consciousness. There are a number of factors that condition a woman's decision to abort—primarily for financial reasons, also for family reasons and for personal freedom—but the sordid and clandestine nature of how abortions are carried out is a testament to the fragmentary, individualized, and guilt-laden character of this act of resistance. In extreme situations, adolescents or young women (the majority of those who abort) vindicate their right to life, but in general, they bend to societal pressures.

6 How do you translate "the Sexual Revolution" into our social milieu? In diverse terrains, the progress over twenty years is surprising: an increasing equality in the treatment of women; new perspectives on cohabitation; information on sexology (we continue to live with prejudices, but now they're a different kind of prejudice); women's use of men's "taboo"

vocabulary; fewer feelings of guilt (it persists, but it's slowing down in some sectors, and is significantly reduced in others); and a diminishing shame with respect to sexual acts, etc.

And yet, we're still a far cry from a fulfilling, civilized relationship. Virginity is no longer overwhelmingly a young woman's primary virtue, and its absolute value hardly exists (proof: the number of Mexican films whose "sociological" objective is to undo this anachronism). See for example, Jaime Humberto Hermosillo's *Amor libre* (Free love), or the behavior of soap opera heroines.[12] But millions of young women continue to be chained to domestic slavery, subjected to uncontested authorities as objects of either sexual use or free labor. In the case of homosexuals, we can see how little we've progressed toward social tolerance given the cruelty of crimes against gay people (normally, acts of social lynching, or assaults against strangers who are savagely robbed of life for the simple crime of disobeying the norm). In the case of women, the violence against them reiterates the widespread precariousness of an antisexist stance. From my point of view, rapists are infrequently (clinically) mentally ill. Most of the time they are individuals who, without much loss of their sense of reality, believe they're exercising their natural rights by forcing themselves on a woman's body. They act within the confines of what's permissible in their worldview, believing that deep down they're satisfying the victim's secret desires. (For such sexism by force, there's no possible rape. If the woman resists, it's only to heighten the violator's arousal).

Something to consider: if rape is reinforced by society's subterranean currents, we must insist on legal punishment to combat it. The root of the solution is an intense and permanent sexual education, but it will be necessary to reinforce this still-very-slow process with legal judgments. Against this machista certainty (that rape is a secret right), we must uphold the judicial and moral notion that rape is a public crime. Until this truth informs our deep social consciousness, the spaces available to adolescents and young women will continue to be limited. They won't have nighttime hours; they'll live—especially in working-class neighborhoods—in institutional terror; they'll overwhelmingly feel how the will of a single macho—or a group of them—can in a single moment nullify everything that has been gained with the rapid and continual shift in mindset, and through their own daily efforts.

7 Who is the adolescent girl of today? In our urban culture, overwhelmingly, someone who already knows that she lacks a place in society (or any society), and that no matter what, and without great conviction, nevertheless attempts to leverage the resources that will allow her to become a part of it. Her reality is harsh, hostile, binding, and sexualized with great

violence. The answer: the invention of her trusting, idyllic, and romantic temperament. The addiction to singing idols, the obsessive consumption of photo-romances and soap operas, owes much to their desire for other psychological models far-removed from their lived experiences. That is to say, what others scornfully call "escapism" is essential to the emotional stability and mental health of millions of pre-teen adolescents without any access to other alternatives.

Who is the adolescent girl of today? Certainly there's no general answer, and categorizing their behavior by social class is not very convincing. Especially because they're being perceived from such a distance, the influences in the national setting are almost always the same: national chaos, electronic media, the presence of US culture, and the idea of fashion as an inflexible reflection of youth (the imposition of fashion by the cultural industry). Beginning in the seventies, adolescents and young people from the working classes have taken to imitating the middle class, and they've put their faith in imitation at all costs, being successively or simultaneously addicted to disco, rock, heavy metal, punk, and break-dancing. Adolescence, in any case, is a series of behaviors that see in their sexual affirmation, in their belonging to subcultures, and in their reproduction of fashion the very definition of their age group. I'm an adolescent because I'm not like a child, because I have clear awareness of my genitalia and my individuality, and unlike young adults, I'm unconcerned with being on the cusp of a fulfilling life. If in the middle classes adolescents and young people tend, ultimately, to justify their existence by being students, in the popular classes, both male and female adolescents are those who are actively educated for failure and who reject this normative grooming with utopias of idealized love, self-destructive rage, codes of body modification and style, simultaneous faith in and hatred of their families, sexist behavior—including to their own detriment, and a reverence to a school system that excludes them. Compared with the most "privatized" families of the middle class, the families that are, so to speak, more "public" and unimportant in the popular neighborhood, produce offspring that collectively create another definition of adolescence, no longer substantially linked to the discovery of sex ("the springtime awakening" of nineteenth-century playwrights) and the right to fool around, but rather a fatalistic acceptance of both personal and class failure. In the frenetic dances, in the prompt memorization of all the popular songs, in the masturbatory contemplation of their pop-idol posters, in the orgasmic cries in the presence of Menudo, Juan Gabriel, or José José, in the daily confrontations with machista vulgarity, adolescent girls learn to divest from childhood by way of participating in fever-dreams and social compensation.[13]

NOTES

1. Title. United Nations designated 1985 the "International Youth Year" (IYY).
2. Álvaro Obregón (1880–1928) was president from 1920 to 1924, prior to Plutarco Elías Calles (1877–1945), and was assassinated in 1928.
3. Women were seen as being easily manipulated by the priests through the confessional and other interactions.
4. A *gavotte* is folkloric line dance with its origins in sixteenth-century France, popular in the court of Louis XIV. Late nineteenth-century Mexico was heavily influenced by French culture because of the Napoleonic invasion that installed Maximilian of Austria as the emperor of the Second Mexican Empire from 1864 to 1867 and ended when he was executed.
5. *Presente amistoso* was the most popular women's magazine of nineteenth-century Mexico, and began circulation in 1847, the year in which its first "anuario" or yearly digest was published. See Marina Garone Gravier, "Nineteenth-Century Mexican Graphic Design: The Case of Ignacio Cumplido," trans. Albert Brandt, *Design Issues* 18, no. 4 (2002): 54–63. The yearly digest to which Monsiváis refers was, in fact, published in 1851, and had many different collaborators, among them Francisco Zarco (1829–1869), who was a liberal Mexican journalist, politician, and historian from Durango.
6. Our translation. Ignacio Cumplido, ed., *Presente amistoso dedicado a las señoritas mexicanas* (Mexico: n.p., 1852), 18.
7. Our translation. Cumplido, ed., *Presente amistoso*, 15.
8. The armed struggle Monsiváis refers to is the Mexican Revolution, which began in 1910 and ended around 1920.
9. Angélica María, known as the "novia de México" (Mexico's sweetheart) was a popular American-born Mexican singer-songwriter (rock), and actress in the 1960s and 1970s. Julissa (Herrera) was a popular actress and singer in Mexico. Patricia Conde is a Spanish actress, model, and television personality. Felix Mendelssohn's "Wedding March" in C major, written in 1842, is one of the best known pieces from his suite of incidental music for Shakespeare's play *A Midsummer Night's Dream* (1605).
10. These are all popular actors and actresses from the Mexican industrial era of filmmaking. *Azahares para tu boda* was a 1950 film directed by Julián Soler (adapted by Mauricio Magdaleno from the 1934 play *Así es la vida* by Argentine writers Nicolás de las Llanderas and Arnaldo Malfatti). It tells the story of a conservative family during the Mexican Revolution whose eldest daughter struggles to obey her parents, refusing to use the same kind of wedding flowers that her mother had used.
11. *Nosotros los pobres* (*We the Poor*) was an iconic Pedro Infante drama directed by Ismael Rodríguez. Monsiváis considered it a critical and influential contribution to the understanding of film in Mexico's Golden Age. See Carlos Monsiváis, *Pedro Infante: Las leyes del querer* (Mexico City: Aguilar, 2008); and Carlos Monsiváis, *Rostros del cine mexicano* (Mexico City: Américo Arte Editores, 1993).

12. See Gabriela Soto Laveaga, "Let's Become Fewer: Soap Operas, Contraception, and Nationalizing the Mexican Family in an Overpopulated World," *Sexuality Research and Social Policy* 4, no. 19 (2007).

13. *Amor Libre* (1979) was a Mexican "sexy-comedy" (*sexicomedia*) by Mexico's premier camp/queer filmmaker, Jaime Humberto Hermosillo, staring Julissa, an actress and superstar of the era.

14. Menudo was a Puerto Rican boy-band that emulated the Jackson Five. It was created in 1977 by producer Edgardo Díaz. Juan Gabriel (Alberto Aguilera Valadez, 1950–2016), also known as Juanga and the Divo of Juárez, was a wildly popular singer, songwriter, and composer whose flamboyant appearance was celebrated despite a generalized cultural homophobia. José José (José Rómulo Sosa Ortiz, 1948–2019) was a popular Mexican musician, singer, and actor, considered one of the best Latin singers of all time.

CHAPTER 6

On Constructing "Feminine Sensitivity"

1987

INTRODUCTORY NOTE

In 1972, I published some notes on sexism in Mexican literature, to demonstrate the patriarchal hegemonies present in our culture.[1] Thirteen years later, I'm admitting the futility of such an undertaking, as in any case in which, a priori, one knows quite well the results of that endeavor: Mexican culture, since its inception, has been structured by machismo. And there's no arguing with this fact. Therefore, I think it's better to explore the multifaceted construction of "a feminine sensitivity."

"TRY TO BE AS DISCREET AS POSSIBLE"

Women have no place in the Nation's liberal project. The Constitution of 1857 and the Constitution of 1917 clearly trace a space of privilege and responsibility that excludes women, the poor, and the Indigenous populations. Beyond the unifying data (territory, laws, language, traditions), a minority guided by noble and important motives knows, or thinks it knows, what's best for the rest of the population. A *Nation* isn't the sum of all the territory's inhabitants, but rather only those endowed with conscience, those who know where the country is headed (socially, politically, economically). What can women do, when according to the country's leaders, they lack participatory qualities, they're fragile and weak with no other destiny than that of being housewives and keepers of their home?

Founding a nation is a matter of virile strength in addition to the refinement needed to enter "the concert of nations." The Porfiristas, for example, think of themselves as an exception in a barbarous country, and see in their recently acquired manners and French education, not a cultural background, but a way of conducting themselves according to the "niceties and brilliance" of their social class.[2] As far as culture goes—the Western version approved in Paris, and to a lesser degree in London, Berlin—the Porfirian government and society grant it an ornamental function in tune with their ideal: the coming-of-age of a civilization!

"A PURE AND ARDENT SENTIMENT"

From the outset, the sensitivity of feminine characters is prescribed, ranging from a lack of alternative morals to a limited and devalued type of artistic creativity. An evident example: the *poetesses* (who were later called "poets" to indicate their "serious" intentions, as the absurd sexist would claim). What is required of a *poetess* in the nineteenth century? Simplicity, spirituality, and a search for values that glorify the home. And if the writer doesn't comply fully with the demands, all the worse for her. Her readers will treat her as unacceptable, they will scorn her sexual outbursts and unorthodox attempts to portray the feminine condition. A quote from Ignacio Manuel Altamirano referring to a female friend is a case in point:

> A pleasing and overwhelmingly delicious impression is the feeling one has reading your poems. A pure and ardent sentiment, robust inspiration, ineffable tenderness in the expressions, profound morality in the subjects, elegance in the descriptive images; these are the qualities that stand out in your poetic compositions.[3]

Feminine sensitivity, "a pure and ardent sentiment," "robust inspiration," "ineffable tenderness," "profound morality," are the defining qualities of those who will never be considered a part of a citizenry known for their genius or talent, but who, at home, repeat the moral lessons learned from men. To be a faithful echo of male instruction, "to sweeten" reality, is to fulfill the requirements of the "feminine condition." Hence the narrative interest in the prostitute, who is both the quintessential woman (she who surrenders) and the negation of true femininity (permanent sexual availability). The prostitute is a woman only biologically, for in relinquishing her spiritual life, she *defeminizes* herself. Femininity is seen as helpless sensitivity, as exemplified in the work of a representative "poetess" of the nineteenth century, Maria del Refugio Argumedo de Ortiz:[4]

Anguish

On the petal of the white rose trembles
a crystal-clear droplet of dew;
the river swiftly crosses humming;
the mist lightly lifting:
the diaphanous breeze softly sighs
among the grove of shady foliage,
and in the warm summer nights
the moon mysteriously passes . . .
Only my soul sadly mourning
wanders in the shadows of mortal agony
with hope and illusions lost;
Suffering without pity assails;
as my mother on her departure
in the hands of anguish leaves me[5]

There is no literary adventure there, and this isn't because of talent or lack thereof, but because of a social decree: don't forsake your poetic vocabulary, don't abandon your recognized and recognizable sensitivity. Another example—a sonnet by Mateana Murguía de Aveleyra:[6]

A Rose

Yesterday fresh, and flaunting fragrance,
displaying its splendid colors,
and from sun to dazzling splendor
swaying on its gentle stem.
Kissed by the loving zephyr
lulled by tender nightingales:
a queen among flowers,
proudly adorning the garden.
But night came, and a storm
its finery furiously strips
leaving it wilted, and sallow:
that's how the hand of sorrow spoils
the flower of my fate, and withered,
hurls it in the abyss of my grief.

Woman is a flower, woman is a beautiful object, woman is the lack of resistance in the face of adversity, and women that are interested in poetry must acquiesce, this is the dictum of literary societies: "If she be a woman, she must write like a woman." In any case, women writers only have one defense: the brilliant mastery of technique. This will be the beginning of their independence. Take for example the case of Josefa Murillo, called the Lark of the Papaloapan, which more than illustrative, was a warning title that signaled her as a woman poet.[7] Josefa Murillo is well-known for technical virtuosity, which lets her express other poetic registers (among others, sexual appetite), but she is a woman (and a "lark") and there's no way to escape a gendered reading. How spiritual and pure! This poetry will be a succession of graceful rhythms, praiseworthy poetic devices, feelings of finitude, an absence of ideas, and a worldview emanating from the position of weakness that lacks the resources that power offers. It's men's place to write vigorous poetry that exalts and educates the spirit. It's women's to write poetry where there can be no "poetry."

CHARACTERS WHO FAIL TO BECOME AUTHORS

Altamirano *dixit*: women, having more time, will read novels, a genre fundamentally dedicated to the fairer sex, who are more quickly moved by the suffering of others. Readers, never authors. In the nineteenth century, in Latin America, there are no equivalents to Jane Austen, George Eliot, or George Sand (two women who cross-dressed their literary names to avoid prejudices). Literary creativity depends on many things, among others, tradition. But as readers, middle-class women easily pick up on the emotional blackmail in the stories they read, and when retelling stories to their children at meal time, they create an oral tradition of melodrama whose "generative function" is also pedagogical.

In the novels, first and foremost, the female characters embody a lack of power. If they are decent, they are de-sensualized or de-sexualized, they are excluded from politics, from the "real world." To make up for this, women readers identify with the heroines, whether or not (most probably not) they enjoy imagining the possibilities of love affairs. As readers, they harness all the sensitivity within their means, the virtues "proper to femininity," spirituality (a synonym in nineteenth-century novels for *submission* or a spirit whose nobility and sacrifice will yield to the dictates of the father, of the priest, of society). These women also believe that the natural inferiority of woman constitutes the foundation of authority, and not even the most notable heroine is exempt from that secondary role, especially as reading novels is starting to become a man's domain.

An example of purity as insignificance: the character of Remedios in

Rabasa's tetralogy (*La bola*, *La gran ciencia*, *Moneda falsa*, and *El cuarto poder*, 1887–1888).[8] In the petty and mean setting of the countryside and the capital, amid uprisings and corruptions, Remedios is the angel who with an air of ecstasy and pain is moved by the winds of fate, bedridden, agonizing, and in a feverish state. Unconscious, she sighs and moans while being contemplated with devotion by he who protects her from reality. Her autonomy and purity are the only dignity she is granted, and her social representation is that of prestigious weakness.

In this literature (and the implacable rule hardly allows any exceptions), if a woman is independent, she has no social dignity. This is not only true for the extreme case of prostitutes, but also for the "flirt," a feminine category so dated that it disappears with new social rules. What is *flirtation*? It's the element of fatal distraction, it's the sexual availability that offends morality and furthers independence by denying morality (therefore, when flirtation stops being a negative characteristic ascribed to femininity, the possibilities for independence expand). In *La Quijotita y su prima* (1818) by Fernández de Lizardi, the novel that introduces women to Mexican society after Independence, a tension arises between the woman who knows and loves her place in the world, and the flirt, who is misguided and wild.[9] Pudenciana, modest, virtuous, and industrious, tends to her home; Pomposita (la Quijotita) exhibits bad behavior: spoiled, flattered, pampered, "confident in her beauty and her charms, always trying to multiply her number of slaves, as she calls her admirers."[10]

RETROACTIVE EFFECTS

To speak of patriarchal thought is to evaluate our entire historical process: the colonial, official independence, liberal, revolutionary, post- and counter-revolutionary eras. Therefore, in Mexican literature, sexism finds an effective and inevitable collaborator. In this case, the reflection of the dominant morality is direct and—almost always—without nuance. If other phenomena of national life (poverty, or political passion, for example) tend to support assimilation and artistic recreation, that's not the case with regards to sexism. This is such a powerful and rooted vision that—judge it as you may—it constitutes an idiosyncratic response to external and internal demands. Thus, when an impassioned Díaz Mirón expresses the following:

> Be content woman! We are here
> in this crushing valley of tears,

> you like a dove, for the nest,
> and I, like a lion, for combat!

He embodies the machismo of his epoch and, at the same time, dramatizes the traditional role accorded to men, an operatic vision of reality, which is necessary to be grasped.[11] (The majority of literature from the Porfiriato resorts to such heightened poetics in order to have staying power).

SENSITIVITY TRANSLATED INTO IMAGES

"Feminine sensitivity" is constructed through fixed roles: the idolized goddess; the vessel of lust; debased and redeemed fragility; the life companion; the repentant sinner; the saint of the stockyard and the bedside of the sick; the relentlessly pursued ingénue; the midnight virgin; the married temptress; the fucking bitch; the beloved mother; the nosy gossip; the praying mummy; the trampled innocent; the poor "holier than thou"; the saintly sweetheart; the patron saint of Mexico . . . thanks to these images, the stereotypes (the clichés and archetypes) are internalized, and become common places of social behavior.

This imposed "sensitivity" requires no specific women, but Woman with a capital W, a spiritual gift, the comforting presence that poetry grants in life's struggles: "I toast to the woman, but not for the one that brings solace to your sadness."[12] And the abstraction ends at Home (that "Sacrosanct Enclosure") where, as a mother, she will continue to be guardian and vestal virgin.[13]

A working hypothesis: in Mexico's cultural process (in this and other contexts, so dependent on Western culture, on Judeo-Christian orthodoxy), the construction of feminine sensitivity adheres to a single tactic: that is, giving "woman" a *visible image* to better render her invisible, and thus confirm—through these symbolic paths—her absence in the true spaces of power.

Take the extreme case of the war years against the dictatorship and the Civil Wars in Mexico (1910–1930, approximately).[14] Until now [1986], the female character par excellence of the Mexican Revolution is the *soldadera*.[15] And if a woman—Nellie Campobello or Rosa Castaño—wanted to write about armed violence, she had to do it with a lavish use of symbols and allegories.[16] Here I quote a fragment from Nellie Campobello:

> Pablo Mares died as he was spraying bullets from his cavalry rifle. They say he was behind a large boulder one sunny day. His face was golden, his forehead

well shaped, his eyes light colored, his nose straight and his hands broad. A handsome specimen. His children would have been grateful for their heritage. Even sickly and unattractive children—poor things—and their parents as well. In fact, both Pablos would have sired beautiful, robust children. I think Pablo Mares stopped spraying bullets from his rifle, and his strong body—the gift he gave to the Revolution—gradually keeled over on his left side; his hands slid down the boulder until they came to rest near the earth. His blue eyes didn't close. His rosy face died little by little. His broad shoulders lay at peace. All the blood running in bubbling red threads over the rock begged forgiveness for not having sired strong children . . . I think his arms fell asleep alongside his rifle after a song of bullets.[17]

Elena Garro and Elena Poniatowska are the first writers that transcend the cultural constraints that have barred women from writing about violence or topics "unrelated to femininity."[18] Thus Rosario Castellanos's efforts to use the thematic and formal possibilities within her reach only clearly succeed when she draws on irony, sarcasm, and self-determination, and invents a character that skirts prohibitions and rejections.[19] During the years of the Revolution [1910–1920] only one culture is encouraged: one that sees in nationalism the major cultural creation of the armed struggle, and finds in muralism, and in the Novel of the Revolution, its maximum expression. The emphasis is placed not so much on national reconstruction, but rather on a nationalist sentiment in which women have no active participation. In novels, proletariat poems, traditional *costumbrista* narratives, theater, chronicles, etc., what drives nationalism is the feeling of belonging that gives rise to the nation, and in this galvanized nationalism, women only have secondary roles, even if it's Tina Modotti distributing rifles in Diego Rivera's mural.[20] Mexican nationalism is made in the image and likeness of the masculine drive to construct the nation, and in their pride of belonging to a nation built on violence.

In "haute couture," women are entrusted with embodying, to the extreme, emotions and sentiments, to be ridiculously "cursi" to the very end, exaggerating sentimentality.[21] The "poetesses" from the provincial areas (those that give such a bad name to both poetesses and the province alike) represent sensitivity as cultural inertia—the defense of family values and the vulnerability sublimated either through suffering or excessive sweetness. The feminine is placid contemplation, a crystal clear stream, a diaphanous sunrise, etc., perfectly in tune with rural culture, lacking in prestige since the 1920s, even as its power in reproduction of these images continued into the 1950s, and in one way or another, until today.

PURITY IS A LIGHT THAT WON'T BURN OUT

In the nineteenth century, women are relegated to a space of "spiritual growth," where they slowly develop their "potentialities" without exerting their minds, without abandoning *the proper duties of their gender* (understanding *women* as those "not morally of-age," blessed by the "respectability" of the middle class and the bourgeoisie). A whole set of rules and prohibitions come into play in the construction of a "feminine sensitivity:" the *Calendarios para señoritas* (Ladies' calendars); the pious readings; the incentive to read only "appropriate" novels; the delicate language men used in their presence; submission to complicated paternalistic hierarchies; the lack of permission to go out unchaperoned; the impossibility of receiving equal treatment under the law; and the duty to model particular qualities.[22] Socially and culturally, women are more object than subject, and in that order of things, patriarchy sees them as mere reflections of their true selves.

In the beginning, there was Tonantzin, our Mother, who would later become Guadalupe.[23] As Guadalupanismo takes hold, both religiously and politically, the terms of her idealization are fixed: the most venerated woman ("I swear, for me, you're the most sacred thing") will be the Virgin, with or without a capital V, the guardian of the inviolable hymen. And in literature (or in reality), this pan-virginal program is solidified: the immaculate is the symbol of respectable womanhood, my mother or my wife or my daughter are, have been, and always will be unsullied virgins beyond reproach, because more than a physical condition, virginity is a patrimonial attribute. All objects in my possession, especially women, are out of reach—beyond all possible desecration. For this reason, and ultimately in the end, feminine virginity is sanctified: it is the most complex and evident manifestation of property rights.

The armed conflict of the Mexican Revolution brings with it a cultural revolution that reorders the terms of "feminine sensitivity." It becomes impossible to portray women only as embodied frailty. In the battlefields and in their survival tactics, women destroyed the myth of endless weakness. Different processes ensue. First and foremost will be the literary. In short stories, poems, novels, and articles, women will be the beloveds who are framed by evocations and sexual euphemisms: the idolized object (whose pinnacle is Fuensanta in López Velarde's poetry);[24] the virginal girlfriend (that must lack personality); the long-suffering mother that relishes her pain (a ubiquitous character that appears from the serialized novel and theatre melodramas to popular poetry in the style of "El brindis del bohemio" by Guillermo Aguirre y Fierro); the repentant sinner Magdalene, who knows the price she must pay to redeem her virginity is death (exemplified

by Federico Gamboa's *Santa*); the man-eater who learns from men's predatory spirit to avenge her loss of innocence (this cliché is present in serials,
and in movies—María Félix makes it her hallmark[25]); the faithful soldadera,
ready to die for her man (la Codorniz in *Los de abajo* by Mariano Azuela);
the flirt who toys with her honor and strays (Micaela in *Al filo del agua* by
Agustín Yáñez); the feverish and inaccessible woman, who is pure poetry
among the ruins (Susana San Juan in *Pedro Páramo* by Juan Rulfo); the
crazed lover whose complete and utter surrender redeems her from her
brazenness (Adriana in *La Tormenta* by José Vasconcelos) . . . The list goes
on and on, but there is no disputing one fundamental fact: the cultural
sphere in Mexico takes a long time to incorporate contemporary notions
of women's freedoms.

In the process of a forced "feminine sensitivity," literature is, for obvious
reasons, a minor element. The principle agents are the State (recalcitrant
on women's rights: their voting rights were finally conceded in 1953), the
Church (that insists on denying women bodily autonomy and psychological
rights), the Family (where there's a curious strategy of calling it a "matriarchy" when the paterfamilias is still in control), and Society (resistant to
all change that might threaten its hierarchical system). Before the 1960s,
Mexican literature was responding to that register of prejudices, with little
resistance to be found.

CHANGE IS DIFFICULT

Modernization puts traditional feminine sensitivity in crisis. There is a
breakdown of the protective shield of magazines that exalt purity; homi-
lies; euphemisms of motherhood that sweeten the wedding night intimacies;
the serious and light scolding from the confessor; the propagandistic advertising by department stores; and the push for modesty and polite blushing
. . . Diverse phenomena act simultaneously: virginity on the wedding day
stops being an inexorable requirement, the extended family under one roof
gives way to the nuclear family, the earlier onset of puberty makes bodies
more precocious, customs evolve (in great part thanks to the demographic
explosion and the international influx of mass media), traditional morality
breaks down everywhere, and a permissive mentality gains strength.

Almost overnight, and all over the country, young women discover their
bodies (with a little help from the cults of sports and advertising), and no
one is embarrassed when confessing to sexual pleasure. In spite of the resistance in traditionalist circles, sex education proliferates (from a scientific
battle to an industry), Freud's theories are disseminated by followers and

adversaries alike. Sexology becomes a horizon of delightful and almost always inaccurate knowledge. The dialectic leap takes place in tandem with the effectiveness of contraceptives. The changing of mindsets is seen in the shift from "abortion as mortal sin," to an "unpredictable misfortune," which implies the Church's decreased control over lives and the gradual elimination of the repressive concept of "Honor."

Profound traces of nineteenth-century feminine sensitivity remain in public language and in literature, where all "didactic" intent has been lost (no one will instruct like Lizardi, nor admonish like Payno, nor scold like Gamboa anymore[26]), and in exchange for this indifference to a feminine sensitivity of sweetness and resignation, which is considered well-lost, the campaign against censorship is unleashed, claiming a new sensitivity in which women have more rights, but are equally subjugated. In novels, characters abound who are as free to sleep with whomever they choose as they are incapable of mental autonomy.

Today the dominant concept of feminine sensitivity is unclear. It is impeded by the democratization of social life (still precarious, but more robust in comparison to before). The cultural industry proposes a "modern sensitivity," consumerist, sporty, freely dependent, and founded on the criteria of beauty and elegance. Traditionalism maintains its basic assumption of subjugation; its greatest success has been convincing millions of young women who have gone through abortions that they should be—under penalty of hell—virgins before marriage, although few have any such offers. And the "feminization of the economy" (the growing entrance of women into the labor market) generates another project of sensitivity, much more adjusted to reality, and ever less dictated from the outside.

Until now, the myth or the sum of myths referred to as feminine sensitivity has been synonymous with the qualities that facilitated domestic life and mystified sexual relations. Although this version still has social force, its replacement is in sight: a more frank, direct, belligerently resentful, ironic, and democratizing sensitivity, as glimpsed in the final poems by Rosario Castellanos, who makes her awareness about alienation the starting point for critical freedom.

NOTES

1. See Chapter 1, "Dreamy, Flirty, and Fiery," in this anthology.
2. *Porfiristas* are followers of *Porfirismo*, the ideological doctrine of the *Porfiriato*, the term for the period of the presidency-turned-dictatorship of Porfirio Díaz (1830–1915). He was a strongman intent on "order and progress," since political

order was necessary for economic development and progress. Díaz opened Mexico to foreign investment, but the benefits did not favor the majority, and economic inequality became increasingly intolerable. Porfirismo ended when Díaz was ousted by the 1910 Mexican Revolution and went into exile in Paris.

3. Ignacio Manuel Altamirano, "Carta a una poetisa," *La Literatura Nacional*, vol. 2 (Mexico City: Editorial Porrúa, 1949), 116–17. Altamirano (1834–1893) was a prominent liberal writer and principal promoter of Mexican literary nationalism, famed for his romantic novel *Clemencia* (1869) and for *El Zarco*, which was published posthumously in 1901.

4. Maria del Refugio Argumedo de Ortiz (1842–1893) was a recognized and anthologized poet of the era and a contributor to the weekly *Violetas de Anáhuac*, a pioneering feminist publication.

5. Our translation of María Del Refugio Argumedo, "Desaliento," *Las hijas de Anáhuac* 1, no. 8 (January 22, 1888): 95.

6. Mateana Murguía de Aveleyra (1856–1907) was a writer, poet, journalist, teacher, and suffragist who directed *Violetas del Anáhuac*, a weekly magazine edited and published by women in Mexico City from 1887 to1889. She participated in literary societies such as *Las Hijas del Anáhuac* and the weekly *La Mujer Mexicana*. She was well known for her essays on education and the social condition of women. Our translation of "A una rosa," *Las hijas de Anáhuac* 1, no, 5 (January 1, 1888): 59.

7. Josefa Murillo (1860–1898) was born next to the Papaloapan River in the state of Veracruz. A poet influenced by romanticism, her themes of life, death, and the passage of time were also often imbued with irony and satire as she expressed the gender roles women had been assigned during that time period.

8. Emilio Rabasa (1856–1930) was a diplomat, politician, and co-founder of the newspaper *El Universal*. He was best known as a novelist in whose tetralogy, *La bola*, *La gran ciencia*, *Moneda falsa*, and *El cuarto poder* (The insurrection, The big science, Counterfeit money, and The fourth estate), Remedios occupies a major role.

9. After three centuries of colonial rule and its war with Spain, Mexico gained Independence in 1810.

10. In this didactic novel on how to educate young women, Pomposita (whose name suggests pomposity or frivolity) was raised by permissive parents and relies on her beauty to make her way in the world. Her cousin Pudenciana (whose name suggests modesty) is raised "properly" following the principles of the Illustration.

11. This is our translation of verses from the poem "A Gloria" by Salvador Díaz Mirón (1853–1928), which is said to have been influenced by Lord Byron and Victor Hugo, and was very influential in Mexico during that time period.

12. This is a quote from "El bríndis del bohemio" by Guillermo Aguirre y Fierro (1887–1949), a much recited poem to this day in which a group of men in a bohemian setting on New Year's Eve make toasts remembering their past loves,

feats, etc., until the last one toasts a woman—the only woman that deserves to be honored—his mother.

13. Monsiváis ironically deconstructs the sanctity of motherhood as portrayed in the poem "El bríndis del bohemio."

14. Here the "war years" are in reference to the dictatorship of Porfirio Diaz, the Revolution of 1910, and the Cristero Wars between the Church and the State from 1926 to 1929.

15. Some of the *soldaderas* took up arms, while others tended to the wounded and provided sustenance and solace to the troops.

16. Rosa de Castaño (1910–1983), a prolific novelist and playwright, was one of a small number of women in the first half of the twentieth century to write about the Mexican Revolution. This group also included Nellie Campobello (1900–1986), recognized for her memoir about her childhood amid the Revolution. In Monsiváis's original, de Castaño mistakenly appears as Castaños.

17. Nellie Campobello, *Cartucho and My Mother's Hands*, trans. Doris Meyer and Irene Matthews (Austin: University of Texas Press, 1988), 76.

18. Elena Garro is considered one of Mexico's foremost writers, known for her short stories, plays, and novels, in particular *Los recuerdos del porvenir* (1963), translated by Ruth L. C. Simms as *Recollections of Things to Come* (Austin: University of Texas Press, 1969). Elena Poniatowska is a well-known journalist, novelist, and short-story writer. Her best-known work internationally is *La noche de Tlatelolco* (1971), translated by Helen R. Lane as *Massacre in Tlatelolco* (New York: Viking Press, 1975), about the violent repressions of the 1968 student movement in Mexico City.

19. Rosario Castellanos (1925–1974), a writer, journalist, and diplomat, is considered one of the most important authors of the twentieth century in Mexico and Latin America. Her work as a novelist, poet, short-story writer, playwright, and essayist focused on gender oppression in literature and reality. It cleared the way for generations of women writers to express themselves freely to contest an oppressive patriarchy for women and other minorities, including Indigenous populations. Her novel *Balún Canán* (1957), central to her politics, was much later posthumously translated by Irene Nicholson as the *Nine Guardians* (England: Readers International, 1992). A selection of her work appears in *Another Way to Be: Selected Works of Rosario Castellanos*, ed., trans. Myralyn F. Allgood (Athens: University of Georgia Press, 1990), and as her reputation has grown, much of her work has been translated and anthologized.

20. *Costumbrismo* was originally a genre of nineteenth-century romanticism that evoked traditional narratives of the folk, but for followers in the twentieth century, it evoked past traditions.

Born in Italy, Tina Modotti arrived in Mexico City with the American photographer Edward Weston and quickly joined the post-revolutionary scene, which included the muralists and pioneering women such as Frida Kahlo, Lupe Marín, and Antonieta Rivas Mercado, among others. As a member of the Mexican Communist Party, Modotti's work became politically charged. As photographer and Revolutionary, her avant-garde corpus has been exhibited internationally.

21. *Cursi*, applied to a person, refers to someone who acts in ridiculously pretentious or overly sappy ways.

22. These ladies' calendars were accepted as appropriate reading material for women, and were instructive about the ways they should behave in society.

23. *Tonantzin*, meaning "our mother" in Náhuatl, is the venerated female goddess of the Mexicas.

24. Ramón López Velarde (1888–1921) was a prominent poet of the "post-modernista" movement, whose muse, Josefa de los Rios, inspired Fuensanta.

25. Monsiváis refers here to María Félix in her portrayal of the title character in the film *Doña Barbara*, inspired by the novel of the same name written by the Venezuelan author Rómulo Gallegos, published in 1929 and considered a classic on the theme of barbarism and civilization.

26. Manuel Payno (1810–1894) was a Mexican author, journalist, politician, and diplomat known for his novel *Los bandidos de Río Frío* (The cold river bandits), first published as a serial in Barcelona from 1889 to 1891 and later as a book in Mexico in 1892.

CHAPTER 7

Love on (the Eternal Eve of an Impending) Democracy

1990

Are love and democracy compatible? Until recently, the immediate response would have been a negative; everyone believed that love, a glorious and painfully subjective experience, could only be understood as the foolishness of two people who had no relationship to politics, and was felt so strongly that it would transcend economic determinism ("I love you even if you're rich"). Love, the supreme notion, was antidemocratic by nature. In any couple, there was always a winner, and equality was a fallacy that only had nominal supporters. A man in love aspired to possession and domination and would accept nothing less.

Institutions supported this version of love, one that imposed a moral tax and physical and/or social persecution on women, while only asking men to keep up appearances in married life. Melodrama was the formative space of an amorous ideology, and everything (idiomatic expressions, plotlines, songs, romance novels, plays, and films) aided in enforcing the idea of romantic love, that peak of human experience, which, whether frenzied or tender, was always hierarchical. For love, in this mythological pageantry, "man" redeemed "woman" from her passive condition; for love, woman ascended to the rank of companion; for love, man obtained a running household.

In the first half of the twentieth century, Freudian ideas undo traditional understandings of love. In light of the successive revelations of the unconscious ("The true motivation of all acts comes from . . ."), how can one defend the beliefs of traditionalists, both liberals and conservatives, who from their pulpits and lay epistles upheld the tyranny of ideal, enchanted, eternal love (if it meant taking vows under divine and human laws), that demanded from women a perennial and spiritual virginity, that is to say, the suppression of any expressed desire, while men were encouraged to sin in order to be forgiven? But questioning the nature of human acts led to the circulation of new ideas and feelings: nothing was as it had seemed, the pervasive expectation of self-sacrifice was crushing free will—to deny desire is to deepen one's self-destruction. And the universe of vows, convictions, weeping at the feet of saints, furtive looks in the dimly lit bedroom, the path from genteel courtship to diamond anniversaries, fell apart (as a true belief, not as the projection of desire nor as a social representation). If the motives were now questionable, love would have to be reclassified.

The dissemination of Freudian theories prompted a questioning of romantic beliefs in which intense and passionate love (love in its strict sense) is by nature ephemeral, and what happens before and after is the tedious and corrosive representation of love in the eyes of society. According to this hierarchal but also ageist version, everyone, for the duration of their existence (especially and almost exclusively for people between the ages of twenty and forty, before maturity goes stale), has very scarce opportunities to find love. And for that reason, one must practice resignation, that substitute for extreme passion. Who can withstand a burning passion for more than a few months?

Along with these general theories, urban couples lived accepting or rejecting the myths of love that were most comfortable to them; in many cases, they tacitly agreed on the experimental nature of marriage; they divorced in order to have another chance; they remarried to reclaim their routine; they believed in and detested the "waning" of feelings; they viewed feminist positions with alarm and/or delight; they washed dishes and cared for children together; they demystified love to the degree that it was no longer needed; and they mythified it to the level of gentle, ironic treatment.

TO WHAT EXTENT IS THE PERSONAL POLITICAL?

From the moment it appeared, the motto "the personal is political" was heavily criticized. Only an extremist—they've said for over twenty years—brings up intimate issues in such an uncomfortable context. The personal is personal, although certainly there are issues in which the personal is political: abortion, legislation about cohabitation and the rights of "natural born" children, labor conditions equal to those of men, etc. Despite the criticism, the motto proved its efficacy by providing the phenomenon of love with landscapes that had never before been taken into account: the subjection to patriarchy, the confusion between love and "ownership" over another, and the use of jealousy as a socially acceptable method to control the other.

In the midst of all that, the Sexual Revolution of the 1970s takes place by advancing and expanding "liberties" (a term completely opposite to the oppressive epithet "libertines," assigned to those practicing "licentiousness") in order to expose the hypocrisy of the traditional notion of love. And just as the libertines of the eighteenth century wanted to make seduction widespread in order to flaunt taboos, to evade the ever-present vigilance of morality, and to make each act of sex an act of war, the Sexual Revolution, by preaching free love, eliminated moral judgment from the "geography below the belt" in their practice, and love became the one great convention—besieged despite its semantic strength. What was the point of using the euphemism "to make love" when much more plainly and simply you could just say "fuck?" One's love life stopped being synonymous with a sex life, and love was understood, ever more, as an aura of feelings.

All this in the midst of major changes. Hedonism stopped being the privilege of the few, and ended, once and for all, that very common concern of being torn between having a wide variety of sexual encounters, and leading a conventional but productive existence. During the Sexual Revolution, the yuppies—whose success depended on never accepting failure— believed that they had created a historical space, one in which their sense of productivity matched their sexual frequency ("The more I work, the more I screw"). Love seemed like an eccentric act of willpower, which in essence fostered discipline: "I'm falling in love to get my life in order," and there was no awareness of the possibility of a relationship between love and democracy, unless we're referring to the very strategic kind described by Mario Benedetti, where love was part of the ritual of militancy and the sentimental repertoire of adolescence. They would sing: "Y en la calle, codo a codo, somos mucho más que dos" ("And in the street, arm in arm, we're many more than two"), and the couple disintegrated into the multitude.[1]

FROM FEAR TO SOLIDARITY

In a single decade, AIDS destroys the Sexual Revolution, and it triggers a growing consolidation of the couple and the first nonreligious reconsideration of love. Social pressure is replaced by a fear of death, and the mistrust in regard to the stranger with whom you're starting a flirtation is almost synonymous with the difficulty of falling in love. Sex itself loses all sense of being carefree, condoms are a bitter reminder of a fear of death, and harassment leads to reconsidering the meanings of fixed roles, a critique of gender fatalism, and freer conceptions of the couple: Adam and Eve are no longer the foundation of humanity, but something slightly less allegorical and therefore much less conventional.

How much ground has been gained regarding the humanization, or the humanistic signification, of the romantic relationship? To speak of, if it's even possible, the relationship between love and democracy also means to examine the ways political and social life incorporate the demands of intimacy and/or private life, whichever you like. In this area, the personal tends to be democratic, not just for the obvious reasons—whosoever takes a stand against authoritarianism must also eliminate it from their own behavior—but because in times of dramatic situations and transformations, love is an essential component. From diverse points of view, this may well be an intangible fact or an astonishingly corny premise, but regardless, what it expresses is an urgent reality. If the PRD, for example, purports to be the grand alternative to the barbarity of neoliberalism and the stubbornness of conservatism, it will need to organically incorporate into its platform what the PRI and PAN would never do: the demands of daily life; the fight to decriminalize abortion; the dissemination of accurate information about AIDS; the fight against rapists; the ideological siege against sexism, etc. In all this—and as difficult as it is to use the most overused and slippery word in language—love is a primordial reality whose deep democratic translation is solidarity that today recognizes its admirable vanguard in the groups that are dedicated to supporting AIDS patients, and who are combatting by any means necessary the propagation of evil.[2]

NOTES

1. Mario Benedetti (1920–2009), influential Uruguayan writer, poet, playwright, novelist, and journalist, was part of the generation of "committed" militant leftist authors of the 1970s. Here, the words are from the refrain of his well-known poem "Te quiero" (I love you).

2. The PRD (Partido de la Revolución Democrática, Party of the Democratic Revolution) was historically the party of Leftist opposition to the right-leaning PRI and PAN. The PRI is an extension of the PNR, Partido Nacional Revolucionario (National Revolutionary Party), founded in 1929. The PRI/PNR held uninterrupted presidential power until the year 2000. The PAN, Partido de Acción Nacional (National Action Party), was the even further-right, religiously conservative party that ended the PRI's institutional stronghold.

CHAPTER 8

How One Day Pro-Lifers Woke Up to the News That They Were Living in a Secular Society

1991

OPENING: NOW EVERYONE IS SPEAKING THE UNSPEAKABLE

On Friday, February 15, 1991, Televisa's Channel 9 is broadcasting "¿Y Usted . . . qué opina?" (And what's your opinion?), a talk and debate show with Nino Canún that aired daily from 11:00 p.m. to 5:00 a.m. (approximately).[1] In the studio, the controversy gets heated and grows cacophonous, with everyone speaking over each other, all convinced of the importance of their viewpoints, aware of the large live audience at their disposal (who are willing to lose sleep over an ideology); in this case, the perspective is autobiographical. There are those advocating for the decriminalization of abortion who see themselves as part of an open, pluralistic society in which beliefs are not at odds with fundamental freedoms, and their opponents, who by calling abortion murder plain and simple, are building a case for an indictment that spares them any argument, protected by their devotion to the venerable traditions of their faith.

Their arguments, both pro and con, have become a part of everyday conversation. First, we have the representatives of Pro-Vida (Prolife; a group emblematic of denial and censorship: "No to abortion, No to condoms, No to sex outside of marriage, No to sacrilegious and sensual representations"[2]): a woman assembly member from the PAN and a few students from schools like the Universidad Anáhuac (looks can be deceiving: likely they're *only* from Anáhuac), all who single-mindedly broadcast the slogan "The embryo is a living being with full rights."[3] They don't listen to opposing rationales, there's no reason to bother hearing them out. They unflaggingly operate on the principle of revealed truths. Next come the opponents: two feminists, a representative from the PRD, a psychoanalyst, and a sexologist.[4] And finally, we have those who are "neutral" and truly defend decriminalization: a lawyer from the attorney general's office in Mexico City and a doctor from El Seguro Social (National Health Plan) who offer statistics and arguments, underscoring the high number of yearly abortions (two million, according to reports), and the women that die as a consequence of these sordid situations. They explain the absurdity of imposing the tenets of a single religion on a secular society, and how it's impossible to prove that terminating a pregnancy is murder. They ask: "Would you put two million women in jail every year?"

There's no response. There can't be one. Dogma impedes the possibility of any dialogue. However, that's not what counts, but rather the existence of the show itself: six hours of discussion on a previously unspeakable topic, and this on the Mexican Family Channel, no less! The incoming phone calls to the station, primarily by young people from ages fourteen to twenty-five, attest to both the intense debate and the hard-won gains over such a short period of time by those who support decriminalization. For the Right, to accept debate would be a step backward, that is, to concede that their position has become just another point of view and is no longer the only morally valid one that shouldn't have to break bread with sinners, because to do so would mean that their views have become just another version of the facts, the traditional one, the one identified with prohibitions and machismo under the cloak of "Buenas Costumbres" (Good Manners), in any case, it would mean that their word alone is no longer enough.[5]

The students (probably from the Anáhuac) repeat hardline slogans: "It's murder. If abortion is legal, it's the same as allowing 'gente decente' (respectable people) to be killed in in the streets."[6] These are not rational arguments, they're dogmatic beliefs carved in stone, like tributes from today's minorities to yesterday's majorities. Other young people ask Serrano Limón of Pro-Vida, "What sexual reality are you imagining? Hysterical nuns praying in the convents? Adolescents feeling guilty for having sinned or for not having sinned?" A feminist asks the representative from the PAN who believes that intercourse is only valid when its purpose is conception: "You are the mother of four sons, so does that mean you only had sex four times in your life?" The Panista blushes (I suppose), and a viewer, still awake at three in the morning, might think that the logical extreme of the Pro-Lifer's position is that each sexual coupling without demographic consequence—lust and carelessness that don't engender a living being with full rights—is also a homicide.

Seeing and hearing to believe, *dearest Saint Tommy*.[7] The Right controls the idea of how the "Buena Sociedad" (Good Society) sees itself, they veto government decisions, they promote intolerance somewhat effectively, but, I think, they no longer hold on to the idea that their own *modus operandi* determines the actions of the rest of society.[8]

THE CONGRESS OF CHIAPAS: THE SPARK AND THE MEADOW

Toward the end of December 1990, the Congress of Chiapas, made up of an of overwhelming majority of Priístas, decriminalizes abortion in that state, or rather, broadens the instances in which it would be permissible.[9] The Right responds immediately: Is this the beginning of another Holy War? How dare the government challenge its greatest ally, the Catholic Church? It's inconceivable for a local legislature, blurred by the historic demands of centralism, to undertake such a far-reaching act on its own. Whether explicit or not, everyone sees it as an experiment, and little attention is paid to Chiapas's particular situation beyond the Church-State confrontation. Poverty defines the state, with its sixteen thousand Indigenous and peasant communities on the edge of famine in many places, its high infant mortality rate, and a daily life ruled by extreme misinformation. Chiapas's own governor Patrocino González Garrido gives us his point of view:

> Are we going to allow women to be nothing more than mere animals? Do we want so see them and treat them this way? Here, at age twelve, they start bringing babies into the world. And they don't stop until they're fifteen or even eighteen. What future awaits these children? Malnourished in the womb. Harmed in life by protein deficiencies. Newborns without brains. Children with low IQs. Is that we want? I hate to talk about such a sordid topic. But the Indigenous women of Chiapas—and we have over a million—try to end their pregnancies using turkey feathers. It's terrible! And we don't want to confront the problem. . . . In Chiapas there are two hundred thousand abortions every year.[10]

In light of the decision by the Congress of Chiapas, there is a tremendous backlash. The PAN goes from politics to theology as it suits them, underscoring their refusal to rationally examine the facts: "You cannot decriminalize what may not be decriminalized," states the congressman Jaime Aviña in his typical manner. The Panista leader José Ángel Conchello sees those that practice abortion as the lowest ilk of criminals and finds any referendum on these cases abominable, "because this is a moral question, and thus, democracy is not acceptable." He expresses this with clarity: dogma is not subject to social reasoning. Now they've moved on to metaphysical topics, and on this subject, the leadership of the PAN overreacts: "Abortion is not justified even in the case of rape . . . to kill the product of a rape doesn't right the wrong . . . it's for loose morals, convenience and hedonism that abortion is accepted . . . we are not accepting any decision, if permission to kill is granted."[11] In tandem with the Catechism of the Catholic Church, the PAN's speculation goes against its own sentimental traditions: "*The gestational being in the maternal womb is neither a biological nor an existential part of the mother* [my italics -C.M.]. Therefore, the mother may not dispose of the unborn child who is not a part of her organism. The unborn child is another human being. The mother, with her unborn child, is part of a transitory symbiosis that doesn't entirely end with birth."[12] Those in the PAN call "transitory symbiosis" what under other circumstances they would qualify as "eternal love."

The Catholic Church threatens, and hesitantly mobilizes, unleashing a moderate deluge of church banns. Their argument is one and the same: abortion is the killing of a defenseless soul. On this they insist: "The commandment *Thou Shalt Not Kill* is absolute," reiterates the spokesman of the Episcopate, Genaro Alamilla, who criticizes the decision by the Congress of Chiapas as an "abuse of authority," demanding that President Salinas de Gortari redress the wrongs of "his" local congressmen.[13] Until now, everything has gone as expected. The political and ecclesiastical Right don't need to update their proclamations because their criteria have always already been set from the beginning to the end of time, and therefore, nothing can escape this, not the incontrovertible fact that no one has an abortion for fun, not the will of the women, nor the misery that awaits their unwanted children who are overwhelmingly doomed to a life deprived of the most basic necessities.

However, there are new developments in the debate, including the position of some government sectors as well as civil society's shift toward feminism. Suddenly, the undesirable, unspeakable word—*abortion*—is expressed freely, because the context is no longer an individual drama but rather a collective tragedy. What in the past would have caused outrage continues to offend traditional sectors, but it is no longer earth-shattering. In spite of the power of the Catholic Church, only three thousand people showed up to protest in Tuxtla Gutiérrez, an unexpectedly low number if you take into account that the event was a call to action by all the parishes, and the bishop of Chiapas, Samuel Ruiz, who lead the march and condemned "the five feminists from San Cristóbal who promoted the law." The threat of excommunication does not prevent the unexpected statements from the Working Group for Decriminalization, nor the avalanche of legal, political, medical, and moral arguments that support decriminalizing abortion. Here's an example from the magnificent essay by Luis Villoro, which I quote here from his conclusions:

> *Fourth. Mother's rights.* The criminalization of abortion cannot be justified by the rights of the fetus, because it is not a subject with rights; on the other hand, it infringes on the individual and inalienable rights of the mother. Let's consider the following:
>
> a) It infringes on the right of all individuals to make decisions for themselves, and therefore, about their own bodies. While the fetus is nourished, breathes and gestates thanks to the maternal organism, it is part of the mother's body. The State has the obligation to guarantee this right.
> b) It infringes on the health rights of all individuals. According to the data of the National Chamber of Hospitals located in Mexico City, illegal abortions cost us the lives of three hundred thousand women per year. The State has the obligation to protect these women and provide them with healthcare so that they may make informed decisions about their own bodies that only they can make, in order to not put their lives at risk.
> c) It infringes on the right of equal opportunity that every individual possesses. Only wealthy women have abortions under satisfactory conditions. The legal punishment for abortion is only applied to those who have no means to pay the necessary costs and who are left on their own with no recourse. The criminalization of abortion is one more element of social discrimination. Abortion is a painful, bloody, sometimes tragic act. No one want this. The solution is not punishment, which only increases the number of clandestine abortions, but rather sex education, the mass distribution of contraceptives, and readily available medical assistance.[14]

Almost all the arguments for decriminalization had already been made and repeated, but never before had they reached such a sizeable audience, nor had they emerged in such spontaneous and varied ways. This is significant. As always, one sector publicly declares itself traditionalist, exercising its right to reject abortion, but public opinion (that yet vague and concrete circle of the press, unions, action groups, public figures, and the social hierarchy of trending topics) advances the idea that by favoring the decriminalization of abortion, they are following what is confirmed by reality: This punitive climate hasn't reduced the incidence of abortion, nor has it increased with the growth rate of the population; the law has been used against doctors and nurses, not against those who abort (two convicted in ten years with fines); criminalization increases corruption, humiliations, and the physical risks of clandestine procedures, which only serve to dramatically impact millions of lives.

Previously, the political lines were clearly drawn. On one side, the feminist groups, with poor access to the press and with no representation on radio and television; on the other, the Catholic Church, with its partisans and unconditional followers, and the fear that secular society has at the mere mention of the topic. But what drives this change in mindsets is the country's cultural internationalization, the increase in intermediate and secondary education, a generalized secularization that makes use of tolerance as a pathway to development, and feminist theories. Another factor in this social process is the attitude of many Catholics who respect and understand the desperation of those having an abortion.

OF PARTIAL DEFEATS THAT ARE SOCIAL VICTORIES

The response from the ecclesiastical hierarchy of the PAN and its para-ecclesiastical agencies delays the passing of the law of the Congress of Chiapas. (Pro-Vida affirms: "We intend to prevent state governments, in their use of sovereignty and freedom, to modify laws that will permit abortion.") The congressional representatives refer the case to the National Commission on Human Rights, whose president, Jorge Carpizo, then calls for a study of the issue. But the Right rushes to celebrate their triumph. The decriminalization proposed by Chiapas opens the floodgates of tolerance, and something akin to a referendum takes place all over the country, and surely in every family.

Take, for example, the case of the political Center-Left. For decades the partisan Left was opposed to birth control, which included, irrationally, an opposition to the decriminalization of abortion, considering it "an imperialist strategy intent on avoiding, at any cost, the birth of the militant masses of the Third World." (On the Ultra-Left, an Ultra-sexist song was popular: "Bear children, Latin American mothers, bear more guerrilla fighters."[5]) The sectarianism that dreamt of fertile wombs as weapons hasn't altogether disappeared, and even today, there are those that oppose decriminalization because it means "taking away the responsibility from the State that should safeguard maternity," but such previously ubiquitous positions are now, if anything, only heard among small factions. The opposite position is what dominates today, as is demonstrated by, among other things, the resolution of the PRD, which was unanimously passed on January 13, 1991, advocating for the decriminalization of abortion.

Since the 1970s, the social Left has backed the humanist arguments of feminism. The message spreads and draws in other sectors, and even if this doesn't immediately translate into legislative action, the social pressure on those who abort is substantially reduced. And the process still continues. Last February 15, 1991, Quintana Roo's State Congress approved a series of guidelines in relation to the practice of abortions, making debate possible there.

NOTES

1. Televisa is a multimedia conglomerate with headquarters in Mexico City. Until 2017, the company was led and owned by three generations of the Azcárraga family, the first being Emilio Azcárraga. The first transmission in 1970 of *24 Horas* (24 hours) with anchor Jacobo Zabludovsky became the most-watched news program in Mexico for decades. Nino Canún was a journalist who became famous in the 1990s for his program *¿Y usted . . . qué opina?* This televised forum on contemporary topics encouraged debate and dissent among its participants, both those in the studio audience and those who called in.

2. Pro-Vida is a movement advocating against the legal practice of abortion. In 2021, the Supreme Court decriminalized abortion in Mexico at a national level, although access to abortion varies by state.

3. La Universidad Anáhuac is a private university with two campuses in Mexico City, which belongs to the conservative Catholic religious congregation the Legionnaires of Christ.

4. The PRD (Partido de la Revolución Democrática, Party of the Democratic Revolution) is a Leftist political party formed in the 1980s by Cuauhtémoc Cárdenas Solórzano that splintered from the PRI, founded in 1929.

5. The phrase *Buenas Costumbres*, understood as "decency," good morals, or behavior that doesn't offend polite company, is used ironically by Monsiváis.

6. This often-used phrase in Latin America privileges "decency" as the moral value that recognizes the importance of living and behaving with dignity in all contexts and places. Again, Monsiváis uses this ironically to point out the unfairness of the terminology, because "decency" is socially classed.

7. This is an ironic reference to Saint Thomas, known as Doubting Thomas for not believing Christ had risen from the dead until Christ appeared and had him put his finger in the hand pierced by nails and his hand in the side gashed by a sword, and told him to stop doubting and to believe. John 20: 24–29.

8. *La Buena Sociedad* is one that is supposed to offer equal opportunity and prosperity to its citizens.

9. The title of this section comes from a quote by Mao Tse Tung, "A single spark can burn down the meadow," and was used as an epigraph on the front cover of the documentary *La chispa y la pradera: El FRAP, una revolución imposible* (The spark and the meadow: The Revolutionary Antifascist Patriotic Front, an impossible revolution), written and directed by José Catalán Deus about the Spanish Civil War (1936–1939) against Francisco Franco.

10. In *Excelsior*, January 13, 1991. Our translation.

11. In *La Jornada*, January 11, 1991. Our translation.

12. Continued quote from *La Jornada*, January 11, 1991. Our translation.

13. Carlos Salinas de Gortari (1948–), a politician and economist affiliated with the PRI, served as president of Mexico from 1988 to 1994.

14. Luis Villoro, "¿Debe castigarse el aborto?" (Should abortion be criminalized?), *La Jornada*, January 11 and 12, 1991. Our translation.

15. From a song called "Marcha de las madres latinas" (March of the Latin American mothers) by José de Molina, a Leftist involved in the 1968 student movement in Mexico.

CHAPTER 9

On Women's Representation

1991

___

WHAT ARE WOMEN DOING IN POLITICS?

In looking for an answer, ask yourself the opposite question—what are men doing in politics?—which you'll find unacceptable or unthinkable: politics, dear sirs, is the business of men, because according to that toxic belief that we call tradition, man is the creator of institutions, a builder par excellence. The prejudice is set in stone, and in order to showcase it, I choose, among the thousands of examples at my disposal, two recent cases.

1) The secretary of social development of the PRI's National Executive Committee prepared an instructional guide for its congressional and senatorial candidates with questions of primary importance as well as answers for them to study and, in the appropriate cases, to memorize.[1] The topics are crucial to the Mexico of today: the North American Free Trade Agreement (NAFTA), modernity, privatization, the informal economy, the financial system, education, salaries, etc. In this repertoire of such important matters, the only mention—shockingly—of women is found in question number 77: "Do you propose any policy for the protection of social groups? What do you propose for children, adolescents, women, Indigenous Peoples, the elderly, drug addicts, and homosexuals?"

In the aforementioned document, the PRI's secretary of social development responds that: a) children, adolescents, and the elderly are social groups, and b) Indigenous Peoples and women are protected *classes*. The responses are, unsurprisingly, on par with the question itself. As one might imagine, homosexuals are not even mentioned. With respect to children, the PRI decides to protect them "from their defenselessness within the home and in the social environment." As for women who are responsible for the "hard work of maintaining a united family," the following plea is made: "With respect to women's participation, the Party proposes the necessary support of women's access to political processes, with equality of conditions to those of men, as well as the effective practice of their right to work, an essential condition of their integration into social life and the basis of their full liberation." If not brilliant and clear, at least the response that was requested or suggested to the candidates was sincere: the social groups of children, adolescents, women, Indigenous Peoples, and the elderly will be safeguarded by *professional protectors*, by the *only* sector that can do so: men between thirty and sixty years of age, the only ones that count in this country. And if women want to liberate themselves, they must find the miracle formula for their right to work, a miracle that doesn't require, according to the PRI, any further stipulations nor legal or social processes beyond well wishes.

2) A fragment from the May 1991 *Manual de imagen* (Style guide), also dedicated to the members of the PRI, keeps us up to date with the essential requirements of a politician who doesn't want to be perceived as tacky:[2]

> A politician must wear clothing that on the one hand symbolizes his identification with the values and the institutions of his forebearers as a platform, infrastructure, or basis for his actions, and on the other, shows him to be a progressive who seeks modern solutions according to contemporary ideals. Therefore, his selection of attire must follow conservative guidelines while at the same time, within these limits, adding fashionable elements. Another important matter to consider are the factors that, within the technical framework of the media (in this case television), are aligned with the aesthetic definition of his image.
>
> Women in General
> Dresses, two-piece suits, or a skirt and blouse that are modern, but not too showy.
> Stockings in the same tone as the suit or dress.
> Matching shoes and purse that go well with the dress, that is, that pick up some of the clothing's colors.
>
> Informal Occasions
> Light colors.
> Cotton, rayon, or linen.
> A simple style.
> Natural makeup.

Formal Occasions (formal public acts or evening events)
Dark colors, or slightly more intense ones.
Silk, wool, or somewhat shimmery textures.
A somewhat more sophisticated style.

Slightly more accentuated makeup.

Politics is not only publicity, it's adornment. These "exterior architects" and "hair architects" are stylists and fashionistas that are taking culture by storm. And though they might appear less rigid, the other parties, trying not to lag behind the PRI, continue to overlook women. You won't find truly developed platforms with respect to the political, economic, and cultural status of women in the PAN nor in the PRD, much less within splinter groups. And in this, the so-called political parties are not inventing discrimination, they're obeying historical conditioning and the process of national consolidation, which has barely permitted the presence of women in public life.

"A HEROINE IS THE HERO'S WIFE"

According to the official story, very few women deserve a spot in the limelight, and only as collateral or complementary heroines: Josefa Ortiz de Domínguez, who informed the "Tata Cura" that the Spanish were already aware of their tactical plan; Leona Vicario, for joining Don Andrés's illustrious family tree; Agustina Ramírez, who offered up all her sons to the Patriotic cause . . . and to that precarious list, add the symbols of the Revolution, the "soldadera" and the "coronela" who are honored with gratitude.[3] In this century, only the writer Rosario Castellanos has become a regular member of the "club" of the Rotunda of Illustrious Men (when it was inaugurated, the adjective seemed superfluous).[4] Thus, successively and obviously, up until recent times, the role of women was just to be witnesses to the greatness of others.

And if we're talking about important dates, the federal recognition of women's abilities is nowhere near reaching its first centennial: in 1979 Griselda Álvarez, the first woman governor, takes office; in 1980 Rosa Luz Alegría is the first woman to be a member of the presidential cabinet as secretary of tourism. Does it make any sense to keep describing women's subordinate position in the historical and social landscape when every situation is an example of discrimination?[5]

Is anybody who is *somebody* a woman? In 1953, President Adolfo Ruíz Cortines concedes the vote to "the females," yes, just like it sounds, he concedes it to "the females" because, as the op-ed columnists of the time—the simultaneous translators of the System—say, a good relationship with the Catholic Church makes any alarm about women ceding their vote to the clergy obsolete.[6] Women will vote for the PRI, which guarantees the stability of their perennial deficiency, and furthermore, since they're half the population, they *should* be given *some* formal rights so that no one can complain. At first, the vote for women was a psychological balm that attempted to soothe the malignant effect of "She was a woman and yet, she could think," but this did little to extend any real benefits to women. It's fine for women to vote, but who could possibly imagine voting for a woman?

"AND NOW THE CONGRESSMAN WILL EXPLAIN TO THE LADIES WHY VOTING DOESN'T GO AGAINST THE NATURAL DELICACY OF THEIR SEX"

For a long time, in the spheres of political monopoly, feminine representation is bureaucratized by force; those who were accepted as the most equal among the unequal must professionalize themselves as symbols. One curricular example, neither too recent nor too distant, is Hilda Anderson Nevares, the public school teacher and leader of La Confederación de Trabajadores Mexicanos (the CTM, Confederation of Mexican Workers).[7] She joined the PRI in 1958, where she was the Secretaria de Acción Femenil (secretary of feminine action) from 1971 to 1973.

She's the founder and leader of the Agrupación Nacional Femenil Revolucionaria (National Women's Revolutionary Group) from 1973 to 1977; secretary general of the Federación de Organizaciones Femeniles (Federation of Feminine Organizations) of the CTM; president of the Comité Femenino de la Confederación Internacional de Organizaciones Sindicales Libres (Feminine Committee of the International Confederation of Free Labor Unions) from 1981 to 1983; member of the Comisión para la Mujer de la Organización Internacional de Trabajo (Women's Commission of the International Workers Organization); and a federal congresswoman, a senator, a candidate for congress again . . . At the end of all that, what do we publicly know about doña Hilda's pronouncements on women's issues? Vagaries, a verbal haze. She is undoubtedly a professional representative, someone who, apart from her merits, has specialized in the job of being a symbol embedded in the bureaucracy.

In the majority of cases, up until now, what has women's representation in the PRI and the opposition done? Until very recently, the answer seemed obvious: it has increased the female or feminine bureaucracy—that is, it has perfected contestatory commonplaces. And more symbols don't mean the end of their symbolic access to politics, only a proliferation of isolated allegorical niches.

The presidents and ministers succeed one another, the tone changes slightly from sentimental paternalism ("woman, the hand that rocks the world") to technocratic paternalism ("woman, the transcriber of noble sentiments"), but fundamentally, with respect to the deeply held beliefs of the political class and of society, the prejudice remains unchanged: politics is a man's game.

How can we destroy this stronghold-idea? Politics is the technique for obtaining power, which requires shrewdness, the moral courage to abandon scruples, access that is only available to men, and a daring based on Testicular Ideology, or, as the elite say, on having *balls*. In Latin America, politics is the business of strong men, for whom any replacement is allegorical. In those societal rules, which we call "the sense of an era," women are still characterized—in an opinion unaffected by facts—by their "virtues of defenselessness": fragility, tenderness, and exacerbated sensitivity.

HOW THEY GOT TO THE WAITING ROOM

Without a doubt, many national and international factors applied pressure to change matters of women's constitutional rights. Here is a list in no particular order:

- Women's growing participation in higher education, the economy, and the police (there are even women "granaderas" on SWAT teams).[8]
- Women heads of state, the New World Order: Margaret Thatcher, Indira Gandhi, Corazón Aquino, Violeta Chamorro.[9]
- Feminism's momentum, whether it's recognized or not, is the theoretical groundwork for all women's participation, which facilitates or demands a permanent analysis of prejudices regarding intellectual and political inequality.
- The proliferation of women leaders throughout the entire country, especially within social movements. Even as many of them turn into despots, replicating tyrannical models without deviation, training women for leadership is a priority; it advances as far as it can (a little, never too much).
- Neverending transformations of the family and society that now demand what used to be discouraged or prohibited: a much greater

development of women's abilities, women who must daily broaden their ideas and horizons. This doesn't happen evenly, it varies by social class, political and ideological background, family dynamics, religion, etc., but the end result is unmistakable: traditionalism in women is a thing of the past.

- The relentless cultural attack on the myths of male supremacy, which doesn't mean, of course, the toppling of the patriarchy, but it does mean the weakening or the disintegration of the truisms and certainties of machismo.

- The electoral support across political parties of thousands of women that has served to prove a) their level of effectiveness; b) the invariably wide gap between their well-known levels of efficiency and their place within organizations; c) the ways their perception of politics has changed, a turn tantamount to the leap from a sacred vision to a profane one; d) the *real* disinterest of organizations (not what they say) with respect to women's status; e) the decorative and luck-of-the-draw nature of the criteria that guide organizations in their selection of female representatives; f) the way the quality of women actually magnifies the difficulty in exercising their positions, from polling station representatives to governors.

"MACHISMO, BRO, IS A BIAS OF OBJECTIVITY"

In the 1991 electoral process, amid unforeseeable clashes, the previous criteria of tokenism has prevailed ("I'm voting for you not based on your worth, but so that no one can call me out"). This, it seems to me, puts in crisis the very idea of representation. If the tendency continues to favor symbolic appointments, who can properly represent women? Why is it important to represent women in parties that so rarely take their problems into account and that retreat from essential topics? An extreme example: the decriminalization of abortion. The PAN is furiously opposed to it, the Chiapanecan sector of the PRI dared to decriminalize it only to be refuted by Centralism, and the PRD unanimously approved the measure but has failed to inform the country of its decision.[10]

The question is obsessive: who owns politics, and where do its owners *do* politics, and what does the term itself encompass? Women can be activists, yes, and in attending to their jobs, they organize the candidates' tours (or, in very few instances, their own tours), they're in charge of campaign meals, they speak persuasively and dogmatically with housewives living in shacks, they cheer, they make impassioned speeches, they call people to vote, and they specify what they see as essential in the meetings. But according to the rules of the game, their job is the politics before the politics, always excluded from the genuine spheres of power, the "palomeo" and the "planchazo," and other strategic considerations in which the women, again, are relegated to the areas of the political party that are suspiciously similar to the classic ones: the kitchen, the confessional, the sewing room, and in front of the television.[11]

In this order of things, what does the common refrain "women haven't been given opportunities" mean? This expression is unfortunate, because an opportunity that is given, or granted as a gift, is an opportunity that doesn't really exist. For example, women were granted the vote, but their delay in truly assuming its exercise has to do with the way many women had to stop seeing the vote as an incomprehensible obligation, turning it instead into an often pleasurable right.

"TWO MORE WOMEN SWEETEN THE FACE OF THE SENATE"

Where do politics take place in Mexico? Up until now in spaces where only a few women are allowed to enter, for short periods, with a restricted invitation and without much power. Perhaps politics engenders rules of the game that are so implacable (with respect to obtaining and retaining power) that, ultimately, the only transcendent actions are those that evade or surpass rigid divisions, both true and false ones, between masculine and feminine, to clear the way for what is "the sex of politics," made up of actions and considerations that emerge from individual psychology, removed from power or the aspiration to it. Simply put, you govern like a politician, which is gendered male even if it's a woman—a conundrum for gender theory—and there lies the specificity of the space in which policies are made, and where women *as women* still haven't had real access.

In this case, in 1991, women's representation has diminished in both symbolic and real terms. The "generosity" of other times has vanished and each opportunity, or lack thereof (let's say they're in thirty-second place on the plurinominal list), was fought for, tooth and nail, and in all the parties, the number of female candidates has decreased.[12] According to the governor of Tlaxcala, Beatriz Paredes, the defeat was sealed long ago when nobody bothered to protest the frivolity used by all the organizations in their documents with respect to women.

Where are politics done, and where do women—and in this case also men—find out about the party platforms? The campaigns don't revolve around programs, but rather procedures, and a candidate thinks about

limiting expenditures for what he sees as "useless programming." Women
don't tend to vote for women, we're told, and while we're determining the
veracity of that statement, what can be observed is a regression or, if you
prefer, the advancement of machismo. In the case of the PRI, of the thirty-
two senatorial candidates, two are women; of three hundred congressional candidates, twenty-one are women, and there are fourteen states in the
nation without female representatives; and of the ninety-five plurinominals,
only eleven are women. In the other parties the same strategy of overrep-
resentation prevails.

Should there be political quotas? Don't these figures still indicate progress
when compared with those of 1960 or 1970? Can anybody be held account-
able (because society and history are not responsible) for this depoliticiza-
tion and women's lack of specialized training? The "off the record" response
is that it's a shame that women who don't belong are included in organizations, but the course of the Republic should not and cannot be forced, and
in twenty or thirty years, the situation will change and then there won't be
any need to insist; society itself will balance its forces.

Realpolitik, cynicism, and indifference adequately convey the internal
workings of society.[13] Women's cause (their rights, their leadership training,
and their response to the serious problems of inequality and subordination)
is reaching its limits, and is constrained by the same forces that oppose
democratization. In politics, as far as I know, feminists' specific objectives
(from decriminalizing abortion to wage parity) will become more effective
only when organically included in a larger project. Otherwise, the cause loses
strength due to its unpredictability, the activists end up as petitioners, the
struggles become myths, and their achievements always seem profoundly
dissatisfying when compared to the totality of the machista monopoly.

Does this mean renouncing their principles? Rather, it means broadening
their radius of action. For women in politics, the feminist perspective, even
if it's the touchstone, should only be a part of their agenda. Otherwise, they
will perpetuate exclusionary practices in the name of theory.

NOTES

1. This was an internal document to the party, not publicly available.
2. Monsiváis uses the term *naco*, which we translate as tacky. It derives from an
   abbreviation of the central Mexican Totonaco Indigenous Peoples (referencing
   all Indigenous groups), encapsulating both a racialized view of the working
   classes whose tastes are seen as tacky and vulgar, and an exclusionary classist
   disqualification of the nouveau riche.
3. Josefa Ortiz de Domínguez (1793–1829), known as "La corregidora" (the

Magistrate's wife), was instrumental in sharing intelligence to and providing a space in her home for the insurgents fighting against the Spanish Crown for Mexico's independence. "Tata Cura" here refers to the revolutionary priest, Father Miguel Hidalgo y Costilla who, because of Domínguez's warning, would famously initiate the war of independence with his "Grito de Dolores" (Cry of Dolores) on September 16, 1810. Leona Vicario (1789–1842) married Andrés Quintana Roo, a notable independentist in 1815, and actively participated in espionage for the insurgents. Agustina Ramírez (Anna Agustina de Jesús Ramírez Heredia, 1813–1879), known as the "dama de ropaje negro" (the woman in black), lost twelve of her thirteen sons to the "cause" against the French invasion. The *soldaderas* bore revolutionary arms alongside their men; the *coronelas* were *soldaderas* that were elevated to military rank.

4. La Rotonda de Hombres Ilustres (The Rotunda of Illustrious Men) was a site established in the center of Mexico City in 1872 under President Sebastián Lerdo de Tejada (1872–1876) as a place to house the mortal remains of those important to the history of the nation. It wasn't until 2003, under President Vicente Fox (2000–2006), that the name was changed by decree to La Rotonda de las Personas Ilustres—The Rotunda of Illustrious People.

5. As a member of the PRI, Griselda Álvarez was governor of Colima, a small state on the western coast of Mexico from 1979 to 1985. Prior to that she had been a senator from 1976 to 1979. Rosa Luz Alegría is a Mexican physicist who studied at the Universidad Nacional Autónoma de México (UNAM, National Autonomous University of Mexico), where she became involved in the Consejo General de Huelga (CGH, General Strike Council). She went on to become the first woman to serve on the Mexican executive cabinet under President José López Portillo who served from 1976 to 1982.

6. Adolfo Ruíz Cortínes (1889–1973) used the word *féminas* to describe women, which can be seen as insulting and derogatory.

7. The CTM, or Confederación de Trabajadores de México, founded in 1936, was the largest confederation of labor unions in Mexico and a central part of the PRI's social program.

8. The term *granadero*, or grenadier, in Mexico refers to a specialized police team that responds to riots and other security emergencies.

9. Thatcher was prime minister of England from 1979 to 1990. Gandhi was prime minister of India from 1966 to 1977 and again from 1980 to 1984. Aquino was president of the Philippines from 1986 to 1992. Chamorro was president of Nicaragua from 1990 to 1997.

10. Centralism is the common political problem in Mexico and Latin America, writ large, in which all the power in a country is concentrated in governments located in the capital cities to the detriment of the provinces.

11. The colloquial term *palomeo* refers to the accounting of how many people you have on your side to be able to push through a vote or show up to a meeting. A *planchazo* refers to the creation of a strategy to destroy a political enemy.

12. The Mexican political system is partially based on proportional representation. This means that if in a given region X party wins 2 percent of the vote, that party has the right to a proportional 2 percent of the representatives/senators. There is a plurinominal (many names) list created by each party, and the number of names from the list that take office is determined by the percentages in the popular vote. Therefore, these candidates themselves are not elected by the popular vote, but rather are determined by the party and its priorities.

13. *Realpolitik* (German) comes out of the European tradition of the mid-nineteenth century, and it is a politics of pragmatism. It has a pejorative connotation that beyond practicality, it is coercive or amoral.

CHAPTER 10

A Crying Lesson

1992

> Indeed they taught me how to weep. But
> crying for me is a broken mechanism: I don't
> weep in front of the casket, on the sublime
> occasion, or when faced by catastrophes. I
> cry when I burn the rice or when I lose the
> latest receipt for the property taxes.
>
> **Rosario Castellanos, "Self-Portrait"**

In 1948, Rosario Castellanos publishes the poem "Apuntes para una declaración de fe" (Notes for a declaration of faith).[1] If you set aside the rhetorical ending (the "finale" that is a hidden call for a culture in need of hopeful messages), the poem already contains all the elements that her work will later reveal: a proven literary language that alternates between cosmogony and irony; an adherence to a "feminine sensitivity" but also a sarcastic rejection of sentimentality. In 1948, a twenty-three-year-old Rosario had spent her childhood in Chiapas, studied philosophy and literature, and exhaustively read the Bible, Paul Claudel, Gabriela Mistral, and the *Contemporáneos* (or more particularly, José Gorostiza and his *Muerte sin fin*).[2] She was educated in a home and social environment where the lives of saints and advice to women about their place in the world were intertwined. From that wealth of experience, a poetry emerges that, surprisingly, combines devotional anguish with sarcasm, a piety with a resounding lack of veneration:

> How implacable God was—his watchful eye
> through a futile fig leaf—!
> Oh, how the archangel came down aglow
> brandishing his ready brass sword![3]

In 1948, in the early stages of full-fledged industrialization, Mexican literature has visibly left the avant-garde and its highly experimental rhetoric
behind. What the *Contemporáneos* achieved poetically in earlier decades
rapidly became the model for the younger generation to follow. Rosario
is not avant-garde, she is disciplined in developing an "orthodox" poetry
of essential words (death, dust, root, mist, memory, love . . .); meta-poetic
reflection; and highly regarded sensations (solitude, anguish, immersion
in the real). Notwithstanding, in "Apuntes para una declaración de fe," her
way of thinking diverges from the prevailing worldview, as she introduces
a different spirit, equidistant from reverence and from profanation, able to
toy with cultural values:

> No one thinks of dying of tuberculosis
> nor of climbing balconies or sighing in vain.
> We're no longer romantics.
> It's this modern and problematic generation
> that drinks Coke and that talks on the phone
> and that writes poems on the backs of checks.
> We are the race strangled by intelligence,
> "she, the unbeatable,
> world-famous trapeze artist
> who flawlessly performs
> a triple mortal leap through space."
> (Intelligence is a whore
> who sells herself for a little bit of glitter
> and no longer knows how to blush.)[4]

Almost a decade after the publication of *Muerte sin fin*, Rosario doesn't feel
the need to celebrate its metaphysical awe ("O intelligence, flaming solitude, / envisioning all without creating!").[5] She rather opposes Gorostiza's
vision of "O intelligence, wasteland of mirrors," with the raw "cynicism" of
one who expresses what she sees, and has stopped having cultural illusions,
even as she firmly keeps her faith in language. But from the *Apuntes* (Notes)
to *En la tierra de en medio* (In the in-between land), her final book of 1972,
the process of finding her own language and making it accessible was quite
challenging. Let's consider her bibliography: *Trayectoria del polvo* (The trajectory of dust), 1948; *Apuntes para una declaración de fe* (Notes for a declaration of faith), 1948; *De la vigilia esteril* (From this sterile vigil),1950; *Dos
poemas* (Two poems), 1950; *El rescate del mundo* (Rescuing the world),1952;
Presentación al templo (An offering to the temple),1951; *Poemas: 1953–1955*

(Poems: 1953–1955), 1957; *Salomé y Judith* (Salomé and Judith), 1959; *Al pie de la letra* (Literally speaking), 1959; *Lívida luz* (Livid light),1960; *Materia memorable* (Memorable matter), 1969; and the collected works in Fondo de Cultura Económica, *Poesía no eres tú* (You are not poetry), 1972.[6]

Aside from the debatable merit of her choice of titles, what comes through is her considerable fidelity to a rhetoric that calls for women's compassion, their painful acceptance of the world as it is, and their commitment to traditions that assure their "purity" and "femininity."

The weight of machismo is so onerous that in order for women writers to break free from determinism, they must make explicit their "feminine condition," and render it central to their poetry or narrative. (Or they have to maintain a neutral tone that is falsely impersonal, which then impedes their growth as literary figures. "I write like a man." That is, she writes like Nobody.) In Rosario, "femininity" is lyricism that is both exuberant and restrained; it is an everyday humor that is jealously guarded, and (at the same time) a display of intimacy; it is a morose sarcasm that doesn't mean to offend, but rather attempts to render "le mot juste"; it is loss and a tearing apart.

> So I licked her shadow until it was gone
> with the abject, sad tongue of a hungry dog,
> and went on insulting the day with my grief
> and dragged my sobs across the floor.[7]

Her self-abandonment reaches its maximum expression in "Lamentación de Dido" (Dido's lament), a pinnacle in her body of work.[8] Dido, passionate and abandoned, invokes Eneas; recounting the stages of her love for him, she cries, she falters, she rises again. Assuming the all-too-common condition of the abandoned woman, Rosario sings her praises with impassioned language, where the neoclassic prosody becomes modern. Expressed with such vehemence, the everyday realities of abandonment are transfigured to become a dramatic tragedy. The housewife, any housewife, is Dido the "guardian of tombs . . . ship of proud sails . . . woman always, to the end." In light of this atonement and catharsis, the abandoned woman is assigned another social and cultural status, and "Lamentación de Dido" announces the author's shifting point of view:

> To die would be the better course. But I know that for me there
> will be no death.
> Because grief—and what other name is left for me—
> has made me eternal.[9]

"ILL-FATED TENDERNESS" AND ITS INVENTION

"Lamentación de Dido," with its biblical, classical, and Claudelian backdrop, is followed by a series of short poems that reveal a hesitant choice between what is clearly recognized as poetry, and the more pronounced literary self-portrayal.[10] Rosario's expressive craft grows, and when she doesn't give in to the then fashionable temptation (of diminishing verbal power in "abstract rhetoric," in exercises of style that pretend introspection or solemn existential reflection), she achieves perfect poems, finely honed masterpieces.

Stone

The stone doesn't move
In its exact place
remains.
Its ugliness there, in the middle of the road,
where all may stumble
and like the heart that won't surrender,
it is the dimension of death.
Only those who see enjoy the order
that the stone supports.
Only in the pure eye of one who sees,
her being is justified and shines.
Only the mouth of the seer praises her.
She doesn't understand anything. And obeys.[11]

Her two dramatic long poems, *Salomé* and *Judith*, unsuccessful as lyric tragedies, are important for the resonance of their language and for their divergent perspective. In both characters, femininity is no longer an imposed destiny and becomes, in the act of surrender and sacrifice, an assumed condition. Salomé will not be repeating her mother's life, one condemned to obscurity and resignation ("And I was educated to obey and to suffer in silence. My mother instead of milk, nursed me on submission"). And Judith rebels against the tasks imposed:

No, I won't go! Let the cataclysm be fulfilled!
Let God nail on my back the most tremendous eye,
let the worst curse rot my entrails![12]

Rosario Castellanos still had to wage an explicit war in order to avoid confining herself to a professionally "feminine" literature. If her theoretical positions are not strictly feminist, her quest for a personal voice is in keeping with a collective will and the free election of topics and viewpoints. In that sense, her poetry is a progression, the conscious register of the shifting meaning of being a woman, and of rejecting, from within, the impositions of a "feminine sensitivity." If, on occasion, it seems like an explicitly ideological battle, that's because the cultural climate demands this in order to guarantee women writers a voice and a public. "We kill what we love. Everything else has never been alive," says Rosario, altering and extending Wilde's phrase, and she, who so profoundly loved a weak and protected sensitivity, destroyed it continuously in her poems, treating it with sarcasm and critical distance.[13]

Accident

I feared . . . not a great love.
I was inoculated in time and forever
with an anachronistic kiss
and a fictitious surrender
—able to fake even rejection—
and for the vow, which is no less convincing
because it's not more solemn.
No, I did not fear the pyre that would consume me
only the match badly lit and this
blister that hinders my writing hand.[14]

In her final years, Rosario memorably destroys many of the pitfalls and manacles of a feminine sensitivity, and writes an admirable poetry that is direct and critical, stripped of any rhetorical masking. It is clearly an autobiographical poetry, clearly not a "confessional" poetry. If she were "confessing," Rosario would remain tied to her early education, relentlessly drawn to feelings of guilt, which are the essence of subjugation. But, she doesn't "confess," she limits herself to affirming that intimacy is neither shameful nor inexpressible. The reader is not the confessor, only a friend or an accomplice, or simply a reader.

Valium 10

At times (and don't try
to make light of it saying
it doesn't happen often)
your measure breaks
the compass goes wild
and you can't make sense out of anything. [. . .]

And you spell out the name of Chaos. And
you can't go to sleep unless you open
the bottle of pills and take one
in which is condensed, chemically
pure, the world's order.[15]

Ten years earlier, this would have been a "Freudian indiscretion." The process of socio-cultural change powerfully contributed to unleashing Rosario's narrative and poetic force, obliged—both with her consent and to her regret—to iconically represent the woman thinker and writer in Mexico. She was an icon tired of gender roles and cultural impositions, determined to be free in her spontaneous conduct and way of being.

There must be another way that isn't named Sappho
or Messalina, or Mary of Egypt,
or Magdalene, or Clementia Isaura.

Another way to be human and free.
Another way to be.[16]

NOTES

1. Epigraph. Taken from Rosario Castellanos's poem "Autorretrato," ed., trans. Julian Palley, with an introductory study by Gabriella de Beer, *Meditation on the Threshold: A Bilingual Anthology of Poetry* (Tempe: Arizona State University, Bilingual Press/Editorial Bilingue, 1988), 120–25. For other translations of Rosario Castellanos's writing, see Maureen Ahern, trans., *A Rosario Castellanos Reader* (Austin: University of Texas Press, 1988).

2. This poem from 1948 opens the collection of Castellanos's poetry in *Poesía no eres tú: Obra poética 1948–1971* (You are not poetry: Poetic anthology 1948–1971) (Mexico City: Fondo de Cultura Económica, 1972), 7–14.

3. Paul Claudel (1868–1955) was a French poet, dramatist, and diplomat known for his verse dramas; Gabriela Mistral (1889–1957), a pen name for Lucila Godoy Alcayaga, was a famed Chilean poet, diplomat, and educator who won the Nobel Prize in Literature in 1945; *Los Contemporáneos* refers both to an influential Mexican "modernist" group and their literary magazine published from 1928 to 1931. José Gorostiza (1901–1973) was a member of the *Contemporáneos* and known for his metaphysical long poem from 1964 *Muerte sin fin* (Death without end).

4. From "Apuntes para una declaración de fe" (Notes from a declaration of faith) in *Poesía no eres tú*. Our translation.

5. From "Apuntes para una declaración de fe" in *Poesía no eres tú*. Our translation.

6. Monsiváis extracts these phrases from the long poem *Muerte sin fin* (1939). We cite the translations from *Muerte sin Fin: Death without End*, trans. Laura Villaseñor (Austin: University of Texas Press, 1969), 17.

7. *Presentación al templo*, a twelve-page plaquette of poetry, was first published in Spain in 1951, and later in Mexico as *Presentación al templo: Poemas (Madrid, 1951)*, together with *Rescate del mundo* (Mexico City: America Revista Antológica, 1952). In Monsiváis's original text the title was printed mistakenly as "*Presentación en el templo.*" This collection of poetry was not included in her complete works, *Poesía no eres tú*. Although there are many translations of individual poems by Castellanos collected in various anthologies, magazines, and websites, none of her poetry books have yet been translated in their entirety as freestanding collections.

8. From the poem "Fábula y laberinto" (Fable and labyrinth), originally published in her 1950 collection *De la vigilia estéril*, and also collected in her complete poetry anthology *Poesía no eres tú*. Our translation.

9. From the poem "Lamentación de Dido," originally in her book *Poemas*, and collected in *Poesía no eres tú* as well as in *Meditation on the Threshold*.

10. All translations of "Lamentación de Dido" in this essay are by Julian Palley, in *Meditation on the Threshold*.

11. In reference to Paul Claudel.

12. The poem "Piedra" (Stone) originally in her book *Al pie de la letra* (Literally speaking) and now also collected in *Poesía no eres tú*. Our translation.

13. This verse is from the dramatic long poem "Judith" in her book from 1959, *Salomé y Judith* (Salome and Judith), now also collected in *Poesía no eres tú*. Our translation.

14. From the poem "Destino" originally in Castellanos's book *Lívida Luz* (1960) and collected in *Poesía no eres tú*. Our translation. The phrase "Yet each man kills the thing he loves" comes from a long poem by Oscar Wilde (1854–1900), "The Ballad of Reading Gaol," published in 1898.

15. From the book of poems *Al pie de la letra* (1959) and collected in *Poesía no eres tú*. Our translation.

16. From the book *En la tierra de en medio* (In the midlands), trans. by Julian Palley in *Meditation on the Threshold*.

17. These are the closing lines from "Meditación en el umbral," which appear in the section "Otros Poemas," in *Poesía no eres tú*. This is our translation. See also Kate Flores's translation in *The Defiant Muse: Hispanic Poems from the Middle Ages to the Present*, ed. Angel Flores and Kate Flores (New York: Feminist Press, 1986).

CHAPTER 11

Let Us Now Praise

1994

Clearly, sound is heterosexist. I'm not sure if it was a misunderstanding on my part, but when Marta Lamas insisted that I present a comparative context today, I didn't hear her say that it was on the topic of women at the end of the *twentieth* century, so here you have me paying homage to the precursors and early militants and activists of feminism, except with a text that addresses women from the end of the *nineteenth* century. I hope I won't contradict today's analytical spirit, which has been well established since our first encounter in Chiapas.[1] In fact, only a few days ago, I was still convinced that the C(h)aste War had been a confrontation to the death between two virgins, and I have been surprised by their evident resurrection.[2]

Let us now praise the women of unutterable or unknown names, who in the era of a femininity that demanded good table manners, singing, piano-playing, embroidery, and dramatic sighs of melancholy, gazing adoringly at their confessor, smiling sweetly with a loving expression, who in the era of "man" being the *only* conceivable phenomenon of the human race, organized, shared complaints and protests, wrote documents that no one outside their group read, and prepared themselves with discipline to freely exercise their individuality.

Let us now praise the women who resisted the pressure to erase and suppress themselves, who didn't restrain themselves at dinner parties while the piano resounded with a sonata, and someone insisted on declaiming Salvador Díaz Mirón's verses with a raspy voice: "Be content, woman! We are here / in this crushing valley of tears / you, like a dove for the nest, / and I, like a lion for combat."[3] And if on concluding the recitation, while drinks were passed around, another voice shouted out amid loud laughter, "a woman's place is in the home, with a broken leg," they kept believing in the existence of their rights, they spent many nights reading the writings of Spanish, French, and North American women like Mrs. Margaret Sanger, for example, and they came to the conclusion for the umpteenth time that yes, indeed, they were right and the others—like their mothers, their sisters, and all the creatures of private strength and public abandonment—were wrong.[4]

Let us now praise the women who, without abandoning their beliefs, still continued to carry out their religious duties, had time to smile first and laugh last when in their get togethers someone would declare: "Man is fire, woman, burlap clothes, the devil walks by and blows"; or when it was said that these maxims were the key to attaining the ineffable: "Between a male and female saint, a wall of song and limestone paint";[5] or that they taught modesty (which was the pride of virgins before marriage), and humility (the containment wall of coquetry), by parroting childhood rhymes: "Getting on the boat and the boat man says to me: / 'Pretty girls don't have to pay, they get to ride for free.' / I am not a pretty girl, nor do I want to be one, / because it is the pretty girls, left ruined and undone";[6] and these women, after hearing all that, were still able to reflect, in this spirit if not these exact words, and decided that servile femininity was a social construct, a long apprenticeship, a pious illumination of dark corners, and that they wanted to be who they were in a different way, taking ownership of their lives by casting doubt on the blindly imposed and *only* form of femininity.

Let us now praise the women who didn't accept any of the roles they were offered, who rejected being the compassionate virgin; or the mother whose autonomy is ceded to her husband, her children, and her confessor; or the virgin-in-mind-only with a long line of descendants; or the faithful wife who only tolerates her husband's body because it's God's will, while in her pre-coital preparations she prayerfully murmurs "What we're about to do, Heavenly Father, / isn't vice, nor fornication, / but to make a child / for your holy devotion";[7] or even those women who inspired fatal attractions, repeating the fate of Rosario who drove Manuel Acuña to cyanide;[8] or great flirts who frequented dance halls: they only wanted to be themselves, something almost impossible to achieve back then, when women were the objects of perfect obsession and endless confessions.

Let us now praise the young woman who, at the end of the nineteenth century, decided to study medicine but wasn't allowed to enroll, who with her mother's support struggled and fought until she finally won, becoming in 1882 the first woman medical student [Matilde Montoya]; she withstood stares of scorn and disdain, accepting, given no other choice, that she wasn't allowed to practice on cadavers in the dissection hall if any men were

present to watch a woman observing a naked body, left to study anatomi-
cal knowledge all alone; she overcame rejections and humiliations, earning
herself a professional degree, but no patients, because who could believe
that a woman would be able to make a diagnosis?

Let us now praise the young women who attempted poetry and didn't
waver in the face of the condescension with which they were received, "It is
natural," wrote Francisco Zarco, "that woman might participate somewhat
in the inspiration of dreams in which their eyes are opened by the light";[9]
and they published their verses without taking credit so as to not embarrass
their families, and didn't persevere because nobody asked for their poems;
or they continued to write but only on topics deemed legitimate or permissible for them: roses, love, motherly or filial sentiments, the passage of
time, an aspiration to equality, all of which gave meaning to their poetry,
descriptions of landscapes, biblical scenes, the sighs and cries of desexualized passion, the courtship of nubile young women, like this one by Refugio
Barragán de Toscano at the close of (almost) two centuries ago: "Don't show
yourself as easy, / keep safe your love's essence, / if he toys with your innocence / tomorrow, his ridicule be. / Girl, enchanting and genteel, / proceed
now with caution, / his words are pure fantasy, / just smoke on the wind";[10]
and they kept writing and their faith in language was indispensable both in
form and temperament, learning by the laws of fire, poetry also served to
ground their sexuality, appetites and desires, while under the yoke of futile
kinds of love.

Let us now praise the women anarchists from the turn of the twentieth
century that little by little (for them there was no other historical time, nor
truth) accepted their husbands' ideas; they deeply understood their mission
to attain rights, and they defended them in workshops by printing at midnight, distributing pamphlets in factories and workplaces, and by speaking against discrimination, even against their own partners; they gradually
occupied battle sites, and with that, more opportunities to be repressed.

Let us now praise Juana Belén Guitérrez de Mendoza, who was born in
1875 and died in 1942, a self-taught woman, a collaborator for *El Hijo del
Ahuizote*;[11] taken as a political prisoner in 1897 in Millas Nuevas, Chihuahua, for her denouncement of worker exploitation; a coordinator of clubs;
a free-lance and high-risk editor for the newspaper *Vesper*, a precursor to
the Revolution;[12] she was also a prison-mate of the Flores Magón brothers;[13]
an exile, a creator of workers groups, a Madero supporter, founder of the
"Club Político Femenil Amigas del Pueblo" (Women's Political Club "Friends
of the People"), a candid woman, who against her own inclinations dressed
as a man to show her rejection of the conceptual prison of femininity; she

was a conspirator of 1911, Zapata's champion, who he elevated to "Coronela" when she organized the Victoria Regiment, a political prisoner of Carranza's regime in 1916, founder of the Consejo Nacional de Mujeres Mexicanas (National Mexican Women's Council), a militant for the Partido Comunista Mexicano (Mexican Communist Party), an editor for *Alba Mexicana* (Mexican Dawn), a great symbol of consequence and tenacity.[14]

Let us now praise the first suffragettes who, before all others, believed that having the vote would confer humanity on them, because it would imbue their actions with that supreme virtue of being able to choose, which is what citizenship is about. They endured it all: mocking, taunting, the condescension of those who weren't prepared to understand them, intolerance, aggressions from machista stupidity and its transactional ideology, bureaucratic delays, political betrayals; they shouldered on, and marched, taking to the streets, not intending to conquer at first, but to publicly abandon their zones of imprisonment and confinement: the confessional, the kitchen, and the bedroom.[15]

Let us now praise Laureana Wright, the director of *Violetas de Anáhuac* (Violets of Anáhuac), that is founded in 1887, and in that same year, demands the vote and equality of rights for women.[16]

Let us now praise the Frías sisters, founders of the Magón club, Hijas de Anáhuac (Daughters of Anáhuac), persecuted, incarcerated, fully obstinate, unable to claim for themselves any fame but that of militancy.[17]

Let us now praise the ex-governor of Yucatán, Salvador Alvarado, who in 1916 convoked the First Feminist Congress in Mérida, and doña Adolfina Valencia de Ávila, its president, and the participants who with a language still in verse, and the supreme affectation of the era with which they were obliged to live, were now able to see themselves as beings radically endowed with freewill.[18]

Let us now praise the poet Antonio M. Plaza, the first standard-bearer in Mexico, if you'll permit me the anachronism, of the combative counterculture, a liberal, a supporter of Juárez, and a literary anarchist; he sang praises to a prostitute when no one recognized even her humanity, he discredited marriage, detested bourgeois custom, and scorned the virtues of the day.[19]

Let us now praise the *soldaderas* who went to battle for the love of their men and cooked, they scared up food however they could, they fought, they breastfed their progeny, they died from stray bullets and targeted ones;[20] all this, and they barely appeared in *corridos*, or as literary characters, but they unknowingly remade a sense of femininity among the popular classes.[21]

Let us now praise the rural teachers, who, in their own words, relevant to this day because of the vast life they sustained, sowed the light of literacy to vanquish obscurantism, and overcame fanaticism with their iron will. They were harassed, raped in front of their students, and humiliated in the name of faith, but even in the most hostile of environments, these women advanced secularization.[22]

Let us now praise the guardians of tradition, who in spite of their limitations and prejudices, the ideological prisons that raised and sustained them, took the time to create networks of female solidarity.

Let us now praise the dissident women who tried only to provide their gender with the basic tenets of freewill and the practice of rational choice. To fully recover their legacy is now absolutely necessary for the civilizing project, on the road to democracy.

Let us now praise.

NOTES

1. Title. Monsiváis's title, "Alabemos ahora," refers to Ecclesiastes 44:1 of the King James Bible "Let us now praise famous men, and our fathers that begat us." We believe it is also a homage to the book by James Agee (1909–1955), *Let Us Now Praise Famous Men* (1941), with photographs by Walker Evans. Considered Agee's masterpiece, it was a verbal and photographic record of poor tenant farmers during the US Great Depression. Here, Monsiváis dedicates his text to praising feminist foremothers, often forgotten by the official record.

2. This speech was an address to the Congreso Nacional Feminista (National Feminist Congress) on January 15, 1994, in Mexico City (DF). It was then published as "Palabras de Carlos Monsiváis" in *fem*, no. 133 (March 1994).

3. *Casta* in Spanish means both "chaste" and "caste," and here Monsiváis is making a play on words. "La guerra de las castas" refers to the Caste War of Yucatán (1847–1901), which began with the revolt of the Mayans of the Yucatan Peninsula against both Euro-descendent and Mestizo populations.

4. This is our translation of the final verse of Díaz Mirón's "A Gloria" (To Gloria) collected in *El Parnaso Mexicano* (1886) by editor Vicente Riva Palacio. It is a poem on the cusp of modernism that extolls the late romantic view of women as "angels of the household."

5. Our translation of the popular refrain "la mujer en casa y con la pata rota" (or its variation "quebrada"), which literally means, "woman at home and with a broken leg." This is similar to the common saying that a woman's place is at home "barefoot and pregnant." In both cases women's mobility is hobbled and they are confined only to the interior domestic spaces in the popular imaginary.

6. "El hombre es fuego; la mujer, estopa; llega el diablo y sopla" is a popular religious refrain warning that men and women shouldn't mix socially because there is inherent danger. "Entre santa y santo, pared de cal y canto" is another refrain that warns of the necessity to keep men and women apart, "cal y canto" being akin to the English expression "under lock and key." Our translation.

7. Our translation of the childhood rhyme: "Al subir la barca me dice el barquero: / 'Las niñas bonitas no pagan dinero.' / Yo no soy bonita ni quiero ser, / porque las bonitas se echan a perder."

8. Our translation of this long-standing religious sarcastic quartet: "Esto que hacemos, Santo Señor / no es por vicio ni por fornicio, / sino para hacer un hijo / en tu santo servicio," collected in Juan Domingo Argüelles, *Breve antología de poesía mexicana: Impúdica, precoz, satírica y burlesca* (Mexico City: Oceano, 2015).

9. Manuel Acuña was a famous romantic poet who died by suicide in 1873. It is believed this was due to unrequited love for his muse, Rosario de la Peña, to whom he dedicated his last poem, "Nocturno a Rosario."

10. Francisco Zarco (1829–1869), politician, journalist, historian, and romantic poet, was a member of the Constitutional Congress of 1856. He was a liberal writer for the newspaper *Reforma* who was later persecuted for his positions and politics.

11. María Refugio Barragán de Toscano (1843–1916) was a teacher, writer, and playwright. We have corrected the error in the original text in which Monsiváis refers to her as Barragán y Lozano. She published the essay "Las mujeres mejicanas," in *Las mujeres españolas, americanas y lusitanas pintadas por sí mismas*, ed. Faustina Saez de Melgar (Barcelona: Editorial Juan Pons, 1881), 325–33. The book was a thorough study on women of the Hispanic and Lusophone world, their customs, education, etc. Among other writings, a fragment of the essay on Mexican womanhood is included in the contemporary collection that takes its title from a line of Barragán's own writing (The pen is, for my soul, a necessity). *La pluma es para mi alma una necesidad: Testimonios de mujeres sobre escritura creativa: ensayos, cartas y otras prosas (México, 1866–1910)*, ed., Leticia Romero Chumacero (Mexico City: Universidad Autónoma de la Ciudad de México, 2017). Our translation of this quote from Barragán's poem "Es mentira" (It's a lie), in *Poetas hispano-americanos*, vol. 1, ed. Lazaro María Perez and José María Rivas Groot, 209–11 (Bogotá, Colombia: JJ Pérez, 1889). "No te demuestres liviana, / guarda de tu amor la esencia, / si hoy juega con tu inocencia / se reirá de ti mañana. / Niña gentil y hechicera / ve con tiento, / lo que te dice es quimera, / humo en el viento."

12. Juana Belén Gutiérrez de Mendoza was a Mexican anarchist and feminist activist, typographer, journalist, and poet. *El Hijo del Ahuizote* (The son of the otter) was a satirical Mexican newspaper founded in 1885 by Daniel Cabrera Rivera, Manuel Pérez Bibbins, and Juan Sarabia.

13. *Vésper* was an anti-Porfirian periodical published between 1901 and 1911, with a brief revival in 1932. It was founded by Gutiérrez de Mendoza and Elisa Acuña Rosete.

14. The three Flores Magón brothers, Jesús (1871–1930), Ricardo (1874–1922), and Enrique (1877–1954), were anti-Porfirian political activists, anarchists, and journalists whose thinking heavily influenced the revolts leading to the Mexican Revolution. Of the three, Ricardo's writings are the most widely circulated, and after his death, Enrique continued to disseminate his message.

15. Emiliano Zapata (1879–1919) was an important agrarian reformer from the southern state of Morelos and *caudillo* in the Mexican Revolution whose demands for the redistribution of land were incorporated into the 1917 Constitution. He coined the Revolutionary motto "La tierra es de quien la trabaja" (The land belongs to those who cultivate it). To become a *coronela* was a high-status marker among the women soldiers, *las soldaderas*, during the Mexican Revolution. It meant that she had earned her stripes in battle. The trope of these women appears in many Mexican films of the Revolution. One famous fictional *coronela* comes in the form of *La negra Angustias* (Black Angustias), directed by female filmmaking pioneer Matilde Landeta in 1950, adapted from the eponymous 1944 novel by Francisco Rojas González, the only such novel to feature an Afro-descendant in the Revolution. Another notable film is Rafaél Baledón's *Las coronelas* (1959), a more comedic take on the topic, in which two young women pass as men to rise in the ranks of the Revolutionary insurgents. Marta Lamas reports that Juana Belén, as the colonel of the Victoria Regiment, sent one of her men to the firing squad for raping a woman. Marta Lamas, "Juana Belén, la transgresora," *Nexos*, Feb. 1, 2004, https://www.nexos.com.mx/?p=11071.

16. Monsiváis uses the term *prostitutario* in his Spanish original. We understand this to mean that at that time, due to the inherent machismo, women were seen as commodities to be purchased. Thus, representations in the public imaginary divided women into groups of "good" and "bad" women—the "good" women were homemakers, pious, and chaste, and the "bad" women occupied public spaces, mainly brothels. This led to the idea that women in the public sphere were automatically equated with "fallen" women, while even women in the domestic sphere were chattel.

17. *Violetas de Anáhuac* was a feminist literary periodical that was first published on December 4, 1887, and lasted through February of 1889. Anáhuac was the pre-Colombian name for the Basin of Mexico.

18. The sisters María del Carmen and Catalina Frías were workers in a textile factory, and in 1911 they founded a women-workers guild called Hijas de Anáhuac (Daughters of Anáhuac) that fought for workers' rights. The Frías sisters, along with other textile workers Justa Vega, Eligia Pérez, Leonila Aguilar, María Gómez, Carlota Lira, Concepción Espinoza, and Josefa Ortega, from the factories La Abeja, S. A., from Puentes Sierra, organized women from other textile sweatshops La Magdalena and Santa Teresa from Contreras, DF, and La Hormiga from Tizapán, DF. Marta Eva Rocha, "La organización obrera Hijas de Anáhuac," *Trabajo y democracia hoy: Las luchas de la mujer trabajadora* 7, no. 41 (1997): 11.

19. The First Feminist Congress Organizing Committee consisted of teachers: Consuelo Zavala Castillo, president; Dominga Canto Pastrana, vice president; Adriana Vadillo Rivas and Rosina Magaña, secretaries; Amalia Gómez Aguilar and Gregoria Montero, pro secretaries; and Adolfina Valencia Ávila, treasurer. During the first congress, Valencia Ávila was elected president. See Secretaría de Cultura and the Instituto Nacional de Estudios Históricos de las Revoluciones

de México, eds., *Mujeres y Constitución: De Hermila Galindo a Griselda Álvarez* (Toluca: Gobierno del Estado de México, 2017), 32–33.

20. Antonio Plaza Lamas (1830–1882), from the state of Guanajuato, was a military officer, poet, and journalist who wrote the famous poem "A una ramera" (To a prostitute), which extolled her virtues and treated her as a beloved, rather than as a denigrated and pitiable subject. Benito Juárez (1806–1872) was a lawyer and politician from the southern state of Oaxaca who became Mexico's twenty-sixth president (1858–1872), and its first president of Indigenous descent. Juárez was a liberal reformer who sought to limit the Catholic Church's economic and political hegemony.

21. *Soldaderas*' role as camp followers was complicated. Elena Poniatowska's novel *Hasta no verte, Jesús mío* (Mexico City: Era, 1969) and her photographic chronicle *Las soldaderas* (Mexico City: Ediciones Era, Conaculta, INAH, 1999) are two major contributions to understanding these women's experiences and their role in the Mexican Revolution. Both were translated into English, the first by Magda Bogin as *Until We Meet Again* (New York, NY: Pantheon, 1987), and again later by Deanna Heikkinen as *Here's to You, Jesusa!* (New York: Farrar, Straus and Giroux, 2001); the second was published as *Las Soldaderas: Women of the Mexican Revolution*, trans. David Romo (El Paso: Cinco Puntos Press, 2006).

22. *Corridos* were narrative ballads that told of the adventures and misadventures of the revolutionary fighters, and, as Monsiváis notes, the *soldaderas* remained largely anonymous in the collective memory of popular culture as no more than symbolic figures. Natalia Gómez Quintero, in discussing the *Adelitas* of the Mexican Revolution at its centenary, marks the importance of naming names, and in 2010 for *El Universal* she writes the first and last names of many of the "lost" Revolutionary women. Natalia Gómez Quintero, "Las adelitas sí tenían nombre y apellido," *El Universal*, Nov. 18, 2010, https://archivo.eluniversal.com.mx/sociedad/6693.html. For an in-depth exploration of this topic, see the chapter titled "The Strains of the Revolution: Musicalizing the Soldadera in the Revolutionary Melodrama," in Jaqueline Ávila, *Cinesonidos: Film Music and National Identity during Mexico's Época de Oro* (Oxford: Oxford University Press, 2020), as well as the foundational text by María Herrera Sobek, *The Mexican Corrido: A Feminist Analysis* (Bloomington: Indiana University Press, 1990).

23. The figure of the *maestra rural* (the rural woman teacher) was important to the nation-building project, which became iconic in the cinema of Mexico's Golden Age. One of the most famous examples is the 1948 melodrama *Río escondido*, directed by Emilio "El Indio" Fernández and starring the famous María Félix.

CHAPTER 12

An Open Letter to Nancy Cárdenas

Exemplary Activist

1994

Dearest Nancy:

Who can break you down, Nancy, you who are a staunch supporter of a marginal Cardenismo?[1] You're a single-minded force of nature in your poems (love guarded by irony), in your plays, in your political activities, in your theater (director, author, translator), in your articles, in your fight for the irrefutable rights of minorities. In preparing my thoughts for this note, I realize who you are and what you mean to your friends, and ask only that in your theatrical purview, you please resign yourself to the civic dimensions of your work. You mean so much to Mexican society.

I'll begin this story of friendship and admiration from the start. I first met you in 1955, in the halls of the philosophy department, and was strongly attracted to your "body language," your way of arguing, and how you heroically mustered the strength to go to classes. The division of labor forty years ago: I was reserved and you were a natural protagonist. Then Luis Prieto Reyes introduced us, and I got the whole story half an hour later: you had been born into a large family of peasant and merchant origins in 1934 in Parras, Coahuila; you studied performing arts and wanted to direct, write, act . . .[2] Oh, the fifties! All of us (who needed to know each other) knew each other, the city was an invitation to conversations and walks, and the national problems weren't really problems, or at least they didn't seem to be because we saw them as distant concerns. (Many situations didn't bother us because we weren't aware that they should.) And we countered the burden of a society regulated by censorship with the tools we had: readings, defiance, rolling our eyes, together with sessions of free "psychotherapy" by playing Spin the Bottle (the Game of Truth or Dare) which, in the early morning hours, led to wild confessions that we couldn't remember later. Ah, to discover our sexual appetites through our emboldened answers! And we were so determined to be different that we didn't feel marginalized.

You joined Poesía en Voz Alta (Poetry out loud), the theatrical experience of a generation, and soon after, you decided to "come out," inspired by the almost Sartrean motto "you only live once."[3] You made unlikely friendships (for those us who lived to read), and you didn't abstain from what, with certain candor, we called "bohemia," which consisted of playfully using "scare quotes" such as: "atypical life," "disorderly schedules," and "ambiguous behaviors." I vividly remember a night in 1956 or '58, when you arrived at Sergio Pitol's apartment on Londres Street, with a group of women friends, among them a woman who seemed to me to be either very unassuming or very authentic, in a *jorongo, calzón de manta*, and *huaraches*.[4] She sang marvelously and introduced me to magnificent songs: "Mi segundo amor" (My second love), "Maringá," and "Macorina."[5] How unique Chavela Vargas was![6] With extraordinary intuition, she followed in the tradition of the great Lucha Reyes, who transformed the *ranchera* genre into something closer to the blues—the same existential suffering, the same autobiographical burden, the same expressive vehemence.[7] By foregoing the mariachi, Chavela also accentuated the connection between the solitary man or woman and music.

Chavela laughed and drank, and I was fascinated by the behavior and style of a group that at the time was more than idiosyncratic. In challenging a society that was not only incapable of accepting much less conceiving of difference, your group's dandyism was necessarily at the forefront, a self-imposed style and lifestyle: from the heights of this commanding elegance, you voiced desires and disdains. In the era before unisex, with outfits labeled as "exclusively for men," you and your friends committed to your decision to live as you damn well pleased, transcending—not without guilt, not without clarity—the limits of a culture known for its repression, that judged diversions from the "norm" on a scale from "disfigurement" to "perversion." Regarding freedom of expression, everything felt new, and in spite of biblical and Judeo-Christian judgments, unorthodoxy wasn't lived fatalistically (in the majority of cases) because its repercussions were necessarily intimate, and because lacking the tools to analyze it, urban expansion had already made the "dissonant" behaviors possible, while the urgency to punish them diminished. Tolerance was sneaking in under the pretext of cynical humor: "Let 'em do what they want as long as they don't mess with me . . . and if they wanna mess with me, gimme a heads up so I can stick around."

Let me interrupt my spiel for a moment to recall that you and I talked about this at length: the world of Mexican lesbians in the early part of the twentieth century, hidden by bias and disbelief that eclipsed even prejudice. How could it even be possible? Women understanding one another without the need for men?! Lesbianism was so inconceivable that those who practiced it were vilified for their "marimacha" (butch) look or for being "professional spinsters," and not for the conduct that society refused to believe possible. Thus, teachers in their predictable tailored suits, political activists in militant attire, and old maids who romantically befriended young women were harassed for not being feminine enough, and for being bitter and stern, but not for exercising their sexuality. Despite the evidence in their lifetime, the lesbianism of Frida Kahlo or Lucha Reyes was never mentioned, much less that of Gabriela Mistral.[8] It would have been sacrilegious.

Now back to my story. In that decade, the 1950s, we lived to surprise even ourselves, and when all is said and done, that mundane premise turned out to be liberating by contrast. We would tell ourselves, albeit using different words, "Today I'm going to give myself a lesson in courage." Our pedagogy of never giving up, of fighting the censoring attitudes of society blow by blow, would lead us to the "Frederic Engels" cell of the Mexican Communist Party, and to the bars on Saturday nights. At the time, any minor incident became an extreme experience, we were young, we were repressed, we depended on our imagination for excitement, and listening to Chavela at El Otro Refugio (directly above El Eco, a mythic bar) or at El Safari was both a personal choice and a risk that turned into social progress.

You were acting: I saw you in a production of *Despertar de primavera* (*Spring Awakening*) by Frank Wedekind.[9] You combined theater performances with what is now known as activism, imbuing it with great eloquence—like someone bent on taking space back from repression. In the Mexico City of the 1950s, political protest was the only accepted dissidence because it could be better repressed. By 1958, a student movement against increasing bus fares had begun. You participated because you had to, you went to marches and meetings, you stood guard. I precisely recall the image of you arriving at the Zócalo at midday in the midst of a demonstration. At the doors of the Palacio Nacional, a discussion was taking place about selecting representatives to meet with President Ruiz Cortines (a politician wise to the ways of the late nineteenth century, but lost in the modernity of blenders and refrigerators[10]). You listened closely to the debates, you made sure you weren't chosen to enter the Palacio, instead you shouted the slogan "Justice for the People!," and followed with: "To the Central Office! Uruchurtu, let us in!"[11] And off you went, emboldened, storming an interview like you would take a city in Northern Mexico, and a deadly rock hit you on the nose, and you sued the Central Office, and I think you actually even won the case. You're impossible, Nancy.

Then you left for Yale and left me your program on Radio Universidad, *El cine y la crítica* (Film and its critics), and on your return, we saw each other more frequently. For a time, you rented a tiny, cramped, but romantic room in El Pesebre, a place that struck me as legendary, where festivities went from biblical chapter to biblical chapter (the triumph of repentance over orgy, the victory of casual sex over morality), and where one night, your friend, the French aristocrat, told us about her heroic participation in the Second World War as a tango dancer who single-handedly distracted more than fifty Germans.[12]

You started directing plays. You were especially interested in acting and staging plays that were cogent and serious in tone, and while you admired Juan José Gurrola, you weren't that into his kind of theater.[13] I remember the small theater in Colonia Nápoles and of your impressive staging of *Picnic en el campo de batalla* (*Picnic on the Battlefield*).[14] There I coined the epithet that you so enjoyed: "Oh, Parras Athena!"[15] And each year we would go to the Reseña de Festivales Cinematográficos (The Film Festival Review) in Acapulco, and each week on Radio Universidad, we would organize sketches and parodies of hot topics for the program *El cine y la crítica*, whose name no longer had anything to do with its original concept.

The events of 1968 changed you and empowered your activism.[16] From the very beginning, we were part of the Alianza de Intelectuales, Escritores y Artistas en Apoyo al Movimiento Estudiantil (The Alliance of Intellectuals, Writers and Artists in Support of the Student Movement), a kilometric title that covered fifty or sixty of us who collected signatures and funds for the manifestos, and who participated in marches and debated issues. You were chosen to coordinate events on Sundays at noon at the Esplanada de Rectoría (University Administration Plaza). You invited poets and singers, you recited short texts, you were thrilled. About five hundred people showed their trust by signing our urgent manifestos—and how about the fights we had with the Guevarista revolutionaries who were demanding that our proclamations be more incendiary![17] And on Saturdays we would record *El cine y la crítica* with impassioned parodies of Díaz Ordaz's ideological apparatus.

On October 2, Beatriz Bueno, Luis Prieto, and you went to the rally at the Plaza de las Tres Culturas (Plaza the of Three Cultures).[18] I showed up late and could only locate Luis, who was determined to find General Lázaro Cárdenas to inform him of the massacre.[19] And it wasn't until 2 a.m. that I finally found you, if memory doesn't fail me or I don't fail memory, and you were desperate, loudly letting me know what you had just gone through. It was, understandably, the only time that you abandoned your optimism, although the next day, fearless as ever, you returned for the car you left in Tlatelolco.

Months later, you explicitly decided to turn your energies to the fight for sexual minorities. You have never worried about what people might say, actually you rather enjoyed it, and the times were a-changin' or we had to change them. I remember a dinner party in 1969 when we talked about what happened in New York on the day of Judy Garland's funeral. At the Stonewall Bar in Greenwich Village, twenty-five years ago, the police once again attempted another one of their raids, and with a frankly historic spirit, homosexuals and lesbians didn't back down; there were confrontations for two days in a row until the police finally withdrew.[20] The gay liberation movement was emerging and you were excited. Then in 1971 and '72, you wrote to me while I was in London to tell me about the first gay meetings at your house, about the unexpected leadership shown by some younger people, the sectarianism inherited from the Marxist Left, and the difficulties or the impossibilities of a non-dogmatic discourse in a movement that was just getting started. As usual, the events were incomparably better than the discourse. So, for example, after a Saturday night raid that was followed by reports and photos in the newspapers, a group of those arrested sued the police for unconstitutional actions. And I couldn't believe when a department store employee, fired for being homosexual, sued the company. I would send you information, and you would surprise me with news about how the sudden consciousness about the rights of the few became legion.

After the frustrating experience of the Gay Liberation Movement, you moved on to focus on the theater, training actors in the staging traditions of England and the United States. Then, in 1973, you thought it important to stage *The Boys in the Band*, the play by Mart Crowley. I argued against it: it's a work based on sentimental blackmail, it's pre-Stonewall, it makes self-compassion the argument. You listened to me with the attention that you gave me when you didn't want to heed my advice and responded (not with these exact words, but with this meaning): "Mexico is still lagging way behind in matters of tolerance, and in such a machista environment, self-compassion is a form of recognition." You were right, of course, as evidenced by the scandals and moralistic outbursts that followed. The delegate Delfín Sánchez Juárez was offended and refused to authorize the staging of the play at the Teatro de los Insurgentes "because it went against morality and 'good manners.'"[21] And in spite of the negative articles and defamations, the intellectual and artistic community (that exists when it organizes) came to your defense, and finally the play was authorized. The scandal continued, but moralism was already on the defensive and resigned to the "shocking" photos and homophobic tantrums: "The queers find each other / The inverted are having their fun / Oh, yes, darling! I also have rights."[22] But you had already royally won.

You believe in the rights of all minorities to follow their own traditions, and in your personal museum, we find inevitable heroines: Gertrude Stein, Virginia Woolf, the painter Natalie Barey, the novelist Radclyffe Hall (whose *The Well of Loneliness* you adapted to theatre), Willa Cather, Janet Flanner, Colette, Chavela Vargas. And you have never been afraid, which perhaps speaks very poorly of your sense of reality. Look at you, believing only in the power of your convictions. That's why in 1974, you accepted Jacobo Zabludovsky's invitation, and for the first time on television, you spoke positively about the rights of minorities, responsible homosexuality, the idea of free choice wholly opposed to the notion of "illness."[23] Millions watched the program (incredulously, I suppose), and later at a restaurant, I witnessed how many people came up to congratulate you. For them, you were starting something in Mexico: a civic courage with respect to sexual options. And then in 1975, during International Women's Year, which was typically presided over by the attorney general of the Republic, I went to hear you at the Centro Médico (Medical Center) at a round table on lesbianism.[24] When the organizers didn't allow us the use of the room, you vociferously protested, and finally, without further ado, a brief discussion ensued in which you argued with the sharp sarcasm and the passion you were known for. And outside, humiliation awaited you. A group of women from the market, paid for by some resentful delegate, was waiting for you with banners and posters. "Get out of Mexico, Nancy Cárdenas! Death to the degenerates! We want a Mexico free from perversions!" They furiously attacked you verbally, and visibly undeterred, you responded by inviting them to a dialogue and scolding them for selling out their conscience. Isabel watched, and admired you. Not for one moment did you let yourself be intimidated; you reasoned with them and got them to back down so we could leave.

How obstinate you are, Nancy, really, how truly unrelenting you are! On October 1, 1978, we talked about the massacre at Tlatelolco, and discussed your participation in the gay contingent of the memorial at length. You agreed not to go in order to avoid opening another chapter of your moral lynching, being that you were a favorite target of the right. The next day, who do I see at the head of the gay contingent? You, of course, joyful and energetic. That day, I thoroughly understood your basic modus operandi: you yield to caution and then grow tired of its tyranny. And how you loved the applause (and you got it) when over the loudspeaker, they announced the arrival of the gay contingent to the Plaza de las Tres Culturas.

You've done theater and had memorable successes (*El efecto de los rayos gamma sobre las caléndulas* [*The Effects of Gamma Rays on Man-in-the-Moon Marigolds*], *La maestra bebe un poco* [*And Miss Reardon Drinks a Little*], *Las amargas lágrimas de Petra von Kant* [*The Bitter Tears of Petra von Kant*]), you haven't escaped failure (I found your version of *Pedro Páramo* so stilted[25]), you've received—as a kind badge of honor—attacks by groups such as Pro-Vida, and you've always been supportive, with unflagging generosity. From that comes your staging of *SIDA . . . Así es la vida* (*AIDS . . . Such Is Life*), which was an internal and external call to attention about the future of your tribe in light of the illness that forced a massive "coming out."[26] And you've organized, convened, discussed, and published stories, scripts, and articles. You've written poems that were published in the literary supplement *El Buho* of the *Excelsior*, and that are now being edited by Consuelo Sáizar, poems both of erotic outpouring and the sarcasm with which you observe your romantic joyfulness.[27] These texts stem from your readings of Salvador Novo and Efraín Huerta, from your taste for the monologue-as-an-aside, and your need to express, almost aphoristically, or chorally, your lived experience.[28] How determined you are: relationships end and you write to remember how they began, and how they enriched you, and allowed you to exercise your masterful calling and your sensual history. You write so that memories can't trap you, and you write to give testimony of your encounters with literature, theater, the courage of being different, your activism, and the humanization of your (our) reality.

How obstinate and amazing you are, Nancy!

CARLOS

NOTES

1. Title. Nancy Cárdenas (1934–1994) was one of the first in Mexico to declare her lesbianism. This essay appeared originally in *Debate Feminista* 5, no.10, September, 1994, six months after her death from cancer.
2. *Cardenismo* refers to the leftist ideological current initiated by Lázaro Cárdenas who served as president of Mexico from 1934 to 1940.
3. A friend of Monsiváis's since their university days at the UNAM, Luis Prieto Reyes (1929–2020) was a well-known attorney and historian recognized for his research and recovery of regional histories. He served as coordinator of the Centro de Estudios de la Revolución Mexicana Lázaro Cárdenas (Lázaro Cárdenas Center for Studies of the Mexican Revolution) from 1976 to 1981, and as general director from 1982 to 2005. Monsiváis remembers that in one

of his autobiographies, Luis Prieto called their group Los Tres Huastecos, the trio made of the two of them plus the writer Sergio Pitol. This is in reference to *Los tres huastecos*, a popular 1948 film directed by Ismael Rodríguez about three brothers (a priest, a soldier, and an outlaw). The Huasteca is a region on the Gulf of Mexico, which includes the Mexican states of Tamaulipas, Veracruz, Puebla, Hidalgo, San Luis Potosí, Queretaro, and Guanajuato, where the Huastec people had influence during the Mesoamerican period.

4. Poesía en Voz Alta was a creative and experimental theater movement initiated by the writer Juan José Arreola in 1956 that presented short theater pieces, plays, and skits around Mexico City, and later included recitations of poems, music, and artistic and stage design. Its participants included Octavio Paz, Elena Garro, Carlos Fuentes, Leonora Carrington, and as mentioned in the essay, Nancy Cárdenas, who, with others, joined in expanding theatrical and poetic spaces. Sartre's actual line is "We have only this life to live," which is the title of a book that collects his essays from 1939 through 1975 on philosophy, poetry, fiction, the arts, and politics, among other topics. Monsiváis's rendition, "se vive solamente una vez" (you only live once), is a line from a now classic popular song entitled "Amar y vivir," written by Consuelo Velásquez, that similarly ponders the brevity of human life.

5. Sergio Pitol (1933–2018) was a well-known Mexican writer, translator, and diplomat who won the prestigious Cervantes Prize in 2005. "*Jorongo, calzón de manta,* and *huaraches*" are a traditional Mexican cotton or wool poncho traditionally worn by peasants, off-white woven cotton pants, and leather work sandals.

6. Maringá is the name of a young shepherdess that dies of unrequited love. "Macorina," a poem by Alfonso Camín set to music, is one of Chavela Vargas's first hits. It invokes Macorina in an erotic play of words, and was originally banned in Mexico. English translations of the lyrics from both songs can be found on the Internet.

7. María Isabel Anita Carmen de Jesús Vargas Lizano, known as Chavela Vargas (1919–2012), was an influential Costa Rican/Mexican singer acclaimed for her soul-stirring performances of *rancheras* (a traditional rural musical genre associated with mariachi bands) and other Latin American popular genres. Although a well-known secret, it wasn't until her 2002 biography that she publicly came out as a lesbian at eighty-two years of age. Subsequently, the multi-award winning film *Chavela* (2017), directed by Catherine Gund and Daresha Kyi, documented her life.

8. Lucha Reyes is the stage name of María de Luz Flores Aceves (1906–1944), a Mexican singer and actress popular in the 1930s and 1940s known as the Queen of the Ranchera, who pioneered a defiant way of singing *rancheras* for women in particular (it was a male-dominated genre at the time). Her influence and legacy continues to be recognized today. See Marie Santa Gaytan and Sergio de la Mora, "Queening/Queering Mexicanidad: Lucha Reyes and the Canción Ranchera, *Feminist Formations* 28, no. 3 (2016): 196–221.

9. Even though today we recognize Kahlo as being bisexual (she maintained love relationships with both men and women), here Monsiváis is referring to her sexual activity with other women. Gabriela Mistral, a pseudonym for Lucila Godoy Alcayaga (1880–1957), was a Chilean poet, educator, diplomat, and the first Latin American author to win the Nobel Prize in Literature (1945). Here Monsiváis is referencing Mistral's relationship with US writer Doris Dana who became her friend and executor, and with whom she lived in Long Island, New York, until her death.

10. Benjamin Franklin Wedekind (1864–1918) was a German playwright, influential in the development of epic theatre and critical of bourgeois attitudes, especially on matters of sex. The work, which was originally titled *Frühlings Erwachen* (1891), was Wedekind's first major play, and is considered a foundational work of modern theater about the lack of sex education for the young. There have been translations of the play to numerous languages, including in English by Ted Hughes and Jonathan Franzen, and an equal number of worldwide adaptations beginning in the early twentieth century and continuing until today. Among them were a musical adaptation entitled *Spring Awakening*, which opened off Broadway and then moved to Broadway where it won eight Tony Awards, and an adaptation for television entitled *The Awakening of Spring*, which premiered in 2008. Monsiváis refers to Wedekind as Fred rather than Frank. We have corrected this in our translation.

11. Adolfo Ruiz Cortines (1889–1973), a member of the PRI, was the fifty-forth president of Mexico, from 1952 to 1958.

12. Ernesto P. Uruchurtu (1906–1997), a member of the PRI, was regent of the Department of the Federal District (Mexico) from 1952 to 1966, serving during the periods of the Adolfo Ruiz Cortines, Adolfo López Mateos, and Gustavo Díaz Ordaz presidencies.

13. El Pesebre (The nativity) is a neighborhood in Iztapalapa, in the Eastern outskirts of Mexico City. It is known as a historically impoverished area with great religious zeal and for staging famous Passion Plays during Holy Week.

14. Juan José Gurrola (1935–2007) was a well-known Mexican architect, dramatist, actor, painter, photographer, and performer. He received the National Prize in Science and Arts in the area of the Fine Arts in 2004. His theater was commercially successful and aimed at entertainment, whereas Nancy Cárdenas was more aligned with political theater and consciousness-raising.

15. Fernando Arrabal (1932–) is a distinguished and prolific Spanish playwright, novelist, poet, and filmmaker living in Paris since 1955. Influenced by the Surrealist movement of André Breton, together with Alejandro Jodorowsky and Roland Topor, he co-founded the Panic Movement inspired by Luis Buñuel and Antonin Artaud's Theatre of Cruelty, plays that pushed absurdity, derision, and violence as a critical response to contemporary issues. Arrabal wrote *Pique-nique en campagne* (Picnic on the battlefield), about the absurdity of war, in 1947, and it was staged in 1959. The play is studied as belonging to the Theater

of the Absurd, in dialogue with Samuel Beckett and Eugene Ionesco, and continues to be staged today all over the world.

Colonia Nápoles is a central neighborhood in the Benito Juárez borough of Mexico City where the World Trade Center complex is located, and the Polyforum Cultural Siqueiros, a performing arts center designed by the muralist David Alfaro Siqueiros that houses his famous work *The March of Humanity*.

16. Nancy is hailed as "Parras Athena" by Monsiváis in a play on words that refers to "Pallas Athena," the ancient Greek goddess who killed Pallas, the god of the Titans, and who is associated with wisdom, handicraft, and warfare. This both speaks to Nancy's heroic endeavors, and by substituting *Parras* (vines) for *Pallas* he seems to be alluding to Bacchus, the god of wine, and hinting at the festive nature of their activist get-togethers.

17. On October 2, 1968, a horrific massacre of students and protestors took place in the Tlatelolco square when Mexican armed forces opened fire on a peaceful demonstration that killed hundreds, though the government officially reported a much lower number. It wasn't until thirty years later when documents were declassified that the full scope of the massacre and the identities of those responsible could be confirmed.

18. This refers to followers of Ernesto "Che" Guevara (Argentina, 1928–Bolivia, 1967), a revolutionary who along with Fidel Castro launched the Cuban Revolution in 1959.

19. The plaza, of the main square in Tlatelolco, is surrounded by a Mexico City housing project that recognizes three periods of Mexican history referenced by its architectural structures: pre-Columbian, Spanish Colonial, and modern.

20. Lázaro Cardenas (1895–1970) was a general in the Mexican Revolution who served as president of Mexico from 1934 to 1940. He is best known for nationalizing the oil industry in 1938 with the creation of Pemex (Petróleos Mexicanos), and for the revival of agrarian reform and land redistribution. His ideological leftist legacy is known as *Cardenismo*.

21. The Stonewall Riots, also known as the Stonewall Uprising, occurred at a time when LGBTQ communities in the US were denied basic rights and were constantly harassed by law enforcement. The riots began in the early hours of June 28, 1969, at the Stonewall Inn, a gay bar on Christopher Street in Manhattan, when New York City police began to make routine arrests for alleged unlawful gathering, selling bootlegged liquor, and serving underage drinkers, etc. But this time, and during the next six days of violent skirmishes, the defenders of gay rights, joined by neighborhood residents and other human rights advocates, fought back. This uprising and subsequent organized resistance is recognized as the catalyst and beginning of today's LGBTQ political movement in the US and around the world.

22. A theater located on Insurgentes Avenue built by José María Dávila in 1953, who commissioned Diego Rivera to paint a visual history of the theater on the building's facade. The Avenue, named after the Insurgent Army who fought for

Mexico's Independence from Spain from 1810 to 1820, is the longest avenue in Mexico City, running from the city center to the southern suburbs. It was originally known as Vía del Centenario, and renamed by President Miguel Alemán during his presidency (1946–1952).

23. Here, as elsewhere, Monsiváis uses quotes as a rhetorical device to collect a sense of a multitude of voices and public opinion.

24. Zabludovsky (1928–2015) was the first anchorman in Mexican television; his program *24 Horas* (24 hours) ran from 1970 to 1998 on the Televisa network.

25. In order to secure women's human rights and support their struggles to reach gender equity, the United Nations named 1975 International Women's Year. The first IWY events took place in Mexico City, launching a series of conversations and publications about women's rights in Mexico, Latin America, and the world. Subsequently, they named 1975 to 1985 the United Nations Decade for Women. Since 1977, March 8 has been recognized as International Women's Day.

26. *Pedro Páramo*, a novel considered one of the masterpieces of Mexican literature, was written by Juan Rulfo (1917–1986) and published in 1955.

27. This is an adaptation of the play *As Is* by William Hoffman that opened on March 10, 1985, in New York, at the Circle Repertory, and was later moved to Broadway for 285 performances. See Sam Roberts, "William M. Hoffman, Who Wrote the Pioneering AIDS Play 'As Is,' Dies at 78," *New York Times*, May 1, 2017.

28. The poems appeared in *Cuadernos de amor y desamor (1968–1993)* (Notebooks of love and heartbreak [1968–1993]) (Mexico City: Raya en el Agua, 1994).

29. Salvador Novo (1904–1974) was an influential gay writer, playwright, poet, and translator best known during his time as the official chronicler of Mexico City. Efraín Huerta (1914–1982) was a renowned rebel, political poet, and journalist. Both were iconoclastic and saw literature as socially transformative.

CHAPTER 13

The Fourth Papal Visit

The Spectacle of Faith Fascinated by Its Own Spectacle

1999

Let no one doubt the strength of faith that moves demographic mountains. Pope John Paul II's visit to Mexico, in January 1999, proved, if there was ever any doubt, the collective need to reclaim origins and search for spiritual sustenance. Absolutely respectable, the devotion and assumed defenselessness of millions of people (the poor, the jobless, the sick, those subjected to diverse types of violence, the orphans, those truly alone in the world) galvanized Mexico City like never before, and during five days they imbued the city with a different energy, neither religious nor secular, not far from the television, but not absent from the streets to watch the pope go by, neither spending the whole day on religion, nor free from parochial zeal. If Mexican society sees itself as fully secularized, it also lives deeply in its past, deriving from this unique condition the solace that religion offers for only a few days a year. The pope's visit was not a reconciliation with celestial forces, nor was it altogether the grand "spectacle" made possible by the (greedy) media and entrepreneurs; it was, all in all, a sublime reminder that at the end of the twentieth century, national mysticism requires an alliance between tradition and live and direct transmissions.

THE PREPARATIONS

The intensity of anticipating Karol Wojtyla's reception builds throughout the year and reaches a fever pitch in the weeks before his arrival.[1] Clips of his previous visits are broadcast, priests and "experts on religion" (also priests) are invited to discuss the good news on television, campaigns to welcome him are prepared, the youth from private prep schools and universities are mobilized, and the Sabritas brand advertises that there will be stickers of the pope and his devotion, the Morenita del Tepeyac, inside their bags of potato chips.[2] The public is reminded of its essential characteristics: that it is Catholic, that it is devoted to the Virgin of Guadalupe, that it holds John Paul II dear to its heart (with parochial school choirs constantly singing "You are my soul-brother"), and that God brought us into this world to receive the pontiff for what will most assuredly be his final visit. The videoclips don't lie: the pope (the Holy Father) (His Saintliness) (the Representative of God on Earth) (the Vicar of God) is quite ill, and he endures this physical suffering so that he may alleviate our spiritual one.[3]

Pressured by their upbringing, or their unwavering faith, or by the sudden revival of their dormant beliefs, or simply to set aside monotony for a few days, Mexicans await the landing of the papal airplane. What's more, this time John Paul II is returning to a different country, with a previously inconceivable presence of the Right, and an emboldened high-ranking clergy ready to belligerently exhibit their fundamentalism. If Catholicism as a collective religious practice has indeed notably declined to the degree that some bishops speak of the "religious illiteracy" of the majority, Catholicism remains the dominant ideology regarding the power of the upper echelons and the exhibitionist anointment of the powerful. (No one from the upper classes would admit to their atheism, that would be tantamount to accepting that their good fortune wasn't a divine gift from heaven.)

At one time, the Jesuits constituted the fundamental order. This happened relatively recently when they were in charge of the principle educational institutions of the elite, the Universidad Iberoamericana and the Instituto Tecnológico de Monterrey, but then the Jesuits were expelled from the capital of Nuevo León; now the preferred universities of the children of millionaires are the ITAM and the Universidad Anáhuac, and there are two orders at the top of the pyramid: the Legionaries of Christ and the Opus Dei, which are the corresponding inventions of *Mon Père* Marcial Maciel and José María Escrivá de Balaguer.[4] When contemplating mortality and immortality, the elite and their resources are in their hands. The logistics and the messaging of the pope's visit is also in their hands.

"WELCOME TO OUR LAND"

At the airport, the president Ernesto Zedillo goes on and on with praises and gratitude. And, as is wont to happen after a huge publicity or propaganda campaign, the tone of the discourse, either consciously or unconsciously, comes from the campaign's focus. From the moment of the plane's descent, everything becomes spirituality, peace, and promises of ecstasy. That's in the best of cases. The radio and television hosts transcend the simple language of praise to enter fully into the realm of transfiguration. Where there was a pope, there now appears a direct and recent emissary of God; where there was a Polish priest elected by the synod, there now appears someone primarily endowed with a divine nature. And the commentators take on the role of prophets, they are all Saint John the Baptist anticipating the illumination that will transform Israel, and immediately, the rest of the world.[5] "The sky was cloudy and gray, but once the papal committee stepped outside, it was one of the most beautiful we've ever seen." "What does this saintly man have that when he walks among the crowds, they feel relief in their hearts?" "This is not a visit from a simple human being. He is the incarnation of religious spirit itself."

In the Museo de la Ciudad the pope is received by Cuauhtémoc Cárdenas, the mayor of Mexico City, and his cabinet, along with five hundred invitees.[6] Engineer Cárdenas's speech is somber, and it ranges from the contributions of Catholicism in Mexico to the diversity that the pope now sees in the country, or rather glimpses.[7] And in the museum, the unexpected but foreseeable phenomenon becomes apparent: after so many years of faking secularism, after a century of being unavoidably secular, it's now time to flirt with mysticism, to go down on your knees and pray, and to throw "official" caution to the wind. The pope blesses the crowd, and a large group seemingly forgets the appropriate response to the act, proclaiming their Catholicism as if they were emerging from the catacombs to confront the lions;[8] they're happy since there's no longer any persecution (quite the contrary, in fact), and now it's time to bravely display their knowledge of the Creed.[9]

"Why do you have so many rosary beads? You have, like, twenty."

"They're for the Pope to bless. They're for my maids and secretaries."

"But the Pope isn't going to bless them."

"Yeah, but how are they going to know?"

"I felt something miraculous. It was like he saw me and I was reminded that I am dust and to dust I shall return."

"You know what? As a kid I wanted to be a priest. Then I got over it, but seeing the Holy Father, I was reminded of the spiritual exercises and the cloistering, and the time I told my confessor that I wanted to go to the seminary."

"I had a horrible car accident. I was miraculously saved, an honest-to-goodness miracle, and I swear I actually saw the Virgin of Guadalupe."[10]

THE METAMORPHOSIS OF THE AUTÓDROMO

The human river is interminable, solid, thick, indifferent to the punishing cold, stoic, and revived every ten minutes thanks to the singular and extensive commentary on the great figurehead. Thousands and thousands, or tens and tens of thousands, join the long chain of beings standing in line to enter the Autódromo Hermanos Rodríguez, today converted into a "great temple" that will host John Paul II's solemn mass on his fourth and final visit to Mexico (according to the predictions by medical enthusiasts).[11] The upper middle class families are proud of their chauffeurs' maneuvering through the stop and go traffic, you can also see proletarian families who, in anticipation of the mass, fill everything with a sense of pious raucousness, parochial groups attached to their spiritual leaders, and the young and ecstatic united in their great expectations for a generationally shared moment.

Surveying the landscape, you see catechists, priests, nuns, lay-people intent on modeling conjugal fidelity, professionals proud to assume their Christianity, workers reminding their children to regard this time as their parents' greatest gift to them, businessmen whose faces reflect the solemnity of this historic moment, religious orders marching as if on a mission ("Preaching by walking"), young, well-to-do women who suspect there must be something more transcendental in life than *discotheques*, fundamentalists who temper their severity when counting how many people in this flock will definitively abandon their hedonistic ways, and above all, believers who return to the source of their beliefs, to the feeling of recovered innocence, "of being again / the clear and barbarous forehead of a child" (López Velarde), of attending mass like before, holding their parents' hands, but this time, at the turn of the millennium, and in the presence of the Holy Father.[12]

In his Epistle to the Hebrews, Saint Paul is both precise and abstract: "Now faith is the substance of things hoped for, the evidence of things not seen."[13] Up until recently this definition was unrivaled, but in the age of mass communication, faith is also the demonstration of things seen in excess. The Fourth Papal Visit, for example, mixes the convincing promises of eternity with the certainty of both electronic and commercial support of belief. And this modifies the landscape of religious experience, not the religious experience itself insofar as the person's connection to transcendence is consistent, but rather the technique for more comfortably approaching spiritual experiences.

> Chiquitibum, a la bim bom ba,
> chiquitibum, a la bim bom ba,
> the Pope, the Pope,
> ra ra ra[14]

There was a time when the news was spread by word of mouth, helped along by parochial announcements and the enthusiasm of congregations. Back then, the tenor of religious acts was fundamental, limiting demonstrations of joy to the bare minimum, and respect for symbols was heightened because there were simply fewer available, and the majority of these symbols were religious. There was a time . . . But now, as the high clergy insists, publicity is indispensable, somewhat different from propaganda, more concentrated, more visual, more aphoristic: a millennium is born. Faith is renewed. And the Fourth Visit is a radiant advance of what religious (or perhaps tele-religious) practice will be at the threshold of the millennium, a practice sustained by parish priests and "floor managers," by the awestruck masses and close-ups of the sacred seal, by the eloquence of holy oratory and a wide-angle pan of the venue and its faithful parishioners. By heartily saturating the television and radio with videoclips, roundtables, special programs, news, advertisements of papal itineraries, convocations, one thing is clear: without technology, the propagation of faith could be stranded in the (extinct) twentieth century. With high tech solutions, the new tradition will be signing autographs like papal dispensations.

On a dark night, kindled in love with yearnings, entering the Autódromo just before the mass are a half million or six hundred thousand souls ready for a taste of martyrdom, withstanding disorganization, darkness, the hammering cold, the scarcity of bathrooms, and the rejection of the provisional saintpeters who go to the extreme measures of scanning IDs to avoid falsifications.[15] Some get lost and cry out for their congregation; others are proud of being able to withstand the low temperatures. As usual, there are those who display their enduring wisdom in the form of sleeping bags, heavy woolen sweaters, scarves, thermal underwear, and their mothers' blessings on the way out the door;[16] there are those that ask in vain for where the usherettes can be found; and there are young men and women with so many badges around their necks that there's no way to miss that they know someone on the organizing committee. The night is truly hostile, and it isn't any more bearable with the singing, cheering, and commentary about the pope on the television, nor with the mutually encouraging stories of the young and faithful. I'll be brief: the night's harshness isn't mitigated even by the certainty that the sacrifice will be worth it.

"John Paul, / traveler, / you are a counselor."

"May Jesus reign forever. / Reign in my heart. / In our fatherland and on our soil, / To Mary, the nation belongs."

Faith moves mountains, it has been said before, but faith can also squeeze in and accommodate. How many people can the Autódromo hold? A million or a million and a half souls that provoke the envy of the idle sitting in front of their TV sets? Maybe the most fitting thing to say is that in this case we have the miracle of the loaves and fishes in reverse.[17] No matter how many people arrive, the space remains wide open. Two hundred, three hundred, eight hundred thousand fit inside, and nothing seems to fill the meters and kilometers of still available space. Faith withstands all, even the chorales that poorly imitate Carl Orff (which arguably gives new composers an opportunity), to the detriment of the listeners.[18]

And the overwhelming feeling is of an urgency that attempts to quell itself. In any massive event for the pope, there are so many important people present that whoever wants to stand out is involuntarily entered into the contest of "Highly Worried Faces," not because something might go wrong, but rather because someone might fail to congratulate those responsible for it all going so smoothly.

The stage is impressive, although because of its dimensions, or the haste with which it was built, or the impossibility of architecturally integrating it with the surrounding area, it is not necessarily majestic. There are two platforms on either side for the high clergy, a small bandstand from which to make announcements, and in the center, a pyramid with the pinnacle reserved for the pope. The feeling is that of a great spectacle, of imperial flashes that devastate the simple and the small. But the plain and simple and small and apparently insignificant are also here, and they counteract and complement the intentions of grandeur that intimidate and subjugate. It is, in effect, faith, that delicate balance between the grandiose and the humble.

Ritual is everything: it is the form of belief, and it is the way that the believer assumes the arc of their spirituality; it is the foundation of the institution, and it is the confirmation of generational memory; it is the confined space in which discoveries are both perpetuated and frozen in time, and it is crystalized and imprisoned emotion; it is the intimate and collective pleasure of repetition, and it is the revival of heritage. And the multitude, or rather, the assembly of multitudes, in a racetrack reborn as a Great Temple, contemplates and adopts and venerates the ritual, and joyfully anticipates it when John Paul II's helicopter comes into view, and when the popemobile passes by, and when the canticles commence. The "wave" and cheers are inevitable given their popularity, as are the enormous, indispensable altar candles, and the rich and varied stoles, and the priestly white that absorbs and encompasses all the other colors, and the "THOU ART PETER!" and the repetition of the hymns:[19]

> I was glad when they said unto me,
> Let us go into the house of the Lord.
> Our feet shall stand within thy gates,
> O Jerusalem.[20]

The complement to and counterpart of the ritual are the millenary and brand new ways of expressing belief: the mother who points out the pope to her small child as if to show him the source of resurrection; the Indigenous woman who kisses the image of the Virgin of Guadalupe and holds it up to the sun; the father that holds back his tears because for the only (and almost certainly last) time in his life, he participates in a mass offered by the Holy Father; the young man who has for days and years meditated on his priestly vocation, and today is here in order to accept that perhaps his decision to marry and have three children wasn't the right one; the group of rural women whose looks of happiness are suggestive of the anecdotes that they will endlessly retell back home. Whosoever may express them, these gestures of faith are the complementary essence of the act, which doesn't displace, but humanizes the ritual.

Sick, tired, and conscious of his mission that the surrounding adoration transforms into a foundational power, Pope John Paul II is what he is, one of the most central figures of the twentieth century, a conservative to the extreme, an anti-neoliberal militant that no longer names his adversaries with the same precision with which he devastated communism, because financial systems are not a Berlin Wall, but rather something more slippery and more ubiquitous, and because the most conspicuous of the faithful in many countries are also the owners of the financial systems.[21] An ardent warrior against modernity and secularism, the pope presides over the display of curiosity, the conditioned responses, the reverent spirits, the paramystic pleasure, and the militancy of millions of Catholics (both long-standing and recent) that are gazing upon him at the Autódromo or from their homes.

One Lord, one faith.[22] The mass commences, reinforcing the era of Mexican Catholicism, in which the desire for homogeneity undermines the gains made by "diversity" and furiously confronts them head-on. But this is merely ideology, and what matters to those seeking solace, relief from pain, a place in life different from the one they're living, is an entirely different thing.

The pope categorically condemns what to his criteria is the greatest crime (all sins in this light are unforgivable offenses, venial sin, it seems, doesn't exist[23]). At the racetrack he leaves no room for escape: "may no Mexican dare interrupt life." And the crowd goes wild, not because every man and woman who subscribes to this thesis believes it to be urgent to condemn those women unable to receive the children that God and machismo have granted them—the rape victims, those who will likely die in childbirth—to tortures and worse damnations, but because before his Ambassador to the Almighty, they must prove their morality, and there is no better way to certify their unconditional religiosity than to subscribe to the punishments of hell. (That's why it was a great disappointment that the Mexican bishop offered absolution to both those who had aborted and were truly repentant, and their collaborators in the "most horrendous of sins," during the 1999 Holy Week of the Year of Grace.[24])

"John Paul / the Second, / the whole world loves you."
"He saw me. I swear."

The "Mexicanization" of Pope John Paul II is even more notorious than the immersion of the country in the conception of Christianity propagated by Karol Wojtyla. The most mind-boggling part of this visit, characterized by intense moments, is the touching urgency of Mexican courtesy—elevated to the galactic plane—"Stay with us!" Chanted in the Autódromo Hermanos Rodríguez, "John Paul, / brother, / you're now Mexican" describes the fundamental significance of the visit: the incorporation of the pope into a national tradition for the first time. What was unforeseeable in prior visits (1979/1990/1993), is consummated in 1999, in this extraordinary mobilization, directed at (in this order, I believe): the Pontiff; Catholicism as a recently acquired public pride; a national community of shared and reiterative emotions; youth's willingness to be at the service of the faith; and the vanity of participating in the most important Catholic happening in the Spanish language at the end of the century, the farewell voyage of the Pilgrim Pope.

Of course, it is not the doctrine being "nationalized," that—as the not necessarily informed Guadalupan historians would say—took place in 1531. Nor is it the religious institution, nationalized by its legion of saints, beatified, martyrs, cardinals, bishops, inquisitors, clergy, theologians, nuns, consecrated, and catechists, and by its notable interventions in acts of intolerance and power. What is "Mexicanized" is the pope, transfigured into the Father, transcendent and affable. According to the available responses, Wojtyla isn't just another Mexican, however notable, but rather the emblem of patriotic faith that is incorporated into the essential repertoire of Catholic homes: a crucifix, a reproduction of the dark-skinned Virgin, a photograph of the Basilica of Guadalupe, the Holy Infant of Atocha (occasionally), and a photo of the "compatriot" pope, no longer just a pope.

This Mexicanization is somewhat akin to a saintly apparition. It is not a miracle in the sense of perverting natural laws, but the multiplied sense of discovery, of the splendor of the very personal experiences: "He saw me, I swear to you. What an indescribable emotion. I couldn't even begin to describe it if I wanted to. It was *the* experience of my life." On the radio, the interviewees let their purified religiosity freely flow: "It was like seeing God. Did you see how radiant? He had a halo. He's a saint! This sinful planet doesn't deserve him! The Virgin of Guadalupe must be so happy her favorite son came to pay her a visit." One by one, the testimonies magnify the wonder of this once-in-a-lifetime event, which has left its indelible mark on the blank canvas of the Fatherland.

All that happened owes a debt to media intervention, the hours, weeks, and months filled with advertising and promotion, and it also relied on the high level of crowd contagion, and on this certainty: to not imitate your neighbor's behavior is to isolate yourself forever from the community. "He didn't do the same for any other nation. He's Mexican now." But above all, as far as I can tell, this emotive commotion is a result of the enormous emotional void—or if you prefer, spiritual emptiness—felt by the people. That affirmation is, perhaps, a bit daring, not because it's heretical, but because it's obvious, like that of a pop psychologist or a prophet disguised as a columnist, but I'm supporting my audacity with abundant testimonies, videos, and chronicles. The crowds that fill and flood the streets, the Basilica, the Autódromo, the stadium formerly known as Guillermo Cañedo, do so in obvious flight from the solitary pleasure of sadness, demanding something more, the nourishment of the centuries, which is the experience of the world crystallized in a few select images.[25] This is what the behavior of millions of faithful tells us: the practice of religion has been missing the element of exaltation that the Pope brings with him; without such enthusiasm, religion was only an immutable monument, important for its stake in eternal life, but incapable of provoking ecstasy or spontaneous tears, and praise the Lord, patience, and sacrifice (the hours and hours of waiting, the torturous cold of the racetrack, the fainting, the impatience turned docile). Now, to experience such exaltation is an attempt to perpetuate the short-lived trance of the event forever more.

One might ask me: and without the pope, how does one manage such exaltation and ecstasy? I'll pass that problem along to those in charge of religiosity, but I will allow myself to predict the zealous and militant preservation of memory, the constant replaying of precious moments, ignoring the chain-link fences, the mistreatment, and the rejections. Ecstasy is also the votive candle of nostalgia, and thus, techniques of preservation—incantations against oblivion—will be applied to this present paroxysm of mystical intentions in the form of masses, videos, special programs, youth gatherings, and choral sessions. If that's not enough, one need only clarify that not all Mexicans, especially not the dead and those absent from Mexico City on those days, have been privy to these celestial sensations. Tough luck, ancestors. Tough luck, countryfolk. Tough luck, travelers.

Girolamo Prigione, ex-nuncio (ambassador) of the pope, has been one of the central figures responsible for bringing the Catholic Church closer to the Mexican government.[26] According to Rodrigo Vera, Prigione used to comment on these interinstitutional marriages: "In life there are certain acts that should be formalized. Like when a man lives with a woman, but isn't married. A legal form must be given to that relationship so that it isn't a 'wild' marriage, *un matrimonio salvaje*."[27] And in the shadows of cohabitation, according to Prigione, were the *Nicodemics*, believers at home, anticlerical in the streets.[28] (The model being Nicodemus, the biblical character who, in order to save face, only sought Jesus Christ by night.) The *Nicodemics* have disappeared, or in any case, are now closeted laypeople, convinced that the worst thing for their children would be to study in public schools, because not only would they lack religious instruction, but more unforgivably, they would be monolingual, they wouldn't make childhood friendships that would set them up for life, and they would have to summer in Mexico. (In Mexican childhood, secularism is sedentary, whereas the religiously educated travel to Disneyland, Aspen, and Europe.) And the *Nicodemics* can now show off their faith, wear it like a badge sewn onto their coats of privilege, making evident that no one is Anyone in this country without their network of influences and social assets, without the aura of "respectability" that guarantees power. A powerful poor man? A powerful disbeliever? A powerful layman? A powerful man publicly opposed to theocracy? Wouldn't we love to see that. The *Nicodemics* are now high-ranking altar boys, proud and devoted.

The priestly invasion of every program and the theological and devotional fervor of their commentators, radio and television hosts, and I mean this sincerely, has shifted the impression that we had of the depth of television personalities. We can no longer take their frivolity and levity so seriously, after witnessing their liturgical spirit and newtestamentarian diligence. So, for example, I think that TV Azteca and the television audience would be greatly benefited if José Ramón Fernández were to make permanent the provisional departure from his program, abandoning sports to dedicate himself exclusively to the edification of the public.[29]

I'm being completely unironic. The roundtables with José Ramón and priests, and I must suppose, consecrated men and women, were the most rewarding even for those of us that aren't Catholic. We're all apprised of how much the suddenly devotional programs gained in those days in both ratings and moral credibility, and there's a generalized fear about the inevitable disappointment of returning to the pagan routine. Wouldn't it be irresponsible to keep on talking about trivialities, and wouldn't it be good to imbue these shows with a more permanent spiritual tone? Why not have private television focus exclusively on catechism? It really is the only choice after everything they said.

The event in the Estadio Azteca, outside the primary activity zone, reiterated the influence of spectacle on the modern world. This isn't new, nationally or internationally, but on January 25, it was taken to its extreme. This said with the utmost respect, nobody had a doubt: politics, faith, and spectacle have essentially mutated before our eyes. They now require super sophisticated lighting, the verve of hip bands, and a Quetzalcoatl "prophet-king of the Toltecs" updated on three massive screens that the missionaries and soldiers follow in their representations of the precursors and the origins of faith in our lands. Technology asserts itself and technology prostrates itself, while the entire stadium does the "wave" in order to feel the emotions of sports which contain, in their way, religious fervor. And the feminine contingents from private schools sing and shout so as not to fail in their historic and artistic observation of the pope ("Mexicans know how to pray, Mexicans know how to sing, but above all, Mexicans know how to shout"[30]). And the disciples of the Legionaries of Christ break out in their arduously memorized Latin: "Rerum Christi! Rerum Christi!" And the rich are certain they're going to heaven, because in the virtual universe, there's nothing simpler than for a camel to pass through the eye of a needle.[31]

Fireworks, cheers, reflectors, wordless swooning, noises, chants, and a succession of virgins revered with applause, which, if you'll excuse me, is not fanaticism but rather an objective baring of their souls. All this comes to its grand finale with the Virgin of Guadalupe. The Estadio Azteca is an enormous, home-grown baptismal font, and after all the messages and promises, Karol Wojtyla becomes Mexican by adopting Mexico: "Today I feel Mexican. I don't feel like a pope anymore. Today I feel Mexican surrounded by so many emotions." And it's up to *Mexico, Always Faithful*, to find the way, not yet clear or even conceivable, to institutionalize this fideist shift once John Paul II is gone.[32]

ON THE CONSEQUENCES OF THE VISIT

"In this home we are Catholic, and we don't allow visits from hierarchies lower than the papacy." It has been abundantly proven: the majority of Mexicans are Catholic, in a lovingly ritual way, and as they used to say, more "pope-ish" than the pope himself. We already knew that, though it was partially forgotten and will be remembered precisely on the occasion of the next (surely even more tumultuous) visit by the pontiff. The Catholicism that took to the streets and catechistically turned sporting venues (the Autódromo Hermanos Rodríguez, the Estadio Azteca) into sites of pilgrimage and penitence, is a pre-conciliar Catholicism focused on exhibiting the joy of faith as if it had never before occurred and this was the first proclamation.[33] Strictly speaking, this much is true: never before had the banner of religiosity been raised so high in a mass gathering in which every single person considered themself the other main character of the encounter.

That is something special. The excitement of sports or the excitement of concerts, while similar, are nevertheless lacking the most important component of religious fervor: transcendence, to have glimpsed for a few seconds or minutes the ineffable, which is a shoe-in on one's "resumé." That ineffable feeling of watching a historic goal or a win for your team, or the ineffable sense of hearing a once-in-a-lifetime diva sing (after all, she's earned the title), cannot compare to the ineffable feeling of fully living your belief, as if the for the first time.

I must insist on that "as if for the first time," despite the centuries of Guadalupan fervor, the saints, the beatified, and those aspiring to sainthood, because what took place was truly without precedent. The pope came to Mexico three times before, and there was no shortage of public acts, but these defining elements hadn't yet connected. In matters of mass faith (something both similar to and different from the faith of multitudes), this papal visit was a sort of "first communion" for the Mexican TV audience, for the ultra-urbanized Mexican, for the Mexican who only thinks of rituals a few times a year. The phenomenon won't be surprising anymore after this, but those dense masses of beings that retained their individuality like the figure on a holy prayer card, searching for the face of their singular "beloved," has marked a decided change in Mexico: a faith that grows sturdier because everyone on your block is on your side, a faith that trembles because the neighbor cries tears of gratitude, a faith that sighs with sadness because not even the videotapes can truly preserve the experience.

Six million people in Mexico City in pursuit of the immaculate figure constitutes a huge happening without conceivable precedent, because nothing like it could have happened except at the end of the millennium, with a charismatic and visibly unwell pope, bolstered by electronic media. All that, however, wouldn't mean much without the element of anguish, a formative resource for the believer, a residual effect of conciliar ecclesiology, and abandonment. No millenarianism invents abandonment; it can, of course, intensify mass exodus, but it doesn't invent it.

NOTES

1. Karol Wojtyla (1920–2005) is the birth name of the cardinal who took the name John Paul II upon becoming pope in 1978, a role in which he served until his death in 2005. He was born in Poland and was the first non-Italian pope since the sixteenth century, known for his conservative interpretations of the Catholic faith.

2. La Morenita del Tepeyac refers to the dark-skinned Virgin, the Virgin of Guadalupe, whose image is said to have appeared to Juan Diego on a hill in Tepeyac, a site where the mother goddess Tonantzin was previously worshipped. In Mexican historical imagination, this episode marks the beginning of the "voluntary" Indigenous conversion to Christendom.

3. Monsiváis offers a critique that often takes on an ironic tone, notable here in his repetition of the epithets for the pope.

4. La Universidad Iberoamericana (La Ibero) is a private Jesuit institution in Mexico City, founded in 1943, with satellite campuses in Guadalajara (Jalisco), León (Guanajuato), Torreón (Coahuila), Puebla (Puebla), Tijuana (Baja California), and Jaltepec (Oaxaca). Though it is a religious institution, it is the most "progressive" of the religious private schools in Mexico. The Instituto Tecnológico y de Estudios Superiores de Monterrey, also known as the Tec de Monterrey, or just the Tec, is a secular private university, founded in 1943 in the state of Nuevo León, with thirty-five satellite campuses around the country. Though it is no longer a religious institution, it tends to be considered politically conservative. The Instituto Tecnológico Autónomo de México (ITAM), founded in Mexico City in 1946, is a highly conservative private institution known for its social sciences, especially economics and political science. The Universidad Anáhuac, founded in 1964 with campuses in Mexico City and Mexico State, is a Catholic institution, affiliated with the ultra-conservative Legionaries of Christ.

All of these institutions, due to their private nature and prohibitive costs, are considered to be universities of the elites.

5. Saint John the Baptist was an itinerant prophet and preacher that dedicated his life to spreading his messianic beliefs in the Jordan Valley during the early part of the first century AD. Many of his followers became the early followers of Christianity.

6. El Museo de la Ciudad (The Museum of Mexico City) is in the historical center of the city, housed in a colonial palace near the central plaza known as the Zócalo.

7. Cuauhtémoc Cárdenas is referred to by Monsiváis with the honorific *Ingeniero*, or Engineer, to denote his highest level of education. This is a practice that is common in Mexico and other Latin American countries, but not in the US.

8. This image refers us back to the early days of Christendom when the disciples of Christ were persecuted by the Romans while staunchly defending their newfound faith.

9. Here Monsiváis refers to the Apostle's Creed, which reaffirms faith in God and the Catholic Church: "I believe in God, the Father Almighty, Creator of heaven and earth, and in Jesus Christ, His only Son, our Lord, who was conceived by the Holy Spirit, born of the Virgin Mary, suffered under Pontius Pilate, was crucified, died and was buried. He descended into hell, on the third day he rose again from the dead. He ascended into heaven, and is seated at the right hand of God the Father Almighty. From there he will come to judge the living and the dead. I believe in the Holy Spirit, the Holy Catholic Church, the communion of Saints, the forgiveness of sins, the resurrection of the body, and life everlasting. Amen."

10. As a chronicler and witness, Monsiváis recreates overheard snippets of conversation here and later in the essay.

11. The Autódromo Hermanos Rodríguez is a 4.304 km motorsport race track in Mexico City, named after the racecar drivers Ricardo and Pedro Rodriguez. This was, in fact, not Pope John Paul II's final visit. He returned to Mexico in 2002 and was received by President Vicente Fox, July 30–August 1, 2002. His prior pastoral visits to Mexico were on January 26–February 1, 1979; May 6–13, 1990; August 11–12, 1993; and January 22–26, 1999. President Salinas de Gortari received the pope twice during his six-year mandate (1990–1996), presidents López Portillo, Zedillo, and Fox once each, as heads of state.

12. Here Monsiváis refers to Ramón López Velarde's poem "Ser una casta pequeñez" (To be a chaste child), in which the poet likens the pure love of a woman to maternal grace and a return to the longed-for childlike innocence that her love inspires.

13. Saint Paul the Apostle, known as Saul of Tarsus prior to his conversion, was an apostle of Christ (though not among the original twelve) who spread the teachings of Christ, founding many Christian communities in Asia Minor and Europe in the early apostolic age. Fourteen of the twenty-seven books

of the New Testament are attributed to him. Here, the translation of Hebrews 11 is taken from the King James Bible, which most closely resembles the quote used in Monsiváis's text.

14. This is a take on the "Chiquitibum," a cheer used at Mexican popular sporting events and stadiums since the 1920s.

15. "On a dark night, kindled in love with yearnings," refers to E. Allison Peers's translation of the opening line of St. John of the Cross's famous long poem "The Dark Night of the Soul" (New York: Penguin Random House, 1985). Here Monsiváis is playing with the mystic poet's opening words to describe the night of the mass. St. Peter was considered the leader of Jesus's twelve disciples, and one of his roles in the early Apostolic Church was that of being judge of religious practice. Acts 5:1–10 in the New Testament.

16. Monsiváis refers to sweaters from Chiconcuac, a town in Mexico state, roughly 10 km to the north of Mexico City's outer limits. It is known for its weaving of heavy blankets and sweaters that are sold by ambulant vendors.

17. The miracle of Christ feeding the multitude, the Feeding of the Five Thousand, known also as the miracle of the loaves and fishes, is recorded in Matthew 14:13–21. In this miracle the multitude is fed by a small amount of food that multiplies. Monsiváis suggests that in the reverse miracle the space is constant, but the people multiply.

18. Carl Orff (1895–1982) was a German composer best known today for his cantata *Carmina Burana*, a swelling choral masterpiece that has appeared in many film scores and is often circulated in classical music venues to this day.

19. "Thou art Peter" refers to Matthew 16:18, "And I say also unto thee, That thou art Peter, and upon this rock I will build my church; and the gates of hell shall not prevail against it." Kings James Bible translation.

20. Psalm 122 (KJV).

21. On November 9, 1989, the fall of the Berlin Wall was the beginning of a physical dismantling of the internal border wall separating communist East Germany from the capitalist West Germany. It symbolized the fall of the Iron Curtain—the military, political, and economic division in place since the close of WWII in 1945, and the decline of communism in Eastern Europe, which had been under the influence of the Soviet Union.

22. From Ephesians 4:5, "One Lord, one faith, one baptism" (KJV).

23. Venial sins, according to the doctrines of Catholicism, are considered lesser sins that do not result in eternal damnation. Unlike deadly sins, these are forgivable with penance, and while they disobey "moral law," may be committed without full knowledge or consent, or in order to avoid a greater harm.

24. While under Pope John Paul II there was no room for priests to absolve women of the "sin" of aborting, under Pope Francis in 2016 there was an explicit Church directive to allow individual clergy to absolve those who are "truly repentant." See "Papa permitirá absolver de 'pecado de aborto' a arrepentidos," *Semana*, January 9, 2015.

25. Here Monsiváis pokes fun at the television conglomerate Televisa that on January 20, 1997, renamed the Estadio Azteca for Guillermo Cañedo de la Bárcena, the Mexican Football Federation president, member of the FIFA executive committee, and network executive who died that day. The name never took, and was quietly changed back after Cañedo's heirs allied themselves in business with Televisa's rival, TV Azteca, the following year.

26. Girolamo Prigione (1921–2016) was an Italian prelate and diplomat in the Holy See (1951–1997) with posts in Nigeria, Italy, Great Britain, the United States, Austria, and Mexico for over twenty years. Monsiváis uses a Spanish version of his name, Gerónimo.

27. Monsiváis cites the journalist from his article in *Proceso*, special edition, January 22, 1999.

28. *Nicodemics* follow in the tradition of Nicodemus, the pharisee, who sought Christ's counsel in John 3, and refers to a hypocritical relationship in which what is stated and what is enacted are at odds.

29. Fernández is a sportscaster and television journalist whose career began in 1970 and who was a household name, covering many Olympics and World Cups. During the pope's visit, his coverage turned religious. He currently works for ESPN.

30. Monsiváis quotes from a famous speech given during Pope John Paul II's second visit to Mexico, on May 5, 1990, from the balcony of the Basilica of Guadalupe in which he closed with "México sabe bailar . . . México sabe rezar . . . sabe cantar . . . pero más [que] todo sabe gritar . . . México, siempre fiel. Adiós." Closing with "Mexico, always faithful." See "S.S. Juan Pablo II En la Basílica de Guadalupe" (D. R. Televisa S. A. de C.V Mexico, 1990). Gloria.TV News, uploaded March 11, 2014, by jahfuentes. https://gloria.tv/post/QGce6wGwSKe66QzzG8YUhpdFB.

31. Here Monsiváis plays with the verse Matthew 19:24, "And again I say unto you, It is easier for a camel to go through the eye of a needle, than for a rich man to enter into the kingdom of God" (KJV).

32. *Fideism* is a philosophical position that posits that faith exists independently from reason and that there is no need to prove what is known through faith.

33. Pre-conciliar refers to what came before Vatican II, known as the Second Ecumenical Council of the Vatican, or the Second Vatican Council. This twenty-first ecumenical council of the Roman Catholic Church was opened in fall of 1962 by Pope John XXIII and was held yearly until December 1965 when it was closed.

CHAPTER 14

The Second Sex

One Is Not Born a Feminist

1999

In 1949, *The Second Sex* by Simone de Beauvoir was published. In the years immediately following its appearance, its impact in Latin America is minimal and the reasons for this delayed reaction are understandable. There isn't the necessary social and cultural space nor the receptive spirit to make decisive transformational changes. Patriarchy is a feudal empire: at that time in Mexico, for example, women don't have the vote; in many countries divorce is not possible; adultery continues shocking the "good" families while titillating them; and even women wearing pants is a battle. In professional fields, women's presence is minimal, and at the UNAM they make up no more than 8 percent of the student body (the percentage of professors is even lower).[1] The heroic suffragists and heroic feminists of the 1920s and 1930s are followed in the '50s by isolated cases of social warriors, often dogmatic Leftists or respected professionals admired, albeit it with a qualifier: "In spite of being a woman . . ."

At the end of the '50s—relying on my testimony as representative of a particular time, rather than an outlier—I read *The Second Sex* with enthusiasm. That said, I consumed the book in a way that now embarrasses me, but that at the time I found normal. It is an excellent essay on "Being a Woman" that examines the nature of her disadvantages. I didn't go any deeper. Today, in retrospect, I can see my "cleverness." I chose to concentrate on the form and expository method: "it's terrible that they're being discriminated against, but what can I do?" Looking back, I'm aware of my inconsistency: How could I be so enraged by this treatise that is a denunciation, without having understood its political consequences? I revisit my copy of *The Second Sex* and find an abundance of underlining, and notes in the margins. But my overarching perspective on women's issues hardly changed. Most likely, the stronghold of patriarchal thought was so overwhelming that it essentially separated my thinking from its practical application, thus reading as "literature" what was the radical examination of the historical oppression and social construction of women.

Nevertheless, I don't think I was an incorrigible sexist in those years. Since adolescence, I was bothered by the signs of a programmed backwardness, most especially the part that tied women to their husbands as slaves: "Mrs. Fulana of Gómez, Mrs. Perengana of Torres."[2] (I felt it was more of a shackle than a marriage.) I had also seen up close and admired the Mexican suffragists from the 1920s, with their stories of how they were pursued by the police, put into patrol cars, and while the police were arresting more of them, the initial detainees escaped, and then everything started all over again. All this while the very same Left continued to discriminate against them. As a militant, I also witnessed women voting in Mexico for the first time in 1955, which moved me or maybe it didn't, but which, for sure, I experienced as a fascinating occurrence: that reverent fear on approaching the voting booth, that hanging on to the paper ballot as if it were the entry key into an unknown world. This much is true, but I had never seriously reconsidered my ideas about women's rights. I accepted them without assuming any responsibility for my point of view. I reacted with anger toward the machista mistreatment of women, the arrogance of rapists, and the disdain toward the activists and their always separate and separable struggles. Nevertheless, my emotional rejection of injustice didn't translate into any personal commitment regarding a perspective on gender.

I owe Rosario Castellanos my rereading of *The Second Sex*.[3] With her masterful style, founded on an obstinate and unrelenting irony, Castellanos made me aware of the book's repercussions. *The Second Sex* had transformed her by changing her overarching understanding of the condition of womanhood. And as had happened to her, so too a generation of university students were finally empowered with a set of precise ideological, historical, sociological, and even scientific tools. If you think that I'm attributing too much value to this one book, please recall the conditions of that era and the political discourse that was still being directed at "Women" from the privilege of paternalism: "These hands that rock the cradle."[4] That is why the influence of *The Second Sex* for Castellanos was so enlightening. She could finally make fun of herself because she could curb her sarcasm by turning it into an ironic critique of machismo.

Many insist that Simone de Beauvoir repeatedly declared she was not a feminist. Without exaggeration, let's remember Marx saying, "I'm not a

Marxist," or the heresy of pointing out that Christ never declared himself a Christian, nor Buddha a Buddhist, it is obvious that the great theoretical renovators weren't angling for personal gain in their projects. Beauvoir is memorable for her intellectual quality, her interpretive courage and her decisiveness in confronting the mindset that structures women's inferiority, as well as the verbal, legal, moral, patrimonial, and physical impunity of machismo. In contesting the canon that has been imposed on femininity both in theory and in practice, in rejecting the essentialism of "femininity," in refusing to consider masculine traditional oppression as deterministic, she exceptionally illuminates the considerable efforts made by women to fully live their condition as human beings.

This had already been partially stated, and repeatedly expressed, but the assertion was generally lacking in hope. Something extraordinary in *The Second Sex* is its dedramatized style, the absence of that melodramatic tinge imposed on women as an "exercise in sensitivity." In rejecting melodrama, Beauvoir casts aside a classic link with essentialism, and by not capitalizing on the "the fineries of fragility," and by choosing the classic objective tone of the French essay, she exposes the fallacy that patronizingly identifies women's writing with its charm, its flirtatious nature, and a certain measure of schmaltzy sentimentality. This is crucial because, among other things, it allows us to reread women's literature, from Jane Austen to George Eliot, from Emily Dickinson to Emily Brontë, from Katherine Mansfield to Virginia Woolf, and to observe how the visible sensitivity is due to the education and customs of the social group, but not to their essential quality. Certainly, only a woman could have written *Pride and Prejudice* or *Mrs. Dalloway*, but women at the time were only allowed those topics, and the writing is not feminine but literary.

THE OTHER IN THE KITCHEN, THE BEDROOM, AND THE CONFESSIONAL AWAITS

The most cited quote from *The Second Sex* is the following:

> One is not born, but rather becomes a woman. No biological, psychic, or economic destiny defines the figure that the human female takes on in society; it is civilization as a whole that elaborates this intermediary product between the male and the eunuch that is called feminine. Only the mediation of another can constitute an individual as an *Other*.[5]

Culturally dismantling the formative and deformed apparatus of patriarchy, Simone de Beauvoir powerfully contributes to the crisis of that dictatorial model in the second half of the twentieth century. It is now possible to say, in the majority of countries and some sectors: "one is not born a woman: there are different ways of becoming one." And these ways also have alternatives. If the Right, as is proven politically in Mexico and in other parts, only admits one way of being a woman—submissive, self-sacrificing, hobbled, and in the kitchen, or at work (but, in that case, acquiescing to male decisions)—then democratic thought has buttressed itself against these essentialisms, and is supported by abundant literature, the experience of social movements, and legal and constitutional gains.[6] But this does not mean that the book by Simone de Beauvoir can be forsaken or relegated to the attic of glorious precursors. It is still requisite reading insofar as its passion and intellectual lucidity continue to be exemplary. Certainly, *The Second Sex* could be updated in several ways, because a half century has passed, and new collective knowledges have arisen, and because in the original there are several moments where sharp observations border on prejudice.

> The lesbian will often try to compensate for a virile inferiority
> by arrogance or exhibitionism, which, in fact,
> reveals inner imbalance.[7]

An inner imbalance is also a social construction. Repression and condemnation, the need to waste energy on defiance, everything that constitutes arrogance and exhibitionism in a group of lesbians, rather than being evidence of an inner imbalance, demonstrates the pitfalls of resistance techniques. Given this harassment, an all-out defensive psychology is not an act of imbalance, but rather a search for space. In a broader sense, this is noted by Kierkegaard in the epigraph chosen by Beauvoir: "What a curse to be a woman! And yet the very worst misfortune for a woman is, in fact, not to understand that it is a misfortune."[8] If one doesn't characterize Kierkegaard as an essentialist, what he says seems perfectly rational: the worst misfortune is not understanding that the imposed condition, so frequently unlivable, is a misfortune that must be fixed. And to transform this gender affliction into a responsible destiny for any person is the job of feminism and those sectors of society influenced by it.

HOW AMUSED ARE WOMEN BY HEROISM?

In the first part of *The Second Sex*, Beauvoir examines both facts and myths. And this, for Latin American readers in the years following its appearance, underscores the enormous difference between theirs and the European experience. In Latin America, the myths and facts have been worse, more degrading, especially in poor and Indigenous women's spaces. And it is not until the collapse of an existing socialism that the ideological myths of the Left take on a superstitious burden similar to the European one, but compounded by functional illiteracy. Therefore, the polemic of Beauvoir with Engel's book (*The Origin of the Family, Private Property and the State*) bothered the cultural Left (the partisan Left never even noticed). The Right, essentially incapable of understanding Beauvoir's book, wasn't aware of her critique of the Catholic Church's positions, the patristics of its French bishops, and above all, they couldn't recognize her ideas about something other than women's natural submission. On the Right, the rejection of feminist positions is fundamental, and on the Left, even with more experience co-existing with feminists, it is only in recent years that the thesis of a diverse and parallel movement has been accepted. Previously, the norm was the sermon: everything must be channeled through the only known path to revolution, and whoever points out alternative routes betrays the proletariat struggle.

In my first reading of *The Second Sex*, the predatory and oppressive quotes by a good number of writers, thinkers, and famous figures caught my attention. How was it possible, I thought, that Nietzsche, whom I had just recently read, but who was still Nietzsche, affirmed, "Woman is the hero's amusement."[9] Do all battles end in orgies? Coitus, the crown of the epic. It took me a while to understand the effectiveness of Simone de Beauvoir's method. She analyzes a process anthropologically, historically, philosophically, and politically, and she uses these quotes like a synthesis of rhythmic writing on the wall. The aphorisms of patriarchy are verdicts without the right to reply, and they don't proclaim wisdom, but are rather a reminder of the relegated, and after all, invisible place of women due to their gender. "One is not born a woman . . .," that is to say, one is not born realizing the tragedy of having been born the wrong gender, or if you don't like such a fatalistic adjective, born a gender that in the 1950s, if considered "decent," received encouragement in a variety of subjugations, or if she dared work, was placed on the margins where no raises were available because how could they be.[10] (If we follow the Freudian thesis of penis envy, in terms of work promotions, then as now, women have lived, so to speak, actually being envious of the advances that the penis awards.)

Biology is destiny. True, but not with such deterministic fury, nor all the time. Today, destiny has notably changed for young women at universities, in the economy, in culture, and it is also transforming the possibilities for Indigenous women in Chiapas who, in finding their voice, acquire a worldview."[11] It is fair to recognize that feminism is the only revolution of the twentieth century that does not end in autocracy (this is not high praise from the point of view of Lenin, Stalin, the Ayatollah, numerous clerics, Fidel Castro, and the PRI), and it is also fair to point out that half a century after its publication, *The Second Sex* retains its vitality because despite their advances, women continue to be in situations of serious disadvantage.

"One is not born a woman." Neither a feminist.

NOTES

1. The UNAM is the Universidad Nacional Autónoma de México (National Autonomous University of Mexico).

2. The original in Spanish reads: "Fulana de Gómez, Perengana de Torres." In Hispanic cultures, it is/was the custom of married women to keep their maiden names, adding their husbands' with the preposition "of "which seems to denote ownership, belonging to. The cognate structure in English would be the use of excluding a woman's given name and calling her Mrs. Juan Torres, rather than Mrs. Maria Torres.

3. Rosario Castellanos (1925–1974), a writer, journalist, and diplomat, is considered one of the most important authors of the twentieth century in Mexico and Latin America. Early on, her work as a novelist, poet, short story writer, playwright, and essayist focused on gender oppression in literature and reality. This cleared the way for generations of women writers to express themselves freely to contest an oppressive patriarchy for women and other minorities, including Indigenous populations. Her novel *Balún Canán* (1957), central to her politics, was translated belatedly as the *Nine Guardians* by Irene Nicholson (England: Readers International, 1992). See Chapter 10 for an analysis of her poetry by Monsiváis.

4. This quote is taken from the 1865 poem, "The Hand That Rocks the Cradle Is the Hand That Rules the World" by William R. Wallace (1886–1960), an Oklahoma district court judge, that praises motherhood. The poem, which resounded internationally, lifted women to an idealized, saintly pedestal that essentialized their role as mothers.

5. Simone de Beauvoir (1929–1980), *The Second Sex* [1949], trans. Constance Borde and Sheila Malovany-Chevalier (New York: Vintage Books, 2011), 283. This second translation of *The Second Sex* was originally published in hardcover in a slightly different form (London: Random House, 2009), and subsequently published in hardcover in the United States (New York: Alfred A. Knopf, 2010). The first English edition was translated by H. M. Parshley (New York: Alfred A. Knopf, 1953). While this first edition was condensed, the 2011 translation by Borde and Malovany-Chevalier is, for the first time, complete and unabridged. We will be citing from this 2011 edition.

6. What we have translated "hobbled, and in the kitchen," in Spanish reads, "en casa y con la pata quebrada"—literally, "at home and with a broken leg."

THE SECOND SEX   167

7. Beauvoir, *The Second Sex* (2011), 425.

8. Kierkegaard's epigraph precedes the introduction to volume 2 of *The Second Sex*. A second epigraph by Sartre follows: "Half victim, half accomplice, like everyone."

9. Beauvoir, *The Second Sex* (2011), 228.

10. *Decente* is a word used and defined as proper, respectable, honest, and upright. This often-used word in Latin America privileges "decency" as the moral value that recognizes the importance of living and behaving with dignity in all contexts and places. Monsiváis points to the fact that it is also socially classed.

11. This is in reference to the EZLN (Ejercito Zapatista de Liberación Nacional) Zapatista uprising in 1994 in the state of Chiapas, an Indigenous rebellion protesting both NAFTA and the revision of Article 27 that protected communal lands from sale or privatization, and the neocolonial conditions suffered by their communities. The Zapatista women, a third of the army, in seeking gender equity presented the Women's Revolutionary Law, a set of ten laws that would grant women rights with regard to marriage, children, work, land, health, education, political and military participation, and protection from violence. These demands were included in the platform that the EZLN presented to the Mexican government.

CHAPTER 15

Women In Power

2000

Following Channel 11's transmission of interviews of women with political trajectories, the interviewers, Sabina Berman and Denise Maerker, go on to publish a series of expanded texts and introductions by Sabina Berman that are incisive and effective.[1] They speak with Elba Esther Gordillo (the conquest of sectorial power), Commander Elisa, a.k.a., Gloria Benavides (the struggle against power), Rosa Luz Alegría (the surprising arrival at power), Silvia Hernández (the discipline of obtaining power), and Rosario Robles (the militant's arrival at an unexpected power, one foreign to Leftist traditions and until recently removed from governmental experiences in general).[2] *Mujeres y Poder* (2000) is a text whose interest lies in the unveiling of five diverse personalities that don't complement one another, and in the sharp critical descriptions, both explicit and implicit, of the masculinist control of politics.[3] Among other things, the following stand out:

- Frequently, though this has decreased, machismo considers it inevitable for women to access power via sex. Their comrades in arms—Elba Esther Gordillo relays—believed that "we were only good for sex." And we must prove the contrary to them.[4]
- For power to no longer be strictly a masculine affair, there must be a great cultural mobilization by women and a normalization of managing leadership positions. Cultural mobilization leads to a resistance against prejudices, and this normalization is aided by the tens of thousands of professionals (women lawyers and doctors, engineers and astronomers), the approved aptitudes of female functionaries and leaders and, especially, though this might not

seem fundamental, the democratization of housework. As long as this doesn't happen, Silvia Hernández, a "professional politician," describes the formula that will prevail: "If you want to win, you need to play by the rules, you can't win with your own rules. This is a man's world: you have to run one hundred meters in nine seconds. So, you want to be a woman and run them in eighteen seconds and still win your place? Well, no, you have to run one hundred meters in nine seconds. And if the record drops a second, you have to drop a second, too. The expressions of this world are masculine and the demands on women are masculine. You have to respect them. And of course never cry, don't laugh too much, women are always smiling, don't suddenly interrupt the boss. You get used to it, those are the rules, so you use them."[5]

- Power is still overwhelmingly a question of hierarchical patience and temerity. (That is, of course, in the case that you don't come from a political or corporate dynasty, or that you don't break forcefully into politics at just the right moment.) Women's place is familiarly relegated to the base of the pyramid. Elisa speaks of her experience on a remote farm in Nepantla, with a guerrilla group, el Frente de Liberación Nacional (The National Liberation Front), made up of people willing to give their lives for the cause of equality: "We were fed up (receiving people, arranging housing, packing, making food), we had already learned to raise chickens and to make nixtamal tortillas and there was no political or theoretical training. We said, what is this? What a scandal. Then we asked for military training, we asked for a political education and the guy in charge of the house, Manolo, asked us what we had read and then gave us something to read. I remember that I began reading, or re-reading perhaps, Lenin's *The State and Revolution* and I don't remember what María Luisa was reading but something along those lines too, right?"[6]

- Power, in the bureaucratized media (and, at this point, what news outlet isn't or won't be within a few weeks?), is resistant to attacks and even to the simplest demonstration of merit. To get close to its milieu, one proven method is cunning: which in men is lauded as wiliness, camaraderie, patriotism, and in women considered dangerously intrepid. Elba Esther Gordillo recounts her first meeting with the magisterial leader Carlos Jonguitud:[7] "One day I decide that I should meet with Mr. Jonguitud, and I do everything in my power to position myself for a meeting. I asked Ramón [a friend] to introduce me to him. But Ramón refused to do it, and he refused because he knew of my history as a dissident. Since he didn't do it, well, I found other ways to get an introduction. I went to an audacious teacher from my region and I said to her: 'I must meet the "illustrious educator," I want to know which version is the truth' [the SNTE's version or that of the magisterial dissidence[8]]. Then we went to wait for him to come out of the Sección Novena in his car.[9] Us in my little car and there we go, and we said hello, and then he invited us for coffee."[10]

- Power is also the great abstraction, that indecipherable thing that runs the gamut from considering its delights ("The forbidden fruit: the apple that we must not eat: that is what power is for women. But we really must eat the apples, they're delicious," Rosario Robles insists[11]) to Rosa Luz Alegría's open depression: "I did know that [Carlos Salinas de Gortari] was annoyed. My presence in the Secretariat of Tourism, my influence on the planning system, my proximity to the president drove him nuts.[12] So when he announces his candidacy for the PRI, I think, 'We're no longer talking about a six-year sabbatical, it's more like there's nothing left, it's over . . . Only then do I have a crisis for about four or five weeks, and a deep depression . . . Absolutely nothing appealed to me. I wasn't even interested in reading or watching television. I just spent it, I don't know, staring out the window."[13]

- Power can be the partial oversight of the feminine condition, understood here as the sum of a long tradition of subjugation, imposed humility, being second or third tier, passivity, lacking the "most important thing" (lest we forget Roberto Madrazo's campaign and his "testicular ideology").[14] With power, the feminine condition is exercised in a different, still very minoritized way. And it is an arduous process. Rosa Luz Alegría finds no model nor ideal woman in history or in literature: "Definitely not. I wanted to be like Alexander the Great, like Pericles. But women? No one. Not Cleopatra, nor Madame Curie. No, no woman."[15] Elba Esther Gordillo points out, "We [women] are only just learning to wield power . . . We are afraid to say, 'We are powerful, yes, I am a powerful woman, yes, I want power.'"[16] And Silvia Hernández reflects, "It's true, Mexican women give very masculine speeches, they never include women's issues; what's more: they avoid the topic of women altogether, and if they come across as less feminine, all the better."[17] It remains to be specified what exactly is the "feminine" and what is the "masculine" topic in a speech removed from any notion of gender, but what is evident is the attempt to be more like men in order to mitigate the limitations imposed on women.

- Power, when referring to women, is always at some level emblematic. A man never represents his gender: a woman does so almost inevitably because to be secretary of state, governor, or senator is an exception or a demographic concession, and this exceptionality confers on her a symbolic quality.

- Power, in women, up until now has translated as conditional success. Each of the interviewed women is successful in her own way. Rosa Luz Alegría, famous during one presidential mandate, is the first secretary of state; Elba Esther Gordillo helms the National Education Workers' Union, has a long history of political posts and representation, including being the general secretary of the CNOP;[18] Elisa, removed from mainstream notions of success, is the survivor of two repressions: the tragedy of the Nepantla Ranch and an arrest because of her affiliation with the EZLN, which then lead to her first triumph before the judge in 1995: "The place was packed with journalists, bursting at the seams of the courtroom, there were family members, friends, coworkers, there were people from the parties, people from the PRD, they had invaded practically the entire courtroom, it was totally full of people that reminded me that I wasn't alone."[19] Silvia Hernández has been a federal representative, senator, director of the CREA, and secretary of tourism.[20] Rosario Robles is the first female head of government of Mexico City. Even with all that, they are still presented as exceptions—"Despite being a woman . . ."—and the awareness of gender limitations is, however you look at it, the diminishment of faculties that patriarchy demands.

- Power stops being the patrimony of one gender because it cleaves to two petrified structures: the masculine monopoly on opportunities, and the generalized mistrust of women's abilities. "Our principal obligation—Rosario Robles affirms—is to show that we are capable, and that it really is a positive thing for spaces to be opened to us."[21]

- Power, according to the collective imaginary, or if you prefer, according to national and international tradition, is a question of negative characteristics: harshness, implacability, excessive complicity, a tendency to plunder, lack of scruples, demagoguery, shady dealings. By not participating in the centrality of power, women avoid that terrible aura, determined by experience, resentment, and

the need to quickly explain disasters. Until now, women—excepting
the contributions by Margaret Thatcher—have been exempt from
a summary identification with politics and fierce authoritarianism, politics and crime, politics and brutal abuses, all things that
have already been said about the behavior of many women leaders
of working-class neighborhoods, unions, and social movements
that proceed in the style of feudal ladies. But despite this tendency
toward a "hard line" feminine leadership, in politics, women are
still considered either easily manipulated or innocent, as is prover-
bial of their sex. This, at the end of the day and given the political
culture in Mexico, translates into a lack of trustworthiness. Women,
it is thought, haven't even had the opportunity to cheat or commit
crimes.

- Power needs to be exercised, and among women, that majority
group treated like a minority, the end and the means of necessary
transformations is *empowerment*, a word that is both dissonant and
inevitable. *Empowerment* is the collective action without which no
social change can take place, it is the most democratic distribution
of power in society.

What is the foreseeable future for women in political parties, in public
administration, in Congress, in NGOs, in situations as conceited and concrete as civil society, in the national debate? *Mujeres y poder* offers evidence
for us to consider. Forced to recognize throughout their careers that the personal (gender) is political (the opportunities that they are denied or receive
sparingly, the efforts that they must always display), women in politics are
aware of their fate in the short and medium term: facing national problems and also sidestepping what they must, from domestic violence to double standards in the workplace. It is not prophetic to point out that in the
coming years women's presence in politics will increase, nor is it visionary
anxiety to affirm that a single woman in the presidency of the republic will
render obsolete the publication of books like *Mujeres y poder*. After all, who
but perhaps a psychoanalyst or a survey researcher would see fit to publish
a book entitled *Men and Power*?

NOTES

1. Title. Monsiváis's title refers to the book *Mujeres y poder* (Women and power)
by Sabina Berman and Denise Maerker (Mexico: Raya en el Agua, 2000). This
book has not been translated into English; all quotations cited herein are
our translations.

2. Canal 11, Mexico's public television channel 11, along with Canal 22, has historically run educational and documentary public television programming for the national audience. Sabina Berman (1955–) is a playwright, novelist, poet, and political journalist who has won the National Prize for Playwriting (Premio Nacional de Dramaturgia Juan Ruiz Alarcón) four times and the National Journalism Award (Premio Nacional de Periodismo) twice. Denise Maerker (1965–) is a Mexican journalist, anchorwoman and board member at Televisa, columnist for *El Universal* newspaper, and radio host at Radio Fórmula.

3. Elba Esther Gordillo Morales is a politician originally from Comitán, Chiapas, who was the leader of the National Education Workers' Union (Sindicato Nacional de Trabajadores de la Educación, or SNTE), the largest labor union in Latin America, since 1989. She was arrested in 2013 for corruption and embezzlement. Subcomandante Elisa (María Gloria Benavides Guevara), from Nuevo León, is here referred to as *commander* by Monsiváis. In the 1980s and early '90s, she served as a subcomandante in the EZLN. She was arrested in February 1995 in connection with the 1994 Zapatista uprising, and was later acquitted. Rosa Luz Alegría Escamilla is a physicist by training and profession. In 1980, she was appointed secretary of tourism, becoming the first female secretary of state in Mexico. Silvia Hernández Enríquez, a long-standing, active member of the PRI, has served in many capacities, including as leader of the PRI's National Confederation of Popular Organizations (CNOP). She served as deputy in the lower house of Congress, and in the Mexican Senate three times. In 1994, she was appointed secretary of tourism. María del Rosario Robles Berlanga is a Mexican politician who stepped in as mayor of Mexico City when Cuauhtémoc Cárdenas resigned to run for president in 2000, making her the first female mayor of the city. She later served as the secretary of social development, and as secretary of agrarian, land, and urban development of Mexico. She was involved in one of Mexico's greatest racketeering scandals, La Estafa Maestra (Master scam), broken by the Mexican political news circular *Animal Político* in 2017.

4. Sabina Bermán and Denise Maerker, eds., *Mujeres y Poder* (Mexico: Raya en el Agua, 2000).

5. "Elba Esther Gordillo o la audacia," *Mujeres y poder*, 88.

6. In *Mujeres y poder*, 185 there is a reference to Silvia Hérnandez speaking about the rules of power, however, the quotation in Monsiváis's original differs significantly from the published text. It is likely that Monsiváis quoted from the documentary television series that gave rise to the book.

7. "Elisa o el imperativo moral," *Mujeres y poder*, 142. Vladimir Lenin's 1917 Russian text, translated into English as *The State and Revolution*, examined the fundamental role of the state and advocated for a proletarian revolution.

8. Carlos Jonguitud Barrios (1924–2011) was a union leader and governor of San Luís Potosí whose actions were often characterized as mafia-like, and thus he was the de facto head of the National Teacher's Union.

9. The SNTE stands for the Sindicato Nacional de Trabajadores de la Educación

(National Education Workers' Union); the "magisterial dissidence" refers to alternative educational projects and organized protests by groups of educators who opposed the educational and curricular measures imposed by the union.

10. The Sección novena, or 9th district, refers to a chapter of the SNTE in Mexico City. See the SNTE official website for Sección 9, updated in 2020, https://snte.org.mx/seccion9/quienes-somos.

11. "Elba Esther Gordillo o la audacia," *Mujeres y poder*, 90.

12. "La manzana prohibida de Eva es el poder: Rosario Robles," *Mujeres y poder*, 260.

13. Carlos Salinas de Gortari (1948–), an economist, institutionalized the neoliberal economic policies of privatization begun under his predecessor President Miguel de la Madrid who led from 1982 to 1988. Continuing the power of the PRI, Salinas was declared Mexico's sixtieth president, serving from 1988 to 1994 despite widespread allegations of electoral fraud that he had stolen the election from opposition leader Cuauhtémoc Cárdenas Solórzano of the PRD. At the close of Salinas's presidency, PRI candidate Luis Donaldo Colosio was assassinated in Tijuana, preceding the 1994 general elections, punctuating a six–year mandate marked by corruption and the erosion of the state.

14. "La verdad de Rosa Luz Alegría," *Mujeres y poder*, 65–66.

15. Monsiváis refers to "lo mero principal" (the most important thing), which is a line from the famous revolutionary *corrido* "La persecución de Villa" (Pancho Villa's persecution) detailing the incident in which Venustiano Carranza (later the forty-fourth Mexican president from 1917 to 1920) allowed US troops into the north of Mexico to find and attack Villa and his batallion; they were ultimately unsuccessful in their mission. Roberto Madrazo campaigned from within the PRI against then president Ernesto Zedillo's "hand-picked" candidate Francisco Labastida during the primaries leading up to the 2000 presidential elections in which the PRI lost for the first time in over seventy years to the PAN candidate Vicente Fox Quesada who became Mexico's sixty-second president from 2000 to 2006. Madrazo has been quoted saying that Zedillo lacked "balls" during his presidency, and subsequently published a memoir to this effect, *La traición* (Treason) accusing him, along with Elba Esther Gordillo, of betraying the PRI. Roberto Madrazo, *La traición* (Mexico: Planeta, 2007). Also see "La Traición," *Proceso*, May 14, 2007, https://www.proceso.com.mx/libros/2007/5/14/la-traicion-730.html.

16. Alegría's quote here is likely taken from the documentary interview.

17. "Elba Esther Gordillo o la audacia," *Mujeres y poder*, 101.

18. Hernández's quote here is likely taken from the documentary interview.

19. Founded in 1943, the Confederación Nacional de Organizaciones Populares (National Confederation of Popular Organizations) is a collective institution of the PRI that aims to represent the middle and lower classes within the party. This is differentiated from the worker and peasant sections of the party structure.

20. "Elisa o el imperativo moral," *Mujeres y poder*, 174.

21. CREA, the Consejo Nacional de Recursos para la Atención de la Juventud

(National Council on Resources for Attention to Youth), was transformed from the Injuve—Instituto Nacional de la Juventud Mexicana (National Institute of Mexican Youth) by President López Portillo in 1976. Hernández became director of Injuve the year it was rebranded as CREA.

22. "La manzana prohibida," *Mujeres y poder*, 247.

CHAPTER 16

Bones in the Desert

Listening through the Eyes of Dead Women

2003

> No one ever told me that grief felt
> so like fear.
>
> **C. S. Lewis, *A Grief Observed***

IN THE FACE OF CRIME: ACQUITTAL

Boastful and violent misogyny has been the most enduring of feudal regimes. Violence isolates, dehumanizes, impedes the development of civilization; it declares a military siege on personal liberties; it physically and emotionally mutilates and elevates fear to unassailable heights; it is, in essence, the perfect dystopia. The weight of patriarchy and all the acquiescence that accompanies it are tantamount to the violence exerted on women by denying them democracy; and the fact that governments, laws, and social norms either don't recognize this, or only ambivalently admit it, is an unequivocal sign of backwardness.

The limits on women's freedoms, and for that matter men's, although with a very different emphasis and reach, is the illegal monopoly on violence. Thus, rape, machismo's *ius primae noctis* was considered "natural" by the "reasoning" that went along with the "right of the first night."[1] "Deep down, what these broads really want is to be raped," has been the enduring dogma of prosecutors at the Public Ministry, police officers, and judges who have until recently held women responsible for the crimes against them, just like the Cardinal of Guadalajara, Juan Sandoval Íñigo, did in 2000 by blaming rape on the women, who in his opinion, go out dressed provocatively, swaying their hips. He stopped just short of saying, "If you don't want anything to happen to you, leave your body at home."

Year after year, global statistics of intra-family violence persist, and the attacks against women who are beaten, tortured, mutilated, strangled, stabbed, asphyxiated, or dismembered in hotel rooms, alleys, and empty lots are unending. This legacy of horror runs through the twentieth century but, nevertheless, hasn't prepared us for the most atrocious homicidal explosion that has ever been known that has been unleashed against young women in Ciudad Juárez since 1993.

THE MAIN PLAYERS IN BONES IN THE DESERT

- From 1993 to 2002, 297 women were murdered in Ciudad Juárez, and those responsible were guaranteed impunity.
- The broken and deceitful legal process attributes all of the multiplying deaths to only one or two supposed responsible parties.
- The governors of Chihuahua see themselves "outside of the conflict" (because politicians only have time for inaugural events and trips to the capital), and serve only to offer platitudes on justice: "We will proceed to the full extent of the law."
- The prosecutors from Chihuahua are (ritually) outraged by the media because they "distort the news and don't report on the progress of the investigation," also hindering the rigorous investigation (which is almost nonexistent).
- The special prosecutor's office for criminal activity distinguishes itself by casting moral judgments on the dead and disappeared women.
- There is no lack of unique characters, such as the Egyptian man accused of several murders who stubbornly declares his innocence while becoming mentally unhinged due to his years in jail.
- The mothers and sisters of the dead women continue to demand justice notwithstanding the threats and mistreatments by the authorities.
- The police chiefs responsible for the investigations are frequently complicit with the drug cartels.
- Ciudad Juárez acts as an open cemetery and battlefield where disputes between the drug cartels are settled.
- The NGOs dedicated to this matter, and the feminist groups that partner with them, remain resolute in their purpose despite the scarcity of resources.
- There are writers, reporters, and videographers adamant about presenting a panoramic overview. For example: Lourdes Portillo and Sergio Gonzalez Rodríguez.[2]

NO RESISTANCE, NO PUNISHMENT

Sergio González Rodríguez's work *Huesos en el Desierto* is an intelligent and courageous approach to this phenomenon. Very well organized, it is an in-depth analysis of the links between the judiciary and organized crime, it is a journey through the devastating consequences of the enforcement of justice, and it is the charting of an endless nightmare. Ultimately, the analysis of these crimes develops between two poles, the unpunished and the defenseless; and impunity, that guarantee of going unpunished, which is the greatest rational incentive for crime, challenges the already powerful national—and to a great extent international—grievance.

I'll keep this short: in this case, the Panista or Priísta administrators have not failed, and this is because they haven't seriously tried to do anything. Their strategy doesn't vary, it entails very clumsy investigations, concealment and destruction of evidence, a moralistic reprimand of the dead bodies ("they had it coming"), a triumphalist showcasing (usually false) of solved cases, and regularly inventing the number of guilty parties. Convinced of their technique—may forgetfulness redeem the record—the authorities yearn for a biblical tone in which the penalty for sin (casual sex, the female condition) is death, and whoever doesn't agree with the official explanation either suffers the consequences or is consumed by frustration.

What is behind the killings in Ciudad Juárez? Are we talking about a single group or an epidemic of serial killers? Is the urge to kill contagious? González Rodríguez chooses adjectival austerity and an unembellished storyline, and by combining extensive information with restrained interpretations, the feelings of indignation and grief in the reader are removed from all sensationalism. The failings of the police and the special prosecutors' office are astonishing, the fear among women workers of the *maquila*, and among other women in the city and their families, is troubling.[3] As if backlit, one can discern panic, the cancelation of a community's freedom of movement, and the pulse of a tradition of physical abuse, possession of weapons, and criminal misogyny.

Why has the government's action, and that of society in general, been so slow and so sadly insufficient in the case of the killings in Ciudad Juárez? On this matter, I present my hypotheses, convinced by the obvious: this hunting of vulnerable young women is an Acteal by accumulation.[4]

THE LIFEBLOOD OF THE CRIMES

A ———

Urban conditions. As the investigator Alfredo Limas Hernández points out, the maquiladora industry "assembles" Ciudad Juárez—an authentic reserve and factory of humankind. Insecurity is exacerbated by the appropriation of private property for public space, and a lack of surveillance in the labyrinth of empty lots, dust, poorly or dimly lit streets, and lack of efficient public transportation, and in the presence of cabarets, bars, and transient hotels that give poverty a bad name. The scenes of the crimes have already been staged.

B ———

The border setting of Ciudad Juárez permeates the collective imaginary with fixed images of lawlessness. Throughout the twentieth century, and this is obvious, crimes occur at a much lesser rate on the northern border than in Mexico City, but prejudice—the border is a lawless land—adds to the insecurity. With or without any evidence, and whether or not they cross the border, there's a conviction in the eternally provisional status of these communities, and film and television mentality recasts the border zones into emporiums of, if not evil, at least criminal fatalism. This primordial fantasy, despicable in itself, goes hand in hand with misogynous oppression.

C ———

It's impossible to accurately pin down the role of drug trafficking and its cartels in this collective tragedy, but in addition to the specific actions of the narcos, the killings are influenced to a great degree by what also drives drug trafficking: the negligible value placed on human life.[5] It's easy to die a violent death, and it's even easier to kill; the worshipping of weapons and armament technology ranges from the destruction of the species (the savage stupidity of hunting) to people actually becoming targets themselves. There are countless people steeped in the tactics of drug trafficking. These are the basic premises: "If they're going to kill me tomorrow, let me kill many today. / If I have weapons, I should use them."[6] The showcasing of weapons, the ease with which hand guns, or AK-47s, or whatever they need, are obtained necessarily leads to killing.[7]

There was already a healthy tradition of barbarism, what was missing was its technological renovation.

D———

Abstractions tend to make criminal activity banal. One killing is already an awful event, but the hundreds of female victims take on ghostly dimensions

from the perspective of the federal authorities (the local and regional authorities, as González Rodríguez well explains, obey another logic altogether). It
is well known that the statistics of mass society tend to downplay the magnitude of any event. Six billion of the planet's inhabitants tend to minimize
everything. It is not, as the hypocritical traditionalists insist, a relativizing
of values as taught through secular education, which is, on the contrary, the
first line of defense against barbarism. Rather, ethical relativism, already
present in the much-idealized and disdainful traditions of human life, is
fomented by the laws of savage capitalism and demography. In order to fully
grasp a tragedy, a human dimension is essential, and therefore epitaphs of
generalization become the rule: "the Perredistas assassinated during the
presidency of Salinas de Gortari," or "the dead women of Juárez" undermine
the link between people and the tragedies—the victims, their hopes, their
trajectories, and their families all disappear.[8] It is always necessary to focus
on the victims, which is, for example, what Lourdes Portillo's documentary
and González Rodríguez's book do.

E ———————

At first, the news media reported the crimes in their "nota roja" sections,
not on the front page where they belonged, and in so doing, they blamed
the victim, who by now was unable to defend her good name, and quite
likely was headed to a mass grave.[9] The steadfast denouncements made by
the NGOs, videographers, and independent writers and journalists pushed
back against the victim-blaming.

F ———————

For González Rodríguez, the key to understanding the "incompetence" can
be traced to the alliance between the governing bodies, the judiciary, the
police, entrepreneurs, and landowners in Ciudad Juárez and El Paso, Texas.
This alliance (not truly) in the shadows begins with the dispossession of
communal lands, with frauds that go unpunished, and with the intimidation tactics and payoffs of drug trafficking that highlight the corruptibility of
judges, police officers (at all ranks), prosecutors, high-level officials, entrepreneurs, merchants, the military, and the clergy. The inescapable destiny
of the drug traffickers includes jail or death after atrocious tortures, but this
doesn't dissuade them because each one considers himself an exception, and
each one believes himself protected by the overall economic power of the
cartel. By demonstrating the vulnerability of the judiciary, the news spreads

prodigiously: crime becomes a taxable activity, and money and networks of interest exonerate the act in advance.

In the case of the dead women of Juárez, beyond individual psychopathy, an organic phenomenon can be observed: impunity is the mother of psychopathic behavior, and the judiciary, anxious to not investigate (for different reasons, none of them admissible) accelerates the avalanche of serial killers.

SEXISM PLUS CLASSISM

The disappeared women and those found in the brush are disproportionately workers in the *maquila*, from families with limited resources. They're barely present in electoral platforms, they're classified as "easily manipulated," and if they're single mothers, they're judged and labeled as "sinful" by the clergy and the Right. How often in their reprimands do the clergy and the Right deny the status of family to those headed by unwed or separated mothers? So, what's happening in Ciudad Juárez obliges us to make women living in poverty visible, and pay them their due respect.

The hate crimes: "I killed her because she had it coming, and she so clearly had it coming that she's dead."

Why have the murders in Ciudad Juárez not been described as "hate crimes," when in the US recognition of hate crimes lead President Clinton to create a specific federal commission in response to the homophobic killings of Matthew Shepard and Brandon Teena?[10]

Hate crimes are directed against a person and what that person symbolizes, represents, and embodies, and in that sense, they're acts of rage against the entire group. The perpetrator has no previous knowledge of the victim, and by wiping her off the face of the earth, he feels possessed of an unlimited power to destroy what he sees as evil (in this homicidal vocabulary, "evil" is the detested behavior and the physical and social vulnerability of the victim). The most known hate crimes are those directed at gay men, and this historic wrong claims dozens of victims each year in Mexico. But nothing surpasses the numbers and persistence of murders of lone women, especially young ones. They're killed because they can't protect themselves, and because their death—which gives men orgasmic pleasure and the audible joy of listening to a woman's dying breath—usually goes unnoticed. (The vast majority of hate crimes remain unsolved.)

The murderers not only feel superior to the fragile beings who are unable to fight off the attack, they also make a mockery of the laws and the society that half-heartedly or pointlessly upholds them. *Strictu senso*, the crimes in Ciudad Juárez are hate crimes because the killers are driven by that ultimate pleasure, which is the power over life and death. The most sordid and degrading aspects of machismo are deposited in women whose principle culpability is their condition as historical victims. That's how reiterative the process is: from the point of view of the murderer, the victims are naturally and constitutionally disposable beings. Hate is the social construction that again and again targets those who can't escape its effects.

"AGAINST OBLIVION, DESTINY WILL PREVAIL"

Each of these murders of women previously unknown to their killers are driven by opportunity and impulsive desire, but the basic facts of the story are always the same: the defenselessness of the murdered women, their family's grief, followed by the demand for justice by varying organizations. González Rodríguez describes the plot from the lower rungs of society as well as from the pinnacles of power, examining diverse trajectories. The conclusion seems inevitable: the bloody serial killings of Ciudad Juárez are affairs of State, because they are empowered by impunity, that great bastion of governments.

Huesos en el desierto is not only great reporting and an act of critical courage, it is also one of the best panoramic depictions of unfettered power that I know. The closing is very eloquent:

> For that reason, I told myself, remember. You are already a part of the dead men and women. You bow before them. Remember, yes. For now, just remember, although in these times it might seem excessive and even inappropriate to remember. Let others know what you remember. So they can read what's written down in red ink in order to understand what's printed in black.
> Of this I'm sure: against oblivion, destiny will prevail. Or memory. In the end, each person's life is a mystery insofar as knowing what will live on after us.[11]

A society paralyzed by killings, that doesn't recognize the murdered women in Ciudad Juárez as their own, is also itself, definitively, a sacrificial victim. Focusing the legal, political, social, and ethical energy of a nation and its institutions on elucidating this phenomenon must be a matter of social justice and reconstruction. Violence is supported in great part by the sporadic and nominal protests that don't expect any real consequences. This, as Sergio González Rodríguez demonstrates, cannot and should not be happening anymore.

NOTES

1. Title. The book by Sergio González Rodríguez (1950–2017), *Huesos en el desierto* (Mexico City: Anagrama, 2002), is about the femicides in Ciudad Juarez from

the 1990s to the 2000s. Following the publication of the book, González Rodríguez was kidnapped, beaten, and warned by assailants that he was being closely watched. González Rodríguez documented the Juárez crimes in a "synthysized" version written specifically for Semiotext(e)'s Intervention Series. This was the first book of his to appear in English translation: *The Femicide Machine*, trans. Michael Parker-Stainback (Cambridge, MA: MIT Press, 2012).

2. In Medieval Europe, this is a supposed legal right that gave feudal lords the prerogative to have sexual relations with subordinate women, and practiced in particular on the wedding nights of women being married to subordinate men. Allegedly, this *derecho de pernada*, as it was called in Spanish, was still practiced in early twentieth-century Mexico.

3. *Señorita extraviada* (2001) is an award-winning documentary by internationally known writer, producer, and director Lourdes Portillo that tells the story of the more than 350 femicides that took place in Ciudad Juárez. As of the first screening, the crimes had not yet been resolved, thus the film served as a critique of an on-going misogyny and machista culture.

4. *Maquilas* or *maquiladoras* are foreign-owned factories in Mexico using cheap labor to assemble products for export.

5. Acteal is a small village in the state of Chiapas where forty-five Indigenous people (Tzotziles), members of Las Abejas, a pacifist group sympathetic to the Zapatista movement, were massacred by the Máscara Roja, a right-wing paramilitary group while attending a Catholic event on December 22, 1997. In September 2020, the government of Mexico finally accepted responsibility for the massacre.

6. *Narcos* has become a popularized term in English and Spanish for those who illegally traffic narcotic drugs.

7. This Revolutionary refrain is reiterated throughout this book by Monsiváis with variations to draw attention to the continued Mexican machismo that evolves over time. "Si me han de matar mañana, que me maten de una vez" (If they're going to kill me tomorrow, let them kill me now) is the closing lyric from "La Valentina."

8. In Mexican slang AK-47s are called *cuernos de chivo* (the phrase used by Monsiváis), literally "goat's horn," in reference to the curved ammunition clip of the weapon.

9. Monsiváis is underscoring the ways that media portray the dead as nameless and numberless. A Perredista is a member of the Partido de la Revolución Democrática (PRD, Party of the Democratic Revolution), which was historically the party of Leftist opposition to the right-leaning PAN and PRI. Carlos Salinas de Gortari's presidency from 1988 to 1994 is seen as continuing the neoliberal free trade economic policies of his predecessor Miguel de la Madrid.

10. The *nota roja*, literally "red news," differs from yellow journalism in that it focuses almost exclusively on bloody stories of physical violence and salacious crimes.

11. Matthew Shepard (1976–1998) was a gay American student at the University of Wyoming who was brutally murdered. Brandon Teena (1972–1993), an American

transmasculine person, was raped and murdered in Humbolt, Nebraska. Also murdered with Teena were Phillip DeVine and Lisa Lambert. After increased lobbying for hate crime legislation, the Matthew Shepard and James Byrd Jr. Hate Crime Prevention Act of 2009 was passed.

12. *Huesos en el desierto*, 172. Our translation.

CHAPTER 17

The Saintly, Long-Suffering Mother

The One Who Loved Mexican Cinema before She Ever Saw It

2004

From the very beginning, as a strategy to expand and retain its public, the film industry—perhaps not in these terms—has attempted to be a larger-than-life mirror for its spectators, reflecting their beliefs and their obstinacy, cataloguing their romantic sentiments, rituals, myths, prejudices, tastes, and attitudes toward festivities and death, and locating Mexicanness, etc. If cinema was and is the domain of the masses *par excellence*, the industry (producers, directors, writers, actors, musicians, composers, set designers) is centrally concerned with recreating, reflecting, adulating, or criticizing, with discretion, its public and the culture from which it derives, and—in ways that were perceived with opening-night enthusiasm—the idea that film enriches, rectifies, and refines. Mexican popular culture—both urban and rural—drastically transforms itself, becoming homogenized over the course of the twentieth century, thanks, in good measure, to the influence of film, radio, the recording industry, and television. This plays out in the daily practices of the community, in the inventory of rites and predilections, in the methods of resistance to consolidated powers, in the Olympus of beloved voices and characters, in the folklorization of the realities of class, race, gender, or simply in what is fashionable and transcends, in a great number of people for an indefinable amount of time in their speech, their clothing, the language for their soul's intense moments, and their treasure-trove of behaviors.

In the early decades of the twentieth century, what is popular is primarily rural and provincial, religiously framed, with an in-depth interrogation of patriarchal norms. It's a long road to what is now definable as urban culture, secularized by technology and the culture of the masses, and with sectors of opposition contesting political and familial authoritarianism accentuated by the rate of growth of cities. At first, the film industry focused on earlier images of its public, selected by deterministic notions of taste that correspond to social origins. "There's no way a poor person could enjoy the opera." The audience is catered to, praised for its morbid fascination with melodrama, encouraged in its prejudices (this tactic fails for multiple reasons), and the changes that are witnessed are sparked by the very dynamics of cinema, whose development requires its public to adjust. In this industry, 95 percent of the time everything is popular culture, and more specifically, it's all about the sentimental, religious, musical, literary, and political patrimony of families.

Inevitably, Mexican cinema is preceded by its primary source: the US film industry, or, to name it by its emblematic site, Hollywood. From there we adapt narrative styles, genres, techniques, and ways of arousing audiences: sentimental blackmail, suspense, music that foreshadows what is to come by intensifying the sense of good feelings or bad omens. And above all, we take from Hollywood the unattainable (and also not) model of the "star system," the idea of the screen as the arena of an Olympus where the magnificence of faces is the most alluring message (the gaze frozen in a close-up modernizes the feeling of prayer). But at the end of the day, our national cinema is attempting to strengthen itself by commercial means, and that demands concessions to the local, and therefore the Mexican film industry strays from Hollywood in two principal ways: the melodramatic formulas, and the free rein given to excess. Without critical reflection, it's decided that only an overflow of lachrymosity and humorous, nationalistic indignation will produce a large local public. Hollywood is the supreme inspiration, but it does not address the sociological, linguistic, nor habitual aspects that make up the specifics of Mexican cinema.

ON MELODRAMA AS AN EXODUS TO THAT PROMISED LAND, CRYING IN COMPANY

The (restricted) variety of themes, characters, and situations is circumscribed by one certainty. The public is exactly as it is portrayed by the industry's expectations, and only in this way can it become a public. Come hither, mothers bathed in tears and self-pity, prostitutes who see themselves redeemed by agony, priests who guide lives as if directing traffic, strict fathers who act as ambassadors of God during dinnertime, cops wholesome as white bread, gangsters who die by the sword because censorship demands their tragic death, families who fall apart because no one told them about the separation of body and soul soon enough, handsome romantic leads and comic actors whose charm relies on their similarity to the spectators, *rumberas* who arouse the entire cabaret with their lascivious outbursts, haughty *charros* and the humble foremen of the Rancho Grande, and revolutionaries who dig their own graves without worrying about measuring.[1]

Accidentally satirical, funny and sentimental by design, the film repertoire that dominated between 1932 and 1955, the era of unbridled industrial growth, marks the positive and negative attributes of the communities, both real and mythical.[2] In this version of the facts, popular culture in Mexico—at that time, still a family tradition—is generous, prejudiced, more emotional than reflective, outwardly and inwardly racist, sanctimonious while satirical of religious hypocrisy, more liberal than it claims to be, genuflective before the Lord-Owner and the Lord-Boss, as rebellious as it can possibly be, close-knit (although the distribution of blessings is unequal), and faithful to its memorized jokes while aware of the pleasures of replaying them in family conversations and favorite comic acts.

"DON'T LOOK AT ME THAT WAY, MAMA, 'CAUSE I'LL THINK YOU'RE GOING TO HEAVEN ANGRY"

Machista attitudes are part and parcel of popular culture in the first half of the twentieth century in Latin America. In the early decades of sound cinema, "Woman," with a capital W, is both archetype and stereotype; from her womb springs the entire race; from the disdain professed about her, hierarchies of treatment are born; and her children's defects derive from her pain or her pleasures. And this flood of prejudices brings to mind the phrase by Roland Barthes: "the Ideological would actually be the image-repertoire of a period of history, the Cinema of a society."[3] In general, actresses interpreted subordinate personalities that, if they had known of it, would approve of John Berger's description in his novel *G.*

A woman's presence was the result of herself being split into two, and of her energy being inturned. A woman was always accompanied—except when quite alone—by her own image of herself. Whilst she was walking across a room or whilst she was weeping at the death of her father, she could not avoid envisaging herself walking or weeping. From earliest childhood she had been taught and persuaded to survey herself continually. And so she came to consider the surveyor and the surveyed within her as the two constituent yet always distinct elements of her identity as a woman. [...] This subjunctive world of the woman, this realm of her presence, guaranteed that no action undertaken within it could ever possess full integrity; in each action there was an ambiguity which corresponded to an ambiguity in the self, divided between surveyor and surveyed.[4]

The ideal and practically only space to represent women is in the melodrama, a scapegoating genre that defends the family by reminding it of the dangers of secularism: adultery, children's rebellion, young women who "fall" prey to seduction or to pay, the transformation of customs that buries tradition in the closet or pushes it to the limits of prayer and revenge. This is one order of things; in another, cinema exalts women with a previously inconceivable emphasis. It extracts them from the temples and ushers them into close-ups, where the experience of beauty is heightened, and the camera serves gaits and gestures (all the feminine ideology necessary). Enslaved and revered, the heroines shine bright. Cinema mistreats and minimizes, it exalts the mirror of virtues and evils that belong only to the dispossessed gender.

The film industry in Mexico during the so-called Golden Age imitates Hollywood as much as possible: in genres, styles, and formats. It imitates it in every way except in the representation of women. In those years, in only a handful of exceptions, are we able to register the female perspective, and women are regarded with contempt or affection or sexual desire, and whether the spectators—men or women—know it or not, women see themselves as part of the scenery, as objects resistant to individualization. Mexican cinema doesn't produce independent characters like those revered in the Hollywood of that time, the likes of Bette Davis, Katherine Hepburn, Rosalind Russell, Joan Crawford, Jean Arthur, the first modern women in the new, irrefutable reality of the screen. And without being modern in the least, Dolores del Río and María Félix become the exceptions due to their imperious nature of goddesses of the silver screen in Mexico, who to the degree that the stories and dialogues permitted, displayed the ambiguity of Greta Garbo and Marlene Dietrich, and thus were already, formally, the creators of individuality.[5]

Dolores del Río, gorgeous and ethereal, is the victim at the zenith, bedazzling, forced, in vain, to be humiliated. In her Mexican filmography, in *Flor silvestre* (Wildflower), *María Candelaria*, *Bugambilia* (Bougainvillea), *Las abandonadas* (The abandoned women), *La malquerida* (The unloved woman), *La otra* (The other woman), *La casa chica* (The mistress's house),

Deseada (The desired woman), *La selva de fuego* (The forest of fire), *La cucaracha* (The jalopy), Dolores lacks any social will, but not the imperiousness of her features. If the meaning of her existence lies in other hands, she is at all times the supreme form. And María Félix's character is disproportionately sustained by the play between person and representation, and by disrupting the norms of femininity, she erects an aura of power. In her, the emotions called for in the script (*Enamorada* is a good example[6]) are thwarted by her tyrannical tone, her voice that belittles the listener, her enslaving gestures, all sustained by beauty. María Félix's character begins its enduring heyday with *Doña Bárbara* (1945, dir. Fernando de Fuentes[7]) because it is there that she assumes the role of the tyrant. She is self-possessed because she has renounced conventional femininity. And the impact is such that the spectators only remember Doña Bárbara, the mistress of the plains, and the civilizing message fades out.

In *La mujer del puerto* (1932, dir. Arcady Boytler), Andrea Palma undergoes "plastic" surgery that turns her into a tropical Marlene Dietrich, with an ambiguity dependent wholly on her distant attitude, her glamour, and notions of sin that are now only a theological window dressing.[8] But the public only slowly accepts women with unpredictable reactions, and it still demands heroines of proclaimed virtues who are fragile, virtuous, joyful in their tears, and despondent because resisting seduction goes against the feminine spirit. Remember the melodramatic and comedic leads, with their shy diction, their beauty immediately undone by their inexpressive voices, their monochromatic characters: Esther Fernández, Gloria Marín, Columba Dominguez, Amanda Ledesma, Marina Tamayo, María Elena Marqués, Amanda del Llano, María Luisa Zea, Irasema Dillian, Miroslava, Elsa Aguirre. Blanca Estela Pavón, Marga López, Rosita Quintana, Lilia Prado, Leticia Palma and Silvia Pinal are partial exceptions. Actresses, who aren't really actresses, are always asked to embody the anachronistic. If film is modernity, Mexican heroines are premodernity, or that which from its own immobility opposes modernity. Therefore, they inhabit the anachronistic space *par excellence*: sentimental blackmail, the safety net of defenselessness.

Blanca Estela Pavón—and here I'm giving a mythological example, "La Chorreada" from *Nosotros los pobres* and *Ustedes los ricos*—the most iconic Saintly Bride, is loyal, solicitous, and eternally faithful despite constant humiliations.[9] Every virtue is hers except that of an individuated psychology and self-possession: she cannot protest, she lacks initiative, she goes along with her mother's will, and only makes her presence noticed in a way that confuses servility with helpfulness. Seeing her misfortune, which maternity both diminishes and accentuates, female spectators approve of her behavior because it responds to tradition, she abides by familiar habits, and in a way, justifies her own subjugation. The sentimental blackmail grows incrementally with the diminishment of sensual displays. The heartbroken mothers make an anchor of femininity, a chain of crucifixions, obedience to the Lord of the House, or the Lord of the Universe ("If you took him from me, there must be a reason, my Lord"). And the industry produces heroic exploits, stereotypical exaggerations, and involuntary mockery of the unreal. That's who Dalia Íñiguez portrays, the mother who never complains of any mistreatment in Ismael Rodríguez's *La oveja negra* (The black sheep), a parody of the sublime parody that is Sara García.[10] At another level, Mexican cinema is increasing its areas of exceptionality by giving a few actresses their own psychology, as long as they gleefully admit their grotesqueness. Thus, for example, the duo of drunks or lumpen ladies, "La Guayaba" and "La Tostada," Amelia Wilhelmy and Delia Magaña in *Nosotros los pobres* and *Ustedes los ricos*, or comic actresses along the lines of Vitola, whose raison d'être was the pleasure of watching them be offended, or the film extras that appear so that at the mere sight of them, the comedian dies of fright.[11] Much later, in the case of "La India María," her starting point is racist humor and brief nullification.[12] "La India María" is not a product of the observation of migrations and of the Mazahua tribe, rather it comes from the tradition of theatrical follies in which the cheap laugh is achieved by imitating the arduous preoccupation with language that many Indigenous people display, and also where the "inditos" (little Indians) make fun of those who observe them with paternalism.[13]

THE STEREOTYPE AS A VARIETY OF OPTIONS

An analysis of the role of stereotypes in film—and cultural studies profligately dedicates essays and books to this topic—is insisted upon. Frequently, these works are quite exhaustive but they tend to make affirmations that are not really demonstrable: characters fulfill functions of a predetermined master plan. The opposite is actually true: in the decade of the 1930s, the film industry in Mexico, desperate to improvise a "national" world and to reproduce Hollywood movies as much as possible, improvises because it has no other option but to pillage the archive of theater and Vaudeville-style follies, the adulterous melodramas, and the sketches of picturesque double entendres. The best of this era are the actresses and actors that developed a new gestural language that the spectators then adopt. In an unspoken agreement, film humor and desperate speech are imposed, and society emerges glued to the grand mirror in which their customs are magnified to the point of becoming forced pleasures, where the images are reworked as premonitions or memories of an inescapable destiny (if you're lucky) at the personal and collective level. Stereotypes don't confirm what already exists, but the excessive emotions on screen infuse reality with a sense of community of faces, bodies, movements, and expressions. The clientele observes their exasperations and defeats, and abides almost as if given orders. They are not asked to or forced to be like the figures on screen; they're made to feel indebted to the social visibility that is quickly learned on the film horizon.

Before film, there are tons of women who are solicitous, self-sacrificing, silent, challenging, and marginal, but there are no canonical ways of interpreting them. That's why, if as Marx affirms in *The German Ideology*, the division of labor only becomes inevitably instituted once the distinction between physical and intellectual labor appears, then, for a long period of time, the distinction between what was "orthodox" and "unorthodox" with regard to filmic morals is derived, not so much from the scripts and dialogues, but rather from the contrasts between theatrical behavior and the uninhibited use of the body by those who arrived at film on their own, with no diploma from the school of innumerable stagings of dreadful adulteries and families who sacrifice themselves so as to not fall apart.[14] And among other novelties that freely permeate film, you can find the melodramas of "bad women" who, despite censorship, affirm their "audacity" and propose a different "feminine condition." On the other hand, if a respectable woman doesn't act like a statue, she's instantly open to suspicion.

Before sound cinema women are, strictly speaking, more shadows of a stereotype than actual stereotypes, society ladies (lacking their own highlights) or, on the opposite end of the spectrum, photos, drawings, caricatures, and oil paintings where marginalized creatures are announced or described by their grotesqueness. The prostitute (the recumbent) (the hetaera) (the whore) tends to be infamy painted like an artist's test canvas, used to explain men's sexual appetite in contrast to the ideal and real virginity of the inhabitants of "Decent Houses."[15] But all together, it is unknown what women are visually and auditorily made of, what faithful spouses are like, how flirts cross a dance hall, how young women from good homes try to orient themselves, and how the stages of motherhood are established, from the joys of pregnancy to the sculptural poses of matrons. Knowing that there are no alternatives to its designs, Mexican cinema establishes a dictatorship of gestures and words where maternity is the midwife of melodrama.

In almost unfathomable films (in too many cases, no one learns by failure), in these over-the-top melodramas that are rewarded by the discovery of emblematic creatures in comedies where—if not for the mediating inventiveness of the comedians—the audience would simply cry; "orthodoxy" loses ground and "unorthodoxy" earns spectators. And the beatification (the *nihil obstat*[16]) of film begins with the cult to the mother:

> If you have a mother yet,
> give thanks to the Lord who loves you greatly
> for it's not all mortals that can get
> a joy so great, pleasure so saintly[17]

"WELL, I GUESS BECAUSE NO ONE HAS EVER LOOKED AT ME THAT WAY AGAIN"

For nonhistorians, reality prior to film's advent is entirely unknown.

What were mothers like before cameras focused on them? We know a little bit about middle-class readers: they read to live, they expressed the tenor of secondary emotions, and they practiced their responses to dramatic situations all day long; they fully knew their children's innocence and pretended to ignore their malicious sides, they were overprotective and allowed mistreatments as the price they paid for domesticity. By codifying them, the film industry sets aside women's ingeniousness, their courage, and their capacity for work, and transforms their daily heroism into a recipe for box-office success. *It's not enough to be a mother*, is the message, *you also have to be hot*. Despite the injustice, women accept these totally false representations and they memorize the expressions of pain that move mountains to the degree of making them verbal institutions that slip into the spheres of conversations, confessions, scolding, advice, and despair.

In *Los olvidados* (1950) Luis Buñuel and Luis Alcoriza's script takes up that tradition, respecting it while offering it in a different, implacable light.[18] Pedro (Alfonso Mejía) has a nightmare. There, looking for a hen that fell from the roof, he runs into Julián (recently murdered by El Jaibo), who is cracking up laughing with his face bathed in blood. Marta (Stella Inda), Pedro's mother, interrogates him:

Marta: Hey, m'ijo, you're a good boy. Why did you do it?
Pedro: I didn't do anything, it was El Jaibo, I just watched. I want to stay with
  you forever, ma, but you don't love me.
Marta: It's just that I'm tired, look at these hands from so much washing.
Pedro: Why don't you ever kiss me? Mama, I swear I'm gonna behave now,
  I'll find work and you can rest.
Marta: Yes, m'ijito.
Pedro: Mama, why didn't you serve me meat the other night?

And in another scene, prior to a sexual encounter, there's the sacralizing and desacralizing dialogue between Marta and El Jaibo (Roberto Cobo):[19]

Jaibo: It must be so nice to have your mom. I see you, and I'm jealous of Pedro . . . I don't even know my name, imagine that. My father, I never knew who he was. My mama, I think she died when I was a little squirt.

Marta: And you don't remember her?

Jaibo: Well, honestly, no. Just once, a long time ago, a long long time . . . they say I would have . . . like, these really strong seizures. One time, once my vision came back, I saw a woman's face. Right up close, she looked at me sweetly and sort of pained, and she was crying, so I think that was my mama.

Marta: How do you remember?

Jaibo: Well, I guess because no one has ever looked at me that way again.

SARA GARCÍA: AGELESS MOTHERHOOD

Today, still, thanks to television, Sara García is an all-encompassing Mother and Grandmother figure, emotionally manipulative, exorbitant, and, being mindful of this particular case, monumental.[20] A brief review of her trajectory: She's born in 1895 in Orizaba, Veracruz, to Spanish parents; orphaned at a very young age, she's sent to boarding school at the Colegio de la Paz Vizcaínas (where she will later teach).[21] In 1917, she has her debut in silent films that are now vanished (*En defensa propia* [In self defense], *Alma de sacrificio* [Sacrificing soul], *La soñadora* [The dreamer][22]) and in the theater, with plays whose titles encapsulate both the plot and the ending (*Pastor y borrego* [Shepherd and sheep], *Las sufragistas* [The suffragettes], *La princesa está triste* [The princess is sad]). Melodrama is her lifeblood, and, again, the titles of her films are a whole ideological and literary project: *El pulpo humano* (The human octopus) and *La sangre manda* (Blood rules), from 1933; *Así es la mujer* (That's a woman for you), *Las mujeres mandan* (Women rule), and *Malditas sean las mujeres* (Women be damned), from 1936; *No basta ser madre* (It's not enough to be a mother), from 1937; *Calumnia* (Slander) and *Papacito lindo* (Handsome papa), from 1939; *Mi madrecita* (My mama), *Ahí está el detalle* (That's the catch), and *Al son de la marimba* (To the sway of the marimba), from 1940; *Cuando los hijos se van* (When children leave home), and *La gallina clueca* (The broody hen), from 1941; *Regalo de reyes* (A gift from the three kings), *La abuelita* (The grandma), *Historia de un gran amor* (The story of a great love), and *El baisano Jalil* (Jalil, the countryman), from 1942; *Resurrección* (Resurrection) and *No matarás* (Thou shalt not kill), from 1943; *Mis hijos* (My children) and *El secreto de*

la solterona (The old maid's secret), from 1944; *Mamá Inés* (Mama Ines),
from 1945; *El ropavejero* (The rag and bone man), *Los tres García* (The three
Garcías), and *Vuelven los García* (Return of the Garcías), from 1946; *Mi
madre adorada* (My darling mother), *Dueña y señora* (Lady and mistress),
and *La familia Pérez* (The Pérez family), from 1948; *Eterna agonía* (Eternal agony), from 1949; *Azahares para tu boda* (Orange blossoms for your
wedding) and *Doña Clarines* (Doña Bugles), from 1950.[23]

Of course I haven't included all her films, rather only those whose title
is a declaration of principles. For obvious reasons, the film that establishes
Sara García's tremendously long reign (that continues to this day) is *No
basta ser madre*, directed by Ramón Peón. The story does nothing more
than show how the biological mother fails by not becoming the spiritual
mother, the multifaceted mother. But the plot is barely the beginning of the
film's strength, which lies in crucifixions of the countenance and shaken
voices.

From *No basta ser madre* on, Doña Sara has essentially resolved her
career (her luck interpreting other roles owes to the wooing of the ideal of
the Sweet Little Old Lady).[24] In 1940, in order to achieve recognition for
her abilities in the theater, Sara García sacrifices herself:

> What's more, I had my teeth removed, more of an accident than an incident
> that I had in a theatrical performance of an unimportant play. Since they
> had given me an unimportant part, that of a little old lady that appears on
> stage for only a few minutes, I decided to show them all that I deserved a
> more important role. I had my teeth pulled, fourteen in one fell swoop! And
> when I came on stage with my mouth all shriveled, "I charted chalking like
> chis," "so naturally." The audience and even my castmates started cracking
> up, 'cause they didn't expect such audacity on my part.[25]

In *Ahí está el detalle* (1940, dir. Juan Bustillo Oro), Doña Sara threatens,
denounces, and courts Cantinflas, and demands that he recognize a dozen
children (not his own) and that he marry her.[26] At that point, at the age
of forty-five, Sara García, the matron *par excellence*, has been completely
desexualized. Her body is an institution, the plumpness of housewives,
which is also a territorial invasion. Sara García: the face full of love and
comprehension, the lap of generations, the impetus of beneficial tears.
Everything is acting and so, in this logic, everything is reality, or better yet,
everything is the coming and going of feelings about that which is lived in
front of the cameras, and that which is barely lived. In 1940 her only daughter, Fernanda, dies of cholera. Her friend José Delgado recalls the situation:

People thought that Sara would make a big deal of her personal drama in real life. But she was solid, contained. She was miserable, really sad, but immovable, and she didn't bat an eyelash, enduring her terrible internal pain. Sometime later, a friend of hers said to her: "Hey, I admired you so much for keeping it together when you heard the news about Fernanda since I've seen you really make a dramatic scene on screen."

She responded: "I act in films, I have to give dimensions to the characters that I portray, because it's what the public expects from me. But in my private life, I'm the one managing my pain."[27]

Why is Sara García unmatchable as Mother and Grandmother? Because she establishes the feminine will under the pretext of a matriarchy, and because her acting can be broken into two tiers: the dissolution and resurrection arising from tears, and the desire to fuse in one character the Housewife and the Petty Tyrant. When Sara García isn't overdramatically afflicted by the fate of her offspring, when she isn't in dialogue with her creator ("Oh, my God, please care for that boy who is so irresponsible and wayward, deep down he's good, but save him from his disobedience"), she tries to behave like she did in *Los tres García* (1946, dir. Ismael Rodríguez), with a cloying severity that guides her children.[28]

She is neither the real mother nor the ideal mother, but rather the institution of motherhood itself. In *Cuando los hijos se van* and *Azahares para tu boda* Doña Sara is the head of a dynasty, the one that all families establish.[29] The breakdown of roles doesn't tend to vary: she is hardworking and submissive, she submits to her husband's plans, she defends her children, she understands that their failings are due to her own weakness (sweetness) of character, and she looks to religion for help and strength. "Ay, my sweet Virgin, care for them, don't abandon them!" For this Ineffable Mother (Protective Grandmother) prayer is life insurance, because in her appeal to God, Jesus Christ, the Virgin Mary, and the Saints, her character is tamed and she learns to converse, to reflect out loud, and to take note of her own thoughts. How can one know how much they're suffering if they don't talk to God?

Quite possibly the height of complexity (both true and false) for the Darling Grandma and Bossy Lady that is Sara García in *¡Vuelven los García!* (1946, dir. Ismael Rodríguez). There she reigns over her three grandsons (Pedro Infante,[30] Manuel Mendoza, and Abel Salazar); she smokes cigars, uses a cane, and hits them "pedagogically"; she is the Last Word. And her "sanction" is one of the Mother's Day hymns, "Mi cariñito" (My darling angel, by Manuel Esperón, with lyrics by Jesús Camacho):

An angel that God gave me to love,
An angel that loves me selflessly[31]

The town of San Luis de la Paz is besieged by a permanent duel between the Garcías and the last two surviving Lópezes. On the day of José Luis's (Abel Salazar) marriage to Lupita (Marga López), one of them, drunk with revenge, shoots and mortally wounds the grandmother. Her funeral is one fit for an angelic soul (*In contemplating her face, I see God*), and the lyrics highlight the mythology of a "purified, or chaste incest." *Heaven sent me an undeserved angel.* The favorite grandson, Pedro Infante, loves her fiercely. "But it's that with you, God polished you to a shine, and then broke the mold." So, when on the day of the burial they ask him to please stop drinking, he responds with loud, howling pain: "You didn't love her like I did," and when they implore him to bravely accept what cannot be changed, he answers: "Bravery . . . but, if she's gone, why bother?" *Long live my angel, that's here with me.* And in turn, the son or grandson in love with their *Cabecita Blanca* (White-Haired One) will serenade her, or he'll play an album, or see a movie again to revive or institutionalize the memory of his loved one. "I loved her so much I didn't realize she's still alive."

To be validated by motherhood is a natural fact; to theatricalize maternity is, in a great number of cases, equally inevitable, but the "maternalistic" operation in Mexican cinema abuses what is natural and inevitable in order to give more credence to the mythology that relies on disrupting the feminine psyche once she has engendered her first child, or even more drastically, her first daughter. In this sphere of maternity as renouncement of an independent mentality, Sara García, multitudinous mother and grandmother, is the infinite example. She's not a woman, nor a friend, nor a citizen, nor a professional, and not even a housewife: she is, simply and totally, the Mother, on a symbolic level with no corporeal structure, she of the vicarious existence, the one who only loses her institutional character if she longs for a life of her own. And the actress accepts this "renouncement of rights" without a fuss:

> *Cuando los hijos se van* (1941) is an immortal picture, whatever might be said against it. Film as we know it will end, and that movie will continue to exist because in every home, children leave to become priests and nuns, or to run off with their boyfriends and girlfriends, or to work outside of the country, or to get married, or whatnot.
>
> In fact, life itself is contained in the title *Cuando los hijos se van*. The audience comes to see it, and those whose children have left really feel it, they cry it out. Whoever still has children at home prepares them because tomorrow they too will leave.[32]

A good mother means an abandoned house . . . in these rules of the game, the consequences of children's departure affect fathers, but devastate mothers. In this zone of emotional determinism, mothers (already totally deperson-alized, joyful embodiments of the domestic) see in their children's departure, more than a patrimonial loss, the proof of their nonexistence. The umbilical cord belongs to the father, the mother finds consolation of the soul. Doña Sara overflows with anecdotes of her authoritarian and painful version of the exercise of maternity. Having just debuted *Cuando los hijos se van*, a man comes out to meet her at the door of a Cuernavaca hotel:

> "Doña Sarita, allow me to embrace you."
> "Absolutely, sir. What's your name?"
> "I'm the owner of Hotel Español and I've come to give you a hug. I saw *Cuando los hijos se van* the week before last. Now, look, Doña Sarita, it's been about two or three years since I left Spain, and I hadn't written to my mother until I watched the flick. I wrote to her and two days ago my mother answered me with a letter full of tears." And that's why I liked making movies about mothers.[33]

Is the story, then, that Alejandro Galindo tells, of a trip he took to Colombia, strange? According to don Alejandro, arriving in Bogotá, a group of busi-nessmen show up at his hotel and invite him to a dinner in his honor. He accepts, convinced of the irrefutable merits of his films. During the toast, they explain the reason: in one of his films, Galindo "killed" Sara García. "It was about time!" they shouted between applause.[34] That's also why, in a mostly failed parodic revenge, in *Mecánica nacional* (1971, dir. Luis Alcoriza), Doña Sara's corpse is promenaded.[35] Her own mythology depersonalized the actress once again, but the spectators' resentment came too late, expressed as filial ingratitude.

"WHY HAVE CHILDREN IF YOU'RE NOT GOING TO TREAT THEM LIKE ROYALTY?"

In 1935, Juan Orol films *Madre querida* (Beloved mother), the movie that would launch a career similar to that of Ed Wood in Hollywood. The story merits the honor of a retelling: the boy Juanito is anguished because with May tenth (Mother's Day) approaching, he doesn't have the money to get a nice present for his Dear Old Mum. The rich kid, Luisito, whose mother has died, gives Juanito fifty cents. Manuel, Luisito's father, confesses to the cam-era that he once fell madly in love with the Cuban singer Adela, but instead married another, and lost track of his beloved's whereabouts. On Mother's Day, Juanito brings flowers to the woman who brought him into the world, while Luisito is lighting a tower of fireworks that starts a raging fire. It goes without saying: the kid who goes to reform school isn't Luisito but rather Juanito, who he blames.

At some point in the film, the school director asks the children, "Who loves us more than anyone?" And the exuberant chorus responds: "Our mother, our mother, our mother!" Meanwhile, struggling with his guilty conscience, Luisito tells his father the truth. Manuel and Luisito visit Juanito's mother, and Manuel recognizes her as Adela, the Cuban singer, now gravely ill and afflicted by her son's imprisonment. Before dying—a favorite technique of the melodrama is to draw out final words into full confessions—Adela confides in Manuel: "Juanito is your son!" Juanito escapes from reform school, and learning of his mother's demise, he becomes a paperboy living on the streets. One day he takes flowers to his mother's grave where he finds Manuel, who with sincerity, reveals his paternity to Juanito, and takes him to live with him, along with Luisito and another paperboy friend of his. Orol himself proclaims, "A mother's heart is never wrong."

Alejandro Galindo shared an anecdote about the opening weeks of *Madre querida*.[36] At the doors of the cinema, they were handing out paper handkerchiefs and a sign saying: "If you return a dry kerchief to us, we'll give you your money back." And it seems there were no refunds. Impossible. The era didn't reward hearts of stone in the theater, and besides, May 10 had only just been created in 1922 (see the magnificent essay by Marta Acevedo on Mother's Day, in which she demonstrates how the infallible combination of ultra-Right ideology and commercialism implanted what is, essentially, Applaudable Dehumanization's Day).[37]

The era from 1932 to 1950 is a very fertile one for honoring The Mother. Only that can explain the melodrama entitled *Madres del mundo* (Mothers of the world; 1936, dir. Rolando Aguilar), and only that can justify the avalanche of films—beginning with the wild success of *Madre querida*—in which mothers die for their children's happiness (they are *Christified*). There's no doubt: man proposes, the group representing God and the box office disposes, and then comes cinema and decomposes it all. The flood of sacrificed mothers follows several courses:

- The epic of subjugation. There the emblematic figure is Dalia Íñiguez's character in *La oveja negra* (The black sheep; 1950, dir. Ismael Rodríguez).[38]
- The public enforcement of degradation. A definitive example occurs

in *Víctimas del pecado* (Victims of sin; 1950), the formidable *rumbera* melodrama by Emilio Fernández, with photography by Gabriel Figueroa, is a tour through cabarets and holes in the wall, centered on the nobleness of spirit portrayed by the *fichera*, Rosa (Ninón Sevilla).[39] The film includes an unrivaled scene. "El cinturita" (The Belt),[40] marvelously interpreted by Rodolfo Acosta, demands that one of his charges abandon the child (of his) that she just bore, and run away with him by herself. "You choose: the baby or me." The *fichera* immediately chooses, and in her delirium dumps the baby in a trashcan. There, minutes later, Rosa rescues the baby, just in time to save him from the approaching garbage truck.

• Sacrifice that turns the martyr into "disposable matter." A representative example of this is *Las abandonadas* (1946, dir. Emilio Fernández), that takes as its title the first verse of a poem by Julio Sesto:

> How I pity those abandoned women who
> loved believing they were loved in return,
> And go through their life mourning a loss,
> remembering a man, with a child in tow![41]

The drama of single motherhood: "Abandoned women are like fruit, fallen / from the tall and leafy tree of life."[42] Margarita (Dolores del Río) exemplifies this, seduced by a wicked man (Víctor Junco) who hides his marriage from her, and protected by a (fake) Revolutionary general, Juan Gómez (Pedro Armendáriz), to whom she declares, "I'll be your smitten shadow." At the end of the film, now aged, after denigrating herself by selling her body, Margarita hears her son's argument, who unknowingly is saving his own mother: "I'm going to remind those in charge of issuing rulings of what they shouldn't forget: where there's a woman, you find the purity of life . . . But where there's a mother, you find God!" For the sake of hearing such judiciary flourish, it was well worth the cost of sending her child to an expensive boarding school, and committing crimes in order to support his class aspirations.

Las abandonadas is amply nourished by *Madame X*, the [1908] play by French author Alexandre Bisson, the story of "Eve expelled from the bourgeois paradise," who completely sacrifices herself in order to give her son an education, the lawyer who will defend her when she falls on hard luck. The theme, a melodramatic dare, directly produces four films: *Madame X* (1920, dir. Frank Lloyd), *Madame X* (1929, dir. Leonel Barrymore), *Madame X* (1937, dir. Sam Wood), and *Madame X* (1966, dir. David Lowell Rich). The fascination is endless with maternal love that suffers through everything, prostitution, poverty, robbery, all for the sake of her son getting ahead (ignorant of the fact that his mother is alive and is a "fallen" woman), and seeing him as an upright man, a respectable lawyer.

The structure of *Madame X* is wide open and supports the luxuries of the female character, her life on top of the world, the tragic act that throws her into the abyss, the daily degradation, and the immoral procurement of money for sending her son to school far from the gutter and the slums. Another variation on the plot can be found in *Salón México* (1945, dir. Emilio Fernández), where the cabaret dancer (Marga López) is consumed and undone so that her little sister (Silvia Derbez) won't experience the degradations of poverty.

BACK WHEN ONLY ORPHANS WENT TO THE MOVIES ALONE

In the Golden Age of Mexican Cinema, it was common practice to see movies with the family, because the cinemas of neighborhoods or rural towns or those in city centers are secular temples in the strict sense: there's no set liturgy, but the way films are watched is liturgical. And without even noticing, families began to shift in their social beliefs. Nothing compares to becoming larger-than-life with the silver screens, and Mexican spectators, under the pressure of both Hollywood and their national cinema, perceive (each in their own way) that women, having become more visible and audible on screen, are now different because in filmic fantasy (for the women, the ultimate reality), they occupy a central role. This doesn't mean that the impositions of the patriarchy are attenuated, but that the change in images foreshadows the change in customs and conditions it.

Sentimental blackmail is shared and assimilated not so much by individual spectators, but rather by diverse family groupings, who use the scenes of crying and pain like behavioral education. When family outings to the cinema cease, the classic melodrama and the Golden Age itself essentially come to an end. And therefore, it's worth reviewing what sentimental blackmail is, and how it functioned during that period, making people feel alive (in solidarity) through tears, forgiving by usurping the place of the victim, incorporating the unfortunate man or woman into their ideal family, which is the only and ultimate honor available to that character trampled by Destiny who can never return home, or else the family that shares in their fate might suffer even worse circumstances.

Without the mother as a central axis of compassion in the Valley of Tears, sentimental blackmail doesn't work. In this mythology that is translated into daily life more forcefully than is acknowledged, the mother understands the world from the kitchen, the bedroom, the dining room, or the living room either real or ideal. She is defeated but never fooled, she is left alone in her bedroom but not left psychologically unaware; she is, always, the one who educates in the language of exasperation, and therefore she's the one decisively rooted in the codes of conduct that are pertinent to every occasion (man must reverse his terms). For that reason, it doesn't make much sense to locate the symbol and its doubling in lead roles based solely on the analysis of films. The great allegories, the mythos, the legendary constructions always happen in the interactive space between the film and its public. The mothers in the front row seats and the galleries receive their filmic models and transform them into their archive of feelings and verbal expressions; the mothers on screen show the archive and resonances of their suffering, and they never contradict the prevailing tastes. Whether for or against her, for quite some time no grandma could ignore Doña Sara García; that would have been like renouncing an identity principle before even knowing it. Aware or not of her points of view, mothers from various generations either become modern or they accept themselves as anachronisms, either rejecting or imitating their on-screen doubles who are bathed in tears and silent reproaches.

For sure, the first modern mom never had kids.

NOTES

1. *Rumberas* were the stars of a genre of studio films in Mexico's Golden Age that relied on large musical dance numbers set to primarily Afro-Caribbean rhythms. These films were melodramatic in nature and generally followed the lives of women who were redeemed through their dancing. *Charros*, or Mexican ranchers, were dressed in elaborate and elegantly embroidered suits with jackets and sombreros. They appeared in studio musical *ranchero* melodramas, and their attire becomes the mariachi's typical outfit. Jorge Negrete, Pedro Infante, Antonio Aguilar, Emilio "El Indio" Fernández, and Pedro Armendáriz are all notable stars of this Mexican Western musical genre. *Allá en el Rancho Grande* (1936; Out on the great ranch; Fernando de Fuentes, dir.) was an early success of the Golden Age. The melodrama portrayed a love triangle between the ranch owner (Tito Guízar as Francisco), his best friend the foreman (René Cardona as Felipe), and the lovely and demure Cruz (Esther Fernández), with photography by the iconic cameraman Gabriel Figueroa. It was so popular that it was remade by Fuentes himself in 1949, with the wildly popular singer Jorge Negrete playing José Francisco, Lilia del Valle as Cruz, and Eduardo Noriega as the wealthy rival for her love, Felipe.

2. The Golden Age of Mexican cinema is an era of major studio productions that flourished both nationally and internationally, launching the careers of many stars. This period (in this essay, defined by Monsiváis as 1932–1955, but sometimes defined as 1936–1950) marks a definitive turn toward Mexican themes, musical melodramas that began to bridge the divide between the countryside

and the city, with the corresponding moralizing and pedagogical agendas. The films that for some mark the beginning of the era are the Revolutionary trilogy by Fernando de Fuentes: *Prisionero Trece* (Prisoner 13; 1933), *El compadre Mendoza* (1933) and *¡Vámonos con Pancho Villa!* (Let's go with Pancho Villa!; 1936); others cite Fuentes's turn toward the musical Western in *Allá en el Rancho Grande* (1936) as the symbolic beginning of the era. In this time there was a marked increase in industrial output. Besides Fuentes, the era's most famous director was Emilio "El Indio" Fernández (who also collaborated with Gabriel Figueroa as director of photography), whose iconic melodramas like *Flor silvestre* (Wildflower; 1943) and *María Candelaria* (1943), both starring Dolores del Río and Pedro Armendáriz, and *Río escondido* (Hidden river; 1948), starring María Félix, Fernando Fernández, and Carlos López Moctezuma, often touched on the theme of a beautiful, young, poor woman subjected to competition for her love, torn between her humble but noble background and the wealth and possibility that her beauty offer. They are films that engage with the changing demographics of the country when mass exodus from the countryside after the Revolution left the culture harkening to a simpler "Mexicanness," or in search of a more cosmopolitan one to which the populace could aspire.

3. Monsiváis paraphrases this quotation as "la ideología es el cine de la Sociedad." Here, we quote Roland Barthes directly, from "Leaving the Movie Theater," trans. Richard Howard, in *The Art of the Personal Essay: An Anthology from the Classical Era to the Present*. ed. Phillip Lopate (New York: Anchor Books, 1995), 421.

4. Here we quote John Berger, *G.* (New York: Vintage International, 1991), in the Kindle version, locations 149, 150. The first edition of the book was published in Great Britain in 1972 by Weidenfeld and Nicolson, and it won the Booker Prize that year.

5. Dolores del Río (María de los Dolores Asúnsolo y López Negrete, 1904–1983) was one of the most iconic actresses of Mexico's Golden Age, and its first Hollywood crossover star, beginning in 1925. She generally played an ingenue, in contrast to María Félix (María de los Ángeles Félix Güereña, 1914–2002) who played a much feistier character, often portrayed as a man-eater or a despotic diva. María Félix's career took her to Europe and other Latin American countries, but she didn't have a career in Hollywood.

6. *Enamorada* (1946) was directed by Emilio "El Indio" Fernández and shot by Gabriel Figueroa, starring María Félix and Pedro Armendáriz. Félix plays Beatriz Peñafiel, the haughty daughter of the wealthiest and most notable landowner in Cholula, where the revolutionary Zapatista troops, under General José Juan Reyes (Armendáriz), have taken the town. The romantic arc of the film has Beatriz finally "tamed," and not only accepting the Revolutionary ideal, but deeply in love. The film was remade in Hollywood by Fernández in 1949 as *The Torch*, starring Paulette Godard, with less success.

7. Fernando de Fuentes's *Doña Bárbara* was the first of many film adaptations of the homonymous regionalist novel by Venezuelan author Rómulo Gallegos

(Caracas: Editorial Araluce, 1929) that sent the author into exile for its critique of the landowning classes and government. It is one of the most widely known Latin American novels, and was translated into English almost immediately in 1931 by Robert Malloy as *Doña Barbara* (New York: Peter Smith). There is a recent reprint with a critical introduction by Larry McMurty (Chicago, IL: University of Chicago Press, 2012).

8. Andrea Palma (Guadalupe Bracho Pérez-Gavilán, 1903–1987), sister to film director Julio Bracho, and cousin to actors Dolores del Río and Ramón Novarro, had her breakout role starring in Arcady Boytler's *La mujer del puerto* (1934), and became a star almost overnight. She was a theater actor as well as a screen actor, and made forays into Hollywood.

9. *Nosotros los pobres* (1948; We, the poor) and its sequel, *Ustedes los ricos* (1948; You, the rich) are the first two films in the trilogy directed by Ismael Rodríguez and are representative of the "slum melodramas" of the latter part of the Golden Age. The saga follows Pepe "el Toro" (Pedro Infante) and his family. His partner, Celia (Blanca Estela Pavón), is pursued by the wealthy, villainous lawyer Montes (Rafael Alcayde), and is mistreated and undervalued by Pepe while remaining humbly faithful to him. Celia doesn't appear in the third film of the trilogy, *Pepe el Toro* (Pepe the Bull, 1953), because the actress, Pavón, died tragically in an airplane accident in 1949.

10. In Rodríguez's 1949 film *La oveja negra*, Íñiguez's character, Vivianita, is systematically humiliated and abused by her narcissistic husband who only pretends to be remorseful when she is on her deathbed where she forgives all of his mistreatment. Sara García (1895–1980) was known as La Abuelita de México (Mexico's grandma) for her extensive roles as an elderly, long-suffering, but disciplined grandmother. She embodied this role from a relatively young age, and it became her claim to fame.

11. Vitola was the stage name for Fannie Kauffman (1924–2009), a Canadian-born singer and actress raised in Cuba and made internationally famous after moving to Mexico City at twenty-one, naturalizing as Mexican, and becoming an actress in the Golden Age of cinema. She was most known for her physical comedic work, especially with the famous comedian Tin-Tán (Germán Valdés).

12. Film director and actress María Elena Velasco (1940–2015) invented and portrayed the fictional character La India María (a.k.a., María Nicolasa Cruz) who appeared in sixteen feature-length films as well as TV spinoffs and cameos. She was portrayed as an Indigenous woman and country bumpkin who migrated to Mexico City and then the US. While the character was immensely popular and commercially successful, Velasco has been criticized for using "brown face" in her insulting portrayal of an Indigenous character.

13. Monsiváis refers to a theater of frivolity (*teatro frívolo*), which is a Spanish-language genre that roughly approximates the follies of vaudeville. It is a theater that focuses on physical comedy and cheap laughs. Calling Indigenous peoples *inditos* is a belittling use of the diminutive form in this case. Calling

them "little Indians" demonstrates a paternalistic view of Indigenous populations espoused by official discourse.

14. Originally written in German by Karl Marx and Friedrich Engels between 1845–
1846, *The German Ideology* was published in 1932 by David Riazanov, and first
published in English in 1970 by International Publishers and Lawrence and Wis-
hart, who hold the translation rights.

15. Monsiváis often uses this term *decente* with significant irony as it speaks to classist respectability politics.

16. In Roman Catholicism, the *nihil obstat* is a certification by an official censor
stating that a book does not violate doctrine or moral codes of the Church.

17. Monsiváis does not cite the author of this poem, and this may be because the
poem is widely circulated in Spanish, with credit to both Heinrich Neuman and
Erich Neuman. However, it was published as E. Heuman, "Si tienes una madre
todavía . . .," *Revista de la Asociación Femenina de Camagüey* 5, no. 53 (May 1925),
10. Monsiváis's text quotes this opening verse: "Si tienes una madre todavía, /
da gracias al Señor que te ama tanto, / que no todo mortal contar podría / dicha
tan grande ni placer tan santo." Our translation.

18. *Los olvidados* (*The Young and the Damned*) is perhaps the most iconic film of
Buñuel's Mexican era. Set in the slums of Mexico City, it follows the lives of a
group of young boys, violent and abandoned by their parents and society. Script
translations are ours.

19. Roberto Cobo (Eleuterio García Romero, 1930–2002) was an actor in the *teatro
de carpas*, or itinerant theater, and later became a screen actor starring in more
than eighty films. His role as El Jaibo (the adjective denotes someone from the
city of Tampico, Tamaulipas) was one of his earliest appearances on screen. He
would later go on to play some of Mexican cinema's most memorable characters, including La Manuela, a gay transvestite in Arturo Ripstein's *El lugar sin
límites* (*The Place without Limits*, 1978). His character runs a small-town brothel
with his daughter, La Japonesita, and is severely punished for resisting attempts
by the local landowner, Don Alejo (Fernando Soler), to purchase his property
as much as for his sexuality by the impoverished, violent, and closeted Pancho
(Gonzalo Vega).

20. While Sara García was married, had a child, and never openly assumed a lesbian identity, she had a close female companion, Rosario González, for over
sixty years, who was also her inheritor. Guadalupe Loaeza mentions this relationship in her book *En el closet* (In the closet), (Mexico City: Ediciones B, 2011).
Notably, Carlos Monsiváis is also included in Loaeza's book, which came out
a year after his death. Monsiváis does not mention Sara García's sexuality in
this chapter, and we believe it is because of his firm belief that no one should
be outed against their will, as he himself did not want to be outed, or seen as
merely a "homosexual writer." See Chapters 12 on Nancy Cárdenas and 18 on
Susan Sontag for mentions about the politics of outing / assuming queer identities publicly. For further discussion of this polemical topic, see also Ileana Baeza

Lope, *Sara García: Ícono cinematográfico nacional mexicano, abuela y lesbiana* (California: Argus-*a*, 2018.)

21. See Morgana (Teresa Carvajal Juárez), "Vizcaínas: De la disciplina del aula al rigor del set," *Somos*, October 2000, 36–41. See also Luis Terán, "Biografía: Drama de la vida real," *Somos*, October 2000, 6–17; and Héctor Argente, "Una mirada a la intimidad de Sara," *Somos,* October 2000, 82–3. We thank Ileana Baeza Lope for providing us with this material.

22. All three silent films debuted in 1917. *En defensa propia* was directed by Joaquín Coss and written by actress Mimí Derba, one of Mexico's pioneer women filmmakers. It was Sara García's debut film. *Alma de sacrificio* was also directed by Joaquín Coss, and also starred Mimí Derba and Julio Taboada. *La soñadora*, directed by Eduardo Arozamena, once again starred Mimí Derba.

23. Here we have chosen to translate the film titles literally, to represent the meanings of the original titles in Spanish. It was, and still is, an industry practice to radically change the titles of films for foreign markets, but in this case, Monsiváis is calling attention to a pattern in the titles that highlights motherhood, self-abnegation, and the family melodrama.

    For a complete filmography, see Luís Terán, "Cine: Encantos de una comediante subversive," *Somos*, October 2000, 42–61. For other performances, see Edgar Ceballos, "Teatro: Actriz con temple, senorío y gracia," *Somos*, October 2000, 62–69; Jesús Flores y Escalante and Pablo Dueñas, "Radio: En voz de la abuelita," *Somos*, October 2000, 70–75; Álvaro Cueva, "Televisión: Mítica imagen de la ternura," *Somos*, October 2000, 76–80.

24. Throughout we retain the use of *Doña* as an honorific that precedes Sara García's name. It is used to signal her importance in the film and cultural industries, as well as to show respect for a woman of a certain age.

25. This quote comes from Sara García, "Entrevista: Anécdotas de una Estrella," *Somos*, October 2000, 27.

26. Cantinflas (Mario Fortino Alfonso Moreno Reyes, 1911–1993) is perhaps Mexico's most renowned comedic actor. His comedy was both physical and linguistic, innovating and improvising with verbal acuity, he riffed on the *ñero* (or low class) accents and speech patterns of Tepito, the rough neighborhood in which he was raised. His acting career began in the *carpas*, or tents, of itinerant theater, which housed vaudeville-style follies and brash, brazen comedy aimed at the working classes. His particular brand of comedy, based heavily on his oral abilities, gave rise to many neologisms, including the verb *cantinflear*, which can be understood in English as a sort of self-defense strategy of "babbling," referring to his ability to perform unending verbal diarrhea without ever saying the thing he means.

27. From Fernando Muñoz, "Así la recuerdan," *Somos*, October 2000, 89.

28. In *Los tres García*, Sara García plays Doña Luisa García whose three grandsons, cousins played by Pedro Infante (Luis Antonio), Abel Salazár (José Luis), and Victor Manuel Mendoza (Luis Manuel), all fall in love with the same

American-born Lupita Smith-García (Marga López). Grandma puts an end to their squabbling.

29. *Cuando los hijos se van* (1941, Juan Bustillo Oro, dir.), initially adapted from a radio-novella, starred Sara García, Fernando Soler, and Joaquín Pardavé. It was then remade by Bustillo in 1957 as *Cada hijo una cruz* (Each child a cross, starring Esther Fernández and Miguel Manzano). Finally, there was an updated version of *Cuando los hijos se van* filmed in 1969 directed by Julián Soler, starring Amparo Rivelles and, again, Fernando Soler. *Azahares para tu boda* (Orange blossoms for your wedding, 1950, Julián Soler, dir.) also starred Sara García, Fernando Soler, and Joaquín Pardavé.

30. Pedro Infante's singing was what made him stand out among his peers. Sergio de la Mora writes extensively on Infante's stardom in his preface, "How I too Came to Love Pedro Infante," and the chapter "Pedro Infante Unveiled: Masculinities in the Mexican 'Buddy Movie'" in his book *Cinemachismo* (Austin: UT Press, 2006).

31. We have italicized the song lyrics as sung by Pedro Infante throughout the paragraph to distinguish them from Monsiváis's words, and from the direct dialogue quoted from the script.

32. Sara García, "Entrevista: Anécdotas de una estrella," *Somos*, October 2000, 30.

33. García, "Entrevista," 31–32.

34. This anecdote appears to have been shared with Monsiváis personally. Galindo cites Monsiváis in his book *El cine mexicano* [1985] (Mexico City: Edamex, 1986), 45.

35. An image of the corpse-manequin of Sara García used in *Mecánica nacional* is featured in García, "Entrevista," 33.

36. This anecdote also appears to have been shared with Monsiváis in a personal communication. Galindo dedicates pages 46–48 of his book *El cine mexicano* [1985] (Mexico City: Edamex, 1985) to a discussion of Orol and the success of *Madre querida* as it impacted the Mexican film industry.

37. Marta Acevedo, *El diez de mayo* (Mexico City: Martín Casillas Editores, Secretaría de Educación Pública, 1982).

38. *Oveja negra* (Black sheep) is a family melodrama in which Fernando Soler plays an unstable father (Don Cruz Treviño Martínez de la Garza) who is perpetually abusive to his wife, Doña Bibiana (Dalia Íñiquez), and son, Silvano (Pedro Infante), who forgive everything.

39. *Ficheras* are women who dance at night clubs and who, for a fee (a token, or *ficha*) act as escorts to the "gentlemen" at the clubs. *Fichera* films were extremely popular and there was some crossover between them and the *rumbera* films, although the *fichera* films grew in popularity in the sixties and seventies, morphing into the genre of *sexi-comedias*. Sergio de la Mora dedicates a chapter to a discussion of the *fichera* films: "The Last Dance: (Homo)Sexuality and Representation in Arturo Ripstein's *El lugar sin límites* and the Fichera Subgenre," in *Cinemachismo* (Austin: UT Press, 2006).

40. Rodolfo Acosta plays "El Cinturita," a pimp who violently abuses the women that work under him.

41. "¡Cómo me dan pena las abandonadas / que amaron creyendo siempre ser amadas, / y van por la vida llorando un cariño, / recordando un hombre y arrastrando un niño!" This verse comes from the widely circulated poem that appears in Julio Sesto's romantic novel *Las abandonadas: Novela humana* (Mexico City: El Libro Español, 1908), 221. Our translation.

42. Sesto, *Las abandonadas*, 221.

CHAPTER 18

Susan Sontag (1933–2004)

Imagination and Historical Conscience

2005

PRESENTATION BY THE AUTHOR AT AN EVENT PROMOTING DIVERSITY

In 1964, Susan Sontag published an essay in *Partisan Review*, "Notes on Camp," dedicated to Oscar Wilde, more as the ideal reader of the text than as the object of another tribute. Sontag borrows the term "camp" from the gay lexicon and presents it as a complex category. Prior to her, the renowned writer Christopher Isherwood had addressed the topic in his novel *The World in the Evening* (1954), in which two characters, whose sexual orientation today would not be in doubt, converse:

"In any of your *voyages au bout de la nuit*, did you ever run across the word *camp*?"

"I've heard people use it in bars. But I thought . . ."

"You thought it meant a swishy little boy with peroxided hair, dressed in a picture hat and a feather boa pretending to be Marlene Dietrich? Yes, in queer circles, they call *that* camping. It's all very well in its place but it's, but it's an utterly debased form . . ." Charles's eyes shone delightedly. He seemed to be in the best of spirits, now, and thoroughly enjoying this exposition. "What I mean by camp is something much more fundamental. You can call the other Low Camp, if you like; then what I am talking about is High Camp. High Camp is the whole emotional basis of the ballet, for example, and of course of baroque art. You see, true High Camp always has underlying seriousness. You can't camp about something you don't take seriously. You're not making fun of it; you're making fun out of it. You're expressing what's basically serious to you in terms of an artifice and elegance. Baroque art is largely camp about religion, the ballet is camp about love. . . . Do you see at all what I'm getting at?"[1]

According to Sontag, Isherwood dedicates "a lazy two-page sketch" to the topic.[2] Incidental, yes, but not lazy, because at least it addresses the central core of what defines "camp": love of what comes naturally, of exaggeration and artifice. Also, and even earlier, in a book from the 1950s, the *Dictionary of Slang* by Eric Partridge, the noun "camp" is peremptorily defined as "effeminate, in reference especially to homosexual mannerisms of speech and gesture," and the adjective is defined as "homosexual, lesbian."[3]

In her essay on camp, as much as she is able, Sontag avoids a direct relationship with the term as used in the gay community, and prefers an association by inference: camp is a sensibility, a taste, an aesthetic trend that—in Sontag's revision—includes the drawings of Aubrey Beardsley (a friend and enemy of Wilde, the cartoonist of *Salomé*), Tiffany lamps, Bellini's operas, *Swan Lake*, King Kong, the singer La Lupe, Flash Gordon comic books, the novels of Ronald Firbank (the very notable eccentric Englishman), the persona of Jean Cocteau, the theatre of Noël Coward, art nouveau, gothic novels, many gestures (in the sense of theatricality) of homosexuals, Busby Berkeley's choreographies, some movies by Lubitsch, Bette Davis's role acting in *All About Eve*, Gloria Swanson in *Sunset Boulevard*, and Marlene Dietrich in the six ultra-baroque films directed by Von Sternberg, the cult figure and myth of Greta Garbo.

Camp, Sontag insists, is concretely an aesthetic experience, and it embodies a triumph of "style" over "content," of "aesthetics" over "morality," of "irony" over "tragedy." In challenging "seriousness," camp offers a ludic vision of the world, and defends snobbish affiliations. In addition, and this is the most radical or subversive part of the essay, camp becomes the taste and the in-group language of gayness, a very marginalized minority, who see in this radicalized aesthetic their best defense. According to Sontag, the flourishing of camp among homosexuals has a definitively propagandistic air to it, given that by promoting an aesthetic sense, it led to societal recognition. In short, "the experiences of Camp are based on the great discovery that the sensibilities of high culture have no monopoly upon refinement."[4]

From the moment of its appearance, "Notes on Camp" was a cultural happening of utmost importance. Thereafter, culture is understood as a kind of secular religion, and great value is placed on camp's inroads into universities and cultural publications that had been suppressed or disparaged by a solemn and rigid vision of the arts and the humanities. Almost immediately, a sector of heterosexual society pays attention to the compendium of aesthetic preferences adopted aesthetically and/or created by the gay avant-garde: They are thrilled by Busby Berkeley's delirious optics; they participate in Judy Garland's melodrama; they listen to the Supremes, and notice the decorations in *The Scarlet Empress* by Von Sternberg (one of them being the prodigious Marlene), they analyze Bette Davis's diction and her stormy spirit, or Garbo's "vapid beauty." Other obligations (admirations) emerge from this cultural modernity. Mae West is a woman satisfied by her sexual teasing and also the parody of femininity, anticipating the popularization of the transvestite; and in the anarchist comedies of the Marx brothers, Margaret Dumont represents vulnerable elegance; and Carmen Miranda *is* the tropics: its parody and its exorcism. The taste was already there, but the expropriation of an aesthetic was huge. Who wouldn't enthusiastically join a game of cultural taxonomy? *Time Magazine* comments that Sontag's essay elicits fierce criticism (some of it quite legitimate), and elitist disdain, and they proclaim the presence of a new intellectual personality. In hindsight, there are some inaccuracies evident in her essay. An example: the authoritarianism of classification that claimed products and attitudes as camp that today would undoubtedly be considered kitsch (by "kitsch" I mean objects and even attitudes of an explosive "aesthetic," focused on the spectacle of bad taste). Nevertheless the fundamental contribution of the essay continues to be current: the reappraisal of diversity, the expansion of the canon (usually well sustained), the integration of another sensibility "not governed by reason but by the logic of taste."[5]

AGAINST INTERPRETATION: AN INTELLECTUAL DEVELOPMENT

Susan Lee Rosenblatt is born on January 16, 1933, in New York. Her father, Jack Rosenblatt, a fur trader in China, dies in 1938 in Tientsin, and her mother, Mildred Jacobson, and her two daughters, Susan and Judith, settle down in Tucson, Arizona. In 1945, Mrs. Jacobson marries Nathan Sontag, an Air Force captain, and her daughters adopt their stepfather's last name. In 1946, they move to California, and Susan studies at Berkeley, and afterward at the University of Chicago. She marries the psychologist Philip Rieff in 1950, begins her work as a reviewer of books, and graduates. Her son, David, is born in 1952. In 1954, she enrolls at Harvard for a Masters in English and then in philosophy. She graduates in 1957, studies a year at St. Anne's College in Oxford and takes some courses at La Sorbonne.

In 1959, Sontag settles down in Manhattan ("I was thrilled, I was like Irena in *The Three Sisters* longing for Moscow.[6] All I could think was New

York! New York!"[7]). Her activities are multiple: she does reports for publishers and writes book reviews, she attends cocktail parties and gatherings, she interacts with writers and artists, meets Roger Straus who will later become her editor and promoter. She also begins her first lesbian relationship with the playwright María Irena Fornés, a relationship that she doesn't hide nor make explicit by "coming out of the closet." She also becomes a close friend to, and in due course an undeniable enemy of, writers whose representation of her in some novels make her out as the image of opportunism or coldness.[8]

In 1969, in New York's Greenwich Village, an uprising known as the Stonewall Rebellion erupted (the mythical resistance of a group of gay folk, several of them transvestites, responding to a police raid that took place at the Stonewall Inn, which launches the gay and lesbian liberation movement worldwide). From that moment on, many come out of the closet and there is an expectation that well-known gays and lesbians will unveil their sexual identity. When this doesn't happen, some radical activists choose "outing" them, a calling out that "renders useless" their remaining in the closet. There's a demand for Susan Sontag, as Rollyson and Paddock state, to make her lesbianism public. She refuses to do so and defends her privacy. Jill Johnston, a militant lesbian, gives her version of the events:

> Successful before Stonewall (1969), they could only have had reason to think subconsciously at least that they had much to lose by coming out after Stonewall provided a consensus for doing so. Another way of putting it: Any controversial (sexual) political identity was liable to threaten their publicly affirmed identity as artists and writers. Susan, of course, became politically identified with liberal left causes that were acceptable.[9]

The above is either inaccurate or simply untrue. Sontag is unrelenting in her political defiance: "coming out of the closet" becomes a personal decision that varies from person to person depending on circumstances and attitudes. Hence the ridiculous or pathetic campaign to "unmask" Sontag, undertaken by the columnist and self-promoter Camille Paglia, a declared lesbian, self-designated as "the Sontag of the Nineties," who sees her "predecessor" as a cornered and defeated deity.

WORLDVIEWS AND PROPHECIES

In 1966, Sontag publishes a collection of essays, *Against Interpretation*, and if the text that gives the book its title does not enjoy the widespread recognition of "Notes on Camp" (also included in the volume), it does spur a polemic in cultural circles. Sontag reveals intelligence, erudition, a panoramic vision of the arts, and she shows herself to be, as she called herself, "a gluttonous reader." Her long-standing admirations make themselves apparent: Walter Benjamin, Kafka, Roland Barthes, Proust, some filmmakers (Cocteau, Ozu, Godard, Bergman), classic mythologies, Greek philosophers, Marx, Freud. Sontag's position is clear-cut:

> Interpretation is a radical strategy for conserving an old text, which is thought too precious to repudiate by revamping. . . . In a culture whose already classical dilemma is the hypertrophy of the intellect at the expense of energy and sensual capability, interpretation is the revenge of the intellect upon art. Even more. It is the revenge of the intellect upon the world.[10]

Later she will qualify these statements without being overly self-critical.

Sontag cites D. H. Lawrence: "Never trust the teller, trust the tale." To support her thesis, she uses examples from abstract art and *pop art* concluding, "The function of criticism should demonstrate *how it is what it is*, even that *it is what it is*, rather than to show *what it means*." And the conclusion of the essay synthesizes this significant provocation: "In place of a hermeneutics we need an erotics of art."[11] Susan delves further, and that's why she recapitulates her observations in the prologue to the paperback edition of *Against Interpretation*:

> I disagree now with a portion of what I wrote, but it is not the sort of disagreement that makes feasible partial changes or revisions. Although I think that I overestimated or underestimated the merit of several works I discussed, little of my present disagreement owes to a shift in particular judgments. Anyway, what value these essays may possess, the extent to which they are more than just case studies of my evolving sensibility, rests not on the specific appraisals made but on the interestingness of the problems raised. I don't, ultimately, care for handing out grades to works of art (which is why I mostly avoided the opportunity of writing about things I didn't admire). I wrote as an enthusiast and a partisan—and with, it now seems to me, a certain naiveté. I didn't understand the gross impact which writing about new or little known activities in the arts can have in the era of instant "communication." I didn't know—I had yet to learn, painfully—the speed at which a bulky essay in *Partisan Review* becomes a hot tip in *Time*. Despite all my exhortatory tone, I was not trying to lead anyone into the Promised Land except myself.[12]

In *Against Interpretation*, Sontag's curiosity and powers of association bring together literature, film, theater, music, and style. Sontag studies, among others, Simone Weil, Albert Camus, Michel Leiris, Georg Lukács, Sartre, Genet, Ionesco, Sade, Artaud. The rejection of narrow disciplinary specializations (that later will be the norm in academia worldwide) is the organizing principal in Sontag's work.

ACTIVISM: CAUSES AS IDEAS, IDEALS AND THE MISTRUST OF IDEOLOGIES

In 1995 in San Francisco, in conversation with the dramatist Tony Kushner, author of *Angels in America*, Sontag's states her position on work and activism:

> I'm not saying truth and justice are in opposition. But I am saying there are situations where they can't simply be mapped one on the other. My way of dealing with this is to live in a certain way, learning from my experiences, which are informed by my principles, rather than first have an idea and then applying it. I'm not just an artist or writer. I'm also someone who has commitments, and when pursuing or implementing them, I bring to these actions certain talents, and the privilege of being heard at all, basically I'm functioning as a human being, a citizen. I believe in righteous action, I believe that one should do good.[13]

Although one takes her stance for granted, Sontag only focuses on feminist themes when circumstances require. Rollyson and Paddock draw our attention to an essay from 1973, "The Third World of Women," published in *Partisan Review*, where Sontag gets to the root of the problem. To simply work for equality under the law will always mean that women will lag behind men, for men have demonstrated their refusal to part with power. True change will only occur when women force men to change "since the very structure of society is founded on male privilege." To attain power, all women should work for pay: "Liberation is power. Homosexuals will be as valid and respectable as heterosexual choices, both will grow out of a genuine bisexuality." Women will have to take to the streets as a sign of protest. They will have to learn karate, whistle at men, attack beauty parlors, organize campaigns against sexist toy companies, conduct male beauty contests, and retain their own names. If reforms are only palliative measures, radical agitation can fundamentally change the conditions that determine women's lives, and at that point it becomes fundamental to change legislation on abortion. Sontag concludes: "I would never describe myself as a liberated woman. Things, evidently, are never that simple. But I have always been a feminist."[14]

In a poll from 1966, "What's Happening in America?" Sontag responds:

America was founded on genocide, on the unquestioned assumption of the right of white Europeans to exterminate a resident, technologically backward, colored population in order to take over the continent. America had not only the most brutal system of slavery in modern times but a unique juridical system (compared with other slaveries, say in Latin America and the British Colonies) which did not, in a single respect, recognize slaves as persons.[15]

This essay was written at the beginning of the large-scale resistance of the US Left to the Vietnam War. Sontag is incisive: "There is something awfully wrong with a *de facto system* that allows the president (Johnson) virtually unlimited discretion in pursuing an immoral and imprudent foreign policy. . . . This is a passionately racist country, it will continue to be so in the foreseeable future."[16] And the next thing you know, she proclaims the phrase that will provoke her harshest critics: "The white race is the cancer of human history . . ."[17]

In 1968, Sontag signs a letter, the first of many protests that she supports, demanding that the shootings in Oakland, California, between the police and the Black Panthers be investigated. In May of 1968, she travels to North Vietnam, invited by the North Vietnamese, and writes a well-intentioned piece, "Trip to Hanoi," although, for the most part, it's not very different from the writings of the hopeful radicals that traveled to the USSR willing to believe.[18] Sontag, for example, attributes their collective uniformity not to the lockstep of an authoritarian society, but rather to the social democratization that unifies people in the city and the rural areas in a popular war. And she continues to cling to her utopia: "it was my impression that the Vietnamese, as a culture, genuinely believe that life is simple."[19] They also believe that "life is full of joy" and that the alienating agonies of existentialism, so prevalent in the US, "aren't found among the Vietnamese."[20] North Vietnam "deserves to be idealized."[21]

Sontag doesn't question the imperialist attitude of North Vietnam toward their neighboring countries, nor the violence exerted against their population, nor the tortures, nor the new bureaucratic class of the party. She only comments on two inconceivable acts: forced collectivization and the purges of dissidents. She sees the Vietnamese as "'whole' human beings, not 'split' as we are."[22] She did not anticipate the obvious: At the end of the war, North Vietnam did not become a democratic society, it would have been impossible, and only economic demands and access to the market modify a totalitarian universe. A democratic change didn't interest Ho Chi Minh and his heirs.

The Cuban Revolution is another regime change she admired, but in this case, Sontag quickly becomes critical. Her only objections to the Castro regime (in an article in *Ramparts* from 1969[23]) are its homophobia and the creation of the UMAP (Unidades Militares de Apoyo a la Producción / Military Units to Support Production), concentration-like camps or "granjas de rehabilitación" (rehabilitation farms) for thousands of homosexuals, "anti-socials," and Jehovah's Witnesses. But in Cuba, the circumstances of harassment require another perspective. True, in Cuba there is no freedom of the press, nor an independent judiciary system, and their militarism is notorious, but in some aspects, [in Sontag's view] Cuba is the most genuinely democratic country in the world today.[24]

In 1971, Sontag, along with fifty-nine other intellectuals, signs the letter addressed to Commander Fidel Castro, "only just" in the twelfth year of his government, protesting the ridiculous trial to which the poet Heberto Padilla is subjected for "being counter-revolutionary," and which results in his Stalinist-like confession. In 1984, she collaborates on *Conducta impropia* (Improper conduct), the documentary by Orlando Jiménez Leal and Néstor Almendros about the persecution of homosexuals in Cuba.

In February 1982, at a rally in support of the Polish labor union Solidarity, banned in Poland under martial law, Sontag criticizes the American Left for not having condemned communism more forcefully. She was mistaken in believing that regimes like Cuba and North Vietnam would finally redeem communism, which if anything, continued to be the same. Wherever they took power, no matter where, they became fascists. She once believed that she could, for example, distinguish Leninism from Stalinism. Now she understands that *Reader's Digest* was correct, and *The Nation* (published by the US Left) was wrong. Communism is intrinsically evil.

ILLNESS AS METAPHOR

In 1975, Sontag is hospitalized for breast cancer. In 1978, she publishes *Illness as Metaphor*, an extensive essay on the relationship among illnesses, language, prejudices, and social certainties.

> As death is now an offensively meaningless event, so that disease widely considered a synonym for death is experienced as something to hide. . . . Cancer patients are lied to, not just because the disease is (or is thought to be) a death sentence, but because it is felt to be obscene—in the original meaning of the word: ill-omened, abominable, repugnant to the senses.[25]

And the essay ends with an enlightened humanistic message:

> [But at that time perhaps nobody will want any longer to compare anything awful to cancer, since] our views about cancer, and the metaphors we have imposed on it, are so much a vehicle for the large insufficiencies of this culture: for our shallow attitude toward death, for our anxieties about feeling, for our reckless improvident responses to our real "problems of growth," for our inability to construct an advanced industrial society which properly regulates consumption, and for our justified fears of the increasingly violent course of history.[26]

The beginning of the 1980s sees the emergence of a new and major menace: the immunodeficiency syndrome whose victims in the US are concentrated in the gay community. The plague spreads to New York, San Francisco, and Los Angeles. Sontag loses many friends, and in 1987, on learning of the death of one of them, she writes an extraordinary piece, "The Way We Live Now," on the experience of the "new families" (of friends, mainly) facing the pandemic and its daily devastations.[27] In 1989, she publishes *AIDS and Its Metaphors*, an important essay, even if its conclusions are shaky given the enormity of the phenomenon. She is moved by the response of the gay community to the pandemic, sees the actions of the radical group ACT-UP as extraordinary, and finds it telling that in such a short period of time, gay men have learned an extensive medical terminology: cell count, antibodies, antigens. She is also saddened "To see a community so medicalized. . . . The fight for gay rights must continue."[28] The title of the book, nevertheless, is not convincing. Unlike cancer, AIDS does not become a metaphor for spiritual decay or the breaking down of the social fabric. The prejudice is so drastic that it cannot be turned into a rhetorical device. AIDS is AIDS, it's that simple or terrifying; and this leads to the traditionalist stance, at the peak of homophobia, where in November of 2004, Pope John Paul II declares: "The spread of HIV, the human immunodeficiency virus, is due to a moral immunodeficiency. It is a pathology of the spirit that must be combatted through a corrective sexual practice and an education in religious values."[29]

ON SERIOUSNESS AT ALL COSTS

In 1963, without too much response from her readers, Sontag publishes her first novel, *The Benefactor*, and in 1967, the second, *Death Kit*. Neither of the two gets the reception that her essays garnered. She directs two films: *Duet for Cannibals* (1960) and *Brother Carl* (1971), both rather tedious if my memory serves me well; and a documentary, *Promised Lands* (1974), on the Arab-Israeli conflict after the Six-Day War, highly regarded by the critics. Her acclaimed essay *On Photography* (1977) engages Barthes teachings, and immediately becomes a reference.[30] In 1978, on returning to the topic, Sontag clarifies:

> in this book, above all, photography is its own artistic medium, its proper language, a language that alters the status of art. Strictly speaking, photography for me is only a pretext to speak about something very different, the problems of our modern society, the complex differences between our thinking and the superficial ability of perception, about the sequence of experience and the capacity to judge that experience.[31]

The book ends with an anti-apocalyptic vision: "If there can be a better way for the real world to include the one of images, it will require an ecology not only of real things but of images as well."[32] She returns to the subject of photography in *Regarding the Pain of Others* (2003), where she examines the images of military atrocities, from photos of the US Civil War, the lynching of African Americans in the South of the United States, World War I, the Spanish Civil War, the Nazi concentration camps, and some images of the barbarity in Bosnia, Afghanistan, Sierra Leone, Rwanda, Israel, Palestine, and September 11. *Regarding the Pain of Others* ends powerfully, reflecting on the dead and those who gaze upon them in photos:

> [There] are two Afghans, perhaps soldiers themselves, who have already stripped the dead soldiers of their weapons. These dead are supremely uninterested in the living: in those who took their lives; in witnesses—and in us. Why should they seek our gaze? What would they have to say to us? "We"—this "we" is everyone who has never experienced anything like what they went through—don't understand. We don't get it. We truly can't imagine what it was like. We can't imagine how dreadful, how terrifying war is; and how normal it becomes. Can't understand, can't imagine.[33]

HABITS OF CONSCIENCE

Sontag directs another film and publishes two successful novels, *The Volcano Lover* (1992) and *In America* (2002), and two books of essays on literature and film: *Under the Sign of Saturn* (1980) and *Where the Stress Falls* (2001). Her assertive and practical activism as an essayist grows exponentially. In 1993, she goes to Sarajevo and returns in order to direct the play *Waiting for Godot*, while pronouncing herself repeatedly against the monstrous dictatorship of Milosevic (having already directed a play by Pirandello in Italy). She defends the rights of Palestinians, censures the politics of Ariel Sharon, criticizes Gabriel García Márquez (whom she obviously admires) for his political positions regarding Fidel Castro, "only just" in his forty-fourth year in power. She criticizes the criminal violence of ETA, and in Germany praises the Israeli soldiers who refused to engage the Palestinians in battle.[34] In 1998, she goes to the conflict zone in Chiapas. In Polhó, she is moved by the survival skills and the poverty of those displaced; in Acteal, she observes and listens. And in Polhó she asks:

> Are you more afraid of something like Acteal happening here, having the army or the paramilitaries do the same thing? Are people more afraid now than a week ago? Is it getting worse? How do they threaten you? And how are people reacting? What are you doing about the fly-overs and increasing Federal patrols?[35]

Her position toward her country's governments is clear: "George Bush is an idiot surrounded by very intelligent people who know what they are doing. I scorn and am fearful of his government. In the United States dissidence is shut down. Clinton is Augustus and now we are truly an empire. Arnold Schwarzenegger is an ambitious cretin and a megalomaniac predator."[36]

Sontag's declarations following the tragedy of September 11 unleash hatred against her in the United States: articles, letters, and threats. She says: "I am aware of what a radical point of view is; very occasionally I have espoused one. But I did not think for a moment my essay was radical. . . . It seemed very common sense."[37]

AN EPILOGUE BEYOND A MERE OBITUARY

Sontag's biography can't be summarized in just a few pages. There are feuds and cultural battles, there is her fame as arrogant (for defending her time or for her elitist temperament), her nomadism, and her sense of entitlement particular to celebrities. In her love life, according to Rollyson and Paddock, María Irene Fornés is followed by the actress and film producer Nicole Stéphane, the dancer Lucinda Childs, and her companion of two decades, the photographer Annie Leibovitz. There was always someone insisting "you should stage a *coming out.*" On that matter, there are several conflicting positions. The writer Fran Leibovitz, Sontag's friend, responds to an article in *Outweek* rallying for the *outing* of Sontag: "It's damaging, it's immoral, it's McCarthyism, it's terrorism, it's cannibalism, it's beneath contempt . . . To me, this is a bunch of Jews lining up other Jews to go to a concentration camp."[38]

In turn, Larry Gross evokes Hannah Arendt's reflection on her experience as a Jew expelled from Germany: "The basically simple principle here is one that is particular to understand in times of defamation and persecution: The principle that one can resist only in terms of the identity that is under attack."[39]

As she herself affirmed with regard to her admired Juan Rulfo, Susan Sontag's body of work is classic in the true sense of the word. In retrospect, it seems it was her duty to write it.

Susan Sontag died of leukemia on December 28, 2004.

NOTES

1. Christopher Isherwood, *The World in the Evening* [1954] (New York: Random House, 1954; New York, Farrar, Straus and Giroux, 2013), 110. Citations refer to the Farrar, Straus edition.
2. Susan Sontag, "Notes on Camp," *Against Interpretation: And Other Essays* (London: Penguin Books, 1961; New York: Farrar Straus and Girard, 1966), 275. Citations refer to the Farrar, Straus edition.
3. Eric Partridge, *The Dictionary of Slang and Unconventional English*, 4th ed. (London: Routledge, 1937; London: Routledge, 1951). Citations refer to the 4th edition.
4. Sontag, "Notes on Camp," 291.`
5. The complete quote by Susan Sontag states, "Taste has no system and no proofs. But there is something like a logic of taste: the consistent sensibility which underlies and give rise to a certain taste." "Notes on Camp," 276.
6. A classic play by Anton Chekhov (1860–1904) written in 1900 and first performed in 1901 at the Moscow Art Theater.
7. Carl Rollyson and Lisa Paddock, *Susan Sontag: The Making of an Icon* (New York: W.W. Norton and Company, 2000), 51.
8. Following the two paragraphs of Sontag's biography, Monsiváis has a starred footnote that reads, "The 'hard data' of this not very private life [appears] in *Susan Sontag*. Rollyson and Paddock, *Susan Sontag*. Translated in Spain in 2002 by Circe Ediciones.
9. Quoted in Rollyson and Paddock, 92–93.
10. Sontag "Against Interpretation," 6, 7.
11. Sontag "Against Interpretation," 14.
12. Sontag, "Note to the Paperback Edition," *Against Interpretation*, viii.
13. In Tony Kushner, *Tony Kushner in Conversation* (Ann Arbor: University of Michigan Press, 1998). Originally part of San Francisco's City Arts and Lectures series *On Art and Politics*, which presented Susan Sontag and Tony Kushner in conversation on April 5, 1995. Monsiváis took the quote from the translation by Carlos Bonfil that appeared in *Debate Feminista*. Tony Kushner and

Susan Sontag, "Sobre arte y política," trans. Carlos Bonfil, *Debate Feminista*, no. 21 (April 2000).

14. In his analysis, Monsiváis paraphrases and quotes Rollyson and Paddock, 148–151, including quotes from Sontag's article "The Third World of Women," *Partisan Review*, 14, no. 2 (1973), 180–206.

15. Susan Sontag, "What's Happening in America," *Styles of Radical Will* (1966; repr., New York: Farrar, Straus and Giroux, 1976), 195.

16. Sontag, "What's Happening in America," 197–98.

17. Sontag, "What's Happening in America," 203.

18. Sontag, "Trip to Hanoi," in Sontag, *Styles of a Radical Will*.

19. Sontag, "Trip to Hanoi," 256.

20. Sontag, "Trip to Hanoi," 256–57.

21. Sontag, "Trip to Hanoi," 259.

22. Sontag, "Trip to Hanoi," 263.

23. Sontag's essay "Some Thoughts on the Right Way (for Us) to Love the Cuban Revolution" was published in a leading New Left publication, *Ramparts*. Susan Sontag, "Some Thoughts on the Right Way (for Us) to Love the Cuban Revolution," *Ramparts* 7, no. 11 (April 1969): 6–19.

24. Sontag, "Some Thoughts." Here Monsiváis paraphases and ironically condenses Sontag's argument in this essay, signaling the hypocrisy of the Cuban Leftist homophobia and repressive techniques.

25. Susan Sontag, *Illness as Metaphor* (New York: Farrar, Straus and Giroux, 1978), 8–9. This essay first appeared in three issues of the *New York Review of Books* in 1978: 24, no. 21–22 (Jan. 26, 1978); 25, no. 1 (Feb. 9, 1978); 25, no.2 (Feb. 23, 1978).

26. Sontag, *Illness as Metaphor*, 87–88. We have added the first half of the sentence from Sontag's original that Monsiváis had elided.

27. Susan Sontag, "The Way We Live Now," *New Yorker*, November 24, 1986.

28. Susan Sontag, *AIDS and Its Metaphors* (New York: Farrar, Straus and Giroux, 1989).

29. *El Pais*, December 1, 2004. Monsiváis documents this reference only with the publication and date, without title or author. However in late 2004, the pope was quoted in many media outlets for claiming that AIDS is a "pathology of the spirit."

30. Susan Sontag, *On Photography* (New York: Farrar, Straus and Giroux, 1978); Roland Barthes, *Camera Lucida* (New York: Hill and Wang, 1981), 180.

31. Unable to locate citation, perhaps from an interview. Our translation.

32. Sontag, *On Photography*, 180.

33. Susan Sontag, *Regarding the Pain of Others* (New York: Farrar, Straus and Giroux: 2003), 125–26.

34. ETA is an acronym for Euskadi Ta Askatasuna (Basque Homeland and Liberty), an armed nationalist and separatist paramilitary group fighting for independence for the Basque region of Spain from 1968 to 2010. Spain, France, the United Kingdom, the United States, Canada, and the European Union classified it as a terrorist group.

35. *La Jornada*, March 23, 1998. Monsiváis documents this reference only with the publication and date, without title or author. Our translation.

36. *La Jornada*, March 23, 1998. Our translation.

37. Interview by David Talbot, "The 'Traitor' Fires Back," *Salon*, Oct. 16, 2001.

38. *Outweek*, January 9, 1991. Leibovitz quoted in Rollyson and Paddock, *Susan Sontag*, 269–70.

39. Rollyson and Paddock, 270.

CHAPTER 19

Mexico at the Dawn of the Twenty-First Century

Globalization, Determinism, and the Spread of Secularism

2006

In 2006, Mexico has 105 million inhabitants (surely the real number is now a few million more). Politically, the triumph of Vicente Fox in 2000 derails the seventy-one-year trajectory of the Partido Revolucionario Institucional's practically single-party rule (previously the Partido Nacional Revolucionario, and the Partido de la Revolución Mexicana).[1] Immediately, Fox implements what will be the norm of his government: to significantly disappoint and defraud. The economic situation, never splendid, highlights its downturn while the macro-economy seems unfazed, and for millions of people the horizon holds unemployment and underemployment. The social landscape, marked by intra-familial violence and delinquency, is quite confusing and depressing, and few believe that there's "any way out." However, a different account of events emerges from renewed definitions of *secularism, nation, minorities, diversity,* and *alternative spaces*. Not only does the US version of globalization cast aside the structures of the nation-state by seeking to redefine sovereignty, but also, from within society itself, what has been postponed for too long finally surfaces: beginning with fundamental demands and human rights.

In these notes, I attempt to synthesize some of the changes that the nation is undergoing with the expansion of globalism, and the fundamental shifts in the imagining of Mexico, different from the accepted version of three decades ago. In the process, several concepts and key terms strongly come into play, underscored by an awareness of human rights. Faced with enormous challenges—the primacy of Bush era imperialism, the catastrophic government and its political parties, the end of formal employment, the devastation of ecosystems, urban violence, drug trafficking—the response can no longer be an absolute lack of commitment or come from a position of helplessness.

The role of ideas is crucial to the survival of societies. Genuine ideas can incite mobilizations and resistance, even if they're worn out and less effective or diluted and muddied. Let's examine the contemporary meanings of some key words—*civil society, tolerance, transition to democracy, programs of inclusion, diversity, plurality*, and *empowerment*—which have profound impact even when presented as platitudes or abstractions deployed irresponsibly and disingenuously. This fundamental vocabulary transcends political formations and brings to light a first attempt at global citizenship, already enacted in demonstrations against the invasion of Iraq, and in the rejection of a sole model of globalization. In imagining alternatives to Single Mindedness, ideas play a fundamental role.

IT HAS BEEN WRITTEN SINCE THE BEGINNING OF TIME . . .

One of the major cultural battles of this era has been that of confronting a deterministic mindset, a narrative interpretation of reality, which deeply internalized, represents a collection of the most entrenched prejudices in Latin America. What do I mean by *determinism*? If it's not the total suppression of consciousness, it *is* the product of a traditional education (religious conservatism, classism, patriarchal ideology), in addition to the mechanisms of authoritarianism in educational and cultural industries. Nothing can be done—that's the message in Colonial times—if you are Indigenous or Mestizo; in the nineteenth century, everything is forbidden—according to the imposed rules—because chaos defines the nation; and in the twentieth century, it's clear that if you don't belong to the elite or if you don't have the privilege of social mobility, you'll be consigned to your fate.[2]

Determinism, fundamentally based on social class, gender, and skin color, minimizes or ridicules the existence of destitution and poverty, which are characterized as "endemic expressions of humanity." Starting with the priests who demand obedience and resignation from Indigenous peoples and the urban poor, the historic aim of determinism (the mindset and desire to control) has been to turn economic and social constraints into idiosyncratic traits. If inequality is an unalterable trait of societies, then emancipatory struggles are futile from the get go.

In laying the groundwork of determinism, there's an insistence on the thesis of original sin. "Man that is born of a woman, is of few days, and full of trouble,"[3] lives under the shame of sin, which is "All thought, word, or act against the law of God" (St. Augustine). And who interprets and knows God's law? The clergy, who in baptizing the nation and its people, subject them from the beginning to the stark judgments of their own condition.

What's the outcome of foretelling the failure of criticism or change? Until very recently, you lived the illusion or myth of a one language, one religion, one political party nation, an inalterable way of understanding the roles of male and female, and a dogmatic body of beliefs, traditions, and practices. Therein lies the search for caudillos, the desperate acceptance of "iron-fisted" governments, the fear of change, and the imagined belief in a National Identity.

IF GOD WANTED US TO BE EQUAL, WE ALL WOULD'VE BEEN BORN IN THE SAME BARRIO

At least in statistics, much is said and known about the marginalized majority, even as their cultural expressions and forms of survival suffer erasure. In the last half century, no one objects to the description of Mexico as "a country founded on inequality," and no government goes beyond passing a couple of egalitarian measures (in the best of cases) or pathetic grandstanding. "To the dispossessed, I ask forgiveness," proclaims President José López Portillo in December of 1976 upon taking office.[4] After the unpayable historic debt is acknowledged, those living in destitution and poverty, about 65 percent of the population, can once again be treated with harshness and indifference.

The marginalized minorities don't even manage to get the attention of governments or the press as they continue enduring racism, sexism, homophobia, intolerance in general, as well as religious intolerance. Until recently, the recognition of diversity has not been the norm; it's only just in 1982, during Miguel de la Madrid's Priista campaign, as a gesture of courtesy toward the social scientists, that the pluralism of the country is recognized.[5] The Liberals define their fellow party members, and Mexico, as a homogeneous whole: Catholics at fiesta time, pilgrimages, and censuses, and a fundamentally Mestizo and heterosexual society. Anything different is hardly acknowledged, and it's extremely difficult to exercise any liberties in matters of morality or daily life.

One must abide by and comply with a proliferation of tyrannical impositions: a monopoly of beliefs, a monopoly of political power, a monopoly of economic power, and a monopoly of acceptable conduct. Majorities and minorities are marginalized, and the "bad luck" we frequently experience is considered "natural or normal." Those excluded from the Visible Nation (the majority) are condemned to a hell in which a lack of opportunities goes hand in hand with the absence of respectability. Religious dissidents, political dissidents, the disabled, the elderly, alcoholics, gays and lesbians, and most notably, the Indigenous populations, congregate in marginal spaces. Occupying an undeclared but relentless marginality are the majority of women, or in spaces of power, all women. Plurality arrives slowly in spite of historic conquests (freedom of religion, freedom of expression, a free and lay education, and secularization). Despite their extraordinary differences, these sectors share fundamental traits: the psychic and/or physical cost paid by assuming or modifying identities defined by outsiders; the difficulties in constructing their own history (the effort required to adapt to hostile environments), and the unending repercussions of "original sin;" *the guilt* of not fitting in with the norm, of being different from the elite.

KEYWORDS

The weight of keywords is noteworthy. Since the decade of the 1930s, at least part of a person or society's true identity depends on their willingness to adapt to terms that many times serve as a constraint: *primitivism, inferiority complex, colonization, underdevelopment, dependency, marginality, Third World, periphery* . . . For almost a century, you can hear these kinds of phrases: "So far from God, so close to the United States." / "What can we do if we're underdeveloped?" / "My third-worldliness came out and I didn't go to work." / "It's true, we're marginal." / "No matter how much I read through the *New York Times*, there's no news about my hometown." (Today you might say: "So global, huh, but still living in the same neighborhood.") These painful or picturesque versions confirm a historical fact: in peripheral countries, because of evident comparison and prejudice, metropolitan cities are idealized. This is intensified by globalization, which turns interpretations of *Alice in Wonderland* into shame-inducing aspirations. Hence, in Latin America at the beginning of the twenty-first century, it's common to label oneself a second-hand global citizen, as international as anyone, but much less so.

In great proportion, old definitions don't apply any longer, or they do, but in a restricted way. In this semantic journey, some words never go out of style, they just express the opposite of their original meanings. And the causes that emerge bring new definitions and words that modify the conceptual map.

The meanings and the rootedness of keywords is overwhelming. I'll quote a few:

- *Sexism*. The ideology of masculine superiority is the dogmatic backdrop (if that's the word) of machismo and patriarchy. The very use of the word marks machismo as the social nightmare that it is.
- *Gender*. The concept that evades historical weight and the prison-houses of male and female identity, and generates a conceptual field that presupposes objectivity. During the decade of the 1990s, the Catholic Church sets out to confront and defeat the term, and at the Beijing Conference of 1995, the Islamic countries and the Vatican reject the word, based on an assumption: God created man and woman, not genders.[6] They fail, and the expression *gender perspective* gains the traction that feminism hadn't been able to achieve in its name.
- *Empowerment*. The notion of the taking of power, such as citizen participation in politics and social movements. This concept is indispensable in the development of feminism, of minority identities, and NGOs.
- *Gay*. The international use of *gay* is a great advance as it doesn't carry the burden of prejudice and the historical contempt that emanates from words like *maricón* (pansy), *joto* (fag), *puto* (bitch, pussy), and their equivalents in each country. The term *gay* connects a national minority with a planetary minority of continuous social and legal conquests.
- *Homophobia*. The irrational hatred of homosexuals acquires a specific name and becomes an identifiable prejudice. This naming considerably reduces the prejudice.
- *Diversity*. A current synonym for minority rights, especially for sexual minorities.

INDIGENOUS PEOPLES: THE LEGACY OF INEQUALITY

If one thing becomes transparent since 1994, it's the evidence of racism in Mexico. To be an "indio" —that is, to belong to communities identified as such because of their endogamous practices, minority languages, and customs seen as "premodern"—is to be in perpetual disadvantage, a segregation "encouraged" by phenotype.[7] Those who deny racism tend to attest to the social mobility of people with prominent Indigenous features, but none of these easily identifiable Indigenous people is secretary of state, governor, renowned politician, first-class entrepreneur, or even simply a celebrity. In his novel *Invisible Man* (1952), Ralph Ellison describes how the prejudice of skin color erases people's individuality, it dehumanizes them. What makes one black person indistinguishable from another is the contempt that a racist society professes. Something similar has happened with the Indigenous peoples of Mexico ever since the time of the Conquest. Why wouldn't it? They're primitive, they're unaware of the wonders of books (much like the racists), and they're considered to be eternally underage, as promoted by institutions (only in 2003 did they close the INI, Instituto Nacional Indigenista, the National Institute of Indigenous Peoples, "tutor" of millions[8]). According to this criteria, they're not marginalized: they were born outsiders and their passive attitude only confirms their remoteness.

Belonging to the "defeated race" denies Indigenous peoples "the possibility of development." Other limitations: the "strange" language shared only by a minority, the "lack" of a formal education, displacement to depleted ecological zones, alcoholism, *caciquismo* (including Indigenous *caciquismo*), the inevitable infighting, and deep cultural isolation.[9] If the subjugation of Indigenous peoples began with the Conquest (notwithstanding the sporadic rebellions and their crushing defeats), the PRI government consecrates fatality. In 1948, Alfonso Caso, the founder of the Instituto Nacional de Antropología e Historia (INAH) and the Instituto Nacional Indigenista, defines the subjects of his advocacy with tautological levity:

> An Indian is an individual who feels a belonging to an Indigenous community, and an Indigenous community is one in which non-European somatic elements are predominant, that preferably speaks an Indigenous language, whose cultural and spiritual culture is proportionately strong in Indigenous elements and that, lastly, has a social sense of belonging to an outlying community within other surrounding communities, that distinguishes itself from white and Mestizo populations.[10]

An *Indian* is one who lives in an Indigenous world, that's how precise Don Alfonso Caso is. The Mestizo has some "European somatic elements," which, in accordance with this argument, is somehow redeeming. "You can still see their 'Indianness,' but they speak a recognizable Spanish." In this universe, economic destitution is complemented by moral degradation or however else you'd like to call the unending drunken fog, the violence, and the brutal treatment of women in spaces that come close to *apartheid*. Oppression radically marginalizes, thus the *ladinos* see it as self-inflicted, and express their opinion: "Indians are that way because they want to be."[11]

Historically, the looters and oppressors enjoy ridiculing their victims. Besides the social climate, racism deploys visual representations (the Indian

tends to be the impossible allegory or the "amusing" caricature) of stereotypes in poetry and narrative, mocking their faltering use of *Castilla*
(Spanish) and, in the twentieth century, parodies of frivolous theater, radio,
movies and television abound.[12] The Indian is seen as a being without sufficient ties to "civilization," a tragic or pathetic individual, only occasionally
humorous and then, unwittingly so. According to those who observe them
but don't really see them, their traditions are merely picturesque, linking
them to "primitivism" either with sarcasm or consternation. The Catholic
Church infantilizes them, Guadalupanismo offers them the refuge of faith,
their "usos y costumbres" (traditional laws) highlight their feudal structures,
the state nominally protects them, and as "orphans of civilization," they are
reluctantly "adopted" without anyone taking any real responsibility.[13]

The Instituto Nacional Indigenista, which during the PRI government
acted at times as "an orphanage" or "cultural heritage site," provides some
benefits and this assures the government's utmost disinterest, confident in
having gone above and beyond their duties by allocating minimal funds
from their budget if they ever do. And the life of the Indigenous population
generally unfolds in very oppressive conditions and amid the indifference of
news outlets, uninterested in reporting murders, unjust incarcerations, the
rape of women, and the continual plundering of lands and forests. *They're
Indians*, they live outside of Mexico. As Enrique Florescano has analyzed,
there's an attempt to justify such dispossession with historical reasoning,
and the oppressive mythology initiated by Lucas Alamán.[14] According to
Alamán and his followers, Mexico doesn't owe anything to its Indigenous
past, and Mexican society doesn't even acknowledge their worth. Florescano
observes that what's eliminated from the historical narrative is "the crucial
participation of the Indigenous Peoples and peasants in the three uprisings
that changed the modern and contemporary history of the Nation: the periods of Independence, Reform, and Revolution."[15] The nation, argues Florescano, has systematically opposed Indigenous claims and has attempted to
impose laws that violate their most sacred rights: racism demands that they
renounce their languages, give up their autonomy and, in short, it encour-
ages them to stop being Indians by obstructing their right to a primordial
identity in which they can take pride.

Destitution and poverty cannot be eliminated by decree, and Indians
are pushed aside and punished for their marginality. In Guerrero, Puebla,
Hidalgo, the State of Mexico, Chiapas, Oaxaca, Mexico City, and Yucatan,
Indigenous peoples live in extreme poverty, and yet their demographic
strength is unyielding, and their numbers still range between twelve and
fourteen million. The Rule of Law doesn't exist for them, and hundreds of

thousands are subjected to semi-slavery. Until 1995, cattle theft was more heavily penalized than murder in Chiapas, and even in 1960, the phrase "gente de razón" (rational people) distinguished Mestizos and Criollos from Indigenous peoples.[16] The disdain is ingrained and, in 1994, Chiapas's highest-ranking official asserts, "The masked fighters of the EZLN can't be Indigenous, because 'Indians' don't use modern weapons, but bows and arrows."[17]

Resistance to this marginality can be seen in labor migration to the United Sates, and more often than not, modernization. Additionally, there are widespread conversions to Protestantism, often due to the social need for new behavioral models, among them, giving up alcohol. Unfortunately, young Indigenous women continue to face both internal and external machismo.

In 1992, the Quincentennial, no longer of the Conquest but—using a political expression—of the "Encounter between Two Worlds," it seems delusional to believe in the resurgence of Indigenous peoples.[18] It's useless, it is said, because they [the Indigenous] neither want to assimilate nor can they learn. Some Federal officials disseminate a theory of "education": because of their inevitable malnutrition, "Indians" are incapable of attaining a solid education, and it's better to encourage them to focus on their handicrafts. Determinism and racism give rise to devastating outcomes: at the end of the twentieth century only 8 percent of Indigenous children finish elementary school. Mexican society doesn't accept that it's racist, but it is, with a caveat: those who look down on, exploit, and consider Indigenous peoples beyond hope don't see themselves as members of a superior race, they're only witnesses annoyed by the inaction of an inferior class: the Indian.

It is in this context of an Indigenous people expelled from the Nation that on January 1, 1994, the EZLN emerges in opposition to the processes of destruction and self-destruction of centuries. And the Zapatista bases show their disgust with their own condition of semi-slavery, Chiapas's feudal economy, and the collapse of their sources of income.

PROTESTANTS: "THERE'S ONLY ONE WAY TO WORSHIP GOD"

As with members of other minorities, Protestants or Evangelicals also suffer a series of exclusions from national identity, legal protection in rural communities, the respect and understanding of their neighbors, and social solidarity. (Any way you look at it, "National Identity" excludes them.) There's no recognition of their cultural, political, and social integration into the country; it was the same at the end of nineteenth century as at the end of the twentieth—there's no major criticism of the intolerance exercised against them. At the close of the nineteenth century, Mexico sees the beginning of a significant presence of Protestantism, and the first converts live the exhilaration of a faith that literally changes their lives, gives them the right to interpret the Bible, and puts them at a distance from what they see as fanaticism. They're watched with enormous suspicion, they're persecuted, and they're forced to gravitate toward the larger cities.

In the early decades of the twentieth century, all the major denominations present in the US can also be found in Mexico, and groups of natives begin to root themselves in the Pentecostal tradition. There are Presbyterians, Methodists, Baptists, Nazarenes, and Congregationalists. From 1930 on, the wave of Pentecostalism that takes precedence is the one that emphasizes religious experience based on emotional connection. As always, intolerant reactions are guided by the criteria of Catholic bishops alarmed at the growth of Protestantism and its "sects." In 1951 and 1952, an anti-Protestant campaign of enormous proportions is unleashed by the Archbishop Primate Luis María Martínez.[19] We have to stop "the advancement of heresy," says Don Luis María, who tells slightly off-color jokes, blesses all new buildings, and is a member of the Academia Mexicana de la Lengua.[20] Incidentally, he is an old-fashioned crusader of faith who, without any remorse, presides over the hunt for religious dissidents.

At that time, there isn't any social script for confronting intolerance. If they're persecuted, it's because they're asking for it, and there's no point in trying to find out why. One exception: the renowned writer Martín Luis Guzmán, director of the weekly magazine *Tiempo*.[21] In a 1952 front cover of *Tiempo*, he declares, "Against the Gospel, the Catholic Church practices genocide." No one else speaks out, and the list of crimes and grievances is considerable: congregations ousted from their towns; churches stoned or burned; ministers hacked to death by machete or dragged by a horse; and the social marginalization of "heretics." The Catholic hierarchy smirks while the Protestants organize a (poorly attended) annual demonstration on the twenty-first of March.

In Mexico City, demographics erase the most conspicuous features of religious marginality (very big town, your choice of hell, depending on luck[22]), but in small and medium-sized locales, religious dissidence is seen as a provocation. The poorest are the most denigrated and, in particular, the Pentecostals have it the worst, because of being branded "hallelujahs," the wailers of a false Lord.[23] There's no acknowledged practice of respecting and *understanding* difference. Closed societies don't understand nuance, and when it's impossible to repress difference, social rejection ranges from contemptuous humor to an essential distrust. A typical joke from that time: a father finds out about his daughter's *non sancta* profession. He gets furious and threatens her: "Damn you daughter! Tell me what you are again, so I can curse my fate. Get out of my house." His daughter is surprised and responds: "Dad, I'm a prostitute." He lets out a sigh of relief and smiles. "Prostitute? Oh good, I thought you had said *Protestant*." And don't forget the classic jab: Hallelujah, hear our song, and let each one grab their dong.[24]

Until the demographic explosion of the masses, Protestants were besieged by incomprehension and the pointing of fingers. "He's a good person but . . ." / "Sure, son, go to their house to eat, but don't let them try to convert you." The door signs distributed by bishops stave off the undesirables: "In this house, we're Catholic and we don't accept Protestant propaganda." What's least acceptable is the phenomenon of conversion, the desertion of the "True Faith" and Juan Diego's unconditional belief as "the humblest of the Virgin's children." Besides that, the nationalist or Communist Left's condemnations accrue: the Protestants are "anti-Mexican, greedy, soul-recruiting agents of the US, and destroyers of national unity." In the attack, the fury of Catholic fundamentalism, the homage of government bureaucrats to their parochial past, and the zeal of Mexican Marxist anthropologists, devotees of National Identity, coincide.

For the majority of nationals, religious dissidence is an unexplored continent, although increasingly less foreign as globalization intensifies. Nevertheless, in the decade of the 1960s, because of the pressures to conform, Protestantism appears to be at a standstill, the minority caught up in the country's period of Americanization, and in the capital and larger cities, Protestants go from being threatening to picturesque, they're the families that walk around with their hymn books and bibles on Sundays, pious people, considered generally trustworthy *if* eccentric. Who would think of converting to a different religion now that not even our parent's faith is particularly practical? Social life assimilates Protestants eager for social mobility, preferring to get married in the Catholic Church; and by the 1970s, growing intolerance makes difference fully unacceptable, and the Instituto Lingüístico de Verano (ILV; Summer Institute of Linguistics [SIL]), an organism responsible for translating sections of the Bible into the Indigenous languages of Mexico, was expelled from the country.[25] In the process of removing the ILV, and without evidence, bishops and Marxist anthropologists called it "an outpost of the CIA," "an instrument to divide Mexicans," etc. There were no protests when the ILV was ousted.

And yet the bishops overlook the prevalence of "idolatry" or "paganism" (the recurrence of pre-Hispanic Indigenous rituals, the hundreds of thousands of followers of Trinitarian and Marianist spiritualism, and spiritism), as well as the varieties of New Age practices.

Around that time, and unexpectedly so, the frenzy of mass conversion to Protestantism sets in. The frenzy of conversions is driven by a need to be integrated into a genuine community; the revelation of individual interpretations of the Bible; the desire for a transformation (a change of life without changing jobs); and Indigenous women's urgent need for their husbands to quit drinking and end domestic violence. Especially in the southeastern part of the country, the conversions become a mass phenomenon and, correspondingly, the Catholic bishops launch hate campaigns against the "sects" characterized by the pope's envoy Girolamo Prigione as "flies" to be swatted with a newspaper. In Chiapas, their churches are burned and the Protestants are expelled from several communities, especially from San Juan Chamula (thirty-five thousand are displaced). Today, in 2006, we continue to see killings in rural areas. The anti-Protestant bashings are accompanied by diatribes against New Age practice and the "diabolical doctrine," nonetheless, the advancement of a diversity of beliefs cannot be stopped, neither can the para-Protestant groups (Mormons or Latter Day Saints, Jehovah's Witnesses) and the Pentecostal churches: "With so many variants, where's the truth?," but in a plural society this question is not enough when roughly ten to fifteen million people participate in these beliefs. (The Catholic Church boasts of having 80 percent of the faithful at its disposal, while at the same time describing a country of "religious illiterates" and "functional atheists.")

GAYS: FROM THE UNSPEAKABLE TO AN INSISTENCE ON NAMING

Since Mexico's adaptation of the Napoleonic Code, its laws do not prohibit homosexuality between consenting adults. (Something very different happens regarding pedophilia, which is highly criminalized for heterosexuals and homosexuals.) Nevertheless, gay men are subjected to horrendous versions of "justice," and whether by commission or omission, persecutions of "the abnormals" are allowed, including multi-year prison terms for the sole crime of appearing effeminate. The bulwark of homophobic witch hunts is a Judeo-Christian tradition, and the legal justification is always a vague term, "lack of morals and good manners," which since the nineteenth century justifies and legitimizes fines, detention from fifteen days to several years, job terminations, police abuse, blackmail, legal kidnappings, in addition to consignment to the penitentiary on the Islas Marías and the concentration camps at the Valle Nacional.[26]

In the history of Mexico, homosexuals have been burned alive, they are morally or physically lynched, they are expelled from their families, their communities, and (frequently) from their jobs, they are incarcerated for the sole offence of being who they are ("a violation of rules," is not required, being effeminate suffices), they are outed without any compassion, they are excommunicated, they are viciously murdered.[27] Just for "being who they are," the twentieth century brings them, in addition to police brutality, an implacable dose of raids, extortions, beatings, murders by stabbing or strangling, and ritual hazing. There is no respect or tolerance for homosexuals or, better yet, "los jotos" (fags), "los maricones" (pansies), "los putos" (bitches), "los invertidos" (inverts), "los larailos" (fairies), and "los volteados" (queers). Aware of the religious and moral discredit of "las locas" (queens), society fully repudiated them until recently, and if anything, it offers a paradoxically magnanimous comment: "Let them do whatever they want, as long as they don't do it in public or mess with me."

Status, talent, or trustworthiness don't matter. Neither, and this is crucial, do human rights. Facing the police or slander, the homosexual loses his personal identity, and becomes a non-person, dehumanized for his instinctual orientation. Therein the need to remain in the closet, or marry (in high numbers), or pursue psychoanalysis to find a "cure," or become religious extremists praying for an "end to this curse." As Sartre says, "hell is other people," but those marginalized also carry hell on their backs.[28] And the absence of human and civil rights multiplies their sensation of nonexistence. "We are nothing, except when what we are is ignored or forgotten."[29] Thus, the absence of reactions in Mexico to the significance of the Kinsey Report (1948), which internationally reorients the idea of homosexuality. If one out of twenty persons is homosexual or has had these experiences, the demographic volume lessens the burden of sin, "If there are that many, maybe they should have rights."

Mexico is officially a secular country, but traditionalism rules in everyday life and, in unison, the liberal politicians, the Leftists, and the conservatives are outraged by the "betrayal of nature." In the offices of the Public Ministry, Judeo-Christian prohibitions are also the rule, and everyone finds it *normal* to send homosexuals to jail because of their tone of voice or gestures, or to victimize them simply out of cruelty—no one defends them or even protests. ("It's a crime of passion typical of homosexuals," assert the press and the police, instead of pointing out, "It's a typical crime against homosexuals.") There's still a long way to go before introducing the term "hate crimes," and each murdered homosexual is followed by the arrests of their friends, and the impunity of the actual criminal. The raids "defend morality and good manners," even if they destroy lives and provoke family crises; such intense bullying leads to tortured psyches, and maybe because of that, tortured psyches are attributed solely to homosexual desire. Before 1969 and the Stonewall Rebellion in New York, no one comes out of the closet if it can be avoided, because such martyrdom doesn't result in any beatification.[30]

AIDS: THE VISIBILITY OF TRAGEDY

By 1985 the magnitude of the AIDS pandemic is clear. Before, everything about the "pink cancer" had been deemed as alarmist and fear-driven. Rock Hudson discloses he's sick and dies shortly thereafter, and the pandemic can no longer be concealed. Fear multiplies prejudices, rejections, and incomprehension a hundredfold, and for example, at the medical center, a young man hangs himself, unable to bear the abuse by doctors and nurses. They relentlessly demonize gay men, the group most affected by AIDS (even today 70 percent of those with AIDS are gay). "Don't eat near a homosexual. You might get infected," reads an ad posted on the streets. The Papal Nuncio Girolamo Prigione categorizes AIDS as "God's punishment"; in several businesses, tests to detect AIDS are required, and those who test positive are given half an hour to permanently leave their jobs. The secretary of health is against campaigns directed specifically at the gay community because, presumably, the State can't or shouldn't recognize that the perversion even exists. (The secretary of health Jesús Kumate has close ties to the Opus Dei.) Only toward the end of 1997 does the first (faint-hearted) prevention campaign for the gay community takes place. In 2003, mass campaigns for the prevention of AIDS are still nonexistent. Let's not get the bishops angry.

These are years of tension, of tragedies, of families who expel the sick, of massive infections due to the negligence of blood banks, of mistreatments at hospitals, and of many family abandonments (though it's not the case for the majority). Added to the motives for hate crimes against homosexuals is the fear of AIDS. An adolescent in Ciudad Neza kills a priest because "he tried to infect me with AIDS." The majority of people are infected because of a lack of information, and in both private and public television, ads for condoms disappear or are reduced to a minimum, while data on the disease is silenced. The Catholic Church and its small advocate groups are opposed to preventative campaigns and undertake a "moral lynching" of the condom, nervously calling it a "preservative," a word that doesn't bother those not yet aware of the existence of genitalia.

Never before had an "adminicle" (the term used by Cardinal Primate Norberto Rivera) carried so much aversion.[31] The Nuncio Prigione calls it "the instrument that drags young boys through the mud," and on denouncing the existence of sex without reproductive purpose, forced abstinence is exalted: "The only response to AIDS is chastity." In 1990, in Monterrey, the governor of Nuevo León Jorge Treviño removes a big ad for condoms "because it can damage the minds of young children." It's not infrequent that the neighbors or even families kick those with AIDS out of their homes. In the rural areas, the problem is greater given the perfect storm of prejudices and medical disinformation, and in farm-working regions, the infection rate among the wives of migrant workers spreads.

Despite their insufficiency, responses are abundant. Anti-AIDS activists persevere in Mexico City and Oaxaca, Aguascalientes, Monterrey, Guadalajara, Querétaro, the State of Mexico, etc., but there are still so many obstacles, even if tolerance is advancing. With worldwide information on AIDS and the "other" sexuality, with numerous movies, TV series, plays, and novels on the theme, with large marches in Washington, New York, San Francisco, London, and Sidney, the spectacle of the perverse shadows of homophobia is no longer so frightening. Being at such high risk, those ill finally disregard the "What will people say?" In addition, the Catholic clergy and the Right, in their obsessive struggle against all diversity, condemn any bodily autonomy (including wearing "provocative" clothing), they spitefully oppose the decriminalization of abortion, they're obstinate in their campaigns to discredit "the sects," and they reaffirm the definition of "Society" that doesn't accept those outside the "Norm." The AIDS pandemic brings out the best and the worst of social attitudes, also calling attention to altruistic young people, many of them seropositive and sick, who are determined to spread preventative measures and support the ill rather than the enemy clergy and the relics of the Counter-Reformation.

WHERE DOES CHANGE BEGIN AND WHAT ABOUT IMMOBILITY?

How real is the much talked about *change of paradigms*? Among the factors that support this hypothesis is globalization (inevitable), technology understood religiously, the collapse of socialist alternatives, neoliberal oppression, and an inescapable reality: the *nation* will continue to be the requisite entry point to globalization. With great arrogance, the neoliberals push the country to transcend its "mediocrity" and become competitive, that is, to renounce its cultural traditions, which will end up seemingly picturesque and folkloric if not abandoned immediately. Here's the edict: no progress is possible without renouncing what the nation has stood for. On the one hand, the warning is late; on the other, a sole model of globalization isn't very effective, especially after the invasion of Iraq.

It's a false dilemma to call for "either nationalism or modernity." This is, if anything, a lesson from the past. Traditional nationalism disappeared or is disappearing fast, and except for sheer resistance to change, no one truly believes in a nationalism founded on a declared homogeneity (National Unity), in the segregation of Indigenous peoples, in the social and political invisibility of women, in the slogans of chauvinistic mythomania, and in machismo. What can a nationalism—whose mythological and sociological vigor depend on the idealization of migrants, or on the illusion of a glorious past for the sedentary—possibly convey today? But if traditional nationalism is as undefinable as "the love of Mexico" (Yes, we all love our country, but without the rhetoric, how do you define this love?), the nation remains and here, again, what's important is the accuracy of the definitions. The nation as we know it has been terribly unjust with its minorities and its oppressed majorities, it has inspired a profound love because it fostered psychological belonging, and is still very cruel in the intensity of its *push factors*. And there's no such thing as "the national" that is valid for all classes and all groups. To each their own homeland, according to their experience.

There is a strong tendency to oversimplify social and political life, and inevitably to confuse Americanization with ridiculous, childish candor. Here's where the tools of determinism come into play, such as self-help manuals, those home-delivered utopias: how to keep the biggest piece of the pie, how to become an entrepreneur without thinking about the minimum wage, how to move up at the office with gifts to your bosses, etc. In the remaking of the country into a big corporation, self-help manuals become the "spiritual" reconstruction of the republic.

Determinism is renewed, supported by *light* Freudian explanations, by the economic imperative of "Be thankful you have a job, whatever it is," and by religious fanaticism. In a variety of ways, in the twentieth century, the following is emphasized: we will never stop being on the periphery, or suffering from an inferiority complex, or living in underdevelopment, or being dependent, or bearing the Cross of the Third World, or being local in the end. Determinism affects the Left and the Right: it influences the bourgeoisie who consider their residential zones "Noah's arks"; it results in situations like the ten-month strike at the UNAM in 1999, with students convinced that the unemployment of radicals also protects those with academic titles; it drastically influences the expectations of the poor, and the peasantry; and in a way, it explains the ease with which narco-trafficking infiltrated to become Mexico's unending nightmare.[32]

The determinism that condemns the country, and the majority of its inhabitants, is driven by the catastrophe of public and private education, the prevalence of functional illiteracy, and the abandonment of reading due to audiovisual media (a performative abandonment, because no one was really reading anyway), the humiliatingly low wages of teachers, the pretechnological condition of a good part of public education, the demographic explosion of students with a lack of qualified educators, in synthesis, the universal crisis of education.

"DON'T EVEN BOTHER BECAUSE IF ALL GOES WELL, YOU'LL BECOME THE COMMERCIALS YOU'RE WATCHING"

Calling for helplessness before the economic "powers that be" may be the worst—the most fatalistic—cultural trait of recent years. In the case of television, fatalism is a success, and a common cliché is spread: in effect, the poor will be forever screwed because they can't afford more with their salaries. If economic power is of utmost importance, its paralyzing consequences are, nevertheless, not "divine law," nor do they devalue or destroy ideas and cultural activity. Despite all this, "the People" (that term that always excludes the one who utters it) are able to develop culturally.

To make poverty tantamount to fatality is power's persistent strategy. President Carlos Salinas de Gortari states, "There is no democracy in poverty," and President Ernesto Zedillo chases off everyone who he thinks doesn't "know what's what" near the ballot boxes, saying, "The poor don't vote."[33] And Vicente Fox's secretary of social development, Josefina Vázquez Mota, explains in her inaugural speech, "Poverty and democratic consolidation are incompatible. Poverty and justice walk in opposite directions. . . . Poverty and human dignity are contradictory, destitution and freedom don't fit in the same space . . ." (November 24, 2000).[34]

So wealth and human dignity are complementary, but if poverty isn't quickly eradicated, human dignity will take a long time to reach the poor, if ever. It goes from the obvious—from the challenges of instilling democratic values in media disinformed, for example, about individual rights—to the latest common belief: daily motivation comes only from the television.

Determinism is renewed by the theory that by dividing the planet into the global and the local, the other classic divisions still remain: metropolis and periphery, development and underdevelopment, first world and third world, colonizers and colonized. Thus, the undeniable is exposed—the chasm between wealthy countries and poor countries—and elevated to the rank of theological truth. Quickly it goes beyond social Darwinism: the loser is already screwed because he never leaves the starting gate. Strictly speaking, these abysmal differences make no attempt at description, but rather turn reality into fatality. "We'll never stop being underdeveloped" was said with the same conviction that is today applied to the local condition. So what writer or painter or filmmaker or architect or actor can "globalize" themselves? A small handful of them do, but the rest of them see the writing on the wall: "No matter what you do, you'll always be local." Even a few years ago, custom bestowed the title of nobility onto those harbored by the Noah's Ark of international fame: "Universal Mexicans." Today one could call them "ringside globals."

"HE'S SO PROVINCIAL, HE REMEMBERS EVERYTHING FROM HIS CHILDHOOD"

The previously rigid borders (cultural, social, moral) between the capital and the province have weakened, and the distinction itself is losing its meaning.[35] However, something of this lack of communication or deep divide between those worlds still remains. Culturally, centralism created a country with only one "true" city. Throughout the twentieth century, successive waves of young men flocked to the capital eager to leave their provincial condition behind and become *capitalinos* (inhabitants of the capital), with universal interests and belonging. The countryside is stripped of any ability to retain the young, and—in spite of the notable culture among their learned minority—of any significant achievement.

Several phenomena (television, communication speed, the emergence of financial centers in regional areas, the internet) phase out the use of a word that has historically been oppressive: "provincial." Cultural activity in the outlying regions increases, and the Global Village is real insofar as information technology is present. True, but 90 percent of cultural offerings are still taking place in the capital. For the State, for regional governments, political parties, and a large number of intellectuals, the democratization of the country is of no concern. The reasons are myriad: it's not considered possible; the attempt is seen as *populist* (almost a legacy of socialist realism); and the imposition of elitist taste is rejected in the autonomous spaces of the popular classes whose natural tastes range from the framed fluorescent prints of the Last Supper to the closeted patriotism that only comes out when the national soccer team wins.

This indifference is acute and costly. Even in poverty, democracy still exists, but this democracy is consolidated without classical music, reading, quality rock, jazz, museums, theater, dance, art exhibits, and some symposiums. This is not addressed because, with a program but no cultural project, the government doesn't believe it possible to increase public attendance, and all the funding is earmarked for the same million people, something notoriously insufficient and disdainful. By omission, minorities that feel "rescued" condemn the majority, who they judge as irredeemable, to a hell that lacks in spiritual alternatives.

ON THE EXPANSION OF SECULARISM

Despite the terrible distortions imposed by the PRI, the Republic is still secular, convinced of the value of tolerance and respect for liberties and community sentiments, with a sense of history essentially sustained by the liberal Reform and the Mexican Revolution, with its mythology of power whose most salient examples are Hidalgo, Morelos, Juárez, Zapata, Villa, and Lázaro Cárdenas.[36] Degraded by corruption and authoritarianism, the Republic has nevertheless preserved a space for the exercise of liberties that is neither a concession to or apartheid from criticism, but rather an irrefutable achievement of social and cultural movements.

Even if it never calls itself by that name, secularism, enriched by socialist thinking and the residue of radical struggles, expands over the course of the last three decades with the development of civil society and nongovernmental organizations (NGOs), as well as with the specific struggles of historically marginalized sectors: first and foremost, Indigenous peoples (recognizing the contributions of the EZLN is inevitable), women of the feminist persuasion, the cultural Left, independent unionization, a considerable portion of the academic sector (especially at the UNAM), regional groups taking on conservatism, certain branches of the PRD (not the [Fidel] Castro supporters nor the bureaucracy that monopolizes opportunities), and the minor political parties, the sexual minorities, etc.[37]

Regarding its principles, at the turn of the twenty-first century, Mexico is an almost unrecognizable entity, while at the same time, a faithful inheritor of its past. There is plurality, feminist theories permeate society, freedom of expression normalizes the presence of a good number of causes, what was once seen as "abhorrent" is now frequently called "the minority," and the political Right in some regions accepts that the terms "moral misconduct" and even "good manners" are no longer applicable. (Who outside of the courts could define *morality*, and what are today's *good manners*?[38])

TESTIMONIES FROM THE RIGHT

"No government plan will work without DI [Divine Intervention]"

A ———

In 2002, on the occasion of the disasters caused by hurricane Isidore, the recommendation from the governor of Yucatán, Patricio Patrón, to a group of those impacted is "I'll pray for you." A Mayan woman responds, "Thank you, but our children can't eat prayers."[39]

B ———————

Toluca. In a sort of Mass where Luis Donaldo Colosio's spirit was invoked, the 373 pre-candidates from the PRI for the 124 boroughs swore to God that they would preserve the unity of their party and recover the faith and creed that had been lost.[40]

"Never again betray society," exhorted the party's state leader, Isidro Pastor, addressing his faithful audience from an altar, brandishing a votive candle, the Mexican flag, and the coat of arms of the State of Mexico.

The Gregorian chants, the tunes of "The Impossible Dream" and "Desiderata" flooded the auditorium of the PRI's state headquarters, where the pre-candidates pledged their allegiance to the state and the national constitutions and to other fundamental party documents.[41]

"Brothers, from pre-candidates to municipal presidents of the PRI: Do you swear by God, by the Nation, and our Party to respect the final results of this selection process, no matter the outcome?" the local senator, Luis Decaro, asked.

"Yes, I swear," came the response from the candidates cloaked in semi-darkness. Pastor returned to the altar, the votive's flame undulating while the artificial mood spread through the air to release those who committed defamation during the political fight.

"I ask all of you to check your consciences and truly repent for having done that," he prayed.

In order to prove their faith to the pastor, the faithful joined hands, and transformed themselves into a dark energy, they swayed from side to side, to the beat of "The Impossible Dream."[42]

C ———————

In a conference held on August 20, 2002, at the Universidad Panamericana (Panamerican University, of the Opus Dei), the secretary of labor, Carlos Abascal, exhorts law students:

> The old liberal saying that you have all heard in different classes is not enough: as long as I respect the rights of others, as long others respect my rights, we can establish a peaceful coexistence: no, it isn't necessary to bash that individualist, pragmatic, materialist vision to be conscious of the fact that today justice demands that we all respond from the position of the rights of others, because their rights are my responsibility and mine are the responsibility of others. Only in this way, with solidarity, can we confront the enormous

challenge that creating jobs for 1,300,000 Mexicans implies. . . . You [the lis-
teners] are children of businessmen, with a comfortable economic situation,
all of you have the blessing of having reached this level of opportunities. . . .
It isn't wrong to have money. On the contrary, it's good that there are wealthy
people with honestly earned money, but that money must be reinvested in
well-remunerated employment, in training, in technological development.
That's your challenge! Look at your future . . . as if you were indebted to
the ninety-seven out of one hundred Mexicans who only attended elementary school, and give back to them through employment that which you've
received in life.[43]

D———

In Guanajuato, the governor Juan Carlos Romero Hicks promotes motiva-
tional speeches backed by the secretary of public education. In those talks,
the proposals are "truly inspired":

> Why do you think Mother Theresa of Calcutta lived so many years? Why do
> you think that the pope speaks seventeen languages? Because they don't waste
> their sexual energy, it goes to their brains. . . . Sexual relations avoid reality,
> like Molotov's music.[44] . . . There are seven reality-avoiders: television, radio,
> newspapers, cheap literature, cigarettes, wine, and sex.[45]

Nice theory, the brain as a deposit of *semen retentum*.

E ———

The private sphere (vengeance) uses the public to make its demands. The
bishop Onésimo Cepeda, on October 5, 2002, pronounced an exemplary
sermon calling the faithful of his diocese to defend themselves against criminals and to take justice into their own hands.

F ———

La Jornada publishes fragments of the homily from October 20, 2002, by the
bishop of San Cristóbal de las Casas, Felipe Arizmendi, who recommends:

- To political leaders, that they should profess their religious convictions without fear of critique or legal reprisal. Regrettably, there are

many of those baptized who are ashamed of their faith; some hide it and deny it, above all, those who hold positions of power and those unable to withstand the taunting of the disbelievers. Whoever holds public office has the right and obligation to publicly profess their beliefs, without proselytism, unless of course their faith is weak, frail, and cowardly. Therefore, they must participate in liturgical celebrations.

- To parents, that they baptize their children and remain attentive so that school doesn't rob them of their faith. On the contrary, their teachers must help them strengthen their faith, as the Catholic institutions do, and if not, parents should get the teachers fired.
- To the government, that they rectify their withholding of subsidies for Catholic centers as is done in other countries. These centers demand monthly tithes that not everyone can pay, though they offer an integral foundation that is worth any and every sacrifice.[46]

G———

In Mexicali, Paulina, a thirteen-year-old girl is raped by a heroin addict in the presence of her family; she is denied her right to an abortion, which is established by the laws of Baja California in the case of rape, because it goes against the fundamentalist beliefs of the director of the public hospital, the secretary of public health of the Panista government, and the governor himself.[47] They win, but the response to their dogmatism underscores the presence of a different social climate.

H———

In Guanajuato, in 2002, the Panista majority in the local congress approves the abolition of grounds for legal abortion: for rape, for threat to the mother's life, and for established genetic defect. Shortly thereafter, defeated, these rights are returned to the Constitution.

I ———

In Guadalajara, in 2002, a young Panista attacks a painting because he considers it offensive to his beliefs (the same ones, one assumes, that lead him to spend the entire day staring at the piece). The disgrace of the action affects both the painting's assailant and the bishop Juan Sandoval Íñiguez, who promises to pay the bail (which he doesn't actually do) and, immersed in theological expenses, accuses female rape victims of being responsible for the action. Sandoval accuses the human rights commissions of being useless and "protecting criminals."

J ———————

At various points in his presidential campaign, Vicente Fox brandishes the image of the Virgin of Guadalupe. He also gives a decalogue to the Catholic bishops, promising them religious education in public schools (which would have to be achieved by modifying the definition of secularism), radio and television stations, tax exemptions, etc.

In all of these episodes, the "liberal republic" (which I insist, is a more accurate term than *civil society*) has come out in force. In the case of Paulina, there was an extraordinary mobilization, and the arguments by the extreme Right were laughable, and furthermore, a frank apologia of illegality. In Guanajuato the governor was forced to curb the fundamentalist impatience of his local representatives, and the law was withdrawn or sent to the limbo of failure.

On December 1, 2000, in his speech at the Legislative Palace, President Fox, who would later declare this repeatedly, says that the twentieth century is like a "lost time" for Mexico (and for him, who, by the way, invested fifty-eight years of his life to it), and that the history of democracy is inaugurated with Francisco I. Madero.[48] The representatives from the PRI and the PRD attempt to jog his faulty memory by shouting "Juárez! Juárez! Juárez!," and the new head of state lets out a mocking reply: "Yeah, yeah, kids, Juárez, Juárez, Juárez, Juárez, Juárez, Juárez, Juárez." Then, in 2005, he writes the prologue to a mass-produced edition of *Apuntes para mis hijos* (Notes for my children) by Don Benito.[49]

THE MURDERED WOMEN OF CIUDAD JUÁREZ

With respect to the treatment of women, in Mexico, violence has been the truest of feudal regimes. Violence isolates, dehumanizes, arrests the development of civilization, enacts a military siege on psychological and physical freedoms, mutilates emotionally, elevates fear to unassailable heights, and represents the perfect dystopia. The strength and historical weight of the patriarchy, and the subsequent resignation it imposes, escalates the violence exercised over one sex to the category of an immense obstacle for the democratic process and, nevertheless, still remains unrecognized as such.

The limitation on feminine freedoms and, in this case, masculine ones, although their emphasis and projection are quite distinct, is the mix of the historical monopoly of power and violence. Thus, rape and the Lord's right, the *ius primae noctis*, were considered "natural" because—the reasoning is itself a solipsism—they brought out the theatrical nature of women's resistance to "protection."[50] And this dogma, across generations, ended up being the chosen one of the courts, the police, and the judges who shifted the responsibility to women, just like the cardinal of Guadalajara Juan Sandoval Íñiguez did in 2000, when he considered that women who, in his very humble opinion, went out with provocative clothing and sensual walks were to blame. He practically said, "If they don't want anything to happen to them, they should go out without a body."

Today, protest is directed against the impunity of violence, whose tragic climax is the approximately four hundred to five hundred young women murdered in Ciudad Juárez over the course of twelve years, from 1993 until now, February 2006. The administrations of the PAN and the PRI have failed with regards to this bloody phenomenon. The PAN governments specialize in victim-shaming, and in 1994 the Chihuahua state prosecutor under governor Francisco Barrio accused the dead women of "giving them a reason" or of "provoking the criminals with their lifestyle," and the governor, as seen in *Señorita extraviada* (2000), the excellent documentary by Lourdes Portillo, bumbles language as he tries to revive the morals of the twelfth century.[51] The consequences of this terribly false theory is biblical; the price of sin (one-night-stands, the feminine condition) is death.

Who are the killers of Ciudad Juárez? Is it a ring or an epidemic of *serial killers*? Are these patterns of extermination contagious? The long and short of it is that the interpretations rely on specific clarifications that never come. The deficiency of the investigators and special prosecutors is surprising, the frequency of the crimes and the similarity of the methods is shocking, and one can imagine the terror among *maquiladora* workers, young women, and their families.[52] Violence immobilizes women, it cancels out their freedom of movement, it underscores their condition as "the weaker sex," and it revives a tradition of abuse, physical force, possession of weapons, and criminal misogyny.

Why is law enforcement still so inefficient? I'll lay out a number of possible reasons:

a) Ciudad Juárez's borderland condition permeates the collective imaginary with images marked by lawlessness. It isn't just the nightmare of narcotrafficking, but the idea of somewhat provisional communities that are built around the possibility or the impossibility of crossing the border.

In some way, we all subscribe to the filmic and television mentality that makes border regions emporiums not of evil, but of illegality and crime. This primary fantasy is, in and of itself, despicable; nevertheless, it's the landscape of reception for this criminal epidemic.

b) The specific role of *narcotrafficking* and traffickers in these occurrences is unknown, but undoubtedly they influence the scarcity of value placed on human life. Since the introduction of mass narcotrafficking in Colombia, Peru, and Mexico, not to mention the United States, the value of human rights, which has never been particularly high, has diminished. It is easy to kill, and even easier to die a violent death, and the cult of weapons, as well as the high tech armaments, demand not only the killing of species in the savagery of hunting, but also to quite literally consider people as potential target practice. Drug trafficking has unleashed a visible and invisible war—the visible part is the body count in its name, the invisible part is the power of dissemination of its tactics that reach far too many. This would be the basic premise: "If they're going to kill me tomorrow, let me kill a bunch of people today."[53] And if they already have the guns, why not use them? I insist: the proliferation of weapons, the speed at which one can obtain revolvers, AK-47s, or whatever is needed, leads to an obligation to murder. The criminal tradition was already in place, why not update it with technology?

c) The fallibility, so to speak, of the judiciary. Narcotrafficking, with its intimidation tactics and its purchasing power, exhibits the vulnerability of judges, police chiefs (at every level), public prosecutors, presumably very high level functionaries, executives, business owners, military men, and possibly clergy. And this, for an indeterminate period of time, permits impunity. The almost ineluctable destiny of narcos includes prison or death after torture, each one considers himself an exception, and each one is protected by the overall purchasing power of the group. And with the certified weakness of the judiciary, the entire criminal sphere gets the news: crime is a taxable action that money and the network of interests absolve in advance.

d) Considering numbers in the abstract carries too much weight. One single death can be a monumental event, even if the results turn out to be as irrelevant as those of the PRI candidate Luis Donaldo Colosio's assassination in 1994, but the many hundreds of murdered women all over Mexico diminish the monstrosity of the phenomenon in the eyes of the authorities. The statistics of mass society tend to dissolve the depth of the tragedy. Six billion inhabitants on the planet is the demographic explosion that minimizes everything. It isn't, as the traditionalists so clumsily insist, that secular education relativizes values; secular education is the first guarantee of a civilized society, and what gives ethical values its relativized perspective is instead the set of facts closely tied to, or structured by, demography. This can be seen in wars, observed in urban violence, and confirmed in the case of Ciudad Juárez, and now in various other cities across the country. A human dimension is always necessary, and by abandoning it altogether, with phrases like "the Leftists murdered during Salinas's mandate," "the dead women of Juárez," the connection between people and the tragedies is lost: the quality of individual identification, the deep relationship to the violated beings, their hopes, their life stories, and their families. What's needed is a more individualized knowledge of the victims.

e) The role of the press is a deciding factor given that until recently it only reported these criminal acts on the crime pages rather than on the front page, where they belonged. And television has barely acknowledged their importance. In this way, the victim's blame is underscored because they can't defend themselves once dead.

All of this is brought to bear in the case of Ciudad Juárez, but nothing is more determinant than the historic disdain for unknown women, that is to say, marginalized women. Let's remember something that happened in Mexico City in 1992. A group of prostitutes organizes to denounce their exploitation at the hands of pimps and police. They go to the House of Representatives in the Federal District, they testify, they name names. Weeks later, two of them are murdered in hot sheet hotels. Their deaths are not connected to their testimony, and they end up in a nameless pauper's grave, that perfect synonym for irrelevance.

Sexism is still the dominant point of view. And add to that, classism. Not only are they women, but in great proportion, they're *maquiladora* workers, and all of them come from families with very few resources. *Poor women* is the term used to essentialize the social invisibility of people not taken into account. They're barely represented in electoral campaigns, and they're classified as "highly manipulable," the councilmen take them into account exactly two days a year, and their autonomy, in the case of single mothers, tends to be seen as a "sinful behavior." How many times, in priestly scoldings, is a family only considered one if it's composed of a father, a mother, children, relatives, and the confessor? Since the beginning, the homicidal epidemic in Ciudad Juárez also foregrounds the urgency of making destitution and poverty visible, as well as the women who inhabit those spaces.

Hate crimes are directed against a person and what that person symbolizes, represents, and embodies. The most noteworthy are those aimed at gay men, a historical abuse that takes dozens of victims a year in Mexico. But nothing surpasses the number and the unending nature of the hate crimes against women who are alone, especially young women. They're murdered because they're unable to defend themselves, because in the eyes of the criminal, their reason for being is to grant others the double pleasure of the orgasm and the death rattle, and because their deaths tends to go unnoticed. (Almost like what happens with gay men, where 99 percent of the murderers go unpunished.)

What provokes such hate? I'll leave that to the psychologists, sociologists, and psychiatrists, but I will venture a hypothesis: to a great extent, what's at play are feelings of omnipotence, which come from an environment of crime without legal or social consequences for the perpetrator. Not only is he superior to these fragile beings, he's also thumbing his nose at the laws and the society that halfheartedly or vainly attempts to uphold them. The crimes of Ciudad Juárez are *stricto sensu* hate crimes because the murderers are taking revenge on their psychic wounds, on their place in society, on every time that they hoped for recognition and didn't receive it, on the daily lack of access to that ultimate pleasure of having life or death power over another. All of the deep-rooted, degraded, sordid sexism pertaining to the most destructive part of machismo is dumped out onto women whose first and foremost guilt is their condition of victimhood. That's how repetive the process of hate crimes is: you victimize the one who, in the eyes of the murderer, is naturally, essentially a victim. Hate is a social construction that over and over again beats down those who cannot avoid it.

THE MARCH OF THE COLOR OF THE EARTH

From 1994 to the beginning of 2001, the EZLN and Marcos embody the rejection of determinism. They're persecuted; President Ernesto Zedillo conspicuously breaks his (signed) pact to respect the San Andrés Larráinzar Accords (which were the result of extensive deliberations between the government, representatives of civil society, and the EZLN); there are huge marches in support in Mexico City; international interest soars; and in the Lacandon Jungle, there are meetings of groups and people from many countries.[54] For the first time in the history of Mexico, one can speak of the Indigenous cause as the result of groups, trends, artists, and intellectuals from various ethnic groups joining forces. Over the period of nine years, more is known about Indigenous life—and its direct complement, racism—than has been learned in half a century of writings and good-faith treaties, or shameless paternalism.[55] Marcos initiates correspondence with US, Latin American, and European publications and intellectuals. He is vehemently criticized (by, among others, Octavio Paz[56]), but a considerable sector finds his work beneficial, and the EZLN defines itself as a social movement.

The Zapatista Caravan of February and March 2001 is a surprising occurrence. A large group of Indigenous people wearing ski masks travels from the Lacandon Jungle to Mexico City, and along the way holds EZLN rallies, informal gatherings, and meetings with representatives from fifty-three (or fifty-six, the data varies) different ethnic groups, to whom they offer Talking Sticks, a deeply symbolic gesture. At each of the caravan's events, women speak and their speeches are translated for the deaf as a gesture toward inclusion of the handicapped. Their language is always simple, attempting to be poetic (sometimes unsuccessfully), and they try to integrate a common language among their listeners, that of the citizenry-in-waiting, always deferred. In Oaxaca City, on February 26, 2001, Subcomandante Marcos proclaims his familiar message:

> They (the powerful) say that we refuse to work and that few, very few, are the pueblos of the earth in which, like many of ours, each person's daily work is combined with the work volunteered to the collective.
>
> They say that we waste the little that we have, but they're the ones who plundered our resources, the ones who contaminated our water with the fecal matter of money, the ones who've destroyed forests to sell lumber, the ones who imposed crops that deplete and damage the fields, who promote the cultivation, trafficking, and consumption of drugs, who grew fat on the blood of our labor.
>
> They are, in short, the ones who've destroyed our home with their ambition and their force. And now it turns out they're blaming us for not having a proper home.[57]

On March 8, the EZLN arrives in Mexico City. In Milpa Alta, Comandante Esther introduces herself: "I didn't know how to speak Spanish. I went to school but I didn't learn anything there. But when I joined the EZLN I learned to write and speak in Spanish, the little that I know, well, I'm doing my best."[58]

On March 11, the Zapatista Caravan arrives at the Zócalo.[59] Nearly a million people show up to receive them, and of those, around three hundred thousand pack into the Zócalo. The principal speech is given by Marcos, and the clear message is that of being included in the idea (the project, the realities) of Mexico. He concludes thus:

> Mexico City: We are here.
> We are here like a rebel color on earth that shouts:
>> Democracy!
>> Justice!
>> Liberty!
> Mexico: We didn't come to tell you what to do, nor to guide
> you in any direction. We came to humbly, respectfully ask
> you to help us. That you don't allow another sunrise without
> a dignified place on that flag for us, we who are the color of
> the earth.[60]

In Congress, there is a week-long debate as to whether or not to allow the ski-mask wearing Zapatistas to speak in the Legislative Palace. In the end, it is approved, and the principal speech is reserved for Subcomandante Marcos. However, he doesn't appear and the key note is carried out by the thirty-five-year-old Comandante Esther, who is, it seems, a bilingual teacher from a small community in the Lacandon Jungle, and a formidable orator. In the National Congress, Esther's speech makes visible the apparent potential and talent of those who have been historically excluded, and this is the fundamental lesson: the ways racism separates large sectors of the population from their own possibilities in order to exclusively favor one of the most limited bourgeoisies known to man.

On March 28, 2001, Comandante Esther speaks before the Nation's Congress, and her speech has a gender perspective:

> That is the country we Zapatistas want.
> A country where difference is recognized and respected.
> Where being and thinking differently is not a reason for
> going to jail, being persecuted, or dying.
> Senators, men and women:
> I want to explain to you the situation of Indigenous woman-
> hood that we live in our communities, today when respect for
> women is supposedly guaranteed in the Constitution.
> The situation is very hard.
> For many years we've been suffering through pain, oblivion,
> disdain, marginalization, and oppression.
> We suffer being forgotten because no one thinks of us . . .

We are, beyond being women, Indigenous, and we're not recognized as such.
We women know which are the good and which are the bad
traditions and customs . . ."[61]

The vindication of Esther's marginality earns her a standing ovation in the
Legislative Palace. At that moment, what was important wasn't the political
or the legislative, but rather the cultural in its broadest sense, which puts
the spotlight on Indigenous women's development, something they weren't
ever even considered capable of before (racism as determinism).

Weeks after the caravan, the Indigenous law that is approved contradicts
the demands by different ethnic groups, and everything seems to return to
"normal." Nevertheless, the rejection of the San Andrés Accords is a great
blow, and the EZLN turns inward, ending its dialogue with society and,
at times, seeing the regression of its discourse through very sectarian and
anachronistic proposals.

IMAGES: SNAPSHOTS FROM THE TWENTY FIRST CENTURY

(Factional) notes on Mexico's landscape at the start of the new century:

- The Right, fully in line with the Vatican, insists on maintaining its
  offensive against the values of secularization, and has mobilized by
  way of its "high priests" [sic] figureheads like Carlos Abascal (successively secretary of labor and secretary of the interior), its governors (the ones from Jalisco and Querétaro), and the bureaucratic
  auspices of the Far Right as it is represented and defended by "El
  Yunque," a semi-secret organization.[62] Nonetheless, time and again,
  the Right has lost its cultural battles.
- At some level, the current debate confronts both liberals and conservatives, but on another, what's most significant is the expansion
  of the concept of *secularism*, which now extends to many aspects
  of daily life: reproductive rights, the rights of minorities who until
  recently were only visible through insults and repressions, and the
  creation of a new vocabulary with its corollary critical spaces (*sexism, homophobia*), etc. The debate has actually been more one-sided
  because the conservatives are expert speakers of "sanctimonyish,"
  which forgives those who know not what they do in the name of,
  I guess, those who know not what they say. Nevertheless, what's
  essential is not just the guaranteed perdurability of secularization,

but also, though it might not be obvious now, the irreversible expansion of secularism, a concept that already forces people to examine their prejudices.

- There are no "historical accidents" nor refuge from societal progress. Therein lies the folly of associating "true religious freedom" with religious education in public schools; therein the inchoate malice of those who praise the secular State, but consider that it should be "in name only" because secularism is pernicious and harms the soul.

- The Catholic Church has insisted on its duty to participate in politics ("Never again will they lock us up in the vestries" is their slogan) and to condemn the political parties that don't "respect life." They've done it before, and they're doing it again with the government's blessing, but they don't get very far because the debate isn't in their favor, and because, among other things, they don't even understand it or accept it. They use "cabalistic" messages offered as "signs" (the unresolvable crossword puzzle that considers itself a hieroglyphic), and their side of the debate is presumably "settled," even though society's is not. Secularism is a material reality, and it is evident that there will not be any holy wars, that the majority of people respect other religions (I say the *majority* because I am not forgetting the persistence of religious intolerance against Protestants), and that it is politically and culturally impossible to return to pre-1860s Mexico.

- It would be, and it is, incomprehensible to have a debate centered on validating the secularization of cemeteries, or the legality of divorce, or the absurd proposal for sex education made by Vicente Fox's government in Guanajuato.[63] The secretary of the interior Abascal wastes our time by commenting on his anachronism, but, at the same time, he squanders his hours with "liturgical traps." He responds to Óscar Mario Beteta on February 2, 2006: "Democracy means liberty, freedom for all, freedom with responsibility and, of course, freedom in the religious sphere."[64] Wait a second . . . Is the *secretary of the interior* affirming that in Mexico there is or there isn't religious freedom? If he says there is, he's contradicting the bishops who are sure of the falseness of the affirmation because Catholicism isn't taught—nor is there praying—in public schools, nor are bishops permitted to run for president of the Republic, even if they renounce their religious vows in observance of canonical law before taking public office. And if he says that there isn't religious freedom, why then does he still remain in his position instead of confronting a repressive government?

- Nobody is stopping government officials from having and proclaiming their religious beliefs; in fact, although this is more difficult to prove, no one stops them from *practicing* their religion. But if faith is proclaimed—and not just faith, but also the prejudices embedded in that faith—from government positions, the officials are confusing their exercise and defense of the law with their belonging to "the flock." Why did Mr. Abascal, secretary of labor, place the institution he directs under the protection of the Virgin of Guadalupe? Why on March 8, International Women's Day, did he affirm that women's place is in the home?[65] Why, as secretary of the interior, did he vehemently oppose, and to this day still oppose, the day after pill without a single shred of evidence that it causes abortion? I still don't know why the secretary, who is a lawyer, doesn't see a denial of the secular State in his behavior.

POSTSCRIPT

In the dedication to Don Salvador Abascal's book *Juárez Marxista 1848–1872*, published by Editorial Tradición, Don Salvador writes, "Great support was generously lent to me in the completion of this project by the following men: [he cites five people] and my son Carlos."[66] At the end of the book, in the concluding remarks, he affirms:

> There are those who think—perhaps out of ignorance about what the Church is—that its first true persecutor in Mexico wasn't Juárez but Calles.
>
> The facts demonstrate that the Zapotec Indian by far surpasses the probably Jewish Turk in that barbaric occupation of hate, in exact correspondence with Karl Marx, against the Catholic Church, and therefore against its masterpiece, Western Culture.
>
> Because Juárez was successful in cutting out the deep roots of religion—of Catholicism—from the Nation, it lead to the following terrible scythe blows:
>
> - the atheistic education of children and youth in official government schools: a sort of terrorism and ideological kidnapping, that on its own was enough to break the spiritual unity of the *pueblo*;
> - legislation that is not only atheistic but that made the Church a slave to the impious government, whose hierarchs have at times even seemed to show gratitude for their chains;

- civil marriage, which will logically and fatally bring with it divorce, and the dissolution of the family, without which there is no Church or Country;
- the introduction, for further confusion, of protestant sects, which mutilate the Faith and dissociate it from action, which remorselessly consecrate the satisfaction of all manner of concupiscence [. . .]

Does the secretary of the interior disagree with these affirmations from the book on which he collaborated? If he doesn't, it's because it accommodates his peculiar vision of objectivity.

NOTES

1. Vicente Fox Quesada (1942–) was the sixty-second president of Mexico from 2000 to 2006. He was the first president since 1929 that was not from the PRI, winning as the candidate of the right-wing PAN (Partido de Acción Nacional; National Action Party), founded in 1939.
2. *Mestizo* is a term used in Mexico and Latin America for a person of mixed Spanish and Indigenous ancestry.
3. Job 14:1 (KJV).
4. José López Portillo y Pacheco (1920–2004) served as Mexico's president from 1976 to 1982. The discovery of oil reserves and the subsequent fall in oil prices brought about an economic and financial crisis, distinguishing his presidency by the default of the country's external debt in 1982, accelerated capital flight, and the nationalization of the banks.
5. Miguel de la Madrid Hurtado (1934–2012) served as president of Mexico from 1982 to 1988. He is known for the neoliberal policies he set into motion to mitigate the economic and financial crisis inherited from the previous administration. Notwithstanding, he was not able to reverse inflation, nor slow the bleak economic growth. He was criticized for his response to the devastating 1985 earthquake in Mexico City, and for fraud in the 1988 presidential elections that declared Carlos Salinas de Gortari winner over forerunner Leftist candidate Cuauhtémoc Cárdenas.
6. Convened by the United Nations, the Fourth World Conference on Women was held in Beijing in September 1995. Considered an empowering and watershed moment, it produced a global policy and document on gender equality that repositioned its emphasis of analysis from "women" to "gender" as the explanatory conceptual framework to re-evaluate and change the patriarchal structures necessary for women to be recognized as the equals of men.
7. *Indio* continues to be a pejorative way of addressing an Indigenous person and refers back to the period of the Conquest when the population of Mexico was so named by the Europeans who thought they had reached the Indies. Today, Indigenous peoples are addressed by their cultural and linguistic identities—Mixtecs,

Mayas, Zapotecs, etc.—and are recognized in the Mexican constitution as citizens of the nation with equal rights.

8. Established by the federal government in 1948, the INI's original purpose was meant to identify and integrate marginalized Indigenous populations (about twelve million people) into the Mexican nation. With time, and given the persistence of these communities, their cultural and linguistic rights have been steadily recognized. In 2003, the INI was replaced by the CDI, Comisión Nacional para el Desarrollo de los Pueblos Indígenas (National Commission for the Development of Indigenous Peoples), as an outcome of the Zapatista uprising of 1994.

9. *Caciquismo* is from the word *cacique*, a Taino term first used to identify an Indigenous authority at the time of the Conquest; today it refers to a local political boss.

10. In Alfonso Caso, "Definición del indio y lo indio," *América Indígena* 26, no. 4 (1948).

11. *Ladinos* are seen as Hispanized Indigenous persons distanced from their cultural and linguistic heritage.

12. *Castilla* refers to the historic region of Spain where Castellano, the language, originated and was used during the Conquest and colonization. Indigenous people identified the language as *Castilla*.

13. *Guadalupanismo* identifies the ways the popular cult and devotion to the Virgin of Guadalupe is imbricated in the discursive construct of the Mexican nation and Mexicanness. *Usos y costumbres* (customary law) is a traditional form of governance based on Indigenous practices. In 1994, this form of governance was contested by a group of Indigenous women who joined the Zapatista Rebellion. Alongside the demands of the EZLN, they presented the Ley Revolucionaria de Mujeres (the Women's Revolutionary Law). Among the demands are the right to choose one's partner and decide for themselves the number of children to bear, the right to health and bodily autonomy, the right to live free of violence, the right to health, education, dignified labor, a fair salary, equal political participation, and economic autonomy—in sum, to be granted the same rights as men. See EZLN, *Documentos y comunicados, 1º de enero/8 de agosto de 1994* (Mexico: Era, 1994). Even so, in 2002, at the Primera Cumbre de Mujeres Indígenas de las Américas (First Summit of Indigenous Women of the Americas) held in Oaxaca, two archbishops and two bishops representing the Mexican Episcopate, fearing the continued spread of the Zapatista women's demands, were adamant about stopping them. The Church hierarchy saw the demands for women's rights as a dismantling of "Indigenous Identity," which, according to them, is based on inalterable rituals, beliefs, and women's permanent subordination in the home. In an article, Monsiváis criticizes the Church's continued defense of patriarchal privileges by quoting from a speech the clergy delivered to the women attending the conference: "Las mujeres (que se apartan de sus deberes) transforman principios y valores milenarios e imponen prácticas a la cultura, propiciando la

pérdida de identidad." ("Women [who abandon their duties] are altering millenary values and principles, and imposing new practices on their culture, which propitiate a loss of identity.") See Monsiváis, "De obispos y geología social," *Proceso*, December 8, 2002, 68–69. For further references on Indigenous women's activism, see Rosalva Aída Hernández-Castillo, "Between Hope and Adversity: The Struggle of Organized Women in Chiapas since the Zapatista Rebellion," *Journal of Latin American Anthropology* 3, no. 1 (Sept. 1997): 102–20; and the special issue of *Cultural Survival Quarterly* 23, no. 1 (March 1999), "Indigenous Rights and Self-Determination in Mexico," https://www.culturalsurvival.org/publications/cultural-survival-quarterly/23-1-indigenous-rights-and-self-determination-mexico.

14. Enrique Florescano (1937–) is a renowned historian of Mexico with numerous publications, among them *El mito de Quetzalcoatl* (1993), *Étnia, estado y nacion, ensayos sobre las identidades colectivas de México* (1997), *Memoria Indígena* (1999), *Memoria mexicana, ensayos sobre la reconstrucción del pasado* (2000), and *Historia de la bandera mexicana, 1325–2019* (2021). Lucas Ignacio Alamán y Escalada (1792–1853) was a Mexican scientist, historian, writer, and conservative statesman, known as an "arch-reactionary," according to D. A. Brading, "who sought to create a strong central government based on a close alliance of the army, the Church and the landed classes." D. A. Brading, *The First American: The Spanish Monarchy, Creole Patriots, and the Liberal State, 1492–1867* (New York: Cambridge University Press, 1991), 642.

15. Monsiváis doesn't reference the text, event, or conversation that the quote and paraphrase he attributes to Florescano comes from, however these ideas can be found throughout, and especially in the "Prologue" and "Final Chapter" of his book *Etnia, estado y nación: Sobre las identidades colectivas en México* (México: Nuevo Siglo/Aguilar, 1996).

16. A term used in colonial and modern Spanish America meaning "rational people" to differentiate those who were culturally Hispanized/Westernized from Indigenous Peoples and those of mixed races. A descendent of Europeans born in the Americas, in this case Mexico.

17. This comment reiterates the persistent racism that continued to see Indigenous peoples as "primitive" or "backward."

18. For the anthropologist Rodolfo Stavenhagen, this resurgence was a call for "the need to reassess relations between Indigenous peoples and the Mexican state … an as yet unresolved and still acute 'national question' in Mexico (as in the rest of Latin America)." Rodolfo Stavenhagen, "The Indian Resurgence in Mexico," *Cultural Survival* 18, no. 2 (1994), https://www.culturalsurvival.org/publications/cultural-survival-quarterly/indian-resurgence-mexico.

19. Luis María Martínez y Rodríguez (1881–1956), a recognized poet, scholar, and member of the Academia Mexicana de la Lengua, was the Catholic archbishop of Mexico City from 1937 until his death. He was the first in Mexico to receive the title of Primate in 1951.

20. The Mexican Academy of Language, established in 1875, is the Mexican institution that corresponds to the Royal Spanish Academy, La Real Academia Española (RAE).

21. Martín Luis Guzmán (1887–1976), a writer and politician, was awarded the National Prize in Literature in 1958 and is considered a pioneer of the novel of the Mexican Revolution. Guzmán founded the magazine *Tiempo: Semanario de la Vida y la Verdad* (Time: A weekly of life and truth) in 1942, and remained editorial director until his death. The magazine contributed culturally, historically, and politically to the construction of the modern post-revolutionary nation.

22. The original saying is *pueblo pequeño, infierno grande* (small town, big hell), which Monsiváis playfully reverses and alters.

23. In Mexico, Evangelical/Pentecostal Protestants were/are often stigmatized by being called *Aleluyas* (Hallelujahs), a denigration that reinforces prejudices against them and their Church.

24. In Spanish this popular refrain reads, "Aleluya, Aleluya, que cada quien agarre la suya," poking crude and cruel "fun" at those who practice Protestantism.

25. The Instituto Lingüístico de Verano (ILV) is a nonprofit organization founded in Mexico in 1948, a branch of the international Summer Institute of Linguistics (SIL), which studied and documented the Indigenous languages of Mexico and promoted translations of the Bible into their particular local languages. Many praised their contributions, but others saw their work as Evangelical proselytizing alongside a US interventionist and political project of conversion and assimilation. For the controversies on their presence in Mexico, see Søren Hvalkof and Peter Aaby, eds., *Is God an American: An Anthropological Perspective on the Missionary Work of the Summer Institute of Linguistics* (Copenhagen: International Work for Indigenous Affairs, 1981). The chapter about Mexico is by André-Marcel d'Ans, "The Art of Evangelization and Political Control: The SIL in Mexico."

26. Here we translate *buenas costumbres* as "good manners," in reference to those that follow "social norms," and don't go against the established order, many times rigidly imposed from above. The Islas Marias, a federal penal colony, is located on an archipelago of four islands belonging to Mexico, located in the Pacific Ocean off the coast of Nayarit. In 2019 President Andrés Manuel López Obrador permanently closed the prison. During the presidency of Porfirio Díaz, the Valle Nacional region in Oaxaca served as a concentration camp for Chinantecas, other Indigenous peoples, and political prisoners from different parts of Mexico. Because the prisoners were treated horrifically as slaves, this region became known as El Valle de la Muerte (Death Valley).

27. A history of executing homosexuals for "sins against nature" by mass burnings during the colonial period has been documented. See Louis Crompton, *Homosexuality and Civilization* (Cambridge, MA: Belknap, 2006), and Federico Garza Carvajal, *Quemando mariposas: Sodomia e imperio en Andalucía y México, siglos SVI–XVII* (Barcelona: Laertes, 2002).

28. "Hell is other people" is a quote from the French philosopher Jean Paul Sartre in his play *No Exit* (1943).

29. Here Monsiváis's use of quotation marks refers to his chronicling of a collective sentiment.

30. Beatification is the step before sainthood when the pope officially declares a person as an exemplary Christian.

31. Here the word *adminicle* means an aid or an accessory and is a euphemism used by the Cardinal to avoid mentioning the unspeakable condom.

32. The strike by students at the UNAM began in April 1999, some months after the university president, Dr. Francisco Bernés de Castro, announced a significant increase in tuition and more demanding graduation requirements. Because this is Mexico's flagship public university, there was a cascade of other sympathetic strikes at public feeder high schools and other universities. A blockade at the main entrance by the students led to the university's prolonged closure. The strike, which lasted through February 2000, saw violent encounters between students, guards, and faculty, leading to Bernés de Castro's resignation, as well as widespread injuries and some fatalities.

33. Carlos Salinas de Gortari (1948–), a Harvard-trained economist and PRI politician, was Mexico's sixtieth president. His election and presidency were marred by scandal, corruption, and fraud. He was in power from 1988 to 1994, at the height of Mexico's neoliberal push. Ernesto Zedillo Ponce de León (1951–) is a Mexican economist and was Mexico's sixty-first president, from 1994 to 2000. His was the last presidency of the PRI's uninterrupted rule. His mandate was marked by scandal, including massacres of Indigenous insurgents and the loss of the PRI's consolidated power at the Congressional level, as well as in the Mexico City government.

34. Josefina Eugenia Vázquez Mota (1961–) is an economist, businesswoman, and politician for the Partido de Acción Nacional (PAN). Vázquez Mota, among other positions held, was a member of the presidential cabinet as secretary of social development under Vicente Fox (2000–2006), and secretary of public education from 2006 to 2009 under Felipe Calderón (2006–2012).

35. When Monsiváis refers here to the "capital" he is referring to Mexico City (Ciudad de México), which at the time was called Distrito Federal (DF; Federal District). There is a long history of centralism in Mexico, which leads to certain resentments from the thirty-two outlying Mexican states.

36. "Heroes" of the 1810 War of Independence: Miguel Hidalgo y Costilla (1753–1811) from Chihuahua, was an insurgent priest, considered Father of the Nation, and José María Morelos (1765–1815) from Michoacán, also a priest, took on insurgent leadership after Hidalgo's execution. Benito Juárez (1806–1872) was a liberal thinker and lawmaker from Oaxaca. He was an important reformist during Mexico's post-Independence period, the twenty-sixth, and first Indigenous, president of Mexico (1858–1872). "Heroes" of the 1910 Mexican Revolution: Emiliano Zapata (1879–1919) was a peasant and agrarian reformist who

became an important *caudillo* among the revolutionaries of the southern states. He implemented land reform through the Plan de Ayala. He is an important symbol and inspiration for the contemporary neo-Zapatista insurgents of the EZLN. Francisco "Pancho" Villa (born José Doroteo Arango Arámbula, 1878–1923), from Durango, was a general and leader of the División del Norte, the largest Revolutionary force in the war. He was instrumental in ousting dictator Porfirio Díaz (1830–1915) from power and instating Francisco I. Madero in the presidency. Finally, Lázaro Cárdenas (1895–1970), from Michoacán, was a general in the Mexican Revolution and Mexico's fifty-first president; he was the founder of the Partido Nacional Revolucionario (PNR, National Revolutionary Party) which would later become the PRI. Cárdenas was perhaps best known for expropriating private (foreign) oil companies and nationalizing Mexican petroleum reserves in 1934, founding Pemex (Petróleos Mexicanos), the state-owned company that maintains a quasi-monopoly to this day.

37. The PRD was founded in the 1980s after hotly contested elections. It has historically been the party of Leftist opposition to the right-leaning PRI and PAN.

38. Here Monsiváis uses the words *faltas a la moral*, which was a legal concept and punishable by law, and *buenas costumbres*, which refers to the "decency" or supposed "goodness" that Monsiváis so often criticizes because of its racist and classist overtones.

39. This citation comes from an article by Jenaro Villamil in *La Jornada*, "En Yucatán 'nuestros hijos no se llenan con oraciones,'" Oct. 1, 2002, https://www.jornada.com.mx/2002/10/01/015n1pol.php.

40. Luis Donaldo Colosio Murrieta (1950–1994), from the northern state of Sonora, was the heir-apparent to the Mexican presidency as the PRI's candidate for the 1994 general elections. His platform included promises of in-party reforms in response to the Zapatista uprising of January 1, 1994, which in turn responded to the implementation of the North American Free Trade Agreement (NAFTA), and the Mexican state's neoliberal economic policies. He was assassinated while on the campaign trail in Tijuana, on March 23, 1994. This marked a watershed moment in Mexican politics.

41. "The Impossible Dream" was composed for the 1965 musical *Man of La Mancha* by Dale Wasserman, with music by Mitch Leigh, and lyrics by Joe Darion. The opening verse of the song in English, "To dream the impossible dream / To fight the unbeatable foe / To bear with unbearable sorrow / And to run where the brave dare not go," differs widely from the Spanish version of the song which opens with much more religious overtones: "Con fe lo imposible sonar / al mal combatir sin temor / triunfar sobre el miedo invencible / en pie soportar el dolor" (To dream the impossible with faith / to combat without fear / to triumph over invincible fear / to bear the pain standing tall). "Desiderata," initially a poem (1927) by US writer Max Ehrman, was introduced as an Episcopalian liturgical reading in the early 1960s and was set to music in 1971 by Broadway composer Fred Werner. It has been widely disseminated (with and without attribution),

and made popular in Spanish translation by Mexican actor and singer Arturo Benavides, in 1972. The poem's denouement reads, "Therefore be at peace with God, whatever you conceive Him to be. And whatever your labors and aspirations, in the noisy confusion of life, keep peace in your soul."

42. Monsiváis cites only the newspaper *La Reforma*, 2002. This episode is also related in Marco Antonio Leyva Piña and V. Francisco Vite Bernal, "¿De qué color es tu campaña?," *El Cotidiano* 19, no. 118 (March–April, 2003): 66. https://www.redalyc.org/pdf/325/32511805.pdf.

43. Monsiváis attributes this quotation of Abascal to Elizabeth Velasco in *La Jornada*. A reduced online version of this note was published as "Abascal pide a estudiantes acabar con el 'viejo enunciado liberal' juarista," *La Jornada*, August 21, 2002, https://www.jornada.com.mx/2002/08/21/010n1pol.php.

44. Molotov is a Mexican heavy rock band, founded in 1995 by Micky Huidobro, Tito Fuentes, Randy Ebright, and Paco Ayala. They are known for their rapping and use of noise, and are still touring today.

45. Monsiváis attributes this quote by Romero Hicks to a presently unavailable article in *Milenio*, October 27, 2002.

46. Alma E. Muñoz, "Exhortan a gobernantes a profesar su fe," *La Jornada*, October 20, 2002, https://www.jornada.com.mx/2002/10/20/009n1pol.php?origen=politica.html.

47. For a detailed account of this case, see Marta Lamas and Sharon Bisell, "Abortion and Politics in Mexico: 'Context Is All,'" *Reproductive Health Matters* 8, no.16 (2000):10–23. The article details the case of thirteen-year-old Paulina del Carmen Ramirez Jacinto and includes an interview with the minor by Elena Poniatowska. Panista refers to belonging to the PAN, Mexico's far-right, religiously conservative political party.

48. Francisco I. Madero (1873–1913), from the state of Coahuila, was a wealthy businessman who became an important revolutionary figure, and later the thirty-seventh president of Mexico from 1911 to 1913 when he was deposed and assassinated. After Porfirio Díaz was exiled and a provisional government was in place, Madero was elected to the highest office in a landslide victory. While he was initially very popular, he was criticized by both the conservatives on the Right and the more radical branch of the Left. His unwillingness to initiate sweeping land reform prompted Emiliano Zapata to rise up against him in the 1911 Plan de Ayala. Nevertheless it was the conservatives, Díaz's nephew Félix, General Bernardo Reyes, and Victoriano Huerta who staged the US-supported coup that led to his demise. His torture and murder, as well as that of his vice president José María Pino Suárez (1869–1913), led to a consolidation of the Left as anti-Huertistas.

49. *Apuntes para mis hijos* is Juárez's most well-known work, which laid out his political philosophy. It was first published in 1819 and has been reprinted and re-edited repeatedly to date. There is no English translation of this work.

50. The *derecho de pernada*, *prima nocta*, or Lord's right was the feudal right of a

monarch, noble, or landholder to have sexual relations with any female subject, especially on her wedding night.

51. *Señorita extraviada* (Missing young woman, 2001) is a documentary film by Lourdes Portillo that examines the phenomenon of missing and murdered women in this time period in Ciudad Juárez, Chihuahua. See Chapter 16 in this volume.

52. Maquilas are foreign-owned factories using cheap labor to assemble products for export. See Wright, *Disposable Women and Other Myths of Global Capitalism*; and Iglesias, *Beautiful Flowers of the Maquiladora*.

53. "Si me han de matar mañana, que me maten de una vez" (If they're going to kill me tomorrow, let them kill me now) is the closing lyric from popular revolutionary song "La Valentina." Monsiváis often refers to this song lyric (and makes playful variations on it, as is the case here), as a shorthand to describe the machismo or toxic masculinity that inspires men to risk death over questions of honor, and especially in this case, to seek violence as a first step in conflict resolution. See Chapters 1, 3, and 16 in this volume.

54. The ratification of these accords, commonly referred to simply as the San Andrés Accords, took place in February 1996. Their purpose was to renegotiate the relationship between Indigenous communities and the federal government, with the latter recognizing Indigenous autonomy and rights in the context of the Zapatista uprising and the low-intensity war that was going on in Chiapas. The principles of this new relationship were to be guided by five principles, "pluralism, sustainability, centrality, participation, and self-determination," in order to heal the relationship of exclusion that had been suffered by all of Mexico's Indigenous peoples, and to promote their full integration into the national project with respect for their particular economic, cultural, educational, political, and ecological concerns. See Natividad Gutiérrez Chong, "La autonomía y la resolución de conflictos étnicos: Los acuerdos de San Andrés Larráinzar," *Nueva Antropología* 19, no. 63 (October, 2003): 11–39. See also Natividad Gutiérrez Chong, *Nationalist Myths and Ethnic Identities: Indigenous Intellectuals and the Mexican State* (Lincoln: University of Nebraska Press, 1999).

55. One catalyzing event that highlighted the institutional racism against the insurgents was the Acteal Massacre that took place on December 22, 1997, resulting in the brutal murder of forty-five Indigenous people from the Chiapanecan village of Acteal. It wasn't until 2020 that the Mexican government acknowledged their role in the massacre, clearly in violation of the San Andrés Peace Accords. See Rosalva Aída Hernández Castillo, ed., *Women and Violence in Chiapas before and after Acteal*, trans. Leslie Clarke, Nick Jones, María Y, et al. (Copenhangen: International Work Group for Indigenous Affairs, 2001).

56. Octavio Irineo Paz Lozano (1914–1998) is recognized as a major literary figure of Mexico's twentieth century. A prolific writer, critic, diplomat, and polemic public intellectual, he won, among others, the Miguel de Cervantes Prize in 1982, and the Nobel Prize for Literature in 1990. Among his most cited and

famous works are *El laberinto de la soledad* (1950; *The Labyrinth of Solitude*, 1961, trans. Lysander Kemp) and his long poem "Piedra de Sol" (1957; translated as "Sun Stone" by several translators, including Muriel Rukeyser in 1962 and Eliot Weinberger in 1987), which were respectively influenced by discussions on Mexican identity and surrealism. He was the founder of two major literary magazines in Mexico City, *Plural* and *Vuelta* (which later became *Letras Libres,* after his death), consistent with his line of thought. He supported the Republican cause in Spain against Francisco Franco. Disillusioned, he became anti-Stalinist, and throughout his life defended liberal democracies against any totalitarian or authoritarian government abusive of human rights. Even as many Mexican intellectuals questioned his political beliefs, Paz continued to consider himself a man of the critical Left as he wrote about major historical and political events in Mexico. While an ambassador to India, he resigned in 1968 to protest the massacre at Tlatelolco. He was married to Elena Garro (renowned twentieth-century Mexican writer), whom he divorced in 1959, and with whom he had a daughter, Helena. Paz was married to Marie-José Tramini from 1965 until his death. His poetry and essays have been translated into numerous languages, including English.

57. This speech by Comandante Marcos is available in its entirety on the Zapatista website. "En Oaxaca: Voltear el país entero y hacerlo por fin el árbol donde los todos que somos diferentes tengamos mañana común como nación," Enlace Zapatista, Feb. 26, 2001, https://enlacezapatista.ezln.org.mx/2001/02/26/en-oaxaca-voltear-el-pais-entero-y-hacerlo-por-fin-el-arbol-donde-los-todos-que-somos-diferentes-tengamos-manana-comun-como-nacion.

58. Milpa Alta (a name that means tall cornfields) is a large rural village in the southeastern extreme of Mexico City. While it remains within the city limits, it bears little resemblance to the urbanized center. This quotation is taken from a joint address by the comandantas. "Comandantas Esther, Yolanda y Susana: Día Internacional de la Mujer Rebelde," Enlace Zapatista, March 8, 2001, https://enlacezapatista.ezln.org.mx/2001/03/08/8-de-marzo-dia-internacional-de-la-mujer-rebelde. Comandante Esther was an important figure in the women's revolutionary movement within the EZLN. Comandante Ramona and Comandante Elisa (see Chapter 15) were other major spokespersons for women's rights within the early movement. They continued to speak out at rallies and as keynote speakers, as well as being interviewed extensively during the decade of the early 2000s. Their participation was a fundamental aspect of the EZLN movement as supporters of the Women's Revolutionary Law and its goals of equity. Other important women in the movement were Comandantes Fidelia, Susana, and Yolanda. See Hermann Bellinghausen, "Si no cumplen, la gente indígena seguirá juntándose: Ramona," *La Jornada,* February 16, 1997, https://www.jornada.com.mx/1997/02/16/ramona.html; and "¿Por qué marchan los comandantes del EZLN?," *La Jornada,* February 17, 2001, https://www.jornada.com.mx/2001/02/17/ezln.html. See also Lourdes Consuelo Pacheco Ladrón

de Guevara, "Nosotras ya estábamos muertas: Comandanta Ramona y otras insurgentas del Ejército Zapatista de Liberación Nacional / We Were Already Dead: Comandanta Ramona and Other Insurgents of the Zapatista Army of National Liberation," *Trayectorias Humanas Transcontinentales*: Special Issue, *Sexe majeur, sexe mineur? "Les femmes qui pensent ne sont pas (toutes) dangereuses,"* no. 6, 2019, https://www.unilim.fr/trahs.

59. The Zócalo is Mexico City's central plaza in its historic center. It has been the center of the city since pre-Hispanic times (the now-excavated Templo Mayor and its museum lie just to the east), and its sides are marked by the colonial palaces that today house the National Palace (the national government's operating base), and the government office of Mexico City, as well as the Cathedral.

60. "Zócalo, Subcomandante Marcos: es la hora de los pueblos indios," Enlace Zapatista, March 11, 2001, https://enlacezapatista.ezln.org.mx/2001/03/11/zocalo-subcomandante-marcos-es-la-hora-de-los-pueblos-indios.

61. "Discurso de la Comandanta Esther en la tribuna del Congreso de la Unión," Enlace Zapatista, March 28, 2001, https://enlacezapatista.ezln.org.mx/2001/03/28/discurso-de-la-comandanta-esther-en-la-tribuna-del-congreso-de-la-union.

62. El Yunque (The Anvil) is a semi-clandestine, ultra-religious rightwing group founded in the 1950s by student groups, primarily in Puebla, a state known for its dyed-in-the-wool conservatism. As it became embedded in the PAN and in some branches of the PRI in the 1970s, it lost much of its condition of a "secret society," but remains to this day, exerting significant social pressure from within high-ranking leadership positions in the ruling right-wing parties. They represent the most aggressive branches of the religious Right, whose agenda is an unabashed rolling back of women's rights to their bodily autonomy and to their participation in politics and the labor force. See Irene Ortiz, "Building the City of God: Mexico's Ultra-Right Yunque," *NACLA Report on the Americas* 41, no. 1 (February 2008).

63. For a brief report on the polemic surrounding Fox's plan for "Así se educa, Guanajuato" (This is how you educate, Guanajuato), in which misinformation in line with Catholic doctrine but not scientific fact was intended to be included in the state's curriculum on sex education, see Rosa Elvira Vargas, "Vicente Fox quiso imponer contenidos educativos religiosos en Guanajuato," *La Jornada*, February 10, 2003, https://www.jornada.com.mx/2003/02/10/012n1pol.php. Ultimately, the plan was not approved by the secretary of education.

64. Óscar Mario Beteta comes from a long line of politicians, and is an influential, award-winning journalist and radio and television host. Trained as an economist, he reports on politics and finance, as well as specializing in interviews with public figures. This was likely a quote from an interview on his longstanding radio show "En Los Tiempos de la Radio" (In the Times of Radio) on Radio Fórmula.

65. March 8, International Women's Day, was first officially recognized by the United Nations in 1977, as part of their agenda on women's equal participation

in politics and society. Its roots were in the labor movements from the turn of the twentieth century in North America and Europe that incorporated many early suffragists. Since 2018, in Mexico there have been massive mobilizations and marches to protest femicide and government negligence regarding women's rights. These protests have had repercussions across Latin America.

66. Salvador Abascal (1910–2000) was a Mexican politician and the leader of the National Synarchist Union, which represented the orthodox Catholic and extreme Right political positions, akin to clerical fascism. He published *Juárez marxista, 1848–1872* (Mexico City: Editorial Tradición, 1984), critiquing Juárez's liberal position on the separation of Church and State. Abascal's son, Carlos (1949–), was the secretary of labor and of the interior.

Frida Kahlo

The Stages of Her Renown

2008

On the esplanade of the Palacio de Bellas Artes (Palace of Fine Arts), the crowd neither blinks nor disperses in the face of a demographic deluge; this could be called the "Great Line of Cultural Time." They all want to see Frida Kahlo's grand exhibit. It could almost be said—and this is only barely an exaggeration—that they're showing up to meet Frida Kahlo personally (her work is her life, her life an indelible memory), and that's enough for them to put up with the frequent downpours, the three- to four-hour lines, the disappointment at not getting tickets, and the deluge of back-and-forth comments, the "Frida always speaks to me," the "Come back tomorrow"—not directed at the unemployed this time, but at those turned away, the "I live all the way out in Matehuala, and I don't want to go home without seeing Frida."

The esplanade is overflowing with joy, frustration at the wait, sorrow, enthusiasm, exhaustion, and the illumination of souls who discover her artistic dimensions, the uplifting of moods when coming face to face with *The Two Fridas*. And the same thing happens, proportionally, at the Casa Azul (the Blue House) in Coyoacán, the place where Frida Kahlo was born and died, with her belongings exhibited for the first time: drawings of Frida and Diego Rivera, photographs, letters, book dedications . . .[1]

OF ALL THE POSSIBLE FRIDAS

Looking at a photo or a self-portrait of Frida Kahlo, looking at the reproductions of her famous paintings, any moderately informed spectator—and this is now true in various countries—knows what to expect: here is the artist ruled by physical pain and artistic genius, the great painter Diego Rivera's partner, both creator and model of these portraits that are strangely moving. And in the Mexico City of 2007, Frida's presence and recognition are re-energized by television programs, flashy ads, and conferences where the artist becomes a necessary referent of culture and of artistic emotion. As her story is retold and rewritten, so too are the fluctuations of her fame, and of the evaluation and revaluation of her work.

FIRST STAGE:
THE 1930S AND 1940S

In a still relatively small Mexico City, in the years of radicalism and battling factions, certain roles are assigned to important figures. Diverse writers, artists, and thinkers are conceded the status of archetypes in the phenomenon in which the revolution (its realities, as well as the interpretations of the armed struggle and the clashes between factions) becomes "The Revolution" (the metamorphosis of institutions and mythologies). The muralists are almost immediately granted the role of archetypes; for the time being, Frida is seen as a secondary presence, the companion to a central figure. Few people know her, but among them, she is highly regarded.

In this first stage, the Frida who will become "Frida" (her last name being superfluous), is defined by her condition as beloved landscape to her lover and husband Diego Rivera—not yet a superstar, a much more recent concept that requires the complicity of electronic media, but rather a protagonist convinced that he occupies the center stage in his own right, and that he must take part in debates, create rivalries, and pontificate. No matter what he does, he immediately garners attention, often with international reverberations. Diego is newsworthy because of his myriad activities and because of what seems to be his total inability to be discrete or keep anything private; even without Diego's extreme notoriety, Frida is a notorious presence in art and cultural circles for her uninhibited behavior in the relatively small city of their shamelessly fashionable new country. Although not readily noticed, her characteristics are unique: she's a painter (an almost exclusively masculine profession back then); a fervent nationalist even in appearance (with her *traje típico*, which rather than reaffirming traditions, renews them[2]); and she's partially handicapped. A great novelty: she's a self-portraitist without vanity, or at least she's never considered egocentric. She's not yet a communist, a dogma that only takes women into account as an afterthought.

The Mexican Renaissance: An Emerging Scene

Between 1922 and 1940, specialized journalists and the illustrious minority start circulating the phrase "the Mexican Renaissance" to describe a land of wonderment, beliefs, and ways of knowing. They celebrate the (literal) appearance of "el pueblo," the stunning images that proliferated during the Revolution and were captured more by visual artists than by writers.[3] Foreigners and Mexicans alike (the latter guided by the overwhelming praise of the former) study the country (more specifically its mythologies), its armed movements, and its aesthetic achievements in deed or potential, and highlight, in their collectivity, an impressive historical leap forward. The Revolution unearths the traditions of popular arts and crafts, previously disdained or not-yet-understood customs, and among other revelations, artists attempting to capture the folkloric as the most visible and defining phenomenon in Mexico, hidden in plain sight because of its "primitive" degree of refinement, according to the Eurocentrists. This is a surprise on many levels: in celebrating the "pueblo" and the popular, artists produce their master works revealing those truths hidden by internalized colonialism. Examples: José Guadalupe Posada's engravings, Hermenegildo Bustos's provincial portraits, popular architecture, and women's traditional dresses.[4]

In the capital, the protagonists of the "Mexican Renaissance" and their immediate spectators (writers, journalists, filmmakers, painters, bourgeois bohemians, and European, US, and Soviet radicals) scrutinize the nation that provisionally emerges, years enlightened by the fall of Porfirio Díaz's dictatorship and the rise of caudillos and peasant armies. It's the moment to grasp and capture the "subverted Edens" (Ramón López Velarde's expression[5]) of nature and of behavior, and to discover that which is meaningful, transcendental, if you will, in what before was judged from a utilitarian or traditional—but always disdainful—perspective. The markets, the altars, the artisanal candies, the straw Judases, the atmosphere in the pulque distilleries, the variety of Day of the Dead celebrations, the popular versions of the "charro" and the "china poblana," the votive offerings, the symphony of colors in small towns, the paper and wax flowers, the piñatas, the refashioning of innumerable traditions into an aesthetics of survival, the masks, the Indigenous traditional dress, the noisemakers, the hand-made toys from the country fair . . .[6]

SECOND STAGE: FEELING AND CONTEMPLATING "MEXICANNESS"

Painting defies marginality, which at the time was considered the inevitable destiny of Latin American societies. To differing degrees, writers and artists challenge the moralistic petite bourgeois milieu, and they construct a *sui generis* nationalism—equidistant from history and everyday life—from both well-known and newly invented points of pride. In this mythology's place of honor, a flexible idea that at its best is more aesthetic than ideological, Mexicanness, in the period of institutional consolidation—roughly 1920 to 1950—is very different from the sentimentalism of that era and from the official and commercial product of today. The Revolution hands out the small and great joys of knowing what is possible; and the visual artists, inevitably avant-garde, promote a "cultural nationalism" that is, above all, an assimilation and reformulation of international trends. Because of that impulse that confuses or joyfully conflates appearance and essence—and not because of some "folkloric" criteria—Frida lets herself be persuaded by Diego, affirms Raquel Tibol, to abandon her customary attire, both conventional and masculine, and adopts the Tehuana dress with its *rebozo* and endless braids.[7] There is a desire to effusively illustrate all of the beautiful objects made invisible by the utilitarian *criollo* traditions, and the typical traditional dress, infrequently used at that time, sits on the razor's edge between respect for vanishing traditions and the gala costume of the bourgeoisie.

In the collective imaginary of an era, Frida is its image, with earrings that are temples or labyrinths or miniature hanging gardens, shawls that are marvels of textile art, rings of pre-Hispanic inspiration that foreshadow metalsmithing museums. In particular, Frida is seduced by the Tehuana dress for very understandable reasons: for quite some time, as many voyagers' testimonials and Sergei Eisenstein's film *Que viva México* affirm, the Tehuantepec isthmus is the diaphanous expression of Paradise Lost, the realm of innocence, the mix between frugality and exuberance, of young women who bathe nude in the river, and of matriarchs with gold-coin necklaces.[8] The Tehuana of legend is the strong woman of the Bible, one free from hypocrisy, with the frank sexuality of the Genesis of Indigenous communities, the matriarch—both fake and genuine (among the Tehuanas, machismo stages its theatrical transfer of authority).

With her attire alone, Frida becomes a public act: the "dolphin polychromies" of her petticoats, the blouses embroidered with golden thread, her braids, an homage to architectural fantasy crisscrossed with multi-color ribbons and earrings.[9] Through a simple formality—the emotiveness of her outfit—and with intentional boldness, Frida sets out to make visible an aesthetic that is one of the last strongholds of a people threatened by modernity. To be Frida or to dress like Frida is to add designs inspired by tradition to the wardrobe that Americanization no longer allows. Therein lies the project: to reconstruct and give a different meaning to tradition by defiantly donning typical dresses, which nevertheless couldn't capture the quickly disappearing landscapes where this clothing had been central to daily life.

"Mexicanness," according to Frida, Diego, and their circle, is a miraculous discovery of what is singular in the collective, and Frida quickly becomes—and this is one of the first expressions of her fame—emblematic of a sector that believes in the possibility of a "Mexican way of life" that, from first sight, resists Western conformity. Though few people are in the know, Frida is already an open secret in the city that chooses to modernize itself, and rejects its now anachronistic "fatal picturesqueness."

THIRD STAGE: A CELEBRITY IN THE CAPITAL AND A (MARGINALLY) INTERNATIONAL FIGURE

A small circle of Mexico City describes Frida's behavior as sinful heroics (the avant-garde underscoring the *heroics* and the traditionalists, the *sinfulness*.) What do they mean by this? They're referring to the power of her persona, to the personality that is shaped by her unique way of speaking and by her physical limitations. Along with Diego, Frida visits the United States and watches him work in New York, Detroit, and San Francisco, interacts with artists and attends bourgeois parties, converses with Nelson Rockefeller and Hollywood actors, recognizes the irresistible halo of Diego's fame as genius, produces notable paintings that cause conflict with her clients, and allows herself to be photographed—a model sought out for being so photogenic . . .

Diego is surrounded by, and in fact caught up in, scandal; Frida achieves fame long before prestige. She's an "unorthodox" artist, exceptional, outside the canon for those years, without an academic school nor direct political messaging; she's Diego's perfect complement, inevitable in a marriage of opposites; she embodies Mexico (her wardrobe) always open to the impromptu tourists that she encounters.

Diego's excesses lead Frida to a divorce and a later reconciliation in San Francisco. All this brings her to live in the heart of what will be History: she will receive Trotsky—exiled in Mexico—and settle him in Coyoacán; she campaigns for the Spanish Republic; she splits her time between singing sessions, drinking, and open-ended love affairs.[10] Her private life could well be public, but her friends and acquaintances prefer not to let on while she comes and goes between heterosexuality and lesbianism, between, let's say, a singer (Lucha Reyes) and a photographer (Nickolas Muray).[11] She is whatever one chooses: surrealist, fantastic, realist, according to the eye of the beholder.

This stage can't be understood without taking Mexico City and the "exotic" aura of the Mexican painters into account. The city is its red-light districts, its bourgeois bohemians, its defense of Respectability with a taste for eccentrics.[12] Diego and Frida supply a considerable sector of the population with juicy stories, they are the couple that abandons the Communist Party and then returns to it, verbally monogamous and sexually polygamous beings, the first urban celebrities that attract other celebrities; they are, all told, the axis of artistic life in the city that with respect to new ideas and progress *is* the whole country. Once again, life-force trumps morbid curiosity, that "rich honey-comb" that attracts tourists and journalists hunting for local color, and guides artists in search of social commitment.[13]

FOURTH STAGE: THE EARLY DISSEMINATION OF HER WORK

Frida in murals, Frida in her paintings, Frida on everyone's tongue. These are the germinating seeds of her mythological explosion, which will occur when multiple factors intersect: her condition as an exceptional woman ready to be consumed by future generations; the perceptions of her radical militancy; the originality of her painting; the ease with which she entangles herself in symbols that never trap her in the end; the suffering that grants her the dual condition of martyr and heroine. In all these combinations, Frida endures. She's a tragedy born of her own survival, such that she becomes the opposite: the spirit of continuity of art and of life, the singular character that contains a multitude. (Frida becomes familiar but this doesn't neutralize her gift of surprising us endlessly.)

The genesis of intertextuality. If Frida portrays herself in order to reject the gloom of her disability that daily degrades her figure, Diego portrays her as the symbol of exceptionalism: at the Hotel del Prado, in the mural *Dream of a Sunday Afternoon in Alameda Park*, and in the murals at the National Palace and the Secretary of Public Education (SEP).[14] By depicting her, Diego anticipates her consecration: this woman, in and of herself, is an epic, she becomes a part of Mexican history.

All for the image in the "Album of Imports." Who doesn't desperately want to be in a photo next to Diego and Frida? Who isn't intrigued by the rumors, the gossip (the roots of rumor), the marriage proposals (Diego's— none are attributed to Frida; at that time, if they weren't self-made widows, women didn't propose)? In the radical decade of the 1930s and later, with even more stage presence, in a city on the brink of internationalization, Diego and Frida are major figures of the "nationalism of daily life," only interrupted when the cultural industry absorbs their repertoire.

The Permanent Passage: Illness

From the *Legends of Frida: Journalist Rosa Castro's Testimony as Told to Hayden Herrera in Frida's Biography.*[15]

Frida spoke of her ills like someone referring to a glass beaker with a strange animal inside it that withstands and withstands the fire. Those corsets that she wore, oh! metal, leather and plaster, made more bearable by painting them a gentian violet, mercury-chrome, studding them with dancing mirrors, and gluing on colored feathers just above her pubis. [. . .] Those corsets that so tortured her, how I remember them! As I remember that afternoon so well; night was falling when she decided to rip it off. Never again!, she had said, and without the corset, without the brace for her fragile backbone, out she went, to the street and straight to a pub. [. . .] The shouting in the street led us to a doorway, to that great entry gate.

How can one describe the whole scene that matched her dazzling bedroom? First came Frida, her hair flowing, excited, arms raised above her head. Then following her, a crowd that was yelling, singing, laughing, and whistling. Between the cloud of dust that they kicked up and the darkness that at times was accentuated, it all seemed like some mad, extravagant rebellion of beings that Frida herself had invented. She struggled to the gate and cried out: "Never again! Never again, no matter what happens! Never again!"

"Loudly the Pain"

In the 1940s, her illness gets worse.[16] Frida is now the patient who refuses to accept her condition as victim. Frida adapts with relative autonomy to her fame (that is, her condition as an obligatory reference). Economically, it's still a difficult time, living off the sale of her paintings to US collectors, loans from friends, and small advances from gallery owners. Her illness advances, and Frida alternates, literally, between agonizing torture and her need to express herself; and her paintings, within their original simplicity, become more complex, or if you prefer, the general knowledge of her trajectory highlights her complexity.

Frida reflects: "Nothing seemed more natural than to paint what had not been fulfilled," and among the things not fulfilled, in her case, is the doubling of her person, that is to say, an escape from her pain.[17] In the self-portrait from her *Diary*, Frida appears as a broken pitcher, she scolds herself: "DON'T COME CRYING TO ME!" and in the next drawing she responds: "YES, I COME CRYING TO YOU."[18] Pain is her supreme militancy, the cause that she leans on in an attempt to minimize it, the baseline for her exploration of reality, and the living hell that death will bring to an end.

Above all others, there is the memory of her trolley accident in 1925. "Some iron bars ran through her entrails the way a pin fixes the weakened body of a museum butterfly," writes her dear friend Manuel González Ramírez in 1954.[19] And already in 1946, in New York, her illness worsens, and in the first operation, they graft a piece of her pelvis to one of her vertebra. For long periods of time, Frida is in traction with her feet tied to weights to avoid paralysis and to separate her vertebrae, which have a pathological tendency to fuse. The operations destroy her, and the morphine stops mitigating her pain.

In the end, the mutilation of her leg defeats her. And according to González Ramírez, "What did worry her, though, was the thought of being lowered into the ground in a recumbent position. She had suffered so often, in so many hospitals, in this posture, Frida explained that she did not want to go to her grave lying down. For this reason, she had asked to be cremated."[20] When it was time, her wish was carried out.

FIFTH STAGE: IN SEARCH OF AN ADJECTIVE THAT DEFINES FRIDA

Work attributed to her legend. What is Frida? Is she a nationalist, a communist, a surrealist, a fantastic painter, an unexpected fabulist of the self? Frida's nationalism has to do with gastronomy, clothing, a sense of color, a love of popular arts and crafts, and songs. Politically, sectarianism is Rivera's fundamental weakness (and truthfully, that of almost everyone during that era), which infects Frida who unperturbed follows her companion, convinced that Diego, better than anyone, can pinpoint the exact place of historical reason. Lola Álvarez Bravo recounts: "Frida was very brave, with a decided and serene courage. I remember that one time she got into a fight during a meeting of the Bread Makers Union, using her handbag and whacking those that criticized Diego. Another time, when Diego was accompanying General Henríquez's presidential campaign, we went to Puebla, and it was rumored that they had set up an ambush near the city, but Frida wasn't worried, she carried a pistol hidden under her thick petticoats."[21] Nevertheless, quite possibly for misogynistic reasons, insistent upon not conceding political value to women, society ignored the radicalism in Frida's anti-imperialist notions, in her moving defense of the Spanish Republic, and in her version of communist religiosity that today is both explicable and inexplicable.

Surrealism is the label that André Breton bestowed upon her and that, strictly speaking, lent her a set of very recognizable symbols; it had little to do with paintings that emerged from dreams, but rather, more specifically, from painful sleeplessness.[22]

On June 2, 1954, Frida attends a protest march against the coup in Guatemala that was carried out under the auspices of John Foster Dulles's Department of State. The military strongman, Carlos Castillo Armas, supported by the CIA, the landowning bourgeoisie, and the Catholic Church, organizes the fall of President Jacobo Arbenz. The coup, a successful imitation of Franco, barely gets any attention in Mexico, and yet, the march is combative and jubilant: "Hands Off Guatemala!" "People Unite!" Diego even dedicates an episode of his mural *The Glorious Victory* to it.[23]

Frida and Diego arrive by pick-up truck, and with difficulty, she's lowered to the ground. Diego and the painter and architect Juan O'Gorman take turns pushing her wheelchair.[24] It's the only time that I ever saw her in person, and her striking impact makes me follow her throughout the march in reverential awe of her celebrity, along with those hoping to relieve Diego of his wheelchair duties. The profound attention that her presence summons makes her the visual center of the march. As I envisage her now, Frida, incandescent, seems to animate a live altarpiece.

In 1954, she is interned at the English hospital on two occasions. Shortly before passing away, she writes in her *Diary* a confession that is a public announcement: "I hope the leaving is joyful—and I hope never to return—FRIDA."[25] On July 13, she dies. Again, nothing in my experience as a high school student had prepared me for the tumult, the constellation of famous people present in the lobby of the Palace of Fine Arts: General Lázaro Cárdenas, David Alfaro Siqueiros, Diego Rivera, and the multitude of women dressed as Tehuanas whose names I learn later and who, with an air of grief and an inscrutable—or at least indecipherable to me—look on their faces, protect the inconsolable widower Dieguito, the froggie-toad, with maternal zeal.[26] "The International" is sung (I think, but am not sure, that this was achieved by handing out mimeographed lyrics), moments of excruciating silence are observed, followed by the din of voices, the Communist Party flag is hung, there is a procession past the coffin, and I feel an uncontrollable sadness, that of not ever knowing her.[27]

The wake is a happening. There are revolutionary nationalists, progressive functionaries, artists, writers, communists, and "el pueblo." The scandalous noise (the murmurs of alarm and excitement) erupts the moment the coffin is covered with the communist flag. Mexican music is played; there is weeping, applause in a compulsive act of Mexicanness, at once a dramatic imposition and an authentic truth for those present. I can vividly evoke the images (or rather, I remember what over the years I've been recalling of that vigil): the women comrades sing *corridos*, the journalists harassing Diego, and the singing: "Por una mujer ladina," "Por un amor," "El abandonado" and "El corrido de Cananea" that Frida so enjoyed:[28]

> Voy a dar un pormenor
> de lo que a mí me ha pasado,
> que me han agarrado preso
> siendo un gallo tan jugado.
>
> *I'm going to give the details*
> *Of my befallen fate,*
> *They've taken me to jail*
> *Being a rooster so well played.*

And a fervent group takes over the melody and adds a more militant lyric:

> Señores, a orgullo tengo ser antiimperialista
> y militar en las filas del Partido Comunista . . .
>
> *Gentlemen, it's my pride to be anti-imperialist*
> *militant in the ranks as a proud Communist . . .*

Everywhere there are anecdotes, tears, and praises for Fridita.[29] The small crowd offers what it has, the proof of nationality that is a cause and an aesthetic trend, that is both style and historical memory, that is art and revolution. Concha Michel, the then well-known singer, composer, and compiler of folklore, sings "Sol redondo y colorado."[30] The songs are the magic words that turn the wake into some other kind of act, not just political, not merely friendly, not only unionist and popular.

This occasion is indefinable, mixing reverence with political scandal. My classmates and I sense something happening when the director of the INBA, Andrés Iduarte, speaks with Diego.[31] Later this dialogue is reported to us:

"The communist flag must come down."

"If you remove it, sir, I'll take the coffin to the streets."

We learned of this later, just as the news of Iduarte's dismissal broke.[32]

The ceremony in the Palace of Fine Arts is brief. Iduarte reads a text: "Frida has died. Frida has died. The brilliant and willful creature that in our days illuminated the halls of the National Preparatory School has died." In the Dolores Civil Cemetery an after-ceremony is held.[33] Carlos Pellicer recites three sonnets.[34] Next to the cremation oven they sing "The International," and the traditional melodies from the mythical ranch, with all of their wells of hope and resentment.[35]

Purgatory

In the following years, Frida is the object of the kind of recognition that tends to look like oblivion. Her paintings are undervalued, little is published on her work, and the critical reception most frequently underscores her pictoric ingenuity and exalts her formidable personality, an everlasting sign of the times of war and militancies. She's never forgotten, but she's also not remembered much. Those who scorn her, in a boldly intellectual pose, are guided by their disdain for "primitivism" and their irritation over her sectarianism, a fair position that when taken to the extreme—denying the artistic quality of Leftist painters—becomes equally sectarian. Modernity, as we know, doesn't discard muralism, it incorporates it, and even makes it an object of ruthless marketing. And modernity positions Frida in the vanguard, as an exception, with the reasoning that she created a different aesthetic.

SEVENTH STAGE: SELF-PORTRAITURE AS AN AESTHETIC

The rediscovery of Frida is definitely aided by the power of her self-portraits. In each one, the exorcism against pain shines through, the desire to persist, the examination of herself that is both absolution and condemnation. This could be her reasoning: "I paint myself, therefore I mark my place in the world; I paint myself, therefore time will perceive me once my suffering is over; I paint myself, therefore these portraits are the prolonging and the metamorphosis of my figure, the figuration of the metamorphosis."

The *Diary* is the succession of writings, drawings, and sketches directed not only to the worthy Diego Rivera, not exclusively to her closest friends (who won't read it), but to all those who in this future without echoes draw close to this pictorial-textual innovation in which the "I" is multiplied, the "I" is split, the "I" gives birth, the "I" descends to the shadows and furnishes them with brushstrokes and colors. In the *Diary* we simultaneously find "a despair which no words can describe," the playfulness that courts "La Calaca," the imaginary memories (the ones that precede real memories), the solitude of the body that wrestles with the gregarious spirit of the soul, the anxious desire to hold onto the poetic (the spirit in its linguistic plenitude), and the will to live.[36]

EIGHTH STAGE: "NO MYTH IS IN-
VENTED WITHOUT ITS CONSENT"

Suddenly, in the 1970s, there's a deluge of admiration.[37] It all coincides: the first details of her relationship with Trotsky and with various women, the exhibits in Mexico and outside Mexico, the film by Paul Leduc with Ofelia Medina, the stream of visitors to the Casa Azul in Coyoacán.[38] The rapid consensus: Frida, singularly unique, is that primordial artist who, lacking any other theme, paints herself obsessively. Frida is a portrait of the era and it's the era in which portraits are in vogue.

The impact is simultaneous: the Chicanos, the feminists, the cultural nationalists, the critics of postmodernism, the radicals, the superstars of entertainment, the writers, the lesbians, the painters, and the theater people, are all drawn to Frida (her work, her figure, her life, her relationship to love and pain). From among the symbols of the legendary decades of the "Mexican Renaissance," Frida is chosen, along with her complementary landscape: the immense, the delirious, the photogenic and antiphotogenic Diego. The inseparable couple and the isolated woman are both love and solitude in flames.

Behold the industry of "miraculous" transformations: take a great artist, an exemplar of moral and political dissidence, a creator of terrestrial and physiological symbologies that pours out her dreams and afflictions in visions of a cosmic pair in self-portraits and secular retablos.[39] Shake up her memory a little and exchange the entire ensemble for an avalanche of biographies, the first by Hayden Herrera, book and magazine covers, calendars, dolls, puppets, plays, two fiction films, various documentaries, t-shirts, postcards, docudramas, paintings that include citations of hers, postmodern analysis, adoring declarations by Madonna and Salma Hayek, astronomic prices at auctions . . .

The inevitable question: is Fridamania a cult of Christian origin, the transmutation of the artist into a virgin of sorrow, and of nation, and of gender? There is no shortage of Christian traces in the work and myth of Frida or, at any rate, the artist portrays herself with the rejoicing piety of one of the retablos that she so gazed upon, collected, and recreated. Nothing in Fridamania suggests an effective transition from the worldly to the celestial, but rather, the inertia of the consecrating practices from centuries of Christian culture and its scaffolding of devotional reproduction. Basically, the myth of Frida is a secular reality of aesthetics from which Fridamania transitions into a popular passion.

First Frida, and then Frida and Diego together, are the icons that complement and give full meaning to the landscape of Zapatas and Villas.

NINTH STAGE: THE COUPLE AND ITS AMOROUS OBSESSIONS

A religion in which divinity, saints, ceremonies, and chapels are simply called Diego Rivera, a credo that goes from love to cosmogony, from afflictions to meditation:

> Nobody will ever know how much I love Diego [. . .] if *I* had my health, I'd like to give it *all* to him, if I had my youth, he could have it all. I'm not just [his]—mother—I am the embryo, the germ, the first cell which = potentially = engendered him—I am *him*, from the most primitive . . . and the most ancient cells, that with time became *him* [. . .] = sense =[40]

It's impossible to know what was really going on, but what we do know is the compulsive manner in which she positioned him, her great model:

> Don't let the tree get
> thirsty, you are its sun,
> it treasured your seed
> "Diego" is the name for love.[41]

Love is the territory *par excellence* of the poetic, exactly as Frida conceptualizes this outpouring.

In her idea of verbal beauty, even new poetic words are justified, as long as the fundamental essence (her surrender) remains. Frida writes:

> The "classic" love . . . .
> (without arrows)
> Just with spermato-
> zoa[42]

Diego is always on Frida's mind: on her forehead in her self-portrait, in the quarrels, the reconciliations, and the anguishes. In the mythology only consisting of images, Frida and Diego are the single being that transcends sex, arguments, numerous infidelities, and becomes the origin of a new species that, for reasons unknown, ends with them.

TENTH STAGE: THE METAMORPHOSIS OF THE MASSES

Since the decade of the 1990s, and very decidedly at the dawning of the twenty-first century, Frida Kahlo becomes the devotion of the masses, for evident reasons (international fame, the multiplication of her images, the transformation of an era into a paradise lost in time, and for secret reasons unique to each individual). The Fridic explosion of 2007 is part of a cultural demand, an informational pressure, a contagious admiration, and an urgency for great referents. Always over-explained and without explanations, she remains permanently "like a rocket like a grenade like a shattered window like a piece of news like a telegraph like blood" (Salvador Novo).[43]

Frida Kahlo lacks statues but, in their place, she gets millions of memory niches.[44]

NOTES

1. La Casa Azul, known as The Blue House, was where Kahlo lived the majority of her life, first with her family and later, with Diego Rivera. It is located in the Coyoacán section of Mexico City. The museography was carried out by curator and famed poet Carlos Pellicer, an intimate friend to the cou ple. See the website for the Museo Frida Kahlo, at https://www.museofridakahlo.org.mx/museo/?lang=en#casaazul.

2. Post-revolutionary nationalism in Mexico revived and made visible the *trajes típicos* or "traditional dresses," which were meant to "typify" regions whose textile crafts and traditions were quickly disappearing due to modernization, industrial production, and internal migration from the countryside to the cities. Some of this attire was adopted based on the cosmovisions of the Indigenous inhabitants of the regions, such as those of Yucatán or the Isthmus of Tehuantepec (Oaxaca), others reflected cultural traditions of the colonial era such as the *charros* (Jalisco) and the *chinas poblanas* (Puebla). Currently each of Mexico's thirty-two states has its own *traje típico*, and they are considered a source of nationalistic pride, appearing in folkloric ballets and community dance events as part of a national cultural program.

3. *Pueblo* here means "the people," both as a social class and a political grouping.

4. José Guadalupe Posada Aguilar (1852–1913) was an artist known particularly for his engravings, illustrations, and caricatures of famous Mexican people and events leading up to the Mexican Revolution (1910–1920). His work demonstrated scathing criticism of dictator Porfirio Díaz (1830–1915), who served seven terms as president for a total of thirty-one years, as well as of the upper class social milieu that kept him in power during the Porfiriato. Posada is most known for his biting social critique that used *calacas* (skeletons), especially the Catrín and Catrina (fancy skeletons that wore the clothing of the social elite including large hats, who rode bicycles and rubbed elbows with the rich). His

use of the skeletons was a way to show that in death, all social distinctions are erased. Hermenegildo Bustos (1832–1907) is perhaps the most recognized painter from Mexico's nineteenth century, thanks in great part to the post-revolutionary nationalism that re-evaluated Mexican greatness. From Guanajuato (the cradle of Independence), he was most known for his still lifes (a cataloguing of local fruits and vegetables) and portraits.

5. The *edén subvertido* comes from a line from the first stanza of Ramón López Velarde's (1888–1921) famous poem "El retorno maléfico" ("The Maleficent Return," 1917) in which the poet laments the destruction caused by the Federal troops to his beloved hometown of Jeréz, Zacatecas, in the wake of the Mexican Revolution. The translation of this poem can be found in Ramón López Velarde, *Poems*, trans. M. W. Jacobs (Moorpark, CA: Floricanto Press, 2013).

6. The *charro* suit, named for the horsemen of Jalisco, is used to this day as a mariachi costume, and is generally made of black velvet with elaborate gold or silver embroidery over pants and a bolero jacket, accompanied by a large embroidered sombrero. The *china poblana* dress includes a white blouse and a colorful and elaborately embroidered and sequined, wide-belled, floor-length red and green skirt. These two styles of dress have become extremely emblematic of Mexico in general, and can be traced back to colonial practice and the mixing of Spanish traditions with those of the local Indigenous populations.

7. Monsiváis paraphrases from Raquel Tibol, *Frida Kahlo: Una vida abierta* (Mexico City: Oasis, 1983). We cite from the biography in English: Raquel Tibol, *Frida Kahlo: An Open Life*, trans. Elinor Randall (Albuquerque: University of New Mexico Press, 1993), 24, 25. It is noteworthy that Tibol's biography was published in Spanish the same year as Hayden Herrera's biography in English. Tibol's biography relies very heavily on direct quotes from people in the Kahlo-Rivera milieu, among which she was an important part, especially in Frida's final years. Tibol published a second biography of Kahlo that draws on her own decades of writings, *Frida Kahlo en su luz más íntima* (Mexico City: Lumen, 2005). Monsiváis wrote the back-cover blurb for the book. A *rebozo* is a woven shawl made of silk or cotton worn by a Tehuana from the isthmus of Tehuantepec in the state of Oaxaca.

8. Sergei Mikhailovich Eisenstein (1898–1948) was a Soviet film pioneer and theorist who traveled to Mexico in 1930 (having befriended Diego Rivera and others in the cultural milieu a few years prior), with the intention of filming an epic, episodic film that would capture many aspects of Mexican culture, with money from US investors including Upton Sinclair, and incorporated under the Mexican Film Trust. The film was to be called *¡Que viva México!* (*Long Live Mexico!*). While Eisenstein ran out of funds and was unable to complete the film, his comrade Grigori Alexandrov (1903–1983) completed a version of the film with Eisenstein's title, released in 1979.

9. "Dolphin polychromies" refers to a verse in Ramón López Velarde's famous poem "La suave patria" (1921): "Suave Patria: en tu tórrido festín / luces policromías de delfín . . ." (Gentle Homeland: in your torrid feast / you flaunt

dolphin polychromies . . .). Translation ours. Velarde's "La suave patria," originally published by El Maestro, was translated by M. W. Jacobs as "Gentle Homeland" in López Velarde, *Poems.*

10. Leon Trotsky (Lev Davidovich Bronstein, 1879–1940), the exiled Russian-
Ukrainian Marxist revolutionary, lived with his wife, Natalia Sedova, at Viena
45 in the Colonia del Carmen in Coyoacán from 1939 to 1940, mere blocks from
Frida's Casa Azul. It was during this time that their romantic entanglement
flourished, and it was there that several attempts on his life were carried out,
including the final successful one by his supposed friend and confidant Ramón
Mercader, who stabbed him to death with an icepick in his study. The house
remained intact and in 1982 was declared a national monument. In 1990, on
the fiftieth anniversary of his assassination, the Instituto del Derecho de Asilo –
Museo Casa de León Trotsky (Right of Asylum Institute – Leon Trotsky House
Museum) was established by the government of Mexico City (under its original
name, El Instituto del Derecho de Asilo y las Libertades Públicas – The Right of
Asylum and Civil Liberties Institute, which was changed in 1996).

11. Lucha Reyes (María de la Luz Flores Aceves, 1906–1944) was an extraordinarily
famous ranchera/mariachi singer from Guadalajara, Jalisco, one of very few
women who dominated these genres. It was rumored, as Monsiváis notes, that
she and Frida had a brief but important affair. Reyes lived a tormented life and
drank herself to death, leaving her young adopted daughter, María de la Luz, an
orphan. Arturo Ripstein's 1994 film *La reina de la noche* is an imaginary biography of her romantic life that focuses heavily on her relationships with other
women, and her abjection. Sergio de la Mora questions this use of her figure in
his chapter "Mexican Abjection: Lucha Reyes and the Politics of Suffering in *La
reina de la noche* (1994)," in *The Films of Arturo Ripstein: The Sinister Gaze of the
World*, ed. Manuel Gutiérrez Silva and Luis Duno Gottberg, 169–95 (New York:
Palgrave, 2019). Likewise, Alma Velasco's novel *Me llaman la tequilera* (Mexico City: Suma de Letras, 2012) is a meticulously reconstructed biographical
novel of the singer's life that investigates the challenges and tragedies of being
a woman alone in show business. Nickolas Muray (Miklós Mandl, born in Hun-
gary, 1892–1965) was an American photographer, also known to be romantically
linked to Frida Kahlo for over a decade (1931–1941). He took some of the most
iconic photographs of Frida during the time that she was in the US traveling
with Rivera and maintaining a relationship with Muray. Mónica Lavín dedicates
one of the short stories in her book *La casa chica* (Mexico City: Planeta, 2012)
to the romance between these two. Lavín's book examines well-researched and
torrid affairs among many of Mexico's most important artists, intellectuals, and
politicians of the twentieth century.

12. Here Monsiváis refers to *zonas de tolerancia* or "tolerance zones," sectors of cities in Mexico in which prostitution is legal, or at least is not criminalized, and
sexual transactions are carried out with little to no police intervention.

13. This quote refers to the fable "Un panal de rica miel" ("The Fable of the Flies")

by eighteenth-century Spanish author Félix María de Samaniego (1745–1801), whose moral is to not overdo it, because the flies drowned in the honey and too much of a good thing can kill you.

14. *Sueño de una tarde dominical en la Alameda Central* (1947) is one of Rivera's most iconic murals, commissioned by architect Carlos Obregón Santacilia for the central dining room of the Hotel del Prado, on Avenida Juárez facing the Alameda park. It strolls through four centuries of Mexican history, from Conquest to the Inquisition, from Independence and the Revolution to modern times. In this mural, Diego paints himself as a child, holding hands with Posada's Catrina, whose other arm is linked with an image of Posada himself. Other notable figures are Frida; Cuban thinker, poet, and revolutionary José Martí; conquistador Hernán Cortés; Emperor Maximiliano; revolutionary Emiliano Zapata; and dictator Don Porfirio Díaz. See *Sueño de una tarde dominical en la Alameda Central* online at Mexicana: Repositorio del Patrimonio Cultural de México, Secretaría de Cultura, https://mexicana.cultura.gob.mx/es/repositorio/detalle?id=_suri:ESPECIAL:TransObject:5bce55047a8a0222ef15d47a.

15. Hayden Herrera's *Frida: A Biography of Frida Kahlo* (New York: Harper and Row, 1983) was an extremely important document in the art history world, and was widely responsible for Frida's international reach as a "celebrity." It was translated into Spanish by Angelika Scherp in 1996. Monsiváis cites heavily from this text, sometimes paraphrasing extensively. In this text, we translate Monsiváis's paraphrase. For example, Herrera describes Castro's narration in the third person, while Monsiváis has included Castro's narration as a first-person account. These are the original texts: "Visitors also signed their names on Frida's various plaster corsets, and decorated them with feathers, mirrors, decalcomanias, photographs, pebbles, and ink. When her doctors ordered her paints removed, Frida painted her current cast with lipstick and iodine. There is a photograph of Rivera watching as his bedridden wife carefully paints a hammer and sickle on a corset that covers her entire torso" (Herrera, 389). "Frida was talking to Rosa about the misery of being enclosed in orthopedic corsets, when suddenly, at dusk, she cried, 'No more!' She ripped off her corset and sallied out to join the festivities, leaving Rosa Castro behind to watch the guests milling about the house. Rosa remembers especially the scene in Frida's bedroom. There, hanging from the rafters—those same rafters from which Frida herself had hung while waiting for one of her plaster corsets to dry—was a multitude of Judases, dressed by Frida in her own and Diego's clothes. They swung and twirled, their cardboard bones jostled by the continuous flow of people moving in and out of the room. Shouting in the street outside called Rosa Castro to the door. There was Frida, her hair loose and flowing over her shoulders, her face wild with excitement that must have been partly the result of drugs taken so that she could endure the pain of walking without the support of her corset. She staggered toward her house, arms raised above her head, her voice joining in the general uproar of the crowd that followed her. In the dim evening light, a cloud of dust

billowed up around the celebrants. And above the noise of the singing, laughing, whistling crowd, Frida's voice could be heard. 'Never again!' she cried triumphantly, referring to her imprisonment in corsets. 'Never again, no matter what happens! Never again!'" (Herrera, *Frida*, 404).

16. Monsiváis's original subtitle is "Dolor, qué ruidoso vienes" (Pain, how noisily you come). This refers to page 131 of Kahlo's diary, where she writes "Calladamente, la pena / ruidosamente el dolor" ("Quietly, the grief / loudly the pain"). Frida Kahlo, *The Diary of Frida Kahlo: An Intimate Self-Portrait*, ed. and trans. Sarah M. Lowe (New York: Harry Abrams, 1995) 273. Hayden Herrera's rendering of this poem from the diary in his biography is "Quietly, the pain / Noisily the suffering." Herrera, *Frida*, 418.

17. This quote appears in "Frida habla de su pintura, an interview with Antonio Rodríguez," in Herrera, *Frida*, 317.

18. These come from pages 100 and 101 of the diary. Kahlo, *The Diary of Frida Kahlo*, 253. Here we quote Kahlo's original diary, written and illustrated between the years of 1944 and her death in 1954, which was not released by the Diego Rivera and Frida Kahlo museums for publication until 1995. The book was released simultaneously in Spanish and in English (telling of her by-then international fame) with an introduction by Carlos Fuentes and an essay by Sarah M. Lowe, as well as the color reproduction of the diary itself, with transcription and comments (and translation in the English version) by Lowe. Frida Kahlo, *El diario de Frida Kahlo: Un íntimo autorretrato*, ed. Sarah M. Lowe (Mexico City: La Vaca Independiente, 1995). The diary page numbers correspond to the original physical diary and are reproduced fully in the text of the book.

19. This quote is not directly cited in Herrera's biography, however González Ramírez appears in her bibliography: González Ramírez, Manuel, "Frida Kahlo o el imperativo de vivir," *Huylate* 2 (1954): 7–25. Manuel González Ramírez was Frida's divorce lawyer and close childhood friend (part of Los Cachuchas, a group of rabble-rousing students named for the baseball caps they wore). Herrera, *Frida*, 27.

20. Manuel González Ramírez is paraphrased in Herrera, *Frida*, 430. Here we quote directly from Herrera's original text in English, although Monsiváis quoted from the Spanish version.

21. Lola Álvarez Bravo (1907–1993) was a celebrated photographer and wife to famed photographer Manuel Álvarez Bravo from 1925 to 1934. She was a close friend to Frida, and was responsible for producing Frida's only solo exhibition in Mexico, on April 13, 1953, at her personal gallery. Tibol, *Frida Kahlo*, 154. Carlos Monsiváis attributes this story to Lola Álvarez Bravo, who we believe he paraphrases from Elena Poniatowska, "Lola Álvarez Bravo": "Frida acompañaba a Diego a los mítines. Fíjate, Frida iba de guarura de Diego, no porque Diego la pusiera, sino porque era bravísima y todo el tiempo estaba al pendiente de cuidarlo con una pistolita que siempre traía en su bolsa. Y de retache iba yo de guarura de Frida para ver que a ella no le sucediera nada. Recuerdo

una tarde en un mítin en un sindicato, creo que de panaderos, sabe Dios de qué, estábamos sentadas Frida y yo y alguien delante de Frida dijo que Diego era un hablador; Frida lo cogió a manazos, a bolsazos, a trenzasos, a aretazos." (Frida accompanied Diego to the meetings. Look, Frida went as Diego's body-guard, not because he put her up to it, but because she was very fierce and was always watching his back with a pistol that she carried in her purse. And as back up, I went as Frida's bodyguard to make sure nothing happened to her. I remember one afternoon in a union meeting, I think it was bread makers, God only knows about what, Frida and I were sitting down and someone in front of Frida said that Diego was full of it; Frida started hitting him with her hands, her purse, her braids, and her earrings.) Elena Poniatowska, "Lola Álvarez Bravo: Los últimos fogonazos de la Revolución," *Todo México, Tomo II* (Mexico City: Diana, 1993), 73. Our translation.

22. André Breton (1896–1966), head of the French surrealist movement, visited Mexico for the first time in 1938.

23. The oil-on-linen mural *Gloriosa victoria*, painted in 1954, was "missing" for more than fifty years, having been gifted by Rivera to the Pushkin Museum in the Soviet Union in communist solidarity, and stored rather than exhibited. It was recovered and displayed in Guatemala for the first time in 2010, and then exhibited at the Dolores Olmedo Museum in Xochimilco, Mexico City, before being returned to Russia. "Exhiben en Guatemala mural recuperado de Rivera" *La Jornada.* September 24, 2010, https://www.jornada.com.mx/2010/09/24/cultura/ao6n1cul.

24. Juan O'Gorman (1905–1982) was a Mexican muralist painter and architect of Irish extraction. His most famous building is the Central Library of UNAM, Mexico's flagship public university. He also designed Rivera and Kahlo's side-by-side 1931 twin functionalist houses that now form the Museo Casa Estudio Diego Rivera y Frida Kahlo (The Diego Rivera and Frida Kahlo House Studio Museum), where part of their collections is housed, in the San Ángel neighbor-hood of Mexico City. O'Gorman's mural *Retablo de la independencia* (1960–1961) is found in Chapultepec Castle and represents the period of 1784 to 1814, and the stages of the Mexican struggle for independence from Spain.

25. "Espero alegre la salida—y espero no volver jamás—FRIDA." This quote comes from page 160 in her diary. Here we quote from Kahlo, *The Diary of Frida Kahlo,* 285.

26. The diminutive *-ito* added to the end of Diego can be both affectionate and also a reference to his infantilization by these women, and Frida herself.

27. "The International" is the hymn of the workers and the socialist/communist movements, taking its name from The First International, a congress in 1864 to unite workers around their labor rights. A mimeograph is a technological pre-cursor to photocopying that allowed for the mass reproduction of text.

28. Originally titled "La mujer ladina" (A beguiling woman), and written by Jalis-can composer Juan José Espinoza Guevara (1890–1974) in 1937, the song was

286 FATEFULLY, FAITHFULLY FEMINIST

dedicated to and made famous by Lucha Reyes. The song laments a woman's abandonment of her lover. See "Juan José Espinoza Guevara," Sociedad de Autores y Compositores de México, accessed on September 27, 2023, https://www.sacm.org.mx/Informa/Biografia/08341. "Por un amor" (For a love) was a wildly popular *ranchera* song composed by Gilberto Parra Paz (1913–2000) in 1940 that laments the loss of love and suggests the lyrical "I" would be better off dead. "El abandonado" (The abandoned man) was composed by Jaliscan pianist and composer José de Jesús Martínez Pérez (1888–1916). "El abandonado" was, perhaps, immortalized by film star and singer Jorge Negrete in 1945. The in-text lyrics here are from the *corrido* "La cárcel de Cananea" (The Cananea jailhouse corrido), written by the Sonoran composer Francisco Romero Santillón in 1917 in commemoration of the Cananea Strike, a June 1906 uprising of local miners that was violently suppressed by the mining company and its cronies. This is considered one of the detonating events for the Mexican Revolution in the north. For a brief history of the jail and its relation to the *corrido*, see Eugenia Meyer Walerstein, ed. *La lucha obrera en Cananea, 1906.* (Sonora: Secretaría del Trabajo y Previsión Social, Gobierno del Estado de Sonora, 1980), 7.

29. *Fridita* is the diminutive; it suggests a friendly familiarity, and in this case, a sort of loving ownership over her and her work.

30. This song was set to music by Concha Michel (1899–1990) from a poem by the socialist poet Carlos Gutierrez Cruz (1897–1930). See León Guillermo Gutiérrez López, "Carlos Gutiérrez Cruz, el poeta socialista de México." *Connotas: Revista de crítica y teoría literarias*, no. 20 (2020): 81–100. https://doi.org/10.36798/critlit.vi20.315. See also "'Sol redondo': Un homenaje musical a una pionera feminista," *Quién*, December 2, 2020, https://www.quien.com/cultura/2020/12/02/sol-redondo-homenaje-musica-feminista.

31. INBA (Instituto Nacional de Bellas Artes; National Institute of Fine Arts), has been INBAL as of 2019, adding the "L" of literature to the fine arts under the national rubric.

32. Andrés Iduarte Fourcher (1907–1984) was a well-regarded and prolific essayist and member of the Mexican Academy of Language in New York. At the time of Frida's death, he was the general director of the INBA, and he lost his job because of his supposed communist sympathies. See Miguel Ángel Sánchez de Armas, "Andrés Iduarte: Una voz necesaria," *Indicador Político*, June 11, 2021, https://indicadorpolitico.com.mx/?p=6897.

33. Located in the third section of the Bosque de Chapultepec (Chapultepec Park), the Panteón Civil Dolores is the oldest and largest civilian cemetery in Mexico City.

34. Carlos Pellicer (1897–1977), originally from the state of Tabasco, was an important poet of the Contemporáneos movement, an avante garde/modernist poetic collective active in the 1920s and 1930s whose notable members—many of whom were homosexual—included its founders: José Gorostiza, Carlos Pellicer, Bernardo Ortiz de Montellano, Enrique González Rojo, and Jaime Torres

Bodet, and later Salvador Novo, Xavier Villaurrutia, Jorge Cuesta, and Gilberto Owen. Pellicer was also a writer, politician, and a museographer who, in fact, established Frida Kahlo's museum at the Casa Azul and Diego Rivera's Anahuacalli Museum.

35. Monsiváis refers to the idealistic idea of "the ranch" fomented by musical films of the Golden Age (1932–1955) that celebrated the Mexican Revolution and mythologized the countryside. Specifically, he is referring to *Allá en el rancho grande* (1936), directed by Fernando de Fuentes and remade in 1949 by the same director.

36. These lines come from page 96 of the diary: "A despair which no words can describe. I'm still eager to live. I've started to paint again. A little picture to give to Dr. Farill on which I'm working with all my love. I feel uneasy about my painting. Above all I want to transform it into something useful for the Communist revolutionary movement . . ." Kahlo, *The Diary of Frida Kahlo*, 252. *La calaca* literally refers to a skeleton. Here, it refers to Kahlo courting her own death in an irreverent manner, on page 16 of the diary. Kahlo, *The Diary of Frida Kahlo*, 262.

37. With the section title, Monsiváis is quoting his own subtitle from a 1992 essay, "De todas las Fridas posibles" (Of all the possible Fridas) in *Nexos*, January 1, 1992, https://www.nexos.com.mx/?p=6393.

38. Paul Leduc (1942–2020) was an important filmmaker in Mexico; his film *Frida: Naturaleza viva* (Frida: Still life), starring the famous actress Ofelia Medina (1950–), was an important catalyst for Frida's international reception.

39. While a *retablo* can also be a large altarpiece in a church, here it is understood as a votive offering, generally a small painting on a panel of wood or metal, through which a person asks for divine intervention, or, more commonly, portrays gratitude for miracles granted. Frida collected many exemplars of this popular art form, and her collection continues to be on display at her housemuseum, La Casa Azul.

40. These lines come from pages 57, 58, and 59 of the diary. Kahlo, *The Diary of Frida Kahlo*, 234.

41. These lines are taken from page 126 of the diary. Kahlo, *The Diary of Frida Kahlo*, 270.

42. These lines are taken from page 67 of the diary. Kahlo, *The Diary of Frida Kahlo*, 238.

43. This quote, "como un cohete como una granada como un vidrio estrellado como una noticia como un telégrafo como la sangre," comes from a poem by Salvador Novo, renowned poet and chronicler, who in 1935 dedicated it to Frida Kahlo in New York and entitled it "Frida Kahlo." The first line begins, "Cuando los pinceles vuelven a ser pinzas" (When the paintbrushes become forceps). It was inlcuded in the Secretaría de Educación Pública (SEP) Letras Mexicanas (Mexican Literature) edition of *Nuevo amor y otras poesías* (1984).

44. There are, in fact, at least two bronze statues of Frida Kahlo and one of Diego in the Frida Kahlo Park (kittycorner to the Plaza de la Conchita) at the corner

of Fernández Leal and Avenida Pacífico in the Concepción neighborhood of Coyoacán, in Mexico City. The park was created in 1984 with the first bronze of Frida seated on a pyramid, evoking the pyramid in the courtyard of the Casa Azul. At the other end of the park stands a life-size pair, cast in bronze, Diego in a suit and Frida in her Tehuana dress, facing one another as if in conversation. All three were cast by sculptor Gabriel Ponzanelli.

Bibliography of Carlos Monsiváis's Writings
in English Translation

"The Culture of the Frontier: The Mexican Side." In *Views across the Border: The United States and Mexico*, edited by Stanley R. Ross, 50–67. Albuquerque, New Mexico: University of New Mexico Press, 1977.

"Travellers in Mexico: A Brief Anthology of Selected Myths." Translated by Jeanne Ferguson. *Diogenes* 32, no. 125 (1984): 48–74.

"Pop Culture and Literature in Latin America." Translated by Lydia Hunt. *Review: Latin American Literature and Arts* 18, no. 34 (Jan.–June 1985): 9–13.

"Landscape, I've Got the Drop on You!" Translated by Julianne Burton and Manuel Rivas. *Studies in Latin American Popular Culture*, no. 4 (1985): 236–46.

"In Defense of Hope." *Voices of Mexico*, nos. 8 & 9 (June–November 1988): 44–48.

"On Civic Monuments and Their Spectators." Translated by Elena C. Murray. In *Mexican Monuments: Strange Encounters*, edited by Helen Escobedo, 105–28. New York City: Abbeville Press, 1989.

"From '68 to Cardenismo: Toward a Chronicle of Social Movements." *Journal of International Affairs* 43, no. 12 (Winter 1990): 385–93.

"Discovering Images: Establishing Point of View." Translated by Roberto Tejada. In "The Art of Gabriel Figueroa," edited by Margarita de Orellana, special issue. *Artes de Mexico*, no. 2 (Fall 1992): 93–95.

"'Just Over That Hill': Notes on Centralism and Regional Cultures." In *Mexico's Regions: Comparative History and Development*, edited by Eric Van Young. San Diego, CA: Center for US-Mexican Studies, UCSD, 1992.

"Mexican Cinema: Of Myths and Demystifications." Translated by Mike Gonzalez. In *Mediating Two Worlds: Cinematic Encounters in the Americas*, edited by John King, Ana M. López, and Manuel Alvarado, 139–46. London: British Film Institute, 1993.

"Globalisation Means Never Having to Say You're Sorry: Popular Culture and National Identity in Mexico in the Age of NAFTA." *Journal of International Communication* 1, no. 2 (1994): 120–24.

"Mythologies." Translated by Ana M. López. In *Mexican Cinema*, edited by Paulo Antonio Paranaguá, 117–27. London: British Film Institute, 1995.

"All the People Came and Did Not Fit on the Screen: Notes on the Cinema Audience in Mexico." Translated by Ana M. López. In *Mexican Cinema*, edited by Paolo Paranagua, 145–53. London: British Film Institute, 1995.

"Dreaming of Utopia." Translated by NACLA staff. *NACLA Report on the Americas: The Immigration Backlash* 29, no. 3 (Nov./Dec. 1995): 39–41.

"Will Nationalism Be Bilingual?" In *Mass Media and Free Trade: NAFTA and the Cultural Industries*, edited by Emile G. McAnany, and Kenton T. Wilkinson, 131–41. Austin: University of Texas Press, 1996.

"Abel Quezada: Cartoons That Became Paintings Overnight." Translated by Roberto Tejada. *Artes de México*, no. 6 (1996): 88–89.

"Ecclesiastic Lotería." Translated by Kurt Hollander. *Artes de México*, no. 13 (1997): 89–90.

"Cultural Relations between the United States and Mexico." Translated by Marjory Urquidi. In *Common Borders, Uncommon Paths: Race, Culture, and National Identity in U.S.-Mexican Relations*, edited by Jaime E. Rodríguez O. and Kathryn Vincent, 99–122. Wilmington, Delaware: Scholarly Resources, 1997.

Mexican Postcards. Edited and translated by John Kraniauskas. London/NYC: Verso. 1997. (First English translation of a collection of twelve essays.)

"Guess Your Decade: A Questionnaire." Translated by Jesse H. Lytle. In *The Oxford Book of Latin American Essays*, edited by Ilan Stavans, 451–56. Oxford: Oxford University Press, 1997.

"Before the Flood: Nacho López and Héctor García." Translated by Esther Allen. *Aperture*, no. 153 (Fall 1998): 40–49.

"Foreword: Anita Brenner and the Mexican Renaissance." In *Anita Brenner: A Mind of Her Own*, edited by Susannah Joel Glusker, ix–xvi. Austin: University of Texas Press, 1998.

"A Fleeting Seduction: Voluptuous and Imprudent You Surrender Yourself." Translated by Michelle Suderman. *Artes de México*, no. 48 (1999), 74–75.

"Cantinflas and Tin Tan: Mexico's Greatest Comedians." Translated by Claudia Serrano, Virginia Rodríguez, and Gabriela Díaz. In *Mexico's Cinema: A Century of Film and Filmmakers*, edited by Joanne Hershfield and David Maciel, 49–79. Wilmington, Delaware: Scholarly Resources Inc., 1999.

"Tequila with Lime and Other Table Talk." In *Tequila: The Spirit of Mexico*, edited by Enrique Martínez Limón, 13–17. Bath, UK: Absolute Press, 1999.

"Toledo and Borges: Complementary Zoologies." Translated by Richard Moszka. In *Fantastic Zoology* [1957], by Jorge Luis Borges and Francisco Toledo, edited by Margarita de Orellana, 15–20. Mexico City: Artes de México, 2013. First edition in English, Galeria Arvil / INBA Mexico, 1999.

"Off with Toledo's Head, Said the Gut-Slashed Iguana." In *Francisco Toledo*, edited by Catherine Lampert, 77–87. Whitechapel Art Gallery, London, 2000.

"The Marriage of the Audience and the Screen." Translated by Lorna Scott Fox. *Artes de México*, no. 10 (2001): 86–87.

"Identity Hour." Translated by John Kraniauskas. In *The Mexico City Reader: History, Culture, Politics*, edited by Gilbert M. Joseph and Timothy J. Henders, 613–18. Durham, NC: Duke University Press, 2002. (Reprint from *Mexican Postcards*.)

"On the Chronicle in Mexico." Translated by Derek A. Petrey. In *The Contemporary Mexican Chronicle: Theoretical Perspectives on the Liminal Genre*, edited by Ignacio Corona and Beth E. Jörgensen, 25–36. Albany, NY: State University of New York Press, 2002.

"Citizenship and Urban Violence: Nightmares in the Open Air." Translated by Heather Hammett. In *Citizens of Fear: Urban Violence in Latin America*, edited by Susana Rotker in collaboration with Katherine Goldman, 240–46. New Brunswick, NJ: Rutgers University Press, 2002.

"From the Subsoil to the Mask That Reveals the Visible Indian." Translated by Mark Fried. In *The Zapatista Reader*, edited by Tom Hayden, 123–32. New York City: Thunder's Mouth Press, 2002.

"Calendars: Cultural Snapshots and Visual Tradition."In *Mexicana: Vintage Mexican Graphics*, edited by Jim Heimann, 3–8. Cologne: Taschen, 2002.

"Where Are You Going to Be Worthier? (The Border and the Postborder)." Translated by Sofía Ruiz-Alfaro. In *Postborder City: Cultural Spaces of Bajalta California*, edited by Michael Dear and Gustavo Leclerc, 33–46. New York: Routledge, 2003.

"The 41 and the Gran Redada." Translated by Aaron Walker. In *The Famous 41 Sexuality and Social Control in Mexico, 1901*, edited by Robert McKee Irwin, Michelle Rocío Nasser, and Edward J. McCaughan, 139–67. New York: Palgrave Macmillan, 2003.

"Would So Many Millions of People Not Speak English?: The North American Culture and Mexico." Translated by Christopher Dennis. In *The Latin American Cultural Studies Reader*, edited by Ana del Sarto, Alicia Ríos, and Abril Trigo, 204–32. Durham, NC: Duke University Press, 2004.

"Laughing Through One's Tears: Popular Culture in Mexico." Translated by Suzanne D. Stephens. In *Literary Cultures of Latin America: A Comparative History*, vol. 1, edited by Mario J. Valdés and Djelal Kadir, 576–97. Oxford: Oxford University Press, 2004.

"The Popular in the Confused Republics." Translated by Suzanne D. Stephens. In *Literary Cultures of Latin America: A Comparative History*, vol. 1, edited by Mario J. Valdés and Djelal Kadir, 640–49. Oxford: Oxford University Press, 2004.

"Enlightened Neighborhood: Mexico City as a Cultural Center." Translated by Suzanne D. Stephens. In *Literary Cultures of Latin America: A Comparative History*, vol. 2, edited by Mario J. Valdés and Djelal Kadir, 335–50. Oxford: Oxford University Press, 2004.

"The Metro: A Voyage to the End of the Squeeze." Translated by Lorna Scott Fox and Rubén Gallo. In *The Mexico City Reader*, edited by Ruben Gallo, 143–48. Madison: Wisconsin University Press, 2004.

"Nightlife." Translated by Lorna Scott Fox and Rubén Gallo. In *The Mexico City Reader*, edited by Rubén Gallo, 175–92. Madison: University of Wisconsin Press, 2004.

"María Póstuma." Translated by Alfred MacAdam. *Review: Literature and Arts of the Americas* 37, no. 2 (2004): 311–14.

"The Hour of the Mask as Protagonist: El Santo versus the Skeptics on the Subject of Myth." Translated by Heather Levi. In *Steel Chair to the Head: The Pleasure and Pain of Professional Wrestling*, edited by Nicholas Sammond, 88–95. Durham, NC: Duke University Press, 2005.

"Foreword. When Gender Can't Be Seen amid the Symbols: Women and the Mexican Revolution." Translated by Paul Liffman and Tanya Huntington. In *Sex and Revolution: Gender, Politics, and Power in Modern Mexico*, edited by Jocelyn Olcott, Mary Kay Vaughan, and Gabriela Cano, 1–20. Durham, NC: Duke University Press, 2006.

A New Catechism for Recalcitrant Indians. Translated by Jeffrey Browitt and Nidia Esperanza Castrillón. Mexico City: Fondo de Cultura Económica, 2007. (The first single work of Monsiváis to be translated as a book.)

"Museums (A Rapid View of Guided Tours): The Ruins of the Future Should Be in Shop Windows." Translated by Francisca González Arias. In *Beyond the Turnstile: Making the Case For Museums and Sustainable Values*, edited by Selma Holo and Mari-Tere Álvarez, 66–71. Walnut Creek, CA: AltaMira Press, 2009.

"Neobaroque and Popular Culture." Translated by James Ramey. *PMLA* 124, no. 1 (Jan. 2009): 180–88.

"Foreword: Anita Brenner: The (Multiple) Story of Origins." In *Avant-Garde Art and Artists in Mexico: Anita Brenner's Journals of the Roaring Twenties*, edited by Susannah Joel Glusker, xi–xxiv. Austin: University of Texas Press, 2010.

"How Do You Say Okei in English? (On New and Archaic Forms of Americanization)." *Norteamérica: Revista Académica del CISAN-UNAM* 5, no. 2 (2010): 161–81.

"El Santo, Being Yourself by Being Someone Else." Translated by Jill Derais. *Artes de México*, no. 119 (December 2015): 75–76.

"One Suffers but One Learns: Melodrama and the Rules of Lack of Limits." Translated by Kathleen M. Vernon. In *Melodrama Unbound: Across History, Media, and National Cultures*, edited by Christine Gledhill and Linda Williams, 151–67. New York: Columbia University Press, 2018.

"The Sidelong World Where Confession and Proclamation Are Compounded." Translated by Marguerite Feitlowitz. Introduction to *Pillar of Salt: An Autobiography, with 19 Erotic Sonnets*, by Salvador Novo, 1–45. Austin: University of Texas Press, 2021.

www.ingramcontent.com/pod-product-compliance
Lightning Source LLC
Chambersburg PA
CBHW060550030726
47498CB00005B/1340